The Nature State

This volume brings together case studies from around the globe (including China, Latin America, the Philippines, Namibia, India and Europe) to explore the history of nature conservation in the twentieth century. It seeks to highlight the state, a central actor in these efforts, which is often taken for granted, and establishes a novel concept – the nature state – as a means for exploring the historical formation of that portion of the state dedicated to managing and protecting nature.

Following the Industrial Revolution and post-war exponential increase in human population and consumption, conservation in myriad forms has been one particularly visible way in which the government and its agencies have tried to control, manage or produce nature for reasons other than raw exploitation. Using an interdisciplinary approach and including case studies from across the globe, this edited collection brings together geographers, sociologists, anthropologists and historians in order to examine the degree to which sociopolitical regimes facilitate and shape the emergence and development of nature states.

This innovative work marks an early intervention in the tentative turn towards the state in environmental history and will be of great interest to students and practitioners of environmental history, social anthropology and conservation studies.

Wilko Graf von Hardenberg is a Senior Research Scholar at the Max Planck Institute for the History of Science in Berlin, Germany, where he coordinates the working group 'Art of Judgement'. He holds a PhD in geography from the University of Cambridge, UK, and has worked at the University of Wisconsin-Madison, USA, the Rachel Carson Center, Munich, Germany, and the University of Trento, Italy.

Matthew Kelly teaches history at Northumbria University, where he is helping to establish the environmental humanities as a broad area of research and teaching within the university. He was an Associate Professor at the University of Southampton, UK, and a Fellow of the Rachel Carson Center, Munich, Germany.

Claudia Leal holds a PhD in geography from the University of California at Berkeley, USA, and is Associate Professor at the Department of History at Universidad de los Andes in Bogotá, Colombia. She was a Fellow of the Rachel Carson Center, Munich, Germany, and co-president of the Latin American and Caribbean Society for Environmental History.

Emily Wakild teaches Latin American and environmental history at Boise State University in Idaho, USA. Her current projects include a primer on teaching environmental history and a monograph on the social and ecological regions of Amazonia and Patagonia.

Routledge Environmental Humanities

Series editors: Iain McCalman and Libby Robin

The *Routledge Environmental Humanities* series is an original and inspiring venture recognizing that today's world agricultural and water crises, ocean pollution and resource depletion, global warming from greenhouse gases, urban sprawl, overpopulation, food insecurity and environmental justice are all *crises of culture*.

The reality of understanding and finding adaptive solutions to our present and future environmental challenges has shifted the epicentre of environmental studies away from an exclusively scientific and technological framework to one that depends on the human-focused disciplines and ideas of the humanities and allied social sciences.

We thus welcome book proposals from all humanities and social sciences disciplines for an inclusive and interdisciplinary series. We favour manuscripts aimed at an international readership and written in a lively and accessible style. The readership comprises scholars and students from the humanities and social sciences and thoughtful readers concerned about the human dimensions of environmental change.

The Nature State

Rethinking the History of Conservation

Edited by Wilko Graf von Hardenberg,
Matthew Kelly, Claudia Leal and
Emily Wakild

LONDON AND NEW YORK

from Routledge

First published 2017 by Routledge

2 Park Square, Milton Park, Abingdon, Oxfordshire OX14 4RN

52 Vanderbilt Avenue, New York, NY 10017

Routledge is an imprint of the Taylor & Francis Group, an informa business

First issued in paperback 2018

British Library Cataloguing-in-Publication Data
A catalogue record for this book is available from the British Library

Library of Congress Cataloguing-in-Publication Data
A catalog record for this book has been requested

ISBN: 978-1-138-71904-0 (hbk)
ISBN: 978-0-367-17260-2 (pbk)

Typeset in Bembo
by Out of House Publishing

Contents

Contributors

Stefan Dorondel has a PhD in history and ethnology from the University Lucian Blaga Sibiu, Romania, and a PhD in rural economy and sociology from Humboldt University, Berlin, Germany. He is Senior Researcher at the Francisc I. Rainer Institute of Anthropology, Bucharest, and affiliated with the Institute for Southeast European Studies in Bucharest. He has published papers on land reform, property issues, landscape changes and land use change in postsocialist countries. Recently he started to work on rivers and state formation in Eastern Europe and on natural disasters and climate change issues. He is the author of *Disrupted Landscapes: State, Peasants and the Politics of Land in Postsocialist Romania* (New York & Oxford, 2016) and co-author (with Thomas Sikor, Johannes Stahl and Phuc Xuan To) of *When Things Become Property: Land Reform, Authority and Value in Postsocialist Europe and Asia* (New York & Oxford, 2017).

Frederico Freitas holds a PhD in Latin American history from Stanford University, USA (2016). He is Assistant Professor of Latin American and Digital History at North Carolina State University and an investigator at the Visual Narratives Initiative. He is currently working on a book manuscript tentatively titled 'Boundaries of Nature: National Parks and Environmental Change at the Argentine–Brazilian Border, 1890–1990'. He has published in South and North America. His work has been featured in *HIb: Revista de Historia Iberoamericana* and *ReVista: Harvard Review of Latin America*.

Wilko Graf von Hardenberg is Senior Research Scholar at the Max Planck Institute for the History of Science in Berlin, Germany, where he coordinates the working group 'Art of Judgement'. He holds a degree in history from the University of Turin in Italy (2002) and a PhD in geography from the University of Cambridge, UK (2007). Immediately before moving to Berlin he was DAAD Visiting Professor of Environmental History at the University of Wisconsin-Madison, USA. Previously he also worked at the Rachel Carson Center and the Deutsches Museum in Munich, Germany, the University of Trento, Italy, and the Scuola Normale Superiore in Pisa, Italy. He has researched and published extensively on issues related to the history of nature conservation in the Alps from a trans-regional perspective and to environmental policies and conflicts in modern Italy.

Michael Hathaway earned his PhD at the University of Michigan, USA, and is presently Associate Professor of Cultural Anthropology at Simon Fraser University in Vancouver, British Columbia. His first book, *Environmental Winds: Making the Global in Southwest China* (Berkeley, CA, 2013), explores how environmentalism was refashioned in China, not only by conservationists, but also by rural villagers and even animals. It also examines the ways that the politics of indigeneity and nature conservation emerged in China, and reflects on how these dynamics can illuminate struggles elsewhere. His second major project examines the global commodity chain of the matsutake, one of the world's most expensive mushrooms, following it from the highlands of the Tibetan Plateau to the markets of urban Japan. He works with other members of the Matsutake Worlds Research Group, looking at the social worlds this mushroom engenders in Canada, the United States, China and Japan.

Matthew Kelly teaches history at Northumbria University, where he is helping to establish the environmental humanities as a broad area of research and teaching within the university. He earned his DPhil in Modern History from the University of Oxford, UK, and has been a British Academy Postdoctoral Research Fellow, an Associate Professor at the University of Southampton, UK, and a Fellow of the Rachel Carson Center, Munich, Germany. His most recent book is *Quartz and Feldspar. Dartmoor: A British Landscape in Modern Times* (London, 2015). Currently he is editing a volume of essays on nature and the environment in nineteenth-century Ireland, completing a project that looks at the Thames Barrier as a response to climate change, and working on histories of women environmental activists and environmental politics in modern Britain.

Emmanuel Kreike teaches African and environmental history at Princeton University, USA. He studied history at the University of Amsterdam, Netherlands, University of California, Los Angeles, USA, and Yale University, USA (PhD, 1996), and Forestry at Wageningen University, Netherlands (PhD, 2006). Recent publications include *Deforestation and Reforestation in Namibia: The Global Consequences of Local Contradictions* (Leiden, 2010) and *Environmental Infrastructure in African History: Examining the Myth of Natural Resource Management in Namibia* (Cambridge, 2013). Currently he is completing two books on the humanitarian and environmental impact of war and refugee displacement on rural societies employing the concept of environcide. The first book looks at conventional wars in global comparative perspective, arguing that total war was no modern invention because rural society and environment were prime targets and tools of war from the sixteenth to twentieth century. The second book extends the argument to unconventional wars in Cold War Southern Africa, demonstrating that 'small wars' may be even more devastating in environmental and social terms than conventional wars.

Siddhartha Krishnan (Sidd) is an environmental sociologist and environmental historian whose research interests are in landscape transformation, conservation and wellbeing and environmental justice. He is faculty at the Ashoka Trust for Research in Ecology and the Environment (ATREE; www.atree.org), Bangalore, India. Sidd is old-school. He believes that history and sociology have much in common. He considers the departmental and differentiated research and teaching in history and sociology as some kind of Foucauldian discipline. At ATREE, Sidd teaches sociology, environmental sociology, field and archival methods and environmental justice. He supervises three PhD students. He hopes to retire after publishing two books.

Claudia Leal holds a PhD in geography from the University of California at Berkeley, USA, and is Associate Professor at the Department of History at Universidad de los Andes in Bogotá, Colombia. She was Fellow of the Rachel Carson Center for Environment and Society, Munich, Germany, co-president of the Latin American and Caribbean Society for Environmental History (SOLCHA). She serves on the boards of *Environmental History* and *Hispanic American Historical Review*. Her book *Landscapes of Freedom*, on the formation of a rainforest peasantry after emancipation in the Pacific coast of Colombia, will be published soon by the University of Arizona Press. She is currently editing a book on Latin American environmental history (with John Soluri and José Augusto Pádua) to be published in English and Spanish, and is researching the history of nature conservation in Colombia.

Veronica Mitroi holds a PhD in sociology from the University of Paris Ouest Nanterre la Défense, France, entitled 'Environmental uncertainties and controversies around fishing degradation in the Danube Delta Biosphere Reserve'. She is currently Associate Researcher at the French National Research Center (CNRS), Institute of Ecology and Environmental Sciences, Paris (iEES Paris), working in an interdisciplinary research project (WasAf) concerning the monitoring and sustainable management of surface freshwater resource conservation in Africa (Senegal, Ivory Coast and Uganda). Her main research interests are the environmental sociology of aquatic environment conservation policies and the moral economy of knowledge (scientific and local) related to the ecological management of these ecosystems. She examines how scientific ecological knowledge on aquatic environment eutrophication is produced in specific socio-political contexts and how this knowledge interacts with management practices in local uses of water.

Ian Tyrrell is Emeritus Professor of History at the University of New South Wales, Sydney, Australia. His books include *True Gardens of the Gods: Californian–Australian Environmental Reform, 1860–1930* (Berkeley, CA, 1999); *Reforming the World: The Creation of America's Moral Empire* (Princeton, NJ, 2010); *Crisis of the Wasteful Nation: Empire and Conservation in Theodore Roosevelt's America* (Chicago, 2015); and *Transnational Nation: United States*

History in Global Perspective since 1789 (revised edition, Basingstoke, 2015). He is working on a history of American exceptionalism as an idea.

Emily Wakild teaches Latin American and environmental history at Boise State University in Idaho, USA. She earned her BA from Willamette University in Salem, Oregon, USA (1999) and her PhD in history from the University of Arizona, USA (2007). Wakild's first book, *Revolutionary Parks: Conservation, Social Justice, and Mexico's National Parks* (Tucson, AZ, 2011) received awards from the Conference of Latin American History, the Forest History Society and the Southeastern Council on Latin American Studies. Her current projects include a primer on teaching environmental history (with Michelle K. Berry), which is under contract with Duke University Press, and a monograph about national parks in South America. Funded by a National Science Foundation Scholars Award and a National Endowment for the Humanities Fellowship, this book strives to account for the ways transnational conservation and scientific research have shaped the social and ecological regions of Amazonia and Patagonia.

Acknowledgements

This project has been rooted in and nourished by many institutions and individuals. The nature state idea was hit upon during a discussion that Claudia, Wilko and Matt had in 2012 at the Rachel Carson Center for Environment and Society (RCC) in Munich. They took the idea to Christof Mauch and Helmuth Trischler, directors of the RCC, who agreed to finance a workshop. Wilko's brother, Achaz, then working for Gran Paradiso National Park in Italy, provided the perfect location. Emily accepted an invitation to act as a fourth editor and Sidd and Stefan, both former Fellows of the RCC, and Veronica, Ian, Michael and Emmanuel soon committed to the project. Emily's newborn kept her from Italy, but she joined those intensive Alpine discussions through Skype. Gran Paradiso National Park offered patronage and a guided hike, and the municipality of Valsavarenche provided the room in which we convened. We owe our gratitude to both. Hiking through spectacular scenery proved as conducive to the production of good ideas as being seated around a seminar table. Frederico, then completing his PhD, joined at a later stage, swiftly producing his essay. Rounds of drafting and editing, and emailing and redrafting, and re-emailing and re-editing followed – including some vital input from Katie Ritson, Brenda Black and the editorial team at the RCC – until in November 2016 it seemed to have come together. A Casita Nepantla Research Grant from Boise State University paid for the production of the map, skillfully designed by Ryan Dammrose, and index, ably created by Timothy Syreen, and permission was kindly given by the Parco Naturale Adamello Brenta for use of the cover image. Above all, whatever the strengths and weaknesses of this volume, it ultimately testifies to the extraordinary sense of global comradeship and shared endeavour nurtured by the RCC.

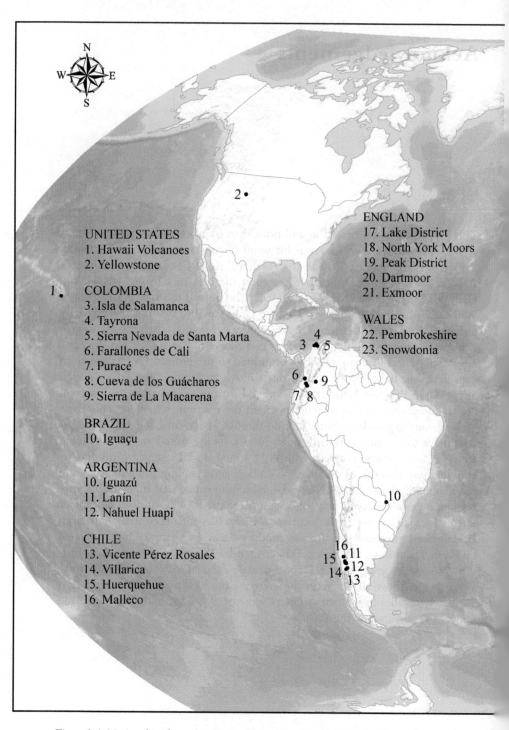

UNITED STATES
1. Hawaii Volcanoes
2. Yellowstone

COLOMBIA
3. Isla de Salamanca
4. Tayrona
5. Sierra Nevada de Santa Marta
6. Farallones de Cali
7. Puracé
8. Cueva de los Guácharos
9. Sierra de La Macarena

BRAZIL
10. Iguaçu

ARGENTINA
10. Iguazú
11. Lanín
12. Nahuel Huapi

CHILE
13. Vicente Pérez Rosales
14. Villarica
15. Huerquehue
16. Malleco

ENGLAND
17. Lake District
18. North York Moors
19. Peak District
20. Dartmoor
21. Exmoor

WALES
22. Pembrokeshire
23. Snowdonia

Figure 0.1 National parks and protected areas mentioned in the book.

Data used with permission from World Database of Protected Areas (WDPA) 2016, www.protectedplanet.net.

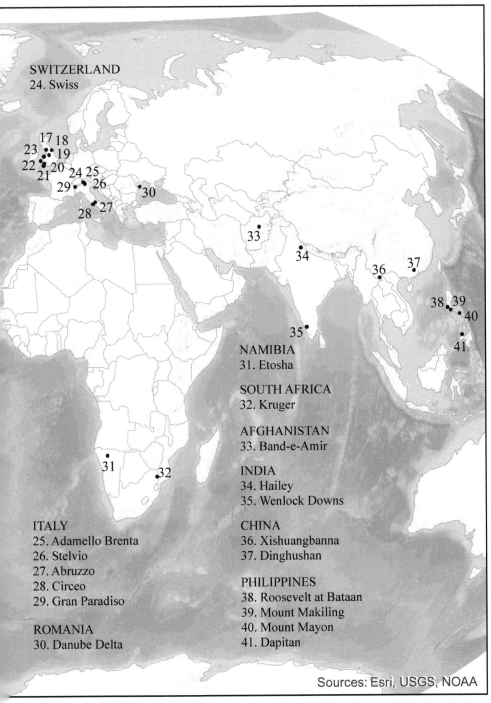

SWITZERLAND
24. Swiss

NAMIBIA
31. Etosha

SOUTH AFRICA
32. Kruger

AFGHANISTAN
33. Band-e-Amir

INDIA
34. Hailey
35. Wenlock Downs

ITALY
25. Adamello Brenta
26. Stelvio
27. Abruzzo
28. Circeo
29. Gran Paradiso

CHINA
36. Xishuangbanna
37. Dinghushan

PHILIPPINES
38. Roosevelt at Bataan
39. Mount Makiling
40. Mount Mayon
41. Dapitan

ROMANIA
30. Danube Delta

Sources: Esri, USGS, NOAA

© Ryan Dammrose of Map Lion LLC

Introduction

*Matthew Kelly, Claudia Leal, Emily Wakild and
Wilko Graf von Hardenberg** *

'Nature made the state, and the state made nature.' This adaptation of Charles Tilly's famous adage that 'war made the state, and the state made war' might at first glance seem ludicrous. Nature surely precedes the state and cannot exercise that kind of agency. But once it is accepted that the state can produce a new nature through its interventions, nature ceases to be the fixed godly entity of the romantic sensibility, and instead becomes profoundly malleable and, as such, a proper subject for historical analysis. Ecologists consider nature to be changing even in the absence of significant human interventions, and environmentalists, transfixed by apocalyptic visions of the Anthropocene's future, highlight the frantic pace of recent transformations. Talk of 'deep history' and the 'big data' needed to make sense of it suggests mainstream historians are beginning to recognize not merely the challenge posed to humanity by climate change, but also how the idea that nature is dynamic should transform how we think about our past. Economists and political scientists have also incorporated nature into their analysis – often as 'local factor endowments' or geographies – to examine its effects on economic development and war (think of the 'natural resource curse'), but these approaches often leave their impact on state formation implicit or ill-developed. Similarly, few have remarked how the varied materiality of national territories has affected states' engagement in nature conservation at different moments of their development. Compare the relatively small and often privately owned 'cultural landscapes' designated national parks by some European states with the large animal reserves of Africa or the huge forested conservation areas of Latin America's frontiers.[1]

This volume proposes 'the nature state' as a term that both describes the varied roles played by myriad states as nature's manager, as distinct from its uninhibited exploiter, and one which is sufficiently flexible to enable comparative historical analyses, whether framed by international, transnational or global perspectives. Creating reserves, controlling hunting or caring about soil recovery are among the numerous activities undertaken by state institutions

* The authors would like to thank Frank Molano and Ian Tyrrell for recommending further readings and Michael Hathaway for commenting on earlier drafts of this Introduction.

that have helped reshape landscapes and ecologies and expanded the state's remit, facing down or accommodating fierce resistance and altering the basis of citizenship in the process. Long aware of the fundamental historicity of the natural environment, geographers and environmental historians have produced insightful studies on this broad topic in which the state is often present, but rarely the focus of analysis. This volume brings together work from around the world by geographers, sociologists, anthropologists and historians on the history of national parks and other forms of nature conservation that place the state centre-stage. It follows the recent historiographical move to locate nature conservation in global and transnational contexts and takes environmental history closer to those other disciplines – political science, sociology, anthropology and, indeed, mainstream political history – that have been at the forefront of studies of state building and functioning.[2]

The concept of the nature state builds on works that have explored how states, as territorial bodies, have always had a hand in the management of nature. The environmental transformations due to these interventions are particularly evident in the way many states have articulated big, bold visions of how nature ought to look and pursued projects of radical change aimed at achieving greater control over local populations in order to make the land more productive, to extract more rent or to render the state more powerful. As such, states have played a significant role as producers of the territory and the nature they claim to control. David Blackbourn's *The Conquest of Nature* is the standard-bearer for this way of thinking historically. In this brilliantly sustained account of the production of the modern German landscape largely through the state's attempts to control water, whether for agriculture, drinking, sanitation, industry or shipping, Blackbourn makes it clear that, among other things, the early modern and modern state was a colossal exercise in civil and military engineering.[3]

Along these lines, in *Seeing Like a State*, James Scott offers what is surely the most influential way of thinking about the state in recent environmental history. Like any seminal intervention, Scott's work has attracted criticism, but many scholars have been impressed by his notion that state-led schemes of improvement failed because they were based on simplified and reductive but politically 'legible' accounts of the natural environment. Scott's archetypal case study is provided by 'German' or 'scientific' forestry, which consisted of a 'forest' with even-aged stands routinely kept clear of animals, undergrowth, or any other messy process that obscured the ultimate goal of producing a uniform timber crop. Orderliness, it seemed, could maximize production, making a modernist aesthetic integral to a modernist efficiency. In practice, scientific forestry, or modern intensive agriculture, produces junky ecologies that require ever-larger interventions (chemical and otherwise) to function productively.[4]

The pioneer generation of environmental historians tended to structure their work as counter-narratives to accounts of progress and improvement, implicitly asserting a distinction between human and nature, producing stories that lamented the harm human developments had caused the natural environment. Now environmental historians are more likely to conceptualize the environment as a hybrid co-production of the human and the non-human, as Blackbourn and Scott aptly demonstrate.[5] The principal agent in the modern production of hybrid natures can be taken to be what, over a decade ago, Adam Rome identified as the 'environmental management state'. Rome deployed the term as part of a larger discussion, centred on the United States in the twentieth century, about the need to take the environment seriously in historical analysis. In just three paragraphs devoted to the topic, Rome pointed out some of the activities that constitute the scope of this kind of state, including predicting the weather, controlling wild fires, protecting cattle from predators, building systems of dams, establishing sanitary services and slowing or halting environmental degradation. In an influential essay on American environmental history, Paul Sutter widened Rome's scope, observing that the reach of the environmental management state goes beyond conservation, preservation and environmental regulation 'to include a broader array of state activities in areas such as agriculture, science, and engineering, public health, internal improvement, warfare and national defense, and international relations'. More recently, Frank Zelko took the term outside US history when he indicated that it could be used to refer to 'the management of environmental affairs [in] virtually every populous, hierarchical society that has ever existed'. The environmental management state thus seems flexible (or vague) enough to include any way in which states, at any time, have dealt with the environment. Furthermore, environmental historians have tended to concentrate squarely on the environmental management side of the equation, while shedding little light on the state itself.[6]

Where this task has been carried out, it has been mainly by political scientists focused on the present, and they have analysed what they variously term the 'environmental state', the 'green state' or the 'ecological state'. Bruce Schulman's skilful analysis of the 'resource management state' in the US Progressive Era is exceptional for focusing on the past. More typical is Andreas Duit, Peter H. Feindt and James Meadowcraft's extended discussion of the 'environmental state', which they define as 'a state that possesses a significant set of institutions and practices dedicated to the management of the environment and societal–environmental interactions', including the agencies, laws, budgets and research organizations that deal with pollution, waste, resource extraction, operation of industrial facilities, energy and transport infrastructure and nature protection. They assert that environmental states emerged in advanced industrialized nations in the 1960s, which chimes with claims made also by historian Brian Drake, arguing that their 'bureaucratic structures, regulatory modes of intervention, and ideological justification were first articulated in OECD-type countries with their privately owned and market-mediated economies and representative democratic political systems.'[7]

However, just as Raymond Williams said of 'nature', so terms like 'environmental', 'green' or 'ecological' need to be historicized. To use them with respect to the activities of state before the late 1960s risks anachronism, and yet to suggest that states did not take an interest in the natural world prior to the emergence of 'environmentalist' discourses in the 1960s is problematic. The chapters gathered here demonstrate that well before the 1960s states, including those outside of the developed world, devised institutions and regulations that took 'nature' rather than the 'environment' as the constituting discursive motif, suggesting that there is an older and continuing political claim by the state that its particular duties included the obligation to care for – and not just use or overcome – nature. The set of institutions, regulations and relations brought about by this responsibility constitute the nature state. In this sense, we move close to our colleagues from political science in identifying 'a distinctive sphere of governmental activity', but argue that the nature state allows us to place this global phenomenon in a longer-term historical perspective. By eschewing a distinctive late-twentieth-century language, we hope to open up a broader research agenda. Our focus might be on the long twentieth century, but our hope is that ancient, medieval and early modern historians might also find the 'nature state' a useful category of historical analysis.[8]

State-led nature conservation, that peculiar form of divination whereby the state endeavours to produce nature according to what its experts perceive to be nature's blueprint, provides the vantage point from which we have chosen to explore the nature state. During the long twentieth century, the urge to preserve or restore landscapes and resources often spearheaded the development of regulations and institutions focused on nature. Since 'the great transformation' induced by the Industrial Revolution, which was then reinforced by the 'great acceleration' of the post-war period and the continuing exponential increase in human population and consumption, conservation in myriad forms has been one particularly visible way in which state agencies have tried to control, manage or produce nature, both physically and symbolically, for reasons other than raw exploitation.

The nature state evokes descriptors of state activity gathered under labels such as the welfare state, the warfare state and the security state, and, like those labels, it is more restricted than over-arching designations like the colonial state, the liberal-capitalist state, the authoritarian state, the communist or socialist state and so on.[9] Whereas the latter descriptors offer a comprehensive description of the state, the former produce the illusion of totality by highlighting just one aspect – however important – of state activity. Such labelling can reflect a significant alignment between what the state did and how it presented or identified what it did, however reductive those representations might seem in retrospect. The British 'welfare state' in the post-war years is a good example of this: whether condoning or condemning, few in post-war Britain doubted the existence of the welfare state. By contrast, historians can articulate an identity for a past state by highlighting particular functions, as, again taking a British example, David Edgerton does in his influential analysis of the British 'warfare state'. Our conception of the nature state takes this approach, but it differs from Edgerton's thesis by not seeking to characterize the general orientation of the state but instead foregrounding a particular realm of state activity, namely the claims the state makes over its constitutive lands, waters and species of plants and animals, with ramifying effects throughout human and non-human histories.[10]

Moving into new areas of activity saw the nature state strengthen more traditional aspects of the state's mandate. For example, it is not new to assert that the modern state is based on the idea of a clearly bounded territory over which it claims total sovereignty and that to exercise control over the citizenry within this bounded space is the pre-eminent way in which a state comes into being. But few historians have followed geographers' lead in thinking about how protected areas – a conspicuous aspect of the nature state – have contributed to territorial state building. Exerting jurisdictional control in the name of conservation over geographically peripheral or economically marginal territories by seeking to restrict or manage development exemplifies a discursive and political shift in how, where and why the state actively exercised its authority. As Emily Wakild shows, the Argentinian government used the designation of national parks as a way of gradually asserting state control over parts of Patagonia, a peripheral and beautiful territory thought to be of little economic value.[11]

Frederico Freitas analyses a similar situation in which the Brazilian state sought to hold sway over its distant border with Argentina by creating Iguaçu National Park. This case also indicates a process by which the state became the proper guardian of nature. The expansion of state authority brought about by the nature state was implicitly predicated on a peculiarly persistent claim that emerged in the past 100 or so years and has been articulated time and again across most landscapes and cultures. The claim holds that the state itself – more so than communities, elite institutions or private consortiums – has the rightful and logical purview to protect nature. This process almost always saw not just the state, but also the central government within it rhetorically obscure the interests of multiple and competing publics in the interest of a single national community by pointing to its unique capacity to determine and designate the use of a certain place or nature. As a consequence, the nature state tends to strengthen the centre at the expense of regional and local state institutions. Rounding out our contributions to the broadly understudied history of conservation in Latin America, Claudia Leal likewise alerts us to the Colombian experience in which regional state authority was partially erased by the universalizing ambitions of the nature state, agent of the centralizing potency of the national government.[12]

Matthew Kelly further shows how the nature state also emerged against other areas of state activity. In post-war Britain, demands that the state take a more interventionist role in landscape and habitat protection generated tension between state-subsidized agricultural intensification, the 'traditional' farming methods that produced the landscapes favoured by the amenity societies, and the professional conservationists whose priority was the maintenance or restoration of flora and fauna rather than a particular landscape aesthetic. In the age of agricultural subsidies, the nature that predominated was the one more strongly backed by the state, with agricultural ministries determined to deliver 'cheap food' and protect the interests of farmers usually outgunning the relatively weak agencies of the nature state. In time, and often in response to European Union directives, successor bodies to the Ministry of Agriculture became agents of the nature state through the administration of agri-environmental schemes. That process was evidence of how the state needs to be seen as a constellation of competing bureaucratic actors that tend to defend their own interests. Importantly, the capacity of bureaucracies to reproduce themselves means state structures can outlive the political formation that led to their creation. As such, interpreting bureaucratic agencies and institutions as semi-autonomous interest-bearers within a fluid state not only helps explain the struggle of the nature state to stake its claims, but it also means individual actors can be located within these broader bureaucratic frameworks without losing focus on their singularity or agency.[13]

The modern nature state justified the expansion of its authority into novel spaces – both conceptual and physical – by advertising that it did so in the public interest. This alleged intention distinguishes the ministrations of the nature state from attempts to manage nature in ways that generally sought to protect or sustain the rights and privileges of particular interest groups, whether these were rights of common or the game reserves set aside for the royal or aristocratic hunt. Seeking to protect natural areas – or, more recently, the functioning of favoured ecosystems – was part of a broader discourse of the common good; the nature state could create a form of commons predicated on citizen rights in processes characterized by the standardizing and bureaucratizing urge of the modern state, although this should not obscure how its actions could equally constitute an authoritarian act of near-total exclusion of citizens, preserving nature for wildlife and restricting access to those tasked with protecting it. Either way, by imposing new rules of access that undermined conventional notions of customary rights or private property, the actions of the nature state were often framed in terms of the national interest, which theoretically allowed all citizens to regard a park as their own, and in some cases non–citizen tourists might invoke their right to a patrimony defined as 'World Heritage'.[14]

The purported public interest was anchored in benefits that could be material or symbolic. By the 1960s and 1970s, states strove to protect samples of different ecosystems present in their national territory and thus guarantee the diversity that many, especially in tropical countries, thought should be promoted as a national symbol and a source of pride. In later decades, biodiversity became a new way of quantifying the value of nature, and nature states used it effectively to promote a sense of their responsibility. Much of this activity was highly performative, the intended audience being the international community, and by the 1990s it could give the Global South access to significant inflows of money linked to international development. Conservation benefits could also be tangible: in Colombia, parks disproportionately protect *páramos* (high Andean ecosystems above the treeline) that constitute the country's primary source of water. Across the world, biodiversity and catchment basin protection delivered benefits to distant and numerous urban people but negatively affected rural dwellers as parks restricted the rights of citizens who had previously made direct use of these same resources.[15]

The problem of restriction of rights and access revolved around an unformulated question: from whom did the state claim to be protecting a common natural patrimony? The answer is: from some of the citizens it claimed to represent. Exercising the state's prerogative to control and conduct conservation was neither a neutral nor an apolitical undertaking; vigorous conflicts often arose between state agencies and resident groups, scientists, bureaucrats and industrialists, and also among these groups. As critics have pointed out, it is often the most disenfranchised citizens, those who live in marginal territories to begin with, who lose sovereignty and security, and more privileged ones who gain rights of access. Costly trade-offs result from, for example, prohibiting traditional extractive activities including hunting and fishing in favour of more modern consumptive uses such as the pursuit of knowledge and tourism, couched as representing the interests of all. In Britain, for example, Parliament allowed, in the eighteenth and nineteenth centuries, private landowners to dissolve common rights to facilitate agricultural 'improvement'; yet in the twentieth century, common rights were more likely to be overturned by the state in the interest of statutory bodies like the water undertakers or, lately, in order to implement environmental management schemes.[16]

As the nature state emerged in tension with various groups of citizens, it lost legitimacy among them. Leal's and Freitas' chapters show how the nature state prevented peasants and elites from the Colombian Caribbean and the Brazilian South from raising cattle, growing crops and building hotels by creating parks. Peasants were evicted, the nature state's most blatant form of absolutism, and such displays of force, here and elsewhere, meant state bureaucrats attracted the animosity of those affected. Subsequent criticism and scholarly attention led in some cases to significant changes in state-led conservation practices. But seemingly as frequent have been the cases in which states have not had the clout to carry out such policies. In these cases, a wholly different configuration exists in which residents have been categorized as squatters without the right to schools, roads and other public services, which compromises both the livelihoods of these citizens and the integrity of the institutions and nature under conservation. Another model is suggested, as Siddhartha Krishnan shows, by how the British in colonial India protected the customary rights of the Toda people because their pastoralism helped create what the British dubbed the Lord Wenlock Downs, an undulating grassland that reminded British officials of much-loved southern English landscapes. Here, colonial self-interest helped protect an indigenous people likely to be squeezed out by commercial forestry, though as the likelihood of Indian independence rapidly approached, pressure came from within the colonial regime to declare the Downs a national park in the hope that this might serve as a defence against anticipated developmental pressures.[17]

While defining and defending a common patrimony constructed a negative state image in the eyes of those who had to bear its costs, it also allowed states to improve their stature vis-à-vis various constituencies, and foster the development of environmental identities. Through the appropriation of a part of the state territory for leisure or education, some gain rights of admittance to places where they previously had none. As such, the state has been called upon to re-value territories, often in response to lobbyists with broadly national agendas, like the Dartmoor Preservation Association (1883) or the National Trust (1895) in the United Kingdom or the Sierra Club (1892) in the United States. The campaigns led by these organizations not only helped re-value upland or mountainous 'waste', but were also part of the constantly evolving discussion about the role of the state, and thus also of citizens' rights and obligations. Arun Agrawal's work is instructive here for it leads the discussion into a new terrain. Taking Kumaon, a mountainous region in northern India, as his case study, Agrawal examines how new forestry policies aimed to decentralize the government and secure the participation of locals, dramatically changing villagers' attitudes and practices towards forests, which contributed not just to better resource management but also to the development of 'environmental subjects'.[18]

The nature state seeks legitimacy not only among its own citizens. Setting aside a specific nature with the express intention of leaving it relatively unchanged in the future allowed states of almost any political hue to announce to the international community their sense of responsibility and affirm their modern character. Across a wide range of social and political configurations – from colonial and decolonizing states in Southern Africa to revolutionary and counter-revolutionary states in Latin America to postsocialist states in Europe – increasingly vocal states claiming the responsibility for and ownership of conservation areas became remarkably common. In the twentieth century, nature conservation became a way in which modern states could project their legitimacy. As Emmanuel Kreike shows, apartheid South Africa, an otherwise pariah state, derived significant credit from its extensive effort to protect nature by designating national parks, combating deforestation and desertification and containing dangerous livestock diseases. In this manner, nature protection helped justify an expansionist South African state determined to consolidate its control over Ovamboland in Namibia.[19] A good recent example of a similar move is the Afghan government's decision to designate the country's first national park in 2009, which made Afghanistan the latest member of a substantial club with an impressive and quantifiable footprint – at the time of writing, 193 countries have dedicated 213,844 marine and terrestrial protected areas covering 32,868,673 km². Or, more vividly, parks and reserves occupy an area larger than the African continent.

To focus on the state rather than individual governments makes it possible to show how, historically, certain institutionalized and bureaucratic functions of the state with respect to nature protection became characteristic not only of liberal democratic states, but of the modern state more generally. Stefan Dorondel and Veronica Mitroi argue that there have been significant continuities in how the Romanian state has managed fishing rights in the Danube Delta in the late nineteenth century's age of nation-building and in its current neoliberal phase. This is not to say that there has been a linear or unidirectional history of the nature state, ever-strengthening once established in any given political context, for as Dorondel and Mitroi suggest, the Romanian nature state expressed itself quite differently under socialism between 1949 and 1991, adopting a radically alternative interpretation of nature. The history of the nature state, fostered by governments of all sorts, is thus erratic and changing, developing in fits and starts rather than showing a steady progression.

The irregular but near-universal character of the nature state can also be appreciated in the way it appealed to various levels of state strength and capacity. In part, building the nature state through the designation of protected areas seemed possible because of the low threshold of expertise and investment required. Rather than a display of power through technology, resource mobilization and spectacle, as exemplified in the twentieth century by the construction of large dams, nature conservation primarily asked the state to decree that particularly valuable places be set aside. Even poor and small states could make such gestures, suggesting that conservation could constitute what Jess Gilbert has termed a 'low modernism', as distinct from Scott's 'high modernist' attempts to reform social and natural systems. The stakes of engaging – but not succeeding – in conservation are deceptively low and ensure this form of state-building remains politically expedient, seductively simple, and therefore astonishingly ubiquitous. Even when attempts at setting land apart for the purpose of nature conservation were unsuccessful, the nature state, as shown by Wilko Hardenberg in his chapter on the preservation of the Alpine bear in Italy, found ways to defend its interests by other means. These processes found expression in complex regulations, often informal, that further affected policymaking in the long term, even beyond radical regime changes.[20]

The universality of the nature state, as the chapters in this volume suggest, has contributed to its coming into being – both materially and conceptually – in myriad different ways. However, with regard to national parks, many historians have emphasized a supposed late-nineteenth-century American model that prioritized scenic preservation and tourism, and became a global prototype. Our conceptualization of the nature state not only allows us to set aside this narrow and sometimes arcane interpretation of American hegemony, but also reorients how we might look at the American case itself. If early American parks should be understood in the context of the United States' imperial expansion, both within and beyond its current borders, so we can recognize the continuities and discontinuities between how the United States sought to establish control over particular natures within its nominal national borders and recently acquired overseas territories. Intentions, however, were not always fulfilled and Ian Tyrrell's chapter shows how overt attempts to develop tropical forestry in the Philippines gave way to a nationalist project for national parks, demonstrating that even the United States could fail to replicate its own model and was not insulated from either local management strategies or the cultural politics of an elite but indigenous nationalism. If the American model is decentred rather than treated as the control for an exercise in comparative history, the nature state becomes a useful means to capture the range of claims, capacities and configurations of states consciously and conspicuously undertaking nature conservation.[21]

A more useful way of integrating the influential US experience is by examining global networks, as can be done by focusing on the relation between science, states and conservation efforts. Knowledge travels, as do the scientists themselves, buttressing nature states across the world. As Michael Hathaway's chapter demonstrates, the scientists of the World Wildlife Fund, under the active patronage of HRH Prince Philip, had little compunction about working in Communist China in the late twentieth century. Emily Wakild opens temporally earlier avenues to think about the role of science in the building of nature states by presenting something like a chicken-and-egg situation; the protagonists of conservation in both Chile and Argentina before the 1930s acquired much of their experience and reputation by working for the state, and then, either from within or from the outside, pushed for the emergence and growth of the nature state. Any consideration of the nature state must take into account the politics that underpin the production of official knowledge, particularly with respect to who qualifies as an expert, and how that changes over time. Hathaway, again, is a good guide here. His discussion of the fall and rise of 'slash and burn' or 'swidden agriculture' in 1980s and 1990s China explores a moment when the scientific consensus was challenged, in this case by a reconsideration of 'indigenous knowledge', and ultimately superseded.

It should be clear by now that we do not wish to reify an interpretation of the state as a discrete entity, clearly bounded from society, which loses sight of the complex systems of networks, actors, structures and institutions that constitute the state in its day-to-day existence. We are influenced by anthropological perspectives that suggest the state is best understood as a space of brokerage and conflict mediation for a constellation of non-state, trans-state, and suprastate actors, institutions and networks. This view is particularly relevant to the historical study of the nature state, since it opens the door to an analysis of governance that is alert to the role of civil society and international relations in defining and shaping the nature state's course of action. Consequently, although we have placed the state at the centre of our analysis, we actively embrace the fact that the nature state emerged and developed in response to the interplay of local, regional, national, imperial or transnational pressures, and suggest that the nature state's claims to authority or ascendancy over non-state actors are part of the constant play of power evident in any polity. Our claim is that during the long twentieth century, states of varied political hues became agents for conservation, and that nature conservation advocates, including influential transnational organizations, generally had to work through the state in order to create the context within which they could function. In this respect, the nature state could operate through its own institutions – most obviously national park authorities and the like, legal and regulatory frameworks, and the bureaucracies that made it tangible – or in collaboration with non-governmental organizations for which state structures and agencies acted as enablers by disentitling or weakening existing vested interests.[22]

If the state did have a hand in the production of nature, where does this leave our opening gambit that nature also had a hand in the production of the state? By developing a comparative perspective on the emergence of the nature state, the concept helps draw out an important component of our analysis: namely the significance of the quite different natures of many twentieth-century states, as suggested by a cursory comparison of the highly developed agricultural landscapes of Western Europe with, say, much of Southern Africa or India. In Europe, large predators were hunted almost to extinction by the late nineteenth century, and wild ungulates are relatively thin on the ground, whereas both are prevalent in large parts of Africa or India. In Latin America, large animals were similarly absent but had been so for millennia, which often resulted in exuberant tropical forests where plants or birds rather than large, charismatic mammals have merited most conservationist attention. Though seemingly elementary, this observation is nonetheless crucial to any attempt to consider comparatively why in Africa big animals became the object of conservation, while the survival of cultural landscapes and endangered colonies of iconic species prevailed in much of Europe, and forests have been the conservation mainstay in Latin America. The radical differences shown by these non-human natures partly reflected the radically different extents to which they had been effected by human intervention. Thinking comparatively about the development of the nature state allows us to consider not only the role of the state as an agent of conservation, but also about nature as a shaper of the social and economic trajectory of a wide variety of states. As such, a relativism born of our historical understanding of the anthropic nature of the most seemingly unspoiled nature should not obscure a key surmise, made in the opening paragraph of this introduction: the nature controlled by the state at the advent of the nature state plays a pivotal role in shaping its future development.

Almost all twentieth-century polities were affected by debates that made nature conservation a question for government intervention. Our case studies fit together around a deepening set of questions concerning the various historical contexts in which the nature state has developed. When does nature acquire political value and why did attempts to conserve nature take particular forms in different places? How can we understand the appeal of conservation through regime changes and transitions in forms of citizenship? What are the local, national and global circuitries that produced and transferred statist approaches to conservation? How has the nature state worked for and against the maintenance of cultural landscapes? Where does a state draw the line between protecting nature and defending livelihoods or increasing the standard of living? How does the state distinguish between the reasonable use and the unacceptable abuse of natural resources? And on what basis does the state, liberal or authoritarian, determine the limits of growth? The discursive frameworks within which the nature state finds answers to these profoundly political questions tell us much about prevailing knowledge regimes and forms in which power consolidates around particular issues. And the degree to which those answers favour the natural environment – and are framed as such – suggests much about the relative strength of the nature state within the constellation of competing state interests.

Given that concern about environmental degradation is likely to increase, and given continuing efforts to achieve international agreements with respect to averting or minimizing the effects of climate change, in the twenty-first century the executive power of the nature state might increase, particularly when it is reinforced by powerful supra-state organizations and institutions. It is possible, if the move away from dependence on fossil fuels increases, as the German example is beginning to suggest, that the nature state might even in some instances achieve the paradigmatic status desired by many environmentalists. Could the nature state become as historically and politically legible as the welfare state, or even the communist state or the capitalist state? This is a question only future historians can answer, but for now it seems timely to enhance our historical understanding of the nation state's trajectory and to try to bring this into the historiographical mainstream.

Notes

1 Charles Tilly, 'Reflections on the History of European State Making', in *The Formation of National States in Western Europe*, ed. by Charles Tilly (Princeton, NJ, 1975), 42. On ecology and ideas of nature see Donald Worster, 'The Ecology of Order and Chaos', *Environmental History Review*, 14/1–2 (1990), 1–18; Karl S. Zimmerer, 'Human Geography and the "New Ecology": The Prospect and Promise of Integration', *Annals of the Association of American Geographers*, 84/1 (1994), 108–25; and Richard White, 'Environmental History, Ecology, and Meaning', *The Journal of American History*, 76/4 (1990), 1115. On history and vast or deep nature transformation, see: Jo Guldi and David Armitage, *The History Manifesto* (Cambridge, 2014); Mark Levene, 'Climate Blues: Or How Awareness of the Human End Might Re-Instil Ethical Purpose to the Writing of History', *Environmental Humanities*, 2 (2013), 153–73; Dipesh Chakrabarty, 'The Climate of History: Four Theses', *Critical Inquiry*, 35/2 (2009), 197–222; and Jamie Lorimer, *Wildlife in the Anthropocene: Conservation after Nature* (Minneapolis, MN, 2015). On nature, development, war and the state, see: John Luke Gallup, Alejandro Gaviria and Eduardo Lora (eds), *Is Geography Destiny? Lessons from Latin America* (Palo Alto, CA, 2003); Philippe Le Billon, 'The Political Ecology of War: Natural Resources and Armed Conflicts', *Political Geography*, 20/5 (2001), 561–84; Terry Lynn Karl, *The Paradox of Plenty, Oil Booms and Petro-States* (Berkeley, CA, 1997).

2 There is a vast literature on nature conservation; these are some outstanding titles (the last two are recent collections of global park histories): Samuel P. Hays, *Conservation and the Gospel of Efficiency: The Progressive Conservation Movement, 1890–1920* (Cambridge, MA, 1959); Alfred Runte, *National Parks: The American Experience* (Lincoln, NE, 1979); Richard Grove, *Green Imperialism: Colonial Expansion, Tropical Island Edens, and the Origins of Environmentalism, 1600–1860* (Cambridge, 1995); Jane Carruthers, *The Kruger National Park: A Social and Political History* (Pietermaritzburg, 1995); Roderick P. Neumann, *Imposing Wilderness: Struggles over Livelihood and Nature Preservation in Africa* (Berkeley, CA, 1998); Bernhard Gissibl, Sabine Höhler and Patrick Kupper (eds), *Civilizing Nature: National Parks in Global Historical Perspective* (Oxford, 2012); Adrian Howkins, Jared Orsi and Mark Fiege,

National Parks Beyond the Nation Global Perspectives on 'America's Best Idea' (Norman, OK, 2016).

3 About the role of the nation-state in shaping nature and vice versa, see: Marco Armiero and Wilko Graf von Hardenberg, 'Editorial Introduction to Special Issue: Nature and Nation', *Environment and History*, 20/1 (2014), 1–8. Examples of this are too numerous to list. For a few representative examples from a variety of projects, see: Judith Shapiro, *Mao's War Against Nature: Politics and the Environment in Revolutionary China* (Cambridge, 2001); Richard P. Tucker, *Insatiable Appetite: The United States and the Ecological Degradation of the Tropical World* (Berkeley, CA, 2000); Paul R. Josephson, *Industrialized Nature: Brute Force Technology and the Transformation of the Natural World* (Washington, DC, 2002). See also David Blackbourn, *The Conquest of Nature: Water, Landscape, and the Making of Modern Germany* (New York, 2006).

4 James Scott, *Seeing like a State: How Certain Schemes to Improve the Human Condition Have Failed* (New Haven, CT, 1998). As predicted by David Laitin when reviewing Scott's book, its core concepts have become a staple of the academic vocabulary. It has thus become exceedingly difficult to pinpoint specific examples of their use in environmental historical scholarship: terms like 'high modernism', 'legibility', or 'mètis' have become almost unavoidable. David D. Laitin, 'Review of Seeing like a State by James C. Scott', *The Journal of Interdisciplinary History*, 30/1 (1999), 177–9. Even when certain aspects of Scott's idea seem not to fit into specific narratives or need to be adapted to specific local conditions, its terminology is apparently adopted almost without criticism. Tina Loo and Meg Stanley, 'An Environmental History of Progress: Damming the Peace and Columbia Rivers', *The Canadian Historical Review*, 92/3 (2011), 399–427; Jess C. Gilbert, 'Low Modernism and the Agrarian New Deal: A Different Kind of State', in *Fighting for the Farm: Rural America Transformed*, ed. by Jane Adams (Philadelphia, PA, 2013), 129–46.

5 Raymond Williams, 'Ideas of Nature', in *Problems in Materialism and Culture* (London, 1980), 67–85; William Cronon, 'The Trouble with Wilderness; Or, Getting Back to the Wrong Nature', in *Uncommon Ground: Toward Reinventing Nature*, ed. by William Cronon (New York, 1995); Donald Worster *et al.*, 'A Round Table: Environmental History', *The Journal of American History*, 76/4 (1990), 1080–420; Paul S. Sutter *et al.*, 'State of the Field: American Environmental History', *Journal of American History*, 100/1 (2013), 94–148.

6 Adam Rome, 'What Really Matters in History: Environmental Perspectives in Modern America', *Environmental History*, 7/2 (2002), 303–18; Paul S. Sutter, 'The World with Us: The State of American Environmental History', *Journal of American History*, 100/1 (2013), 94–119; Frank Zelko, 'The Politics of Nature', in *The Oxford Handbook of Environmental History*, ed. by Andrew C. Isenberg (Oxford, 2014), 716. See also Paul S. Sutter, 'Tropical Conquest and the Rise of the Environmental Management State: The Case of US Sanitary Efforts in Panama', in *Colonial Crucible: Empire in the Making of the Modern American State*, ed. by Alfred W. McCoy and Francisco A. Scarano (Madison, WI, 2009), 317–27; and Christine Keiner, 'The Panatomic Canal and the US Environmental-Management State, 1964–78', *Environmental History*, 21/2 (2016), 278–87.

7 Bruce J. Schulman, 'Governing Nature, Nurturing Government: Resource Management and the Development of the American State, 1900–1912', *Journal of Policy History*, 17/4 (2005), 375–403; Andreas Duit, Peter H. Feindt and James Meadowcroft, 'Greening Leviathan: The Rise of the Environmental State?', *Environmental Politics*, 25/1 (2016), 5, 8; Brian Allen Drake, 'The Skeptical Environmentalist:

Senator Barry Goldwater and the Environmental Management State', *Environmental History*, 15/4 (2010), 587–611. See also: Arthur P.J. Mol and Gert Spaargaren, 'Ecological Modernization and the Environmental State', in *The Environmental State Under Pressure*, ed. by Arthur P.J. Mol and Frederick H. Buttel (Bingley, 2002), 33–52; John S. Dryzek, *Green States and Social Movements: Environmentalism in the United States, United Kingdom, Germany, and Norway* (Oxford, 2003); James Meadowcroft, 'From Welfare State to Ecostate?', in *The State and the Global Ecological Crisis*, ed. by John Barry and Robyn Eckersley (Cambridge, MA, 2005), 3–23; Lennart J. Lundqvist, 'A Green Fist in a Velvet Glove: The Ecological State and Sustainable Development', *Environmental Values*, 10/4 (2001), 455–72.

8 Williams, 'Ideas of Nature', 67–85; Duit *et al.*, 'Greening Leviathan', 6.

9 In this regard, see also Duit *et al.*, 'Greening Leviathan', 6.

10 A Scottian analysis can be offered here. The welfare state was made politically legible for ideological reasons, particularly with respect to political mobilization, but was in actuality a simplified account of the post-war British state. David Edgerton, *Warfare State Britain, 1920–1970* (Cambridge, 2006).

11 Roderick P. Neumann, 'Nature–State–Territory: Towards a Critical Theorization of Conservation Enclosures', in *Liberation Ecologies: Environment, Development, Social Movements*, ed. by Richard Peet and Michael Watts (London, 1996); Lary M. Dilsaver and William Wyckoff, 'The Political Geography of National Parks', *The Pacific Historical Review*, 74/2 (2005), 237–66.

12 In a similar fashion, Tina Loo has explained elsewhere how wildlife management in Canada shifted from fractured, local efforts to unitary control. Tina Loo, *States of Nature: Conserving Canada's Wildlife in the Twentieth Century* (Vancouver, 2006). Similar processes can be noticed for the United States according to Louis Warren, *The Hunter's Game: Poachers and Conservationists in Twentieth-Century America* (New Haven, CT, 1997).

13 Tony Bennett and Patrick Joyce, 'Material Powers: Introduction', in *Material Powers: Cultural Studies, History and the Material Turn*, ed. by Tony Bennett and Patrick Joyce (London, 2013), 2–3. On the state as disunity, see Philip Abrams, 'Notes on the Difficulty of Studying the State (1977)', in *The Anthropology of the State*, ed. by Aradhana Sharma and Akhil Gupta (Oxford, 2006). On state autonomy, see Theda Skocpol, 'Bringing the State Back In: Strategies of Analysis in Current Research', in *Bringing the State Back In*, ed. by Peter B. Evans, Dietrich Rüschemeyer and Theda Skocpol (Cambridge, 1985), 3–37.

14 Tom Mels, 'Nature, Home, and Scenery: The Official Spatialities of Swedish National Parks', *Environment and Planning D: Society and Space*, 20/2 (2002), 136; Paul Betts and Corey Ross, 'Modern Historical Preservation: Towards a Global Perspective', *Past & Present*, 226/suppl. 10 (2015), 7–26.

15 David Takacs, *The Idea of Biodiversity: Philosophies of Paradise* (Baltimore, MD, 1996); Claudia Leal, 'Uneasy Bedfellows: Water and Conservation in Chingaza National Park, Colombia' (presented at the 8th European Society for Environmental History Conference, Versailles, France, 2015). Much the same occurs in Europe, where upland parks contain vital watersheds.

16 Arun Agrawal and Kent Redford, 'Conservation and Displacement: An Overview', *Conservation and Society*, 7/1 (2009), 1–10; Matthew Kelly, *Quartz and Feldspar. Dartmoor: A British Landscape in Modern Times* (London, 2015); Harriet Ritvo, *The Dawn of Green: Manchester, Thirlmere, and Modern Environmentalism* (Chicago, 2009).

17 Dan Brockington, Rosaleen Duffy and Jim Igoe, *Nature Unbound: Conservation, Capitalism and the Future of Protected Areas* (London, 2008); Mark Dowie, *Conservation Refugees: The Hundred-Year Conflict between Global Conservation and Native Peoples* (Cambridge, MA, 2009). Latin America is often referred to as a region in which environmental authorities have not been able to expel residents from national parks, see Stephan Amend and Thora Amend, *National Parks without People? The South American Experience* (Gland, 1995).

18 Arun Agrawal, *Environmentality: Technologies of Government and the Making of Subjects* (Durham, NC, 2005), 17.

19 Marine Deguignet et al., *2014 United Nations List of Protected Areas* (Cambridge, 2014). It is telling that to be included on this list, a protected area has to be officially designated by a country. This list was first presented at the first World Conference on National Parks held in Seattle in 1962. Present terrestrial coverage is 15.4 per cent of the earth's surface, excluding Antarctica. The number of sites has nearly doubled each decade since 1962.

20 Emily Wakild, *Revolutionary Parks: Conservation, Social Justice, and Mexico's National Parks, 1910–1940* (Tucson, AZ, 2011); Jane Carruthers, 'National Parks, Civilization and Globalization', in *Civilizing Nature: National Parks in Global Historical Perspective*, ed. by Bernhard Gissibl, Sabine Höhler and Patrick Kupper (Oxford, 2012), 257; Jess C. Gilbert, *Planning Democracy: Agrarian Intellectuals and the Intended New Deal* (New Haven, CT, 2015).

21 For a bibliographic overview of the topic, see Richard White, 'American Environmental History: The Development of a New Historical Field', *Pacific Historical Review*, 54/3 (1985), 297–335. Classic contributions to this debate include Roderick Nash, *Wilderness and the American Mind* (New Haven, CT, 1967); Richard West Sellars, *Preserving Nature in the National Parks: A History* (New Haven, CT, 1997). The idea of America's exceptionalism is greatly stressed in the series of documentaries by Ken Burns, *The National Parks: America's Best Idea* (Arlington, VA, 2009). For a comparative perspective, see also Libby Robin, 'Being First: Why the Americans Needed It, and Why Royal National Park Didn't Stand in Their Way', *Australian Zoologist*, 36/3 (2013), 321–31.

22 Aradhana Sharma and Akhil Gupta, 'Introduction: Rethinking Theories of the State in an Age of Globalization', in *The Anthropology of the State: A Reader*, ed. by Aradhana Sharma and Akhil Gupta (Oxford, 2006).

1 The export of the American national park idea in an age of empire

The Philippines, 1898–1940

Ian Tyrrell*

Applying the concept of the nature state to the United States is inherently difficult. Getting in the way is the leathery notion of American exceptionalism, in which the United States is considered outside the supposed normal path of historical development. Under this influential idea, the United States is considered a prototype of civil society, while 'Europe' is characterized as dominated by big states. In exceptionalist thought, the United States is also considered a republic, not an empire, a dichotomy that complicates discussion of any colonial nature-state project. To work one's way through this ideological thicket, great attention has to be paid to the specific articulation of American power. This is not to say that the United States lacked a state apparatus at any time in its history as a nation, but that the composition of the actually existing 'state' has changed over time. In the nineteenth century, federal power was limited, though the individual state and local authorities had a disproportionate role in both regulation of the economy and promotion of public welfare. Nevertheless, as the century wore on the institutions of the 'state', particularly the federal state, focused increasingly upon the harnessing, rationalization and disposition of natural resources, particularly land, to the private sector. Within political economy, their chief function was seen as enabling capitalism to grow boundlessly. Abundant natural resources have played a key role in underpinning this political economy.[1]

On the basis of the historical record, many Americans felt by the end of the nineteenth century that capitalism's further growth was far from assured. One reason was the expected future diminution in the availability of natural resources. As a result, reformers, scientists, politicians and members of the wider public worked to develop conservation organizations and policies that would regulate the exploitation of natural resources, making more efficient use of them to prolong supplies. Since the largest landowner in the American west was the federal government, there was still ample opportunity to use the federal state to ensure the future survival of the republic, albeit in a modernized

* Ian Tyrrell wishes to thank the Australian Research Council for support of project DP0986538 – The International Context of American Conservation Policy, c.1900–1920 – from which this work is drawn.

form that ran counter to the certainties of American exceptionalism. But that required precisely the development of a state apparatus in which the regulation of natural resources was key. Arguably the United States became a nature state in ways not completely dissimilar to what happened in Germany, or to some extent also in some other European countries over water and timber policies as well as broader issues of nature conservation.[2] Whether that be true or not requires a comparative treatment almost entirely absent in the current literature. Nonetheless, 'nature' understood as the physical resources available to the human race probably played a more important part in the reconfiguration of the US state in the early twentieth century than in practically any other country. Only since 1941 has the warfare state intruded dramatically upon the nature state for greater prominence in the configuration of the American polity and power.

This is not the way American historians have cast the issues of conservation. They have not recognized the pivotal role of nature conservation in the so-called Progressive Era, *c.*1898–1917, and have typically used the language not of 'state' but 'nation'. They have certainly emphasized the pioneering role of national park legislation in creating what could be termed a nature state. This national park concept has been described as 'America's best idea', and, so the mythology goes, was exported to the remainder of the world.[3] The national park movement spurred an important bureaucratization process popularizing the idea of the United States as 'nature's nation'.[4] The latter term has been used in US historiography but not problematized as an analytical category grounded in the peculiar development of a state rather than a transcendent idea embodying American nationalism.[5] That this outcome was achieved with the National Park Service (1916), a US government bureaucracy, and through the exercise of political power and legal force to remove lands from commercial use or indigenous occupation for several decades before that, shows that a nature state within the United States both existed and yet was not purely utilitarian in emphasis. The national parks operated *within* the confines of the wider conservation of natural resources. To succeed politically, however, the movement for national parks had to embody ideas of efficiency and utility through promotion of both tourism and human physical wellbeing more than just an intrinsic appreciation of nature.[6]

With the establishment of the National Park Service, the project of identifying and protecting a unique American nature became thoroughly institutionalized in the nation-state apparatus. Almost simultaneously, during the so-called Progressive Era from around 1900 to US entry into the First World War, the American nation-state itself was shaped in a global engagement with the wider world of 'high' or 'Victorian' imperialism. Part of this broader engagement concerned the appropriation of nature in the colonies that the United States acquired after the Spanish–American War of 1898. The two themes, empire and nation-state building through regulation of the natural world, have rarely, if ever, been brought into the same frame within the historiography.

As already noted, the United States itself was in the process of creating a nature state in which the conservation of natural resources, particularly water and forests, would occur under national government purview. The means was the creation of a federal bureaucracy. The most prominent example was the Forest Service, which became, between 1898 and 1909, a major instrument of nature-state management. Its numbers rose dramatically from just 10 to 2,500 employees over that period, and the acreage covered jumped by nearly 400 per cent in the same period, to reach almost 200 million acres by 1910. The Forest Service was self-consciously a national project from the point of view of its champions, led by Gifford Pinchot, the Chief Forester of the United States (1898–1910) and main adviser on domestic policy to President Theodore Roosevelt (1901–9). Under the leadership of Pinchot and Roosevelt, both efficient use and conservation by withdrawal of public lands for future use where possible became the guiding principles of a nature state. In the continental United States, national parks and monuments fell outside the control of the Forest Service, but the service had more influence over these matters in the colonial possessions. The efficiency form of conservation, not national park promotion, was critical to the complicated nature state that the US government attempted to project upon the nation's new colonial possessions.[7]

The key bureaus of the US nature state were duplicated in the colony, though not connected directly to their US equivalents, since they reported to the Philippine Commission (established in 1900). The latter was in effect the colonial government, and a body with a majority of non-elected US representatives. In turn, Philippine government bureaucrats (initially largely Americans) reported not to the US Congress or individual specialized departments such as the US Department of Agriculture, but the Bureau of Insular Affairs within the War Department in Washington. In this 'insular' nomenclature, the United States concealed its embarrassment over the colonial relationship and avoided the use of the term 'Colonial Office'. These complicated manoeuvrings were a concession to ideological American exceptionalism and its political force within the US Congress.

In the same exceptionalist vein, Americans trumpeted their form of colonialism as one of temporariness and modernity in comparison with the empires of old Europe. Yet national parks never became an important part of the colonial regime's enterprise, nor were other forms of protection such as wildlife reserves or national monuments prominent in the possessions acquired between 1898 and 1917. Only Hawaii, which became an incorporated territory eligible for statehood, was a partial exception to this rule. Given that the claim of originating the national park idea is a deeply rooted one in US historiography and popular thought, and given that colonial national parks have come to be identified in historical literature with the promotion of modernity, symbolizing national identity, development and citizenship in the making, this absence is a curious one.[8]

Delving deeper into the history of resource management in the US-occupied Philippine Islands from 1898 to the creation of the Commonwealth of the

Philippines in 1935 is necessary to supply answers to these apparent anomalies. Thereby, light can be thrown on how American policymakers understood the place of national parks within wider nature protection and utilization. This case reveals that US colonial nation-building was indeed premised on utilitarian conservation. Nature and nation were closely related, but nature in the colonial setting was to be fashioned as rationalized space and resources for the sustainable economic development of the colony. But it was also expected to be a colonial state that paid for itself. For this fiscal reason, much of the responsibility for the enforcement of conservation and other policies was – especially after the passage of the Jones Act in 1916 to Filipinize the lower echelons of the civil service – delegated to these officials or to local municipal authorities dominated by Filipinos. This was another legacy of American exceptionalism as, despite the defeat of anti-imperialists in the US presidential elections of 1900, 1904 and 1908, there was little stomach in the US Congress for an expensive external empire.[9] Empire was expected to operate on the cheap. Educated colonials could easily live with a relatively light colonial bureaucracy, since it quickly served to augment their local power and underpinned the emergence of a savvy political elite that campaigned within parliamentary means for eventual self-government.[10]

The colonial elite had a different view, however, of the role of the colonial state. It was not simply there to cover the expenses of stationing American troops and putting down rebellions, but to spread a Philippines-wide consciousness in a polity fragmented ethnically and regional. The colonial state needed to be converted into an instrument for the gradual assumption of indigenous power that had been lost in the so-called Philippine Insurrection after the American occupation. The educated elite, heavily Catholic and Filipino, saw national park and monument creation as important to the colonial state due to its promotion of nascent national feeling. They drew upon American national park ideas but modified them to incorporate traditional Filipino peasant mythology concerning humans and the wider natural world, and to suit a story of heroic resistance to both European and American imperialism. From their point of view, the state should use national parks to promote a cohesive national identity necessary to foster economic and social development. In practice, this would mean cementing the colonial elite's power. One might express this process as a form of legitimation for the nature state in its anti-colonial guise.

This was not the only modification in the American model of a national park that occurred in the US colonial empire. The emphasis on natural resource management faced a challenge not from preservationist sentiment, but indigenous traditions and prerogatives of land use. The outcome was a compromise over land management that incorporated traditional human use of forested areas that, because of the pressures of economic modernization, impinged heavily upon national parks when they were finally proclaimed in the 1930s. This was a different pattern from national park development in the United States, and the concessions made by the colonial government towards land use within all reserved spaces, notably the forest reserves, spilled over into the management of parks. One can conclude that the provenance of park spaces is essential to understanding park outcomes.

Nature and protected spaces in the American colonial rule

The American 'Insular' government in the colony, with the American-dominated and unelected Philippine Commission at its apex, treated the Philippines as a natural resource cornucopia. Forests were regarded as key to the islands' development as a colony and proto-nation. The United States inherited as much as 55 million acres of forested land from the defeated Spanish. It was the duty of the Bureau of Forestry, working under the Philippine Commission, to assess this land as suitable for forestry, and to transfer to the Bureau of Lands unsuitable parcels that could be disposed for agriculture or mining. Sugar plantations and other commercial farming already existed in the Philippines, and the colonial state extended this and peasant cultivation to make the islands self-sufficient economically. Such land could be clear-felled, but so could forest land in the following ways. 'Forest' land was to be mapped, setting out timber concessions for development of a commercial industry, but other areas, treated as 'reserves', would be withheld from immediate or even medium-term use. Such land could be reserved for future use or preserved as essential to support agriculture, that is, to prevent erosion and to conserve water supplies. None of this land was originally intended for scenic or ecological purposes. The characteristics of the Philippine nation-state in the making under American rule would thus be interconnected with the transformation of nature. They would depend upon the scientific classification, rationalization, supervision, and disposal of resources to various economic ends. As well as bureaus of lands and forestry, those of science and 'plant industry' (studying plant introductions such as rubber trees) made American Progressive Era utilitarian conservation central to this imperial mission.[11]

Americans regarded the forests as the most obvious natural resource to be studied by these bureaus and to be exploited. Because of inter-imperial competition and because the colonial takeover coincided with the rise of Progressive Era conservation at home, policies of efficient and rationalized use of forests were as prominent in the objectives of the colonial officials as among their superiors back home.[12] Very important in this process was the ebullient, wealthy and highly ambitious Pinchot, who engineered the appointment of Colonel George Ahern, a close supporter, as chief of the new Philippine Islands Bureau of Forestry in 1900.[13] Pinchot himself visited the colony in late 1902 to appraise the situation and to recommend action to Governor-General William Howard Taft, and to the US government in Washington.[14] Under Ahern and with Pinchot's connivance, colonial forestry policy aimed to attract American capital using timber concessions. A forestry law authored by Pinchot was proclaimed (1904), requiring licences for timber removal. Formerly unknown tree species were investigated, the proposed forest reserves began to be mapped and proclaimed, and mechanized logging was encouraged in concession areas. By 1911 a vigorous commercial marketing campaign was underway to make the islands the centre of an East Asian and Pacific timber trade. The expansion was based upon research into the *Dipterocarp* family, of which Red Lauan (*Shorea* sp.) was the most prominent.[15] A forestry school was established at Los Baños, Luzon, in 1910, to experiment with this and other tree species and to guide the scientific study of the forests. In these ways, Americans pursued their longer-term objective: a new model of efficient colonial development for global imperialism, with forestry as a key component.[16]

The administrative position of forest resources was different in the Philippines from the mainland United States, however. In the latter case, Pinchot and his allies fought against preservationists and advocates of tourist interests wishing to take charge of the management of national parks. Parks and forest reserves were each under different management and with different objectives by 1916. By contrast, in the Philippines, economics took precedence and the Bureau of forestry controlled all forested land. This location militated initially against any plans to create national parks. It also meant that when national parks were declared, they were greatly influenced by the bureau's policies, rather than a preservationist agenda, and by the social compromises with elites and peasants that the Insular government as a whole made to effect its utilitarian plans.

This did not mean a total absence of interest in protecting special natural features and 'wonders'. Rather, such interests (slowly) developed within and subordinate to social and economic utility. In no way did the establishment of park reserves concern wilderness preservation, but the first attempts to engage in park creation came with strong connotations of garden landscapes tied to economic botany. The turn-of-the-twentieth-century US environmental aesthetic placed high value on ornamental gardens that embraced 'natural' and informal plantings, as had been famously used by Frederick Law Olmstead in his plans for Central Park in New York, and at other locations by the 1890s.[17]

The timing supports the view that the US government and private American citizens resident in the Philippines linked national park creation – American-style – with a constructed national identity represented in an imagined *national* space in which nation was identified with scenic beauty or other 'natural' space. The only purported attempt at creating a national park in the first quarter-century of American rule was the tiny Dapitan site in Zamboanga del Norte, proclaimed by the governor-general in 1910; this was the house and garden of nationalist hero José Rizal before his execution by the Spanish in 1896. The choice of a moderate from the liberal elite that had opposed the Spanish reflected the desire of American officials and US residents in the islands to create proto-nationalist pride without compromising American legitimacy. American schoolteacher Austin Craig worked in 'semi-public service', wrote his biographer, George F. Nellist, to establish 'Rizal National Park' in Dapitan.[18] A teacher with the Philippine School of Arts and Trades and from 1915 an associate professor of history at the University of the Philippines, Craig was one of several private American citizens who endorsed the idea of national parks as a move towards national status for the Philippines.[19] Craig's commitment to Philippine nation-building on a liberal, democratic model nurtured by the colonial state was clear in his hagiographical works on Rizal, where Rizal's musing on nature were identified with the growth of Philippine consciousness.[20]

Yet, despite Nellist's testimony, the colonial government did not create a *national* park. No national park legislation existed for Dapitan in the colonial period. The Philippine Commission called it simply a 'park', noting expenditure of funds to honour Rizal's memory, under an Executive Order of the governor-general. American authorities subsequently neglected the site until Manuel Quezon's Commonwealth of the Philippines resurrected it in 1940.[21] The Americans did establish a commemorative site in Zamboanga, employing a prominent landscape architect to design it. But the site was named for the governor of the province, John J. Pershing (1909–12), who prosecuted the war against the Islamic rebels on the island of Mindanao. With attractive hanging gardens, Pershing Park was 'of special note' and, colonial officials claimed, it helped to make Zamboanga one of the most beautiful cites of the 'Orient'.[22] But, as 'Pershing' Park, it memorialized the bloody subjugation of the Muslim-dominated island.

Where the American regime did move to establish quasi-national reserved spaces, the impetus was more renovationist in regard to nature than preservationist or conservationist. This stance was perfectly represented in botanic gardens. This aesthetic emerged as early as 1903, when Thomas Hanley, a landscape gardener with the Bureau of Plant Industry, proposed a national garden for Lamao in Bataan, on the island of Luzon. Henley recommended parks and gardens for the Lamao site to combine scientific, economic and aesthetic interests. The space created would instruct businesses on likely agricultural prospects, throwing 'light upon many questions affecting the industrial resources of the Islands'. Indeed, the entire 'scientific world [was] awaiting the result of botanical investigations in the Archipelago', asserted Hanley. But, without any hint of contradiction, Hanley recommended that sections for 'pleasure gardens' also be set aside.

The plan was hierarchical and supervisory. The colonial state attempted to educate the Filipino people in the ways of Western social and economic advancement. Hanley intended to instruct the people not only in Bataan, but also on a 'national' level, because 'a national garden' would start from an 'educational standpoint' and improve public health through strategic planting of trees that would purify unhealthy air. Here, Hanley illustrated the lingering belief in the miasmatic vapours theory on the transmission of tropical diseases. In Manila especially, he lamented that 'no place of healthy recreation for the people' existed, and there was 'no escape from the evil-smelling ditches, malaria breeding swamps, and impure atmosphere that surrounds them'. No wonder that Manila's 'Civil Hospital' was 'always crowded', and Americans developed 'a longing to leave for "God's own Country"'.[23] A start needed to be made to convince the Philippine people of the prophylactic utility of parks and gardens.

Though Hanley's plan for Lamao was not adopted and the site proceeded no further than becoming an agricultural experiment station, the underlying themes in his proposal continued both to influence and to reflect American ideas of the appropriate spaces of nature for the Philippines. Hanley's approach was almost duplicated in the plans to renovate Manila as a City Beautiful. This would overcome the absence of any 'place of healthy recreation for the people', and free them from those 'evil-smelling ditches' that Hanley referred to as in need of the City Beautiful design. The colonial government called in Daniel Burnham, the noted Chicago Beaux-Arts designer and architect, to draw up ambitious plans for parkland laid out on a geometric basis, with garden landscape ideas incorporated. The implementation of this plan was never completed but several stately buildings were erected, and landscape areas and boulevard construction began before the First World War. These ordered yet 'natural' landscapes were intended to express the creation of a model city, appropriate to a modernizing colonial state. As a colonial engineer put it: 'We have now [begun to create] not only one of the most beautiful cities in the world, but one of the healthiest and most conveniently arranged.' Aesthetics and utility would work together.[24] Similarly, Forbes Park in the planned city of Baguio, the summer capital, featured a detailed plan 'based upon both a practical and the artistic application of landscape design', and 5.5 kilometres of hedges were planted.[25]

At the basis of both Burnham's well-known and Hanley's little-known plans was a Euro-American aesthetic of parks and gardens, rather than appreciation of a 'natural area', but the latter could be preserved as part of this aesthetic just as cultivation of the wild was encouraged in the English and American Romantic landscape gardens of the nineteenth century. It was from this kernel of interest in the wild among landscape gardeners and economic botanists that colonial moves towards national parks for the Philippines would grow in the 1920s. Hanley stated that parts of the Lamao site that were still untamed should be left so. These sections displayed 'a scene of wild grandeur that I should be sorry to see disturbed'. The 'colonial government should extend paths from the cultivated section of the garden into the wilder places' because the latter 'will always afford pleasure to ordinary people' and to the botanist these wild sites would be 'a most prolific field of study'.[26]

This proto-national space to instruct and uplift the Filipino people was not created at Lamao, but a national garden was eventually established elsewhere in Luzon in 1920 to incorporate the same values. The Makiling National Botanic Garden at Los Baños near Mount Makiling reflected this aesthetic and the growing appreciation of tropical plants and landscapes,[27] a situation that conformed to the utilitarian and scientific priorities of the state. These imperatives were to classify and exhibit large numbers of previously undocumented species for economic utilization. The background to this enterprise, like the plan for the Lamao garden, began after 1898, when American botanists travelled to the famed Buitenzorg Botanic Garden in Java to study the tropical flora with which the Dutch had so much experience, and to import plants from there for the economic development of the American colony.[28] The entire Southeast Asian region was scoured for specimens, including trips to Borneo, Singapore and the Malay States. By 1911, the US government in the Philippines was engaged in a complex multilateral exchange programme to spread the benefits of tropical plants that might have military, commercial, medical or industrial uses. The Los Baños Botanic Garden primarily served these scientific purposes of economic botany. The Yale Forestry School and other institutions began to study tropical flora, and some bureau officials – such as Harry N. Whitford, who returned to an academic position at Yale – became apostles for the development and dissemination of rubber and other tropical plants on a global basis. From forestry alumni who worked in the Philippines, a nucleus of tropical forest experts emerged in the United States by the 1920s.[29]

While Americans were not interested in pushing the national park concept in the colonial era, they did begin in the 1920s to move towards such an idea by setting aside a nature 'reserve', and initiated discussion on others. They focused first on the 'scenic beauty' theme, starting with the tiny (4 ha) Cave Forest Reservation in Baguio (1922). Tellingly, Baguio was the American hill station used by senior government officials; it was built on European colonial lines to avoid the oppressive summer heat, and the Cave Reserve would benefit colonial administrators and their families. But it was more significant that the national park concept found its Philippine origins in the National Botanic Garden, the nucleus of the Mount Makiling National Park, proclaimed as the first national park. The origins of this park from a working botanic garden drew less upon American ideas of national parks and more upon the local environment and the natural resource management context that dominated colonial policy.[30]

Also important in official thinking was the utilitarian objective of the control of water to preserve irrigation opportunities and stop flooding and soil erosion. This was classic multiple-use conservation in the style of Gifford Pinchot. In his 1928 annual report, Henry Stimson, the Philippines governor-general and a protégé of Pinchot and former President Roosevelt, recommended a reservation that would protect, for utilitarian reasons, the catchments in the Mountain Province of Luzon. That area was threatened by peasant or tribal agriculture that led to deforestation and consequent impact upon water supplies for farming. The other reserves established in the 1920s served utilitarian forestry purposes. Only at Los Baños was there a different agenda, because of the location of the Forestry School there as an institution that encouraged the scientific study of plants.[31]

A sudden change towards national park development came only in the early 1930s. Mount Makiling was first proposed as a national park in 1930 and designated as such under a special Act in 1931, though it was almost immediately subsumed within a broader plan for a series of parks.[32] Part of the impetus for change came from the practical forestry officials whose interest in preserving 'natural' areas grew as they mapped forest reserves, and encountered impressive scenic places such as Pagsanjan Gorge and waterfalls in Laguna Province.[33] In 1923, foresters had been ordered for the first time to collect data on 'all caves, waterfalls, hot springs and other natural resources located within the public forest', to encourage their use for 'industrial, health, recreational, or other public purposes'.[34]

Experience of grand and beautiful places such as mountains, gorges and waterfalls recalled the nineteenth-century Romantic inclinations towards worship of the sublime in nature. Foresters' attitudes also reflected growing interest in and knowledge about the tropical vegetation. Influential among the American officials in both regards was Arthur F. Fischer, director of the Bureau of Forestry in Manila from 1917 to 1935 and a Yale Forestry School graduate of 1911. Working at Los Baños, he became, through practical experience in the field, fascinated with tropical plants and developed a love of the archipelago's rich biodiversity.[35] From 1929, he cooperated closely with indigenous officials to plan a national park programme. Fischer joined Philippine Senator Camilo Osias on a tour of the islands from Luzon to Mindanao in 1931, where they reportedly 'explored the country, identifying natural wonders that should be set aside for public enjoyment'.[36] The Mount Makiling National Park came under the new unified park system after its creation (Act No. 3915 of 1932). The latter Act, however, did not come into force until 1 January 1934 through the Forestry Administrative Order No. 7 (National Park Regulations), which provided rules for the establishment, supervision and special uses of national parks.[37]

Filipinos and the reworking of the national park idea

The real impetus for this change came from Filipinos seeking to promote a national identity for their projected independent country. These liberal nationalists were members of the Hispanicized and Catholic elite. Often wealthy, influential and educated people, they were well-represented in the Philippines legislature and wished for independence, but worked with the American administration to achieve it. The popularly elected Philippines legislature (instituted in 1907) proclaimed in 1931 that because 'Progressive countries of the world have their own national parks which are considered as one of their national treasures', the Philippines should have its own as part of its move towards self-government. Here the elite followed the European and American idea of national parks and attempted to mimic its effects. 'Following in the footsteps of such countries and in line with the policy of conserving public properties which are of national interest' was an objective of nation-building and national status, according to this educated group.[38] Osias was the leader of these national park enthusiasts. He was a liberal nationalist in the tradition of Rizal. An American-trained teacher with a degree from Columbia University, Osias was 'a member of the first Independence Mission to the United States in 1921'. After becoming a Philippine senator in 1925, he went four years later to the United States as resident commissioner to the US Congress and 'worked assiduously for the Independence Bill'.[39]

The importance of Filipino support for national parks was accentuated by the continuing low priority that the Bureau of Insular Affairs in Washington placed on this issue. Though agreeing to sign the bill creating the parks, the US government refused to provide funding. Governor-General Frank Murphy vetoed the implementation of the proposal in 1934 for a national park budget.[40] He cited financial stringency at the height of the Great Depression. But economics did not deter Filipino politicians. Once Commonwealth status was achieved in 1935, the new government initiated an intensive campaign to create national parks. In all it proclaimed 26 of these, covering a total area of 167,706 hectares by 1939; another 68 sites were under consideration.[41] All but a handful were created out of Bureau of Forestry land and many were to be administered by the bureau, whose mission continued to be utilization of the forests for commercial timber production.

The Filipino nationalists borrowed elements of the American stateside interest in 'natural wonders', tourist opportunities and the growing appreciation of the wild. The Act establishing the parks described national parks in terms familiar to American advocates:

> a portion of the public domain reserved or withdrawn from settlement, occupancy or disposal under the laws of the Philippine Islands which, because of its panoramic, historical, scientific or aesthetic value, are dedicated and set apart for the benefit and enjoyment of the people of the Philippine Islands.[42]

In theory at least, they were to be free of human settlement, as in the United States. Filipino officials also drew upon the developing aesthetic of wilderness as a place for recreation that coalesced in the 1930s in the United States. National parks were promoted in the pro-modernizing *Philippine Magazine* – a vehicle for the elite – as a means to satisfy the needs of 'vacationists' and 'nature lovers'. Forester and sometime journalist Fidel Paz publicized the parks in that magazine. He noted places of 'esthetic, scientific and historical interest' in Visayas that might become national parks by government action and he explicitly praised Filipinos because they were mimicking Western sensibilities: 'We have followed the example of other countries in preserving our historical and natural beauty spots.' To emphasize the point, he quoted the Romantic antebellum poet William Cullen Bryant on the wilds of nature. Wilderness advocate Arthur H. Carhart, a recreation engineer in the US Forest Service, was also invoked on the importance of recreation so that the Filipino people could 'take part in the strenuous contest of life'.[43] Nations must have a vigorous people if they were to stand on their own feet, and the development of a healthy and recreation-oriented 'race' would further this aim of national self-sufficiency. Americans remaining in the colony after the establishment of the self-governing Commonwealth in 1935 backed this approach. College of Agriculture professor at the University of the Philippines and former Philippine Islands Bureau of Plant Industry official Hugh Curran publicized the newly designated spaces in terms similar to those applying to American parks: 'for those who love nature in its untamed form'.[44]

Yet neither the support of Filipinos for the national park concept nor the enthusiastic endorsement of individual Americans meant wholesale implementation of an American idea of a racially improved nation through encounters with wild 'nature'. Instead, Filipino park advocates focused on the importance of a variety of park types, monuments and gardens as an integrated system for the production of national identity. They drew upon the diverse legacy of US park history, not just national parks. The new Commonwealth of the Philippines imported an American national park expert Louis P. Croft in 1939. The Utah-born and Harvard-educated Croft came to work as an adviser to the new government (he remained and was interned by the Japanese in 1942). Croft was a landscape architect, the first such expert employed in the US National Park Service. The idea to hire him came from another nationalist politician, Senator Sergio Osmeña, then vice-president to Quezon, and later Philippines president. Osmeña visited the United States in 1939 and observed the full range of park varieties. Croft was appointed to plan city parks and monuments as well as national parks. Filipino legislators saw little practical difference between the various categories of 'nature' reserves. They sought to use all of these to build national feeling in a country composed of many different ethnic and language groups spread across 7,000 islands.[45]

The 'national' monuments proposed in a public discussion of the issue in 1940 showed how a nationalist elite constructed its own sense of nature and nation, and attempted to impose it upon the diverse population of the country as a whole. There was a marked preference for sites of revolutionary significance in the struggles against both Spain and the United States by 'illustrious Filipinos', as well as sites of religious significance for the largely Catholic population of the areas apart from Mindanao (Islamic) and the tribal areas of the Mountain Province (animist religion). The built environment of the Catholic Church was incorporated into this sense of the cultural landscapes that needed to be preserved as part of the 'sacred ground' 'where blood [had] been spilt' in the struggle for national uplift. One such site proposed in 1940 was Barasoain Church in Malolos City, Bulacan, known as the Cradle of Democracy in the East for its role in the creation of the first independent Philippine constitution in 1898 that the Americans had refused to recognize. However, little was achieved before the Japanese invasion of 1941, since no preparation for this work had been undertaken, and during the Pacific War some of the sites marked to become historical parks and monuments, such as the Jesuit Church of St. Ignatius in Intramurus, were destroyed by Japanese torching or bombardment.[46] However, the establishment in 1940 of the Zamboanga site of José Rizal's house as a national park, despite its tiny size and appearance as a shrine, testifies to the intersection of the monument aesthetic and that of national parks, Philippine-style.

In addition to mixing the different types of recreational spaces available from the Euro-American legacy, Filipinos themselves claimed these spaces and redefined them. As in Europe in the medieval period, the forests of the Philippines were sites of folklore symbolic of indigenous religious beliefs. Mountains and forests were traditionally considered sacred and possessed of spirits. 'Maria Makiling', also rendered as Mariang Makiling, was a diwata or lambana (a fairy or forest nymph) inhabiting the land of the Mount Makiling National Park. Similar 'mountain deities' were Maria Sinukuan of Pampanga's Mount Arayat and Maria Cacao of Cebu's Mount Argao.[47] Maria (or Mariang) Makiling was and remains in Filipino folklore a guardian of the mountain. This mythology went alongside the anthropomorphic rendering of the landscape, especially in the case of the volcanoes that often provided the nucleus of a national park site. These were treated as volatile spirits, as in the case of the most active and 'wonderful' Mt Mayon, a major national park. 'Mt. Mayon, some people declare, is symbolic of the Bicolano character. Definitely beautiful, peace loving and kind, but also capable of violence when provoked.'[48] It was often said that Mount Makiling resembled a woman's profile, and this became a tangible source of the legend. To the local inhabitants, 'The mountain's various peaks' were said to be 'Maria's face and two breasts, respectively', with her hair 'cascading downwards a gentle slope away from her body'.[49] Some of the powers attributed to these places derived from the indigenous folkloric tradition of them as brooding volcanoes possessing their own will and magic.

Filipino elites in the 1920s and 1930s tried to tap this interest in the myths and symbols linked to forests and mountains. Forestry official Fidel Paz took up the story of Mariang Makiling that had been popularized by Rizal as a source identifying nationalism with the distinctive topography and flora of the islands.[50] Paz recommended that his countrymen visit the newly created Mount Makiling National Park because of the legends of 'Mariang Makiling', the bountiful but elusive goddess. She rewarded visitors who accepted the sovereignty of Mariang over nature, and who hunted within her prescribed limits, but punished those who did not. It was she, said Paz, 'who guides the [fishermen] on Laguna de Bay' and gave them fruitful harvests that campers could enjoy. This Filipino myth translated and subverted the impulses in American parks ideology that would otherwise have created separate national spaces rooted in a modernist ideology of the nation state in place of indigenous myths.[51]

This appropriation of Filipino folklore was one way in which the educated elite sought to create, out of the islands' diversity, a nation that valued nature and that through nature attained its own identity. Yet the Philippines included many different ethnic groups and tribes whose interests cut across this liberal nationalist objective.[52] Conflict among the people of the islands was inevitable over the purpose and status of the parks. The appropriation of folklore was highly specific and tended to shape perceptions of the parks as local in significance. This contradictory tendency towards fragmentation within the integrationist nationalist ideology was further highlighted by a different subversive impulse, coming squarely from local practices, though duplicated in similar ways across most of the Philippines. Local practices in the use of forests and water contributed to a further Filipino reshaping of the national park idea. They pitted the nation-shaping agenda of the Filipino elite, like the US authorities before it, against indigenous use of the forests, mostly by Igorot tribesmen and other ethnic and tribal minorities.

Not far from the surface, the popular Filipino conception of nature resisted the compartmentalization of the secular and the sacred into ordinary space and 'national' space. The practical uses to which forests were put defied the creation of national parks as objects for preservation of nature separate from humans. But there was an irony here. The Commonwealth of the Philippines inherited in 1935 a nature state that had already made compromises with indigenous people. The ways in which the American rulers treated the natural resources from 1898 until 1935 conceded spaces within which popular practices of resource use within the parks could be preserved. These practices now frustrated the nationalist leaders in effecting a national park programme on the ground. Thus the provenance of the parks in the form of the prior administration of the Bureau of Forestry and its compromises in the interest of political stability and economic growth proved decisive in the local legacy of American conservation. The original Act of the Philippine Commission governing the forests, passed in 1904, provided for draconian penalties against illegal use of timber and burning of forests for *caingins* (a form of swidden agriculture today rendered as *Kaingin*). Yet just a year later the bureau had to issue rules to extend free local peasant access to the forests for personal and village use without licence for five years: for removal of wood and stone and for cultivation and hunting. There were several reasons. On the one hand, the forests, especially in the South, were sources of refuge for rebels still opposing American rule. Any attempt to prohibit local indigenous forest harvesting threatened to undermine the security or social stability of the colonial state. On the other hand, the lack of adequate manpower and funding from the United States meant that the forestry administration had limited supervision of the forests in practice. The bureau simply lacked the resources to police the land, and the power to prosecute illegal use was vested from 1906 in municipal officials, who proved lax. Moreover, the introduction of commercial logging on an industrial scale (upon which taxes or licence charges could be exacted to support the colonial state) put further pressure on the peasant use of marginal lands, as did general economic development and population growth that American rule and its improvement of medical conditions fostered.

The forest fires that accompanied the shifting cultivators certainly changed the land, yet this was far from new. They had done so since before European occupation. Scientists and anthropologists still dispute just how damaging *caingins* can be, since the effects vary with ecological conditions and with the intensity of modern capitalist development.[53] As the report of Governor-General Stimson noted in 1928, the pressures of a growing population and marginalization of the poor by rich landowners in the towns and villages had made it inevitable that there would be further incursions on the forests for swidden agriculture.[54]

Because of the social and political complications, colonial authorities began to change tack as early as 1906, and worked to accommodate the realities of peasant and landless occupation of the public lands acquired in 1898. The destruction of forested land for swidden agriculture was regulated rather than suppressed, and 'legal' *caingins* were allowed. As a result, the public forest 'reserves' of the 1920s were not quite what they appeared to be. They contained a great deal of economic activity that had nothing to do with rational resource management of timber, and everything to do with growing peasant and landless occupation.

For this reason, forest management prior to 1932 contributed to the traditions of forest use that survived into the national park period. In Makiling National Botanic Garden, the conflicting utilitarian interests produced detailed regulations that aimed to supervise rather than suppress indigenous use of the forests within this supposed national space. Swidden agriculture bequeathed environmental problems under conditions of colonial economic development. The *caingineros* (shifting agriculturalists) failed to control the tough and almost impenetrable cogon grass (*Imperata cylindrica*) that sprang up as soon as the fired areas were abandoned by itinerant cultivators seeking 'virgin' forest to clear.[55] For this purpose, in 1922 the Bureau of Forestry introduced a system of forest planting in return for the right to clear other areas. Makiling National Botanic Garden's regulations included such *caingin* permits under a reforestation project with specific requirements for labour in exchange for clearing rights, and requirements for ipil-ipil (*Leucaena leucocephala*) planting to combat cogon infestations. As a result, a good deal of what became the Mount Makiling National Park in the 1930s was planted forest, and, indeed, non-indigenous forest, as ipil-ipil was a native of Central America used in the Philippines because it could grow faster than cogon grass and had several economic uses, including as firewood and insecticide products. These plantings were harmonized with continued peasant occupation and harvesting. In effect the colonial state was creating the 'nature' which was now to be protected.[56]

These practices had legacy implications for the national parks created from within such spaces. The new national parks included provision for forestry, manufactures (for example the making of wooden shoes), numerous *caingins*, and communal firewood concession zones. Some of these uses pre-dated the 1932 Act, with licences that had several years to run. Pig-hunting permits were honoured too, while the extinguishing of the fires lit by poor people and illegal hunting required more policing than the available Forest Bureau funding could allow. The struggle to combat forest decline was, therefore, an unending one and continued within the Makiling National Park and others declared after the passage of the national parks Act. Timber could be taken freely under 'gratuitous' allowances, but in other cases *caingins* were sites of 'illegal cutting'.[57]

Different indigenous constructions of nature – symbolic and religious on the one hand and subsistence agricultural on the other – profoundly affected the national parks that American officials and Filipino legislators tried belatedly to assemble in the 1930s, as the survival of illegal wood taking and settler occupation demonstrated.[58] The contested nature of the use of the lands inherited from the colonial state meant that park creation and policing reflected confusion over the boundaries of the parks, disputes over titles within them, and ambiguities in the legitimacy of the entire enterprise. These ambiguities were underpinned by the division of protected land between Bureau of Forestry control and local municipal authorities who had to enforce regulations, depending on the provenance of any particular national park's creation. The very meaning of the term 'national park' was often unclear in its application.

Together with the disruptive impact of Japanese occupation and significant post-independent economic pressures, peasant use in the colonial era severely compromised the parks after 1945. They underwent frequent and bewildering changes of administration and nomenclature thereafter, and their status remains fuzzy as a result of different Filipino understandings of such 'natural' or 'protected' spaces. In a notorious example revealed in 2010, criminal elements controlled a prominent national park and administered informally the distribution of domiciles to poor people camped illegally within its confines. This case was the 'protected landscape' (ironically) known as 'Roosevelt National Park' in Bataan.[59] In other instances the post-1945 parks faced depredation through rezoning by the Philippine state itself in the aid of crony capitalism's business interests, a pattern reflecting the colonial heritage that built the power of local elites in cooperation with the colonial state.[60] Moreover, the importance attached to practical forestry and the economic pressures contained therein limited the extent of parks created, which before the Second World War covered a very small proportion of forested land, despite the proliferation in the numbers of parks. Indeed, the tendency over time was for the area of pre-war parks to be reduced, as happened to Mount Makiling before its total decommissioning as a national park in 1963, when it was returned to its earlier mission as a forest reserve for 'advancement of scientific and technical knowledge on natural resources conservation and watershed protection'.[61] Mostly the parks that remained were in mountainous and volcanic landscapes unsuitable for close settlement, even as settlement continually encroached upon them.

What happened in the Philippines was different from American rule in the new territory of Hawaii. The contrast is telling for the American understanding of national parks as a particular type of national space, and can be conveyed in a brief summary of the much better known Hawaiian introduction of a national park. The legal position and prognosis of that territorial acquisition in 1898 for incorporation in the American state differed from the start. This difference was reflected in the treatment of spaces as suitable for national status and legislative protection. Whereas Filipinos were never citizens but subjects, and were 'foreign in a domestic sense' according to the US Supreme Court's Insular Cases,[62] the occupants of the new territory of Hawaii acquired in the same epoch of empire were US citizens, with an elected territorial government. This different outcome reflected the strength of the white Americans who dominated Hawaiian politics, and who had engineered the islands' annexation.[63] They succeeded in imposing a Euro-American aesthetic preserving the 'wonders' of their own volcanic region. The proposal for Hawaii National Park first received endorsement from Theodore Roosevelt's Secretary of the Interior, James Garfield, in 1908. Enthusiastic support came later from both wilderness advocate John Muir and Roosevelt, and congressional action followed in 1916.[64] Hawaii benefited from significant lobbying by the sugarcane planter elite in the islands, and Hawaii's status as an incorporated US territory made the idea of a national park there as non-controversial as the Philippine one was anomalous until the 1930s.

These two cases on the periphery of American empire are instructive. From the point of view of the American state, having a national park required not only a culturally constructed perception of natural wonders, but also participation in the body politic.[65] Though endorsed and often strategically chosen from the top, the process of US park (and national monument) nomination was highly particular. It reflected power relations through access to congressmen and lobbying capacity. Without these features, preservation of scenic beauty could not apply to any of the insular possessions until the 1932–41 period in the Philippines.

Nevertheless, the outcome was not simply the product of legal hairsplitting of subjects and citizens such as asserted in the Insular Cases, precisely because the (contrasting) Hawaiian outcome reflected white American dominance in the islands. Rather, the colonial history of American rule and its compromises was important. The Philippine case shows the need for historians to consider a wider range of reserved spaces than 'national parks', including forests and monuments, and above all, to pay attention to their provenance in the colonial period. The Philippine experience shows how colonial rule promoted a certain kind of national space in the making, linked to rationalized resource management. A strong tradition of national parks as spaces of preservation was difficult if not impossible to develop in this context. The impetus for national parks came principally from colonial Filipino politicians seeking parallel symbols of national development to those of the United States, symbols that inevitably underwent change when translated into the daily practices of forest occupation by ordinary peasants and tribespeople. Though not necessarily incompatible with sustainable agriculture and forestry, the impact under population growth and economic development that US colonial rule stressed made these traditional practices corrosive of the colonial state's simultaneous desire to create viable forest reserves. Moreover, the compromises that had cemented the power of local landed elites encouraged tendencies towards resource degradation that marked the environmental history of the Philippine Republic after the achievement of full independence in 1946.[66] The objectives of Philippine nationalism and the neocolonial role of the post-independence state in resource management merely further militated against an American-style park ethic. The nature state that the independent Philippines Republic inherited was profoundly colonial and Filipino at the same time.

Notes

1 The underpinning role of natural resources is associated with Frederick Jackson Turner, *The Frontier in American History* (New York, 1920), chap. 1, though the idea runs deep in American culture. See Alexis de Tocqueville, *Democracy in America* (New York, 1961), 343–44. For the state, see Brian Balogh, *A Government out of Sight: The Mystery of National Authority in Nineteenth-Century America* (Cambridge, 2009); William J. Novak, *The People's Welfare: Law and Regulation in Nineteenth-Century*

America (Chapel Hill, NC, 1996). The role of the state was mediated through law: James Willard Hurst, *Law and Economic Growth: The Legal History of the Lumber Industry in Wisconsin, 1836–1915* (Cambridge, MA, 1964).

2 David Blackbourn, *The Conquest of Nature: Water, Landscape, and the Making of Modern Germany* (New York, 2006). See also James Sievert, *The Origins of Nature Conservation in Italy* (Bern, 2000).

3 Roderick Nash, 'The American Invention of National Parks', *American Quarterly*, 22/3 (1970), 728. The phrase was adapted from Wallace Stegner, 'The Best Idea We Ever Had', in *Marking the Sparrow's Fall: The Making of the American West*, ed. by Page Stegner (New York, 1998), 137.

4 John Opie, *Nature's Nation: An Environmental History of the United States* (Fort Worth, TX, 1998).

5 Opie, *Nature's Nation*; Ian Tyrrell, *Transnational Nation: United States History in Global Perspective since 1789*, revised edition (Basingstoke, 2015), 143–7.

6 Alfred Runte, *National Parks: The American Experience* (Lincoln, NE, 1979); Karl Jacoby, *Crimes against Nature: Squatters, Poachers, Thieves, and the Hidden History of American Conservation* (Berkeley, CA, 2001); Louis S. Warren, *The Hunter's Game: Poachers and Conservationists in Twentieth-Century America* (New Haven, CT, 1997); Mark David Spence, *Dispossessing the Wilderness: Indian Removal and the Making of the National Parks* (New York, 1999); Robert H. Keller and Michael F. Turek, *American Indians and National Parks* (Tucson, AZ, 1998).

7 Brian Balogh, 'Scientific Forestry and the Roots of the Modern American State: Gifford Pinchot's Path to Progressive Reform', *Environmental History*, 7/2 (2002), 198–225; Bruce J. Schulman, 'Governing Nature, Nurturing Government: Resource Management and the Development of the American State, 1900–1912', *Journal of Policy History*, 17/4 (2005), 375–403; Adam Rome, 'What Really Matters in History: Environmental Perspectives in Modern America', *Environmental History*, 7/2 (2002), 304; Greg Bankoff, 'Breaking New Ground? Gifford Pinchot and the Birth of "Empire Forestry" in the Philippines, 1900–1905', *Environment and History*, 15/3 (2009), 369–93; Samuel P. Hays, *Conservation and the Gospel of Efficiency: The Progressive Conservation Movement, 1890–1920* (Cambridge, MA, 1959).

8 Cf. Bernhard Gissibl, Sabine Höhler and Patrick Kupper (eds), *Civilizing Nature: National Parks in Global Historical Perspective* (Oxford, 2012).

9 'An Act to Declare the Purpose of the People of the United States as to the Future Political Status of the People of the Philippine Islands, and to Provide a More Autonomous Government For Those Islands', 64th Congress, 39 Stat., 545, c. 416 (29 August 1916).

10 For the wider social, political and economic context, see Alfred W. McCoy and Francisco A. Scarano (eds), *Colonial Crucible: Empire in the Making of the Modern American State* (Madison, WI, 2009).

11 Administration of Philippine Lands, *Report by the Committee on Insular Affairs of the House of Representatives of Its Investigation of the Interior Department of the Philippine Government Touching the Administration of Philippine Lands and All Matters of Fact and Law Pertaining Thereto, in Pursuance of House Resolution No. 795*, 61st Cong., 3d Sess. House. Report 2289, 2 vols (Washington, DC, 1911), I. On the Bureau of Forestry, see Brendan Luyt, 'Empire Forestry and its Failure in the Philippines: 1901–1941', *Journal of Southeast Asian History*, 47 (2016), 66–87. For forest estimates, see Greg Bankoff, 'One Island Too Many: Reappraising the Extent of Deforestation in the Philippines Prior to 1946', *Journal of Historical Geography*, 33/2 (2007), 314–34.

12 Ian Tyrrell, *Crisis of the Wasteful Nation: Empire and Conservation in Theodore Roosevelt's America* (Chicago, IL, 2015), chap. 4.

13 Char Miller, *Gifford Pinchot and the Making of Modern Environmentalism* (Washington, DC, 2001).

14 Bankoff, 'Breaking New Ground?', 369–93.

15 George Ahern to G.B. Sudsworth, 29 November 1911, fl. 1191/128, box 242, Entry 5, RG 350, National Archives and Records Administration, College Park, MD (hereafter NARA); Ahern to F.E. Olmsted, 14 April 1910, fl. 1191/100, ibid.; Donald M. Matthews, 'Lumbering in the Philippines', with acting director of forestry W.F. Sherfesee to Bernhard Fernow, 26 August 1911, fl. 1191/119, ibid.; H.N. Whitford, 'Studies in the Vegetation of the Philippines: I. The Composition and Volume of the Dipterocarp Forests of the Philippines', *Philippine Journal of Science*, 4 (1909), 699–725.

16 Tyrrell, *Crisis of the Wasteful Nation*, chap. 4; Bankoff, 'Breaking New Ground?', 369–93.

17 Anne W. Spirn, 'Constructing Nature: The Legacy of Frederick Law Olmsted', in *Uncommon Ground: Rethinking the Human Place in Nature*, ed. by William Cronon (New York, 1995), 91–113. See also Ian Tyrrell, *True Gardens of the Gods: Californian–Australian Environmental Reform, 1860–1930* (Berkeley, CA, 1999). On European approaches to cultural landscape and nature, see Caroline Ford, 'Nature, Culture and Conservation in France and Her Colonies 1840–1940', *Past & Present*, 183 (2004), 173–98; Thomas Lekan, *Imagining the Nation in Nature: Landscape Preservation and German Identity, 1885–1945* (Cambridge, 2004).

18 George F. Nellist (ed.), *Men of the Philippines: A Biographical Record of Men of Substantial Achievement in the Philippine Islands* (Manila, 1931), 71.

19 *Cornell Alumni News*, 25 March 1908, 297; Charles C. Walcott, Jr., Bureau of Insular Affairs to Esther Peterson, 24 April 1923 and Peterson to Walcott, 5 April 1923, file 27857/1, box 1267, General Records relating to more than one Island Possession, General Classified files 1898–1945, Entry 5, RG 350, NARA.

20 Austin Craig, *Rizal's Life and Minor Writings* (Manila, 1927), 161–5. See also Austin Craig, *The Story of José Rizal, the Greatest Man of the Brown Race* (Manila, 1909), 2.

21 Nellist, *Men of the Philippines*, 71. *Cornell Alumni News*, 25 March 1908, 297; 'Report of the Governor General of the Philippine Islands [1910]', in *Report of the Philippine Commission to the Secretary of War, 1910, [in One Part]* (Washington, DC, 1911), 4.

22 Francis Lejeune Parker (Bureau of Insular Affairs) to Jenn A. Pall, 31 March 1931, with file 27857/2, box 1267, Entry 5, RG 350.

23 Thomas Hanley, 'Report on the Proposed Botanical Garden at Lamao, P. I.' 2, Bureau of Agriculture, 17 February 1904, folder Forests. Philippine Islands Reports, box 587, Gifford Pinchot Papers, Library of Congress.

24 Cristina Evangelista Torres, *The Americanization of Manila, 1898–1921* (Manila, 2010), 59–65; Thomas S. Hines, *Burnham of Chicago, Architect and Planner*, 2nd ed. (Chicago, IL, 2009), 200–8, esp. 200; Thomas S. Hines, 'American Modernism in the Philippines: The Forgotten Architecture of William E. Parsons', *Journal of the Society of Architectural Historians*, 32/4 (1973), 316–26; A.N. Rebori, 'The Work of William E. Parsons in the Philippine Islands', *Architectural Record*, 41 (1917), 305–9; 'Manila Engineer Tells of City Beautiful Plan', *San Francisco Call*, 25 March 1913.

25 *Annual Report of the Director of Forestry of the Philippine Islands for the Fiscal Year Ended December 31, 1922* (Manila, 1923), 67–8.

26 Hanley, 'Report', 5.

27 Burnham, quoted in Hines, *Burnham of Chicago*, 207.

28 Elmer D. Merrill, *Report on Investigations Made in Java in the Year 1902*, Department of the Interior, Forestry Bulletin 1 (Manila, 1903), 8–9.

29 Lawrence Rakestraw, 'George Patrick Ahern and the Philippine Bureau of Forestry, 1900–1914', *The Pacific Northwest Quarterly*, 58/3 (1967), 149; Harry Nichols Whitford, *The Forests of the Philippines: Part 1. Forest Types and Products* (Manila, 1903).

30 Proclamation no. 16, 27 April 1922; Charles C. Walcott to Esther Peterson, 24 April 1923 and Peterson to Walcott, 5 April 1923, file 27857/1, box 1267, Entry 5, RG 350.

31 *Annual Report of the Governor General of the Philippine Islands 1928. Message from the President of the United States Transmitting the Report of the Governor General of the Philippine Islands, Including Reports of the Heads of the Departments of the Philippine Government, For the Fiscal Year Ended December 31, 1928* (Washington, DC, 1930), 202.

32 *Annual Report of the Director of Forestry of the Philippine Islands for the Fiscal Year Ended December 31, 1930. Arthur F. Fischer Director of Forestry* (Manila, 1931), 385.

33 Proclamation of the President, Manuel Quezon, no. 392, 29 March 1939.

34 *Annual Report of the Director of Forestry of the Philippine Islands for the Fiscal Year Ended December 31, 1923* (Manila, 1924), 18.

35 *California Garden*, 38 (Autumn 1947), 1–2.

36 Sonata Dulce F. Restificar, Michael J. Day and Peter B. Urich, 'Protection of Karst in the Philippines', *Acta Carsologica*, 1/35 (2006), 122.

37 IUCN, *Protected Areas of the World: A Review of National Systems: Indomalaya, Oceania, Australia and Antarctic* (Gland, 1992), I, 113.

38 Raf. R. Alunan to Governor General of the Philippine Islands, 16 June 1931, file 27857/5A, box 1267, Entry 5, RG 350, NARA.

39 www.senate.gov.ph/senators/senpres/osias.asp.

40 Frank Murphy to President of the Philippine Senate, 1 December 1934, file 27857/11/A, box 1267, Entry 5, RG 350.

41 *Annual Report of the Director of Forestry of the Philippine Islands for the Fiscal Year Ended December 31, 1939* (Manila, 1940), 51.

42 IUCN, *Protected Areas of the World*, I, 113.

43 Fidel Paz, 'Our Philippine National Parks', *Philippine Magazine*, 33 (1936), 67, 97.

44 Hugh McCullum Curran, 'Makiling National Park', *Philippine Magazine*, 34 (1937), 69, 91, 94. 'Curran, Hugh McCullum (1875–1960)', *JSTOR Plant Science*, http://plants.jstor.org/person/bm000001758.

45 Fidel Reyes to Resorts and Playgrounds of America, 8 July 1925; Richard R. Fly (assistant to the governor-general) to the director, Alabama Archives and History, 6 December 1934; Sergio Osmeña to Oscar Chapman (assistant secretary of the interior), 15 August 1930, file 27857/2, box 1267, entry 5, RG 359.

46 See file 27857/16, box 1267, Entry 5, RG 350; *Sunday Tribune Magazine* (Manila), n.d. (received 28 October 1940), ibid.; 'San Ignacio Church' at http://intramuros2007.wordpress.com/2007/02/19/san-ignacio-church.

47 Resil B. Mojares, *Waiting for Mariang Makiling: Essays in Philippine Cultural History* (Quezon City, 2002), 5–7, at 7; F. Landa Jocano, *Myths and Legends of the Early Filipinos* (Quezon City, 1971), 60–1; Malcolm Cairns, 'Ancestral Domain and National Park Protection: Mutually Supportive Paradigms? A Case Study of the Mt. Kitanglad Range National Park, Bukidnon, Philippines', *Philippine Quarterly of Culture and Society*, 25/1–2 (1997), 31–82.

48 Entry for 3 November 1902, Philippine Diaries of Gifford Pinchot, microfilm, Pinchot Papers; 'Mount Mayon National Park', http://en.wikipilipinas.org/index. php?title=Mount_Mayon_National_Park.

49 'First Quarter Topical Issue featuring Maria Makiling', www.phlpost.gov.ph/stamp-releases.php?id=3102.

50 Gregorio F. Zaide, *José Rizal: Life, Works, and Writings* (Manila, 1957), 8, 102; Laong-Laan [Josè Rizal], *Mariang Makiling: A Philippine Folktale*, trans. by Charles Derbyshire (Manila, 1916).

51 Paz, 'Our Philippine National Parks', 67.

52 Cf. Resil B. Mojares, 'The Formation of Filipino Nationality Under U.S. Colonial Rule', *Philippine Quarterly of Culture and Society*, 34/1 (2006), 11–32.

53 Cairns, 'Ancestral Domain and National Park Protection', 31–82; Michael R. Dove, 'Smallholder Rubber and Swidden Agriculture in Borneo: A Sustainable Adaptation to the Ecology and Economy of the Tropical Forest', *Economic Botany*, 47/2 (1993), 136–47; David Henley, 'Swidden Farming as an Agent of Environmental Change: Ecological Myth and Historical Reality in Indonesia', *Environment and History*, 17/4 (2011), 525–54; Gregg Bankoff, '"Deep Forestry": Shapers of the Philippine Forests', *Environmental History*, 18/3 (2013), 523–56.

54 *Annual Report of the Governor General of the Philippine Islands 1928*, 202.

55 See Frederick L. Wernstedt and Joseph Earle Spencer, *The Philippine Island World: A Physical, Cultural, and Regional Geography* (Berkeley, CA, 1967), 331, 364, 431,441 for the *caingineros* and their long-term impact.

56 *Annual Report of the Director of Forestry of the Philippine Islands for the Fiscal Year Ended December 31, 1922*, 54–55, 61, 69.

57 *Annual Report of the Director of Forestry of the Philippine Islands for the Fiscal Year Ended December 31, 1933* (Manila, 1934), 63 ('gratuitous') and 64 ('illegal cutting'); *Annual Report of the Director of Forestry…1935* (Manila, 1936), 62 ('illegal').

58 *Annual Report of the Director of Forestry… 1935*, 60, 62.

59 'Settlers Asked to Leave Bataan Park', *Manila Times*, 5 June 2010; Republic of the Philippines. Proclamation No. 273 (1992). Declaring the Roosevelt National Park … as a Protected Area.

60 Patricio Abinales and Donna J. Amoroso, *State and Society in the Philippines* (Lanham, MD, 2005), chaps 5–6; Richard P. Tucker, *Insatiable Appetite: The United States and the Ecological Degradation of the Tropical World* (Berkeley, CA, 2000), chap. 6.

61 Republic Act 6967 (1990); Republic Act 5323 (1963). The full range of Acts and Executive Orders governing Mount Makiling is at http://mountmakiling.org/index.php?page=gov_law.

62 For the legal position, see Christina Duffy Burnett and Burke Marshall, *Foreign in a Domestic Sense: Puerto Rico, American Expansion, and the Constitution* (Durham, NC, 2001); Bartholomew H. Sparrow, *The Insular Cases and the Emergence of American Empire* (Lawrence, KS, 2006).

63 Roger J. Bell, *Last among Equals: Hawaiian Statehood and American Politics* (Honolulu, HI, 1984), 198.

64 Nash Castro, 'The Land of Pele: A Historical Sketch of Hawaii National Park', *Hawaii Nature Notes: The Publication of the Naturalist Division, Hawaii National Park and the Hawaii Natural History Association*, 5/2 (1953), at www.nps.gov/hawaii-notes/vol5-2f.htm.

65 Cf. Warren, *The Hunter's Game*, 135.

66 Tucker, *Insatiable Appetite*, chap. 6.

2 Protecting Patagonia

Science, conservation and the pre-history of the nature state on a South American frontier, 1903–1934

*Emily Wakild**

Between 1903 and 1934, Argentina and Chile became two of the earliest countries in Latin America and the world to create national parks. Federal governments created these parks in the transnational cultural and ecological southern region of Patagonia, a place that still today holds the largest conservation areas in either nation. The landscape here is temperate, windswept and stark. Jagged and glaciated peaks, a southern extension of the Andean range, form a north to south spine that gives way to steppes and drylands to the east and thick forests and fjords to the west. The entire region, stretching southward from roughly the Río Biobío in Chile and the Río Colorado in Argentina to the shared island of Tierra del Fuego, is about three times the size of Italy (about 400,000 square miles) and today has fewer than two million inhabitants. The emergence of national parks in Patagonia is related to at least two factors: the growth of state institutions and the existence of frontier territories. State institutions included the emergence of scientific societies (funded in part by the state), the passage of federal laws and the development of governmental agencies to manage nature in place. Combined, these created the social and institutional infrastructure required to design, support and administer national parks. Importantly, despite the similar national contexts, the constitution of these state institutions reflected distinct national priorities.

In Argentina, the national park concept privileged tourism while in Chile it centred on forestry. In 1903 the Argentine government received a private land donation for designation as a national park at Nahuel Huapi Lake, but the park existed without funding or personnel until 1922, when President Hipólito Irigoyen signed a decree creating the park and extending its boundaries.[1] This decree designated a provisional director within the Ministry of Agriculture, local engineer Emilio Frey. In 1934, Law 12.103 was passed, creating the first national park administration in Latin America, the Dirección de los Parques Nacionales, and Exequiel Bustillo became its director. Bustillo

* Funding for the research and writing of this chapter was provided by the National Science Foundation Science, Technology, and Society Scholars Award (#1230911) and a National Endowment for the Humanities Fellowship (2015–2016). I am grateful for comments by Claudia Leal, Matt Kelly and Lisa Brady, which greatly improved the chapter.

focused intently on using national parks as mechanisms to develop elite tourism.[2] Across the Andes Mountains in Chile, forestry rather than tourism drove national park policy. Chile's federal government declared its first conservation law in 1879, but the legal mandate for protecting forests did not acquire specific territory until the creation of a national forest reserve, Malleco, in 1907 and another at Villarrica in 1912. The first national parks were declared in 1925 and 1926 as part of a general reorganization of forestry's position within the federal bureaucracy. For instance, the first Forestry Department was the Sección de Aguas y Bosques of the Ministerio de Industria y Obras Públicas in 1906, which became the Inspección General de Aguas, Bosques, Pesca y Caza in 1911. In 1925, this was moved to the Subsecretaria de Tierras y Colonización, still within the Ministerio de Agricultura, Industria y Colonización, but in 1927 it was transferred to the Ministerio de Fomento (Public Works). The passage of the Ley de Bosques in 1931 marked a new era of state investment in forestry that recalculated the importance of forests as separate from agriculture and more in the domain of public goods.[3] In both nations, the necessary tools to allow the state to manage nature were in place by the 1930s, and from there parks and conservation began to acquire a footprint on the ground.

This abbreviated chronology of national park creation exposes the ways in which states grappled with nature on a territorial frontier. That the first three decades of the twentieth century brought the extension of state governance to the southern borderlands is hardly a new idea, but the manner in which the state came to use, manage and control nature for reasons other than raw exploitation opens a new perspective onto frontier expansion as one whose social effects are more mixed. A diversity of encounter, plurality of social groups, and multiplicity of cultural forces shaped the Patagonian frontier such that these lands never constituted a blank slate onto which national or economic agendas could be drawn.[4]

Never a fully formed tool, the deployment of a national park idea was both connected to global systems and adapted to local and national conditions. The national park idea acquired global circulation after the creation of Yellowstone National Park in the United States' Wyoming territory in 1872. By the 1880s, Canada, New Zealand and Australia had created national parks and it seemed a model was born as Sweden and Switzerland followed suit. In examining the Swiss National Park, historian Patrick Kupper has suggested that a 'myth of Yellowstone' indicates both historical continuity and linear development, which do not play out in the history of protected areas.[5] Patagonian parks help to contextualize this supposed model in part by revealing how adjacent states, with distinct goals for development, used the idea of a national park to suit their own purposes. Perhaps one reason for the reinforcement of a supposed Yellowstone model is an overemphasis on institutional histories of national parks that foreground landmarks such as the passage of laws, articulation of decrees, and creation of bureaucratic structures rather than situating the parks in their full social and cultural contexts.

Although policymakers were the historical actors most intimately tied to the erection of the nature state apparatus, this chapter looks at the actors who preceded the bureaucrats but whose activities nevertheless represented the growth and outreach of state institutions such as natural history museums. In investigating this pre-history of the nature state, it analyses the work of the first generation of state-sponsored scientists exploring and explaining the Patagonian region as a way to chart both conservation and development. Scientists, as explorers and experts, helped provide an alternative to extractive schemes although they generally favoured applying their expertise to the development of frontier territories. These scientists contributed a template for a nature state that could then articulate specific claims to territory for inclusion in national parks. That is, by the 1930s, the information provided by scientists gave added legitimacy to the extension of a centralizing state apparatus by calling for the creation of national parks in places once far from reach. As William Adams has pointed out, over the course of the twentieth century, *ex-situ* locales for conservation such as zoos lost favour to *in-situ* ecosystems and habitats.[6] Patagonia provides a comparative lens on this slow transition. After addressing some of the issues involved in scientific expeditions, this chapter turns to two development projects – demarcating the international boundary and managing forests – that highlight the circulation of scientific knowledge in Argentine and Chilean Patagonia. It then turns to the creation of institutions for conservation in parks on both sides.

This process was not without contradictions. Conservation created justifications for an expansive government apparatus necessary to engage in long-term resource management. Yet, especially in the earliest years, scientists and state managers had at best liminal authority over frontier areas. Their endeavours did less appropriating of long-term residents' interpretations of the landscape and more integrating of worldviews derived from centuries of contact and exchange. Scientists transported natural curiosities (such as fossils and animal skins) to the metropolitan cities and they translated understandings (and misunderstandings) derived from the back and forth of conflict, conquest and commerce in distant lands. In doing so, scientists on the ground helped convince governments of conservation's expediency for agendas from forestry to tourism. Scientists minded the distinction between exploitation and conservation in a way that opened an intellectual and practical space for prioritizing nature in place. Temporal gaps existed between ideas for parks and the institutional supports that facilitated their implementation, yet scientists and their lingering legacies solidified the perceptual apparatus that came to buttress the nature state.

Sociable scientists[7]

If there is one man responsible for stitching the Patagonian territory to the Argentine nation, this man is Francisco 'Perito' Moreno.[8] Explorer, scientist, boundary commission leader, museum director, national park founder and more, Moreno is the emblematic national figure for Argentine Patagonia. In fact, one contemporary suggested that the entire cordillera region be named 'Moreno

Territory'.[9] Born in Buenos Aires in 1852 to a British immigrant's daughter and an Argentine father, Moreno had the heart of a naturalist from a young age.

In January of 1876, Moreno became the first Argentine to reach the shores of Lake Nahuel Huapi. He walked the rocky shore, gazed up at the glaciers, and recorded plant names. His was by no means an uncharted, solitary voyage. In addition to his personal assistant, Moreno hired a mestizo guide, Mariano Linares, and four Indian escorts, Amhillil, Gerrú, Cayunao and Caríleo.[10] Moreno afforded great attention to the scientific particulars of the journey, including the basalt rocks which created rapid waterfalls and coniferous forests so prodigious they attracted view-obscuring fog. Moreno chose the course by following the explorations described by George Musters, Guillermo Cox and Basilio Villarino. Along the route, Moreno noted extensive wild apple forests, a legacy of Old World plants sowed by prior settlers but now growing in untamed orchards. The party routinely sent scouts ahead to ask permission to pass among the various native settlements.[11] In addition, Moreno acutely observed the rituals and practices of people he encountered and recognized that the objectives of his own journey relied upon negotiating effectively. For instance, to secure permission for this initial visit to the lake, Moreno left his most personal belongings – including his wallet, photos of his family and letters he intended to send from Chile – with the presiding regional leader, Shaihueque. Moreno listened to Shaihueque's warnings (including threats of attack by mountain monsters, cavern-dwelling dwarfs and organ-seeking lightning), but conveyed his intentions all the same: 'As a curious man, I desire to collect samples and pass into Chile' and to return to Buenos Aires by sea. Native leaders convened several meetings and determined that their ancestors would not approve of giving him permission to cross the pass. Moreno returned via the route from which he arrived, but not before leaving his Argentine flag with Shaihueque, who hoisted it to the top of his hut.[12]

One might expect Moreno to be party to military reconnaissance, such was the brutal Conquest of the Desert that asserted military authority in Patagonia. Military expansion and modernization contributed to the context of the frontier, but Moreno's journey was instead tied up with new scientific institutions.[13] The distinction matters because although scientific exploration contributed to the militarization of the frontier, the two state objectives were not one and the same and scientific inquiry contributed to enterprises beyond direct conquest. Exploratory science was nascent in Moreno's day. In 1872, a group of young scientists at the University of Buenos Aires founded the Argentine Scientific Society. One of their early objectives was to create a museum and sponsor expeditions to fill it. Moreno was trusted with the expedition.[14] He belonged to a growing set of international scientific and geographical societies and participated in their networks of research and exchange. The provincial legislature provided for the construction and inauguration of the La Plata Museum, which opened in 1888 using Moreno's collections, and placed him as director. Moreno came to administer the nation's most complete sampling of Argentine science in the peak years of museum collection.

Nearly three decades after his first journey, the Argentine government sym-bolically gave Moreno territory along the shores of Nahuel Huapi Lake as compensation for his work negotiating the international boundary line with Chile. In 1903, Moreno returned three leagues to the Argentine nation with the explicit demand that it be incorporated as 'National Park of the South', the continent's first. The proposal was accepted but governmental funds to support and maintain the project were slow to come.[15] Moreno did not live to see the creation of Argentina's National Park Service in 1934, nor the creation of a different park in his honour three years later. This uneven cadence reveals an experimental journey rather than a march towards a known goal. Importantly, Moreno's position as a scientist shaped this march. Due to his background and what he had experienced from a young age, Moreno's work bridged empiri-cal studies and sensational travel narratives. The personal element of his work captures the combination of humanistic inquiry, rational science and touris-tic desires that emerged in early-twentieth-century writings about Patagonia, especially in places that became reserved for conservation.[16] This scientist's experience and enthusiasm fostered the park vision and set out a prototype for state-based nature conservation.

To understand both the craft of science and its contribution to state-building, we must attend to Moreno and other scientists' commitment to studying the land and its contents. The young governments of Chile and Argentina charged these men with demarcating legible territory and explaining what it contained. This has been seen as a stage in the violent erasure of native peoples from the region and the opening of the land for enormous private land consortiums.[17] Yet, this deletion and concentration was so widespread it hardly explains why conservation also occurred when and where it did. In addition to the narrative that paints national parks as one shade of conquest, I suggest that a related but separate consequence of these cumulative scientific expeditions was how they created authority for the state-based science that would come to support nature conservation. In other words, these scientists paved the way for both Chile's and Argentina's institutionalization of national parks. Science could be appropri-ated for business and it could also be appropriated for aesthetic, recreational or ecological objectives. Rather than interpret these naturalists, geographers and geologists as pawns of politicians promoting development or tools of capitalists exploiting workers, we should see these scientists as complicit in these first two developments but not beholden to them.

Scholars have shown that exploratory science is hardly a neutral endeavour; however, to take a critique of science seriously means to also consider that sci-entific observations could have merit beyond strategic uses by other interests.[18] Conservation areas arose as both a complement to and a critique of simul-taneous land transformations such as settlement and economic development. Scientists, and the conservation areas they advocated, connected to these other activities but did not completely coincide with them. Scientists served as guides to a vision of that world by mediating imperial relationships on the frontier. These men – and a few women – who advocated and facilitated conservation on the Patagonian frontier nurtured the nature state. By asking how the world worked and describing what they saw, scientists laid bare reasons why nature constituted the national interest and, by doing so, contributed to the creation of a world order in which raw nature had an articulated place.

Although their expeditions are conventionally shortened to solitary biographies, men like Moreno were rarely alone. Moreno was one of many scientists and explorers sent by state bodies south from Buenos Aires (and Santiago in Chile) to bring back information about the natural resources, native populations, mining prospects, watercourses, and settlement possibilities in the sparsely settled lands of Patagonia.[19] Not all of these expeditions were the same, but one cannot overlook the explicit connection to nation-building in this pattern of team work, exploration, description and publication. For instance, Moreno's third major trip to investigate Patagonia in 1896 was sponsored by the La Plata Museum, which he then directed.[20] He oversaw a hand-picked group of 17 scientists – including topographic engineers, geologists, naturalists, landscape artists and their assistants – with the objective of producing a 'geographical and statistical study of the region from the point of view of population and the elements that can add to national wealth, roads, and aspects of terrain that converge with the interests of the Nation'.[21] Over five months, this mainly geologic and geographic survey took place over 7,155 kilometres and ten degrees latitude; pairs of men explored, described and studied assigned points and reported back to Moreno, who synthesized their observations with his own, shaping a single narrative.[22] The men noted the vast changes in landscape as they travelled over sand dunes, lava fields, glacial ice, dense forests and fertile valleys. Moreno managed the team of researchers on this rapid but thorough assessment and oversaw epistemic habits of scientific collection and expeditionary research make critical transitions in field practice.[23] In particular, Moreno signifies early efforts to leave landscapes in place at the same time artefacts and measurements were taken from them to contribute to broader systems of knowledge. A generation of scientists sponsored by state institutions such as museums added to the constitution of a government apparatus and, concomitantly, the development of scientific networks and practices with applied uses.

Scientific lines and knowledge tracks

Scientists left intellectual marks as they criss-crossed Patagonia and grappled to make sense of it. They accumulated information about northern Patagonia quickly and attempted to apply new scientific practices to international boundary demarcation, forest management and more. The most obvious of these scientific applications came with negotiating the boundary between Argentina and Chile in Patagonia, an endeavour that immediately preceded the area's first national park. Chile argued that the boundary should follow the '*divortium aquarium*', or the watershed divide, meaning waters that drained to the Pacific would mark Chilean territory and those to the Atlantic would mark Argentine territory. In self-interested arguments, Argentina defended the notion that the boundary should follow the highest peaks in the range, the '*encadenamiento principal*' or main chain where the western slopes were Chilean and eastern Argentine. At its heart, this was a geographic debate where direct, firsthand knowledge of the specific points of dispute came into play in a lengthy process of demarcation. Highlights in this debate included: an agreement signed in 1881 that set the cordillera as the working border; a series of meetings over several months held in Santiago in 1898 at which specific interpretations of the landscape were addressed; and arbitration in 'neutral' London in 1902, where a final boundary line was delineated. Scholars have addressed the diplomatic and political challenges of such negotiations, the economic implications of the outcomes, the spatial rivalry such claims entailed, and even the cultural processes it set in motion.[24] The question of boundaries also relates to the scientific practices unfolding, especially the premise that the political line between the countries should coincide with the geographic boundary in one form or another – high peaks or watersheds.

The boundary commission allowed the nations and their scientists to face-off over their geographic reconnaissance. Moreno served as Argentina's representative at the London Court of Arbitration, while the Chilean expert was Hans Steffen, an Austrian-born geographer employed by the Chilean government. Steffen and Moreno corresponded privately as well as publishing their studies of the specific mountains in question.[25] As Carlos Sanhueza has argued, the exchanges, transfers and mobility of firsthand scientific knowledge exposes the social side of science.[26] No small amount of posturing over the names of specific rivers, lakes and inlets took place, and suspicions were frequently cast upon the inaccurate mapping of the other side. The series of reports published in 1899 in the *Geographical Journal* (the publication of record for the Royal Geographical Society) reveal as much. Hans Steffen outlined his approach in 'Exploration in South America' and Moreno responded in the subsequent issue. Among specific critiques of Lake Pueyrredon (Lake Cochrane to the Chileans), Moreno cast doubt on the thoroughness of Steffen's survey, challenged his experience on site, and politely disputed his honesty, insisting that 'Surely Dr. Steffen saw our encampments in the inlet.'[27] More than an argument about precedence and getting there first, these claims gave voice to a desire to authenticate knowledge with the expectation that experience created authenticity.

Specific knowledge also gave scientists a chance to invoke their ancestors.[28] Steffen and Moreno acted as historical chroniclers by giving lists of prior geographic knowledge in their summaries.[29] By doing this, they bolstered their own authority but they also resurrected an ancient landscape, recovering traces of trade routes, glimpses of transportation corridors, even environmental changes. They rarely positioned origins of knowledge – indigenous, settler or scientific – in strict hierarchies or as more authentic than another. Rather than translating or appropriating vernacular knowledge, they wove it into the fabric of their stories and their selves. Just as Moreno had noted, Steffen pointed out how missionaries planted apples on some of the earliest expeditions to Nahuel Huapi Lake and the trees remained in the landscape and gave him comfort.[30]

As much as a political debate, the arbitration was a scientific one resting on specific evidence – mapping coordinates and soil samples in particular. River charts, climatological evidence and botanical inventories served the arbitration at various moments, but these compilations existed beyond the political debate, in particular as reference points for future inquiry housed in both Argentina's Museo de la Plata and Chile's Museo Nacional de Santiago.[31] The domestic collection and storage of this evidence proved a significant endeavour in the process of accumulating a national identity taken from territorial claims. To give but one example of many, a large glacier-fed lake straddles the alpine border and Moreno and Steffen debated the name: Chileans argued the lake should bear the name Lago Cochrane after an independence-era British naval officer turned rebel organizer for Chile. Argentines insisted the lake bear the name Lago Pueyrredón, after their own early-nineteenth-century general and politician.[32] Specific knowledge of the land allowed the experts to argue for wresting land away from the other country both symbolically through names and practically through border arbitration. Further north, Nahuel Huapi Lake formed a strategically important site for Moreno to claim because although it resided within the Andean range and proximate to the watershed dividing line, it also lay more than twice as far from the Atlantic coast as from the Pacific. It is no wonder that most of the colonists sparsely dotting the area were Chileans and that the routes through the Andes had been fiercely guarded. With no firm boundary line, the fertile foothills might have gone to either nation.

Forests and plains

Part of the finagling for territories in the southern lands and the transportation corridors through them meant coming to terms with the varied landscapes, especially distinct between the wetter, heavily forested western side of the Andean cordillera and the drier, grassland plains of the eastern side. The environments shared proximity but had important distinguishing features. In sum, one region had too little water and the other too much. The vast portion of Argentine territory consisted of arid plains, but across the cordillera water from melting glaciers, rivers and lakes fed forests. Argentine scientists went to Patagonia charting rivers and scouting for water; Chileans' interest resided in the trees.

In Chile, a network of German scientists played an essential role in developing state-based institutions for forestry as well as attending to the growing problems of erosion in certain areas. Foreign expertise created a dominion for science in various government institutions, including the National Museum of Natural History, Botanical Garden, Horticultural School, and the General Direction of Forestry, Fishing and Hunting, which were all funded by the state and established between 1890 and 1910 with assistance by naturalists of German origin.[33] But the privilege and prestige afforded to these foreign scientists – invited and employed by several democratic administrations – did not always translate into social acceptance of them. This group of foreigners had detractors and some felt displaced, although there was little reason to doubt the Germans' commitment to Chile. These men trained Chilean students within these new state institutions, probed deep intellectual and comparative questions, and maintained professional conscientiousness that cannot be overlooked.[34] Most of them even endured personal hardship to continue their work, finding their salaries cut in half after currency devaluations in 1908.[35] Although some developed their own entrepreneurial activities – creating new industries in map production, for instance – many were simply infatuated with the scientific questions and opportunities that Chile had to offer a curious mind with time and resources to investigate.

Although Chile has a long and important history of forest use, forestry only became a necessary endeavour to the Chilean government at the beginning of the twentieth century.[36] The western slope's mainly wet forests presented challenges, including fierce erosion when the trees were removed.[37] Part of the shift to forest policies can be attributed to the cluster of German experts brought in by the government.[38] Among these scientists was Frederico Albert Faupp, who was born in Berlin in 1867 and came to Chile in 1889 with a doctorate in natural sciences from Hamburg University. Albert arrived in Chile to work at the National Museum of Natural History under the invitation of José Manuel Balmaceda's government, and was later naturalized as a Chilean citizen.[39] He is recognized in some circles as the 'father of conservation' in Chile.[40] His various labours included work in dune recovery, species introduction (salmon in particular) and attempts to foster concern for the value of natural resources.[41] Although Chile had forestry legislation pre-dating his arrival, Albert's writings and work were influential in changing perceptions of forests into a necessary resource for the economy and public wealth.[42] Albert was a scientific force by any reckoning – before the age of 30 he had published more than 50 articles, books, booklets and conference papers promoting ideas of how to best take advantage of renewable resources, all the while designing and directing public works.[43]

Albert found himself in a situation similar to Moreno in that the national government was pushing for development on the southern frontier and this development had environmental and human consequences. For Chile, this meant the clearing of large extensions of public land south of the Bío Bío River to expand agriculture. Tragically, the colonizing desire did not correspond to the physical reality of the land. Forests were cleared but the lands proved inadequate for crops, especially wheat. In turn, colonists abandoned the land and left behind denuded hills susceptible to torrential floods. Albert saw this as a geographical nightmare and demanded that the state create forest reserves with conservation and reforestation works in areas unsuitable to agriculture.[44] In doing so, Albert demonstrated a widespread and creative understanding of forests, including designing regulations to promote forest plantations as substitutes for the faltering wheat economy.[45] Although he often advocated the repopulation of forests using native species, he also promoted exotic trees, especially the fast-growing eucalyptus varieties. He generally advocated keeping livestock away from reforestation works, arguing that 'you cannot just take a plot of agricultural land and plant trees. It must be fenced off from animals.'[46] Nor was Albert opposed to forestry industries developed to meet the country's demand for lumber and firewood. However, he advocated separate processes linked to larger projects of rationalization. For example, he advocated railroads to facilitate the transport of lumber and to avoid overharvesting in the areas most convenient to markets. Other organizing principles included the idea that industrial lumber should be labelled according to species and quality to facilitate sale, and that special cutting rules should be enforced for fragile species best harvested at the end of winter. Such recommendations and flexibility characterized Albert's commitment to developing the state capacity to manage forests in conjunction with conservation areas. In Albert's prolific writings, he consistently revealed forceful arguments for state intervention in forest management. Yet, his expansive view of the landscape reveals a complex pastiche of native and exotic species, restricted and regulated uses, primitive and repopulated nature. As a trained academic, he used scientific knowledge as a lens for understanding, but he also applied that knowledge as one of the first state managers of these resources. He was a scientist and the representative of nascent state claims to nature on a frontier that came to take the form of conservation legislation.

Albert and his various government divisions advocated prohibiting logging on slopes greater than 35 degrees and terrain less than 25 metres from river banks, as well as during the spring and summer months (October through April). They replanted along fences, roads, canals and irrigation ditches with wood seen as useful for construction or forage, and prohibited cutting vulnerable species.[47] Like most conservationists of his generation around the world, Albert envisioned a close connection between rational exploitation and resource conservation. In other words, natural resources were meant to be used, but they were also fragile and in need of stewardship. He recognized this seemed contradictory, insisting that 'to conserve, it is necessary to cut' and that 'the exploitation and conservation of the forests is intimately linked with the planting and restoration of forests'.[48] This central focus on use and conservation did not keep him from advocating certain cases of stricter non-use. For instance, he recommended in 1913 that the country 'ought to establish small national parks in distinct regions to conserve samples of native species in their primitive form'.[49] Such small sites revealed a conception of parks as one component of a larger landscape managed for many uses.

Albert and Moreno both embodied the nature state in their commitments to knowing nature for state purposes. They were under no illusions of returning to a pristine state or creating areas untouched by people. As a result, the landscapes that came to hold national parks were conserved, reforested and reimagined not just by the centuries of habitation in various places, but by the vigorous state initiatives to craft and rescue the quality of the forests seen by government scientists as valuable to the country's future.

Applying science to conservation

By the 1920s, what emerged from the multidimensional state-building work of people like Moreno and Albert was an assemblage of conservation areas scattered across Northern Patagonia. Federal entities created national parks, forest reserves and public lands which turned scientific observations into policies. Connected by tenuous boundaries that crossed national borders, differences of nomenclature and contrasting uses, the assemblage that emerged in this area formed an impressive medley of parks set among other uses. With a population density of about three people per square mile, these designations were linked by latitude lines, shared histories and cultural exchanges.[50]

Scientists could see the value of arid plains, scenic lakes and dense forests for alternating objectives of settlement, exploitation and conservation. For Argentina, Nahuel Huapi Lake formed the nucleus of the first park, although this was mostly an intellectual endeavour at the beginning. In a few decades of gestation, neglect and transition, the parks went from notions and fragments to a cohesive system. The three leagues of the original parcel donated by Moreno included the western fjord of Nahuel Huapi Lake, south to the Pérez Rosales pass (over which he was prohibited from crossing in 1876) and east to include several smaller lakes. The designated area reached to the Chilean border and included the highest, glacier-covered peak in the area, Cerro Tronador (Roaring Mountain, 3,470 m). Moreno's 'National Park of the South' was expanded in 1922 to an area of about 440 leagues (half the size of Yellowstone). By 1933, under the presidency of General Augustín P. Justo, an administrative commission was reorganized and tasked with getting the parks going.[51] On 9 October 1934, both houses of Congress approved Law 12.103 which created, organized and governed the administration of the parks. It called for a directorate of eight members chosen by the executive branch plus a president selected by the Senate. The law laid out the duties of the National Park Service, including regulating access and concessions, conducting scientific studies, conserving fauna and flora, authorizing censuses and topographic surveys, as well as budgeting and reporting functions. The law afforded an annual budget but also allowed additional revenue through fees, permits and a portion of railroad fares.[52]

While it took 30 years to get from Moreno's donation to an administrative structure that could manage parks (a firm nature state), the law that supported them was well done and Argentina became the third country in the Americas (after Canada and the United States) to build a park service. Exequiel Bustillo headed this new national entity from 1934 to 1944, and through a great expansion of parks nationwide, including four new parks in Patagonia. Derived from this new law, Bustillo believed that his charge was to conserve nature and create public access, so he set out to seed villages along the frontier and promote tourism by building roads or other means of access, all while 'affirming Argentine sovereignty'.[53] Notably, he credits the notion of the national parks to 'the simple desires of some scientists, patriots at once, that knew and appreciated the great natural beauty of our national soil'.[54] The law made the parks work, but the origins – even for their most famous administrator – remained in the hands of the scientists.

In one of Bustillo's initial achievements, he oversaw the declaration of Lanín National Park, adjacent to the north of Nahuel Huapi Park. In March 1936, after their survey of the area, a park study and proposal was generated by park service scientists Pedro C. Denegri and Gustavo A. Eppens and the park ranger, D. Martín Escalona.[55] The men noted the similarities of climate, terrain and natural richness to Nahuel Huapi Park. Scenic panoramas, dense forests, prodigious rivers, 25 lakes, abundant fish populations, ample Pehuen (*Araucaria* trees), apples and berries defined the natural character of the park. Rugged and beautiful, Denegri, Eppens and Escalona did not see the proposed park as empty. They pointed out that diverse groups of ranchers lived throughout the proposed region and that they would remain there after the park was created. One property owner, on the shores of Lake Huechulafquen, lent the scientists a boat to tour the lake and its many elongated branches that were surrounded on all sides by thick forests.[56] In addition to ranchers, they noted that 'in certain points there also exist relatively numerous indigenous populations whose conditions of life would not be difficult to improve greatly'. They reported on the usurious relationships with merchants that had developed, resulting in uneven trades of labour for alcohol or simple foods. Chileans also resided in the park. After its official declaration on 11 May 1937, Lanín and Nahuel Huapi formed a contiguous park, adjacent to the border and replete with natural and human elements that had played out for centuries in tandem.

Across the cordillera, on Chile's western slope, temperate rainforests were home to Chile's earliest nature protection areas. Federal legislation protecting forests dated back to 1859 but the first declaration for conservation came in 1879 and required that a 10 km swath of forests was legally mandated to remain unused in any sale of state lands in either the coastal or Andean mountain range, from Angol to Llanquihue.[57] This was a mandate for conservation that did not match the reality of settlements on the ground, but it laid the groundwork for the first swath of protected land, Malleco Forest Reserve, created on 30 September 1907 at the suggestion of Albert and other conservationists.[58] Executive powers expanded forest regulations as a way to reclaim lands from concessions and colonization companies that were foundering. By instead forming public reserves, exploitation could be regulated.[59] The result was a small collection of parks nestled up against the cordillera, but unconnected to each other, at least initially. Malleco was buttressed by seven additional reserves of 600,000 hectares in the next five years.[60] Villarrica Forest Reserve was declared on 18 October 1912, but Chile's landmark date for its first national park is 22 December 1925 with the creation of Benjamín Vicuña Mackenna National Park out of territory already existing within the Villarrica Forest Reserve, plus additional lands.[61] The park involved 71,600 hectares of public land in the province of Cautín and the objectives stated in the decree promoted stricter protection for the natural beauty of the area, investments in tourism and prohibitions on agriculture, although the park was not to curtail government colonization plans.[62] Support for the park came from some members of the resident immigrant population, including Otto Gudenschwager, who authored a detailed map of the park demonstrating historic uses of the region and idealizing animal and landscape features.[63]

Unlike Nahuel Huapi Park, the initial Chilean protected areas shrank before they grew. This can be attributed to resistance on the ground as well as the nascent form of the nature state which proved unsuccessful in challenging interests in other government arms. In 1929, administrators rededicated approximately 90,300 hectares, the majority removed from the forest reserve and the national park, to colonization (including settlements of Chileans repatriated from Argentine lands). Essentially, the forest reserve laid a conservation footprint and it was then carved into three parts: one strictly a national park, one remaining a semi-restrictive forest reserve and a third reverted to individual property, including some native settlements. Historian Thomas Klubock has shown how state officials faced continual conflicts with peasants who sought lands in this contradictory expansion of conservation and colonization.[64] As a result, the continuity of the park and reserve dissolved, leaving small islands of reserved forests among riverine settlements of new and older residents. In the next few decades, the first park virtually evaporated and two additional national parks (Villarrica and Huerquehue) were added to the area. These were Chile's first trials with protected areas, but upon creation neither Malleco nor Villarrica neighboured Argentina's Nahuel Huapi Park. Over time, this too changed. Villarrica National Park did include the western slopes of the Lanín volcano, the object at the centre of Argentina's Lanín National Park, making those contiguous and by extension part of the larger Nahuel Huapi park complex, although these shared boundaries seem more incidental than strategic. Such contestation, confusion and wavering over boundaries and designations demonstrates the absence of a clear ecological purpose (to combine designations into contiguous transboundary units, for example) and also the weakness of the nature state in such early formulations.

In 1926, Chile's second (and now oldest) national park, Vicente Pérez Rosales National Park, was created adjacent and directly to the west of Nahuel Huapi Park. Unlike Villarrica, this protected area was expanded five years after its creation since nearly all the lands contained rocky volcanic soils, unsuitable to agriculture and vulnerable to erosion if deforested.[65] This park involved another set of constituents – skiers and recreationists. On behalf of the Alpine Club of Osorno, its president Carlos Bushmann offered to have club members act as honorary guards enforcing conservation regulations in the park. Bushmann explained the ongoing development of a ski resort on the skirts of the Osorno volcano and proposed aligning interests between the park and the resort for recreational land uses.[66] A territorial extension was declared for the park in 1950, using some of Bushmann's arguments.[67]

On the whole, once national parks began to inhabit this landscape, their presence continued and strengthened, bringing a stable form of land use – conservation – that solidified the development of a nature state. By 1934, Argentina's parks had a federal agency, a budget and presence on the ground that marked a new era in park development. For Chile, the intimate association between parks and forests meant that the legal institutions appeared earlier, but the parks had little visible presence on the ground until the 1950s.[68] This long history of management hardly amounted to a forceful, strategic takeover. The parks have been in flux since the beginning, changing with pressures and without dogmatically enforced rules. As argued in the Introduction to this volume, the development of nature states has not been unidirectional and neither has conservation provided a singular onwards march for state development. Tensions with residents or competing economic interests sometimes obligated the state to reform or repeal its conservation policies, while in other areas new lands were incorporated into conservation areas according to social and political criteria.[69] Such dynamism of response helps account for the different flavours of nature states even across similar and shared territories.

Conclusion

In autumn of 1968 the International Union for the Conservation of Nature (IUCN) held its first conference on Latin America in Nahuel Huapi National Park. The site had been chosen to highlight the historical depth of conservation in the region, to show the agreeable scenery the park provided, to demonstrate the problems and solutions of environmental management within the park, and to display the results of the prideful and forward-thinking initiative of a single citizen – Francisco Moreno.[70] Such a showcase delighted attendees. The head of the Mexican delegation, noted conservationist Enrique Beltrán, remarked at the conclusion of the conference that this final personal aspect had the most lasting result. 'Believe me gentlemen', he noted on the boat trip to the island in Nahuel Huapi Lake where Moreno's remains rest,

> all the conservationists felt something within ourselves that made us put more emphasis and effort if possible in not betraying the heritage of Moreno and this place that he gave to Argentina, to the world, because the Parks belong to everybody.[71]

This first park created a series of referents for national progress and for future conservation. There is more to the context of Nahuel Huapi Park than a search for origins; the idea for the park created new ideological space for frontier conservation.

Historians have long employed expeditions, maps, railroads and cities on the march to chart capitalist development in frontiers. Rather than a fringe fixation, national parks and conservation formed a part of the growing state purview in Argentina and Chile, driven alternatively by tourism or forestry. But despite the existence of national parks elsewhere, parks did not have a fixed definition or a clearly defined model. Yellowstone itself would change in form, footprint, and administrative policies over time, making it more of an idea than a prototype.

The Swiss National Park developing simultaneously would place scientific research at its core. Argentine and Chilean parks followed neither model, but mixed many of the same elements. Early park sentiments encouraged the incubation of parks informed by and applied to each nation's situation. Such values contributed to a continual reinvention of what a national park meant to the local, national and international public.

Notes

1 President Julio A. Roca accepted the donation from Francisco Moreno on 1 February 1904. The original donation was 7,500 hectares. It was expanded on 7 January 1907 to 43,000 hectares by President José Figueroa Alcorta and then again to 785,000 hectares on 8 April 1922 with President Irigoyen's decree. On 9 October 1934, during the presidency of Augustin P. Justo, Law 12.103 was passed creating the park administration and changing the park's name to Nahuel Huapi.

2 Eduardo Miguel E. Bessera, 'Políticas de Estado en la Norpatagonia Andina. Parques Nacionales, desarrollo turistico y consolidación de la frontera. El caso de San Carlos de Bariloche. (1934–1955)' (unpublished BA, Universidad Nacional del Comahue, 2008) and 'La Nacionalización de las fronteras patagónicas. Los Parques Nacionales como herramienta estatal de ocupación e integración territorial', in *Procesos históricos, transformaciones sociales y construcciones de fronteras: Aproximaciones a las relaciones interétnicas*, ed. by Graciela Maragliano *et al.* (Buenos Aires, 2011), 67–88.

3 Pablo Camus Gayán, *Ambiente, bosques y gestión forestal en Chile, 1541–2005* (Santiago de Chile, 2006), 167.

4 Germán Palacio, 'An Eco-Political Vision for an Environmental History: Toward a Latin American and North American Research Partnership', *Environmental History*, 17/4 (2012), 725–43.

5 Patrick Kupper, *Creating Wilderness: A Transnational History of the Swiss National Park* (New York, 2014), 18.

6 William M. Adams, *Against Extinction: The Story of Conservation* (London, 2004), 4.

7 I borrow this term from Patience A. Schell, *The Sociable Sciences: Darwin and His Contemporaries in Chile* (New York, 2013).

8 For an introduction to the abundant biographical literature on Moreno, see Roberto Hosne, *Francisco Moreno: una herencia patagónica desperdiciada* (Buenos Aires, 2005) and Antonio Requeni, *Francisco P. Moreno: perito en argentinidad* (Buenos Aires, 1998).

9 Bailey Willis, 'Recent Surveys in Northern Patagonia', *The Geographical Journal*, 40/6 (1912), 615.

10 Francisco P. Moreno, 'Viaje a la Patagonia setentrional', *Anales de la Sociedad Científica Argentina*, 1 (1875), 187.

11 Guillermo E. Cox, *Viaje en las regiones septentrionales de la Patagonia, 1862–1863* (Santiago de Chile, 1863); George Musters, 'A Year in Patagonia', *Journal of the Royal Geographical Society of London*, 41 (1871), 59–77; Basilio Villarino, *Diario de la navegación emprendida en 1781, desde el Río Negro, para reconocer la Bahia de Todos los Santos, las Islas del Bueno Suceso, y el Desagüe del Río Colorado* (Buenos Aires, 1837).

12 Moreno, 'Viaje a la Patagonia setentrional', 197.

13 Jens Andermann, *The Optic of the State: Visuality and Power in Argentina and Brazil* (Pittsburgh, 2007).

14 Alejandro Winograd, *Patagonia: mitos y certezas* (Buenos Aires, 2008), 174.

15   In a three-year term as a national representative, Moreno drafted projects to create experimental agricultural stations and tree nurseries and expand protected areas in 1912. Claudio Bertonatti, 'A Naturalist Devoted to the Common Good', in *Perito Moreno National Park* (San Francisco, 2015).

16   See the works of explorer, photographer and priest, Alberto Agostini, including *El cerro Lanín y sus alrededores (parque nacional)* (Buenos Aires, 1941) and *Andes patagónicos: viajes de exploración a la cordillera patagónica austral* (Buenos Aires, 1941). See also the analysis in Bessera, 'La Nacionalización de las fronteras patagónicas. Los Parques Nacionales como herramienta estatal de ocupación e integración territorial', 67–105.

17   Susana Mabel López, *Representaciones de la Patagonia: colonos, científicos y políticos, 1870–1914* (La Plata, 2003), 77. The most notable family monopoly is the Braun-Menendez family of Punta Arenas.

18   Neil Safier, *Measuring the New World: Enlightenment Science and South America* (Chicago, IL, 2008); Eileen Crist, 'Against the Social Construction of Nature and Wilderness', in *The Wilderness Debate Rages On: Continuing the Great New Wilderness Debate*, ed. by Michael P. Nelson and J. Baird Callicott (Athens, GA, 2008), 504–23.

19   Chris Moss, *Patagonia: A Cultural History* (New York, 2008), 181; Susana Bandieri, *Historia de la Patagonia* (Buenos Aires, 2005), 114.

20   The museum received sparse funds from the legislature and Moreno eventually saw to it that the museum was attached to the University of La Plata to provide it with greater financial stability.

21   Francisco P. Moreno, *Apuntes preliminares sobre una excursión a los territorios del Neuquen, Rio Negro, Chubut, y Santa Cruz hecha por las secciones topográfica y geológica, bajo la dirección de Francisco P. Moreno, Director del Museo* (La Plata, 1897), 18.

22   Moreno, *Apuntes*, 145.

23   Robert E. Kohler, *All Creatures: Naturalists, Collectors, and Biodiversity, 1850–1950* (Princeton, NJ, 2006).

24   There is an immense literature that touches on this subject; for an introduction see Pablo Lacoste, 'La guerra de los mapas entre Argentina y Chile: una mirada desde Chile', *Historia*, 35 (2002), 211–49; Francisco Le Dantec Gallardo, *¿Cooperación o conflicto? relación argentino chilena* (Santiago de Chile, 2008); Álvaro Fernández-Bravo, *Literatura y frontera: procesos de territorialización en las culturas argentina y chilena del siglo XIX* (Buenos Aires, 1999); Richard O. Perry, 'Argentina and Chile: The Struggle for Patagonia 1843–1881', *The Americas*, 36/3 (1980), 347–63; George Victor Rauch, *Conflict in the Southern Cone: The Argentine Military and the Boundary Dispute with Chile, 1870–1902* (Westport, CT, 1999).

25   Carlos Sanhueza, 'Un saber geográfico en acción: Hans Steffen y el litigio patagónico 1892–1902', *Magallania*, 40/1 (2012), 21–44, offers an excellent reading of this correspondence.

26   Ibid., 35; Irina Podgorny, 'Fronteras de papel: archivos, colecciones y la cuestión de límite sen las naciones americanas', *Historia Crítica*, 44 (2011), 56–79.

27   Francisco P. Moreno, 'Dr. Steffen's Exploration in South America', *Geographical Journal*, 14/2 (1899), 219–20.

28   Julie Cruikshank, *Do Glaciers Listen? Local Knowledge, Colonial Encounters, and Social Imagination* (Vancouver, 2005), 11.

29   Hans Steffen, 'The Patagonian Cordillera and Its Main Rivers, between 41° and 48° South Latitude', *Geographical Journal*, 16/1 (1900), 14–38. This is not unique to Steffen; Cox and others do this as well.

30 Steffen, 'The Patagonian Cordillera', 17.
31 Sanhueza, 'Un saber geográfico en acción', 42. For instance, different soils might demonstrate that a region was not geologically consistent with the Argentine claim of a single range of mountains.
32 For Chile, the national hero was Admiral Thomas Cochrane, 10th Earl of Dundonald, known as Lord Cochrane, who organized rebel troops during Chile's independence movement from Spain. For Argentina, the eponym refers to Juan Martín de Pueyrredón, who served as supreme director of the United Provinces of the Río de la Plata after independence. See discussion of conflicting names in Moreno, 'Dr. Steffen's Explorations', 219.
33 Federico Albert Faupp, *La necesidad urjente de crear una inspección general de bosques, pesca i caza* (Santiago de Chile, 1911); Fernando C. Hartwig, *Federico Albert: Pionero del desarrollo forestal en Chile* (Talca, Chile, 1999), 16.
34 Jean-Pierre Blancpain, *Los alemanes en Chile, 1816–1945* (Santiago de Chile, 1987).
35 Hartwig, *Federico Albert*, 16; Carlos Cabaña Chávez, Michele Benavides and Nancy Pizarro Núñez, *CONAF: su historia y rol en el desarrollo forestal y ambiental de Chile 1972–2013* (Santiago de Chile, 2013), 31.
36 Camus Gayán, *Ambiente*.
37 Albert Faupp, *La necesidad urjente*, 5.
38 On foreign scientists in the earlier years, see Schell, *The Sociable Sciences.*
39 Cabaña Chávez, Benavides and Pizarro Núñez, *CONAF*, 39.
40 Rafael Elizalde Mac-Clure, *La sobrevivencia de Chile: la conservación de sus recursos naturales renovables* (Santiago de Chile, 1970).
41 Hartwig, *Federico Albert*, 11.
42 Cabaña Chávez, Benavides and Pizarro Núñez, *CONAF*, 40; Camus Gayán, *Ambiente*, 150.
43 Elizalde Mac-Clure, *La sobrevivencia de Chile*, 4.
44 Albert Faupp, *La necesidad urjente*, 8.
45 Thomas Miller Klubock, *La Frontera: Forests and Ecological Conflict in Chile's Frontier Territory* (Durham, NC, 2014), 18.
46 Albert, 'Mi opinión profesional', 3.
47 Camus Gayán, *Ambiente*, 158.
48 Federico Albert Faupp, 'Los bosques, su conservación, espoltacion i fomento', *Boletín de Bosques, Pesca, y Caza*, 2 (1913–14), 11; Ángel Cabeza Monteira, *Aspectos históricos de la legislación forestal vinculada a la conservación, la evolución de las areas silvestres protegidas de la zona de Villarrica y la creación del primer parque nacional de Chile* (Santiago de Chile, 1988), 23.
49 Albert, 'Mi opinión profesional', 3.
50 'Conditions in Northern and Central Patagonia', *Journal of the Royal Society of Arts*, 70/3633 (1922), 601–2.
51 Exequiel Bustillo, *Huellas de un largo quehacer: discursos, artículos y publicaciones diversas* (Buenos Aires, 1972), 78.
52 Dirección de Parques Nacionales, '12.103, Ley de Parques Nacionales' (Buenos Aires, 1935).
53 Exequiel Bustillo, *El despertar de Bariloche: una estrategia patagónica*, 2nd ed. (Buenos Aires, 1971), 18.
54 Exequiel Bustillo, 'Treinta años de la ley de parques nacionales', *La Nación*, 8 October 1964.

55 Gustavo A. Eppens, Pedro C. Denegri and Martín Escalona, 'Informe de la primera comisión exploradora: Parque Nacional "Lanín"' (Buenos Aires, 1937), 13.

56 Ibid., 27.

57 Cabeza Monteira, *Aspectos históricos*, 19, 29.

58 Shifting international priorities, including involvement in the War of the Pacific and feuds over nitrates in the north and borders in the south, likely accounts for the long delay between the initial legislation and the first reserve.

59 Klubock, *La Frontera*, 86.

60 Camus Gayán, *Ambiente*, 151.

61 Villarrica Forest Reserve was originally declared in an area of 127,444 hectares. Benjamin Vicuña Mackenna was dissolved as a national park.

62 Cabeza Monteira, *Aspectos historicos*, 38. See also Ministerio de Bienes Nacionales, Decreto Supremo (henceforth MBN-DS) 3654, 18 May 1929, Archivo Nacional, Chile (henceforth ANC).

63 Otto F. Gudenschwager, Map, Ministerio Agricultura, 1949, Decreto Supremo 1353, ANC. Detailed map is of a 300 square metre section and includes trails of Spanish conquistadors on the left and cattle running towards the park from Argentina.

64 Klubock, *La Frontera*, 72.

65 Decree dated 30 June 1931, MBN-DS 338, 27 February 1950, ANC.

66 Carlos Bushmann Z. to minister, 12 May 1949, MBN-DS 338, 27 February 1950, ANC.

67 Decree dated 2 February 1950, MBN-DS 338, 27 February 1950, ANC.

68 Klubock, *La Frontera*, 174. Elizalde Mac-Clure, *La sobrevivencia de Chile*, 478.

69 Cabeza Monteira, *Aspectos historicos*, 28.

70 'Introductory note', in *Proceedings of the Latin American Conference on the Conservation of Renewable Natural Resources, [Held in] San Carlos de Bariloche, Argentina, 27 March – 2 April, 1968: Organized by I.U.C.N.* (Morges, 1968), 4.

71 Enrique Beltrán, 'Closing Session' in *Proceedings of the Latin American Conference on the Conservation of Renewable Natural Resources, [Held in] San Carlos de Bariloche, Argentina, 27 March – 2 April, 1968: Organized by I.U.C.N.* (Morges, 1968), 466.

3 Another way to preserve

Hunting bans, biosecurity and the brown bear in Italy, 1930–60

Wilko Graf von Hardenberg[*]

On 26 May 1999 a truck snaked up the narrow mountain roads of the Val di Tovel, a secluded valley at the core of the Adamello Brenta Natural Park in the Italian province of Trento. It had a very special load: a male bear from Slovenia. This was the first of many trips organized by the park administration as part of an EU reintroduction programme to avoid the complete disappearance of the brown bear from the Italian Alps. The last litter had occurred in 1989 and by the mid-1990s only three bears were left in the area. The relict population was, because of its inability to reproduce, considered effectively extinct. Only the translocation of bears from the thriving Slovenian bear communities could grant continuity to the presence of bears in the Italian Alps. As a result of this effort, the local colony now boasts a viable population of 40–50 individuals. This, however, is only the latest intervention by which the Italian nature state has attempted to save the local bear colony from total demise. The earliest attempt at reintroducing bears to the area, for instance, dates back to 1959. Debates about the presence of brown bears in the Eastern Alps of Italy have an even longer history: the local bear population has, in fact, been at risk of extinction, and its protection a pivotal issue in the conservation debate in Italy, for most of the twentieth century.[1]

In this chapter I look at previous attempts made by government agencies to preserve the brown bear in the Italian Alps through various means, including the planning of natural parks, the issuing of hunting bans and the payment of monetary compensation. By doing so I reframe the complex social relations among the bear, local communities, conservationists and the state in the years around the Second World War. I also aim to address the role of formal and informal policies and practices of species preservation within the nature state. While – possibly – postponing the end of the bear's presence in the region, some of the policies put in place in those years laid the foundation for an

[*] Essential archival research for this chapter has been performed thanks to generous funding provided by the Autonomous Province of Trento for the Postdoc PAT2007 Na.T.U.R.900 research project. I want to thank Emmanuel Kreike, Matthew Kelly and Emily Wakild for the insightful comments on earlier iterations of this chapter, which have helped to greatly improve my narrative and argument.

enduring conflict between farmers and the state over the risk posed by bears to livestock and to the biosecurity of the local communities. Finally, in this chapter I discuss the continuity and disruption of the agencies, rulings and philosophies that made up the nature state when faced with regime change, such as the post-war transition from fascism to democracy.

When the nation-state assumes the role of the nature state, charging itself explicitly with the preservation of environments and species, it inevitably chooses which nature deserves protection, often losing, in the eyes of other involved parties, its ability to act as a neutral arbiter. This can lead to confrontation and the need for mediation not only between the representatives of the nature state and local actors, but also among different sectors within the state. It would indeed be misleading to interpret the nature state as a monolithic structure, bound to the implementation of one clear and straightforward nature protection agenda. It rather acts as a combination of agencies and regulations at various levels of state administration, ranging from the local to the national (and beyond, as in the case of supranational EU programmes), and from the official to the informal. The variety of involved actors and the need to give different answers to the representatives of different interest groups has led to a scenario in which many conflicting stances act against one another: conflict is as inherent to the nature state as it is to any other form of politics and administration.

The preservation of species perceived to be somehow dangerous to humans is often unwelcome to local stakeholders such as farmers and herders, who may perceive nature conservation as undermining their right to biosecurity. In this chapter I interpret biosecurity from the same 'visceral' perspective of 'not being eaten by big and ferocious wild animals' adopted by Henry Buller in his discussion of the reintroduction of wolves in southern France. Security in this context does not encompass only physical safety, however, but also the defence of economic interests and animate and inanimate property from possible damages caused by these same animals. Claims made by local communities about the need to ensure this kind of biosecurity comes into conflict with state-ensured protection of even the most iconic species.[2] Questions faced by the nature state include: what is the species being saved from? Who will be the saviour? How and where will it be saved? And who will experience the costs?[3] Each and every one of these issues has potential for unleashing confrontation between the nature state and other actors, effectively putting at further risk the animal species or ecological niches to be protected.

Among the instruments adopted to preserve the environment, national parks play an iconic role in how the nature state physically expresses its power on the territory, but they represent only the apex of a more complex system, which extends well beyond the limited boundaries of nature reserves and affects entire regions at different scales. Within this broader setting the most common form of animal species conservation enacted by the state has historically been the regulation of hunting, ranging from species-specific bans to the subdivision of the year into hunting and closed seasons. With the dismissal of royal prerogatives and the passing of the hunt's sacral aura, the long nineteenth century saw hunting management become one of the many prerogatives of the state.[4] Legal mandates such as hunting bans or the determination of preservation areas are empty bureaucratic efforts if they are not accompanied by the power to actually implement them on the ground. From this perspective, *state capacity* – i.e. the ability of the state to achieve its aims through the effective management of its territory and resources – is pivotal in determining the effectiveness of government action in shaping animal conservation.[5] In the Italian Alps, for instance, an agrarian region characterized simultaneously by a transhumant and a resident livestock economy, as well as a burgeoning tourism industry, the cohabitation of the interests of local communities alongside the preservation of large carnivores requires active state intervention, on both the legislative and the administrative level.

Being a bear in man's world: appearance, behaviour and ecology

Alpine brown bears (*Ursus arctos arctos*) can vary decidedly in appearance: the smallest females can be just 130 cm long and 75 cm high at the withers, and weigh 50 kg, while the largest males can reach 250 cm head to tail, a height of 120 cm, and be 300 kg in weight. The optimal habitats for brown bears are deciduous or coniferous forests with a lush underwood. They prefer elevations between 700 and 1,800 metres above sea level and visit areas above the timberline mostly just for transit. Scholarship shows clearly that the main factor in the decreased bear population in the Alps has been the radical change in the area's environmental conditions since the nineteenth century. European bear populations typically have a low density and relatively large home ranges. In the area of study, the Alps of Trentino-Südtirol/Alto Adige, the average extension of each bear's home range is 300 square kilometres for males and 100 square kilometres for females. Since the species is also characterized by a low level of resilience, mainly because of its long reproduction times and extreme sensitivity to disturbances to its habitat, its survival chances in modern times have been increasingly impeded by the negative impact of human land use patterns on the availability of isolated forested areas.[6]

Human transport networks and resource extraction activities, as well as increased tourism, livestock grazing and hunting, can all critically affect the species' survival chances. Human activities disturb the bears' seasonal migrations from the foraging terrains of spring and summer to their wintering areas, or can force them to roam over huge areas beyond their home ranges. Any human impact on the bears' life is thus able to shift the survival chances of the species at the local level. Since bears have been forced over the centuries to live in ever smaller regions or closer to human settlements and economic activities, the number of conflicts between humans and bears has risen exponentially, leading to an increase in bear killings as a form of property defence. As Buller argued happened to the wolf, so animal husbandry also 'provided the most effective rationale for the demonization, exclusion, and ... disenchantment' of the bear.[7]

The disappearance of the European brown bear on a continental scale has been a long-term process: its numbers have been in serious decline in Western Europe since the Middle Ages. By the eighteenth century widespread deforestation limited the European brown bear's habitat to mountain regions. The bear became extinct in the British Isles about 1,000 years ago and disappeared from northern Germany by the end of the eighteenth century. As regards the Alpine range and neighbouring regions, the brown bear was already extinct in Bavaria by the mid-nineteenth century, while the last Swiss and Austrian bears were hunted down in the first third of the twentieth century, as were those in the western Alps of Italy and France. The last bear colonies left in the Alps by the Second World War were thus in north-eastern Italy and Slovenia (where the Alpine and the Dinaric bear population overlap). In particular, in Trentino-Südtirol/Alto Adige the last stronghold of the brown bear was the wild and remote Val di Genova, in the Adamello Brenta massif.[8]

Estimating the actual dimension of the population of a secretive, forest-dwelling species is still considered extremely difficult. Even very small populations or single individuals can, in fact, give the impression of a well-established colony. It is even more difficult to give a solid estimate of past populations when confronted with scarce historical data. In any case, coeval estimates put the bear population of the Adamello Brenta region around the year 1940 somewhere between 5 and 15 individuals.[9]

Hunting legislation that treated bears as pests and rewarded hunting them with a bounty had been drafted in the Hapsburg Empire, Italy and Switzerland since the early nineteenth century. In 1890 the naturalist Agostino Bonomi reported an increase in the number of bears in Trentino–Alto Adige/Südtirol and the consequent attempts made by local farmers and herders to hunt them down, as well as their requests to Hapsburg state authorities to intervene in defence of their economic interests and their communities' biosecurity. Besides being hunted as nuisances, European brown bears also attracted trophy hunters; however, no explicit mention in the sources suggests there was a market for bear meat and furs in Trentino–Alto Adige/Südtirol. The steady modification of the Alpine landscapes and the low reproductive rate of the European brown bear, combined with a state-supported extermination policy, was enough to radically reduce the bear population.[10]

Herders have consistently presented themselves as the foremost victims of incidents involving bears in the Alps, while being primarily responsible for creating the conditions for heightening the risk of encountering bears in the first place.[11] In fact, the 'spatial proximity' forced upon bears by the expansion of the livestock economy was the main factor in increasing the sense that bears were a threat to the biosecurity and livelihood of the mountain communities of Trentino. Ironically, the more bears became accustomed to humans, resulting in an increased level of encounter, the more the bear came to be regarded as wild, dangerous and noxious.[12]

Although the European brown bear is omnivorous and its diet is highly dependent on seasonal conditions, it mainly lives on fruits and plants. Species sensitivity to changes in the quality of its diet, especially when getting close to hibernation and gestation, may encourage a move towards a more mixed diet. Among European brown bears, those living in temperate forests, like on the eastern Alps, are reportedly the least dependent on vertebrates as part of their diet. From the human perspective, the brown bear is thus less threatening or dangerous than the other big predators in the Alpine range, such as the wolf and the lynx. Only when wounded, or if its cubs are threatened, will the European brown bear attack humans. The scientific literature suggests the species' impact on livestock is minimal as well. Usually, it does not kill domestic animals, even when its habitat overlaps with livestock economies that could represent a handy source of nourishment. Bears are mainly active from the afternoon onwards, and when they hunt live animals they almost exclusively do so at night or under the cover of adverse atmospheric conditions.[13] Data from the 1980s and 1990s gathered in areas where brown bears share their habitat with well-developed herding economies tell us that, on average, each year a bear kills between 0.4 and 3.4 head of livestock, mainly sheep.[14] Recent data for the Adamello Brenta, which account not only for livestock losses, but also for raids on beehives and encounters with humans, give much lower numbers: 250 incidents in six years for an estimated population of about 30 bears, or an average of 1.4 incidents per bear per year.[15]

Protecting an icon

At the dawn of the twentieth century an increasing number of Italian scientists, intellectuals and politicians became aware that the brown bear was on the brink of extinction. Immediately after the First World War the desire to preserve one local subspecies, the Apennine brown bear (*Ursus arctos marsicanus*), contributed to the creation of the Abruzzo National Park as an integral reserve. This was the product of a broader debate about the need to actively involve the state in the preservation of endangered species that also led to the creation of a national park on the Gran Paradiso massif, intended to protect the last colony of Alpine ibex (*Capra ibex*).[16] Earlier attempts to protect this species had been made, but the definite passage of conservation from a matter of debate among scientists and enthusiasts to direct state intervention reflected, to simplify a complex story, the decision of the recently instated Fascist regime to support and promote the institutionalization of these parks. This decision was taken mainly for reasons of national pride and propaganda, and although the regime's interest in the matter proved neither durable nor stable, the fact that new agencies were created to preserve nature for its own sake entrenched these tasks within the purview of the state.[17]

At the same time, the urge to protect the brown bear (*Ursus arctos arctos*) in the Alps of Trentino-Alto Adige/Südtirol, annexed as a consequence of the First World War, triggered a debate about the possible institution of a national park around the Adamello Brenta massif.[18] In the 1930s, Oscar de Beaux, director of the natural history museum in Genoa, and Guido

Castelli, conservator at the one in Trento, published two well-received essays on the European brown bear in the Alps.[19] Castelli even appealed directly to Mussolini in an attempt to convince him of the urgent need to protect the brown bear through the institution of a national park on the Adamello Brenta massif – the bear's 'last stable refuge' in the Alps.[20] The coalescence of the domestic debate about the need to protect the bear, growing international pressure to preserve one of the last bear colonies in the Alps, and the regime's self-appointed role as the defender of the nation's nature, may have helped induce the Fascist government to slowly proceed with the introduction of stricter hunting regulations.

Various sources, including Castelli, mention that bear hunting had been forbidden already for a few years by 1935.[21] The Italian hunting laws of 1923 and 1931 actually stated that the hunting and capture of bears was forbidden only in winter, when bears hibernate. The rationale behind this policy is not clearly stated, but it may be safely assumed that it reflected the desire to protect the bear in the season when it was most vulnerable. Only the bears of the Abruzzo National Park, about 500 km south, were formally protected all year. The only piece of legislation mentioning a total ban on bear hunts, limited to the 'new provinces' of Trento and Bolzano and not renewed in the following years, was a ministerial decree of 10 July 1931. Not until 1936 did the Ministry of Agriculture and Forestry, in an attempt to 'adopt exceptional measures that may allow the protection and increase of the Alpine brown bear', include in its hunting calendar a nationwide ban on the hunting and capture of bears. Such temporary decrees were included in a coherent legislation only with the Consolidation Act of 1939 that banned the hunt of the bear over the whole national territory, without exceptions and in all seasons.[22]

A first proposal to annex the Adamello Brenta massif to the recently founded Stelvio National Park was made as soon as the latter was instituted in 1935. This proposal was thwarted by Edmondo Rossoni, minister of agriculture and forests, on the pretext that Mussolini himself had already denied the Italian Touring Club's requests to further expand the Stelvio National Park and that the existing hunting ban was already effective in protecting the bear population.[23] After the institution of Stelvio National Park, which followed shortly on the creation of the Circeo National Park in the area of the Pontine Marshes near Rome, the Fascist government proved unwilling to fund a further national park, at least until the effectiveness of the four existing ones had been proven. It must also be noted that all early plans for a national park on the Adamello Brenta or for the enlargement of the Stelvio, allegedly aimed at saving the bear population, encompassed mainly higher elevations and not the actual habitat of the brown bear. This was in part an outcome of the primary preoccupation of so many Italian conservationists with the protection of aesthetically pleasant landscapes, rather than animal species. Indeed, in contrast to what Peter Alagona says of California, where concern for species preservation preceded concern for habitat conservation, in most of Europe the two existed in different but sometimes opposed strands of conservationism.[24]

Proposals for the stricter preservation of the diminishing bear population through the institution of a national park were also thwarted by the widespread fear that actively favouring the repopulation of the bear stock, in addition to limiting its hunt, could critically endanger livestock and thus negatively affect the local economy.[25] Acceptance of the brown bear by local communities appears to be inversely proportional to its (perceived) presence.[26] In 1938 Bruno Parisi, director of the natural history museum in Milan, wrote about the prevailing negative popular attitude towards bears in the Adamello Brenta region. In particular, he stressed that hoteliers, hunters and herders alike strongly opposed any form of protection for the bear or to institute a bear reserve in the region. The widespread fear was that next to limiting local customary rights to access resources and use pastures, the preservation of the bear could increase bear predation of livestock. Parisi reported that bears were also commonly perceived as dangerous to humans and many women feared for the safety of their children. Moreover, it was widely believed that an increase in the bear population would hurt the nascent tourist industry.[27] Guido Castelli also reported that herders were convinced that, with the institution of a park, they would lose access to their Alpine pastures in the summer as well as their customary rights to collect wood from the forests.[28] Besides this, Parisi reported that even prominent local representatives of the state – such as the president of a commission charged with the enforcement of the new hunting legislation – believed that the existing ban was sufficient and instead of a park promoted the introduction of monetary compensation for the damage caused by bears, as had been paid in the Abruzzo before the royal hunting reserve was de-designated in 1912. This, it was thought, would reduce the animosity of the local communities towards the bear,[29] an animosity that surfaced in 1939 when some herders alleged that the local hunting association had freed a number of bear cubs in an attempt to repopulate the stock, causing a panic among the locals. This was sternly rebutted by state officials,[30] and since bear hunting was by then forbidden it does seem unlikely that the hunting association, of all possible clubs, would have attempted to restock the bear population. In 1940, a state commission to study the feasibility of a park on the Adamello Brenta massif was established and, despite the debate in the Senate lasting until 1942, nothing came of the initiative.[31]

Even after the end of the Fascist regime, it took a long time before a park was instituted on the Adamello Brenta massif. In the immediate post-war years, Guido Castelli, together with other conservationists, inspired by the renaissance of the Gran Paradiso National Park enforced by its director Renzo Videsott, took up again the struggle in favour of instituting a national park on the Adamello Brenta massif. Castelli claimed that, since it had not been thoroughly implemented through the hiring of wardens, the hunting ban had proven not to offer enough protection to the bear colony.[32] The president of the regional council, entrusted with new powers as part of the post-Fascist move towards decentralization, set up a committee charged with drafting a detailed plan in this regard. For the first time, people living in the Adamello Brenta area started to openly support the idea of preserving the local bear population. A group gathered around leading glaciologist Vigilio Marchetti petitioned the regional government, wondering whether the renewed plans for a park in the area would actually lead to its institution before the bear went extinct. They also highlighted the irony of the possibility that a new reserve would merely serve to protect an 'empty cove' because too much time had been spent discussing the issue without acting to save the bear.[33]

During 1949 and 1950 the regional administration set up a commission charged with evaluating the proposals for the institution of a national park on the Adamello Brenta massif. The commission was asked to pay particular attention to the park's role as a scientific endeavour, rather than as a tourist attraction.[34] Tourism, however, remained a central motive, convincing many of the necessity to set up a protective park in the area. In a letter sent by the Milan section of MIPN (*Movimento Italiano per la Protezione della Natura*), the 'good-tempered' bear was presented as 'one of the most original attractions' of the region.[35] Even some critics of the hunting ban had by then become supportive of the institution of a park, in the hope that creating an area where the protection of the bear was strictly enforced would end the hunting ban outside its borders.[36] Plans for the institution of a park around the Adamello Brenta massif gained national attention, but local communities, fearing its designation would too heavily restrict their access rights and thus further damage an already suffering economy, insisted that any plan for a park should first be vetted by the involved municipalities.[37]

In the 1950s the government attempted again to enlarge the Stelvio National Park by including the Adamello Brenta massif and granting the brown bear statutory protection. The project failed, in part because the regional administration claimed that the central government had no rights to modify the park's boundaries. It was not until the late 1960s that a regional nature reserve was finally instituted in the area.[38]

The consequences of the Fascist hunting ban

If the early attempts to create a national park explicitly dedicated to the preservation of the brown bear in the Alps were unsuccessful, by the end of the Fascist regime Italy could nonetheless boast one of the world's first total bans on bear hunting. As a form of preservation this was nominally much wider in scope, but risked in practice being much less effective than the institution of a park because of the practical and economic difficulties of implementing such a ban. In particular, conservationists lamented the fact that there were not enough game wardens to grant the actual protection of the bear.[39] It is difficult to evaluate the actual effect of the ban: the average number of bears killed per year had halved since the introduction of the seasonal ban in 1923, and a possible slight reduction in killings after 1936 seems hardly significant.[40] Still, in April 1938, the Ministry of Agriculture and Forestry told Italian newspapers, contrary to scientific opinion, that the ban of 1936 had allowed the bear population to recover in a 'satisfactory way'.[41] The reduction in the number of killings after the First World War, rather than marking the success of Fascist conservation policies, may have been actually due to there being fewer bears in the first place. It might be a false conclusion in a further way as well: bear killings were obviously more likely to become public when bounties were granted rather than under a total hunting ban. It must also be added that, even if these laws, and the much later institution of a nature reserve around the Adamello Brenta, might have helped ensure the survival of a local bear colony, neither expression of the nature state proved very effective in promoting the bear's revival over the long term: the estimated number of bears in the area remained extremely low throughout the period we are looking at, dropping, as already noted, to just three individuals by the mid-1990s.

In the years following the ministerial decree of 1936, the *Milizia Nazionale Forestale* – the Fascist paramilitary corps charged with forestry and nature conservation police tasks – intensified its surveillance activities in an explicit attempt to guard against the 'worrying diminution of the few Alpine brown bears still existing in the Brenta massif'.[42] Only one bear was reportedly shot in Trentino between the spring of 1938 and 1943, against the six killed between 1935 and 1937.[43] When the nature state committed enough resources and intensified policing, apparently it was able to efficiently enforce protection; as Fascist control over the territory diminished during the Second World War, the number of bears illegally shot soared again. Increased poaching, facilitated by the increased number of weapons in circulation and often masked under the presumption of self-defence, was described by some conservationists as forming a wilful and malicious 'mania for destruction'. Four bears were killed in 1945 alone.[44] That said, we cannot be absolutely sure whether the reduction in poaching in the last years of the Fascist regime was due to underreporting rather than the actual effectiveness of Fascist hunting laws.

Beside the actual impact on the bear stock, the Fascist regime's hunting legislation had an enduring impact on the preservation policies of the Italian Republic after the war. It is thus in the years following the regime's fall that it is first possible to assess the impact of the legislation on conservation and the local economy, and to evaluate how it contributed to social conflict. In particular, it is in those years that the nature state became a prime actor in the ongoing conflict between local communities and the bear, carrying most of the blame for the loss of biosecurity suffered by the former.

Before the total ban of 1939, herders already held the state and its local representatives responsible for losses to their herds allegedly caused by bears. No formal piece of legislation was passed to regulate how damages caused by bears should be compensated, but the Ministry of Agriculture and Forestry evaluated petitions on a case-by-case basis and occasionally granted non-recurring subsidies.[45] The Ministry continued this customary practice in the post-Fascist era, in particular when it appeared that attacks on livestock affected the herders' main means of livelihood. Compensation was offered on the condition that in the future the shepherds should take active precautions against bear attacks, like corralling sheep, getting sheepdogs or keeping lights on at night.[46] The total ban on bear hunting had thus transformed the traditional conflict between herders and bears, introducing a new set of actors. Now that it was illegal to kill bears, the herders began to struggle also with the nature state.[47]

Your money, or the bear! Of livestock, damages and compensation

By 1950 the effectiveness of the hunting ban was still questioned, particularly with respect to the consistency of its enforcement. The press alleged that poachers had been allowed to continue with their 'vandalic destruction' leading to a situation in which it was uncertain whether the brown bear of the eastern Alps could survive.[48] After 1950 the regional administration of Trentino-Alto Adige/Südtirol gradually took on the responsibility the central state had for managing hunting and was confronted with an increasing number of requests for monetary compensation for bear predation on livestock.[49] At the same time, old and new representatives of the conservation movement lobbied the authorities to introduce better ways of preserving the bear colony. In addition, the local press widely discussed both the risks posed by the bear to the local economy and the need to preserve the last bear colony in the Italian Alps.[50] Between 1952 and 1958, three local newspapers (*L'Adige*, *Alto Adige* and *Il Gazzettino*) published at least 65 articles on the brown bear, including reports on bear sightings in Trentino's western Alps, alleged bear attacks on livestock, and discussions about the need to preserve the bear. The newspapers reported 29 livestock attacks by bears between 1952 and 1958, which caused the loss of at least 100 cows, sheep and goats. Requests for compensation, reports about incidents compiled by regional game wardens and yearly lists of granted settlements filed by the regional administration suggest the frequency of incidents might have been even higher. In fact, there were more than 100 reported incidents, causing the loss of 211 animals between 1952 and 1958, an average loss of about 30 livestock per year. If we assume the average European annual per capita livestock loss figures for the 1980s–1990s to be indicative also for earlier times, this level of loss suggests a population of nine or more bears, which is slightly higher than the number assumed by most preservationists, but still within the upper limit of existing estimates.[51]

Partial compensation for damages was awarded by the regional administration in 85 per cent of cases.[52] Only six requests were explicitly rejected, mainly because they had been presented too late or it had not been possible to gather enough evidence about the incidents.[53] For another ten requests there is no answer from the regional administration preserved in the archives, so it is not possible to determine why compensation was refused.[54] Over a seven-year period, the regional administration, even if it was not compelled by law to do so, granted two and a half million lire (about €35,000 at current value) in subsidy to herders who claimed losses due to bear attacks on livestock.[55] In 1955 the regional administration inquired with an insurance company whether the risk of bear attacks could be covered by a private insurance policy, rather than through the existing system of compensation. This attempt failed, but it shows how keen the state administration was to find alternative ways to cover such extraordinary and unregulated expenses.[56]

Judging by those requests in which the herders declare the value of the loss (about 60 per cent of the total), the regional administration typically compensated only half the value of livestock involved in incidents. This was in conformity with the suggestion of its own hunting and fishing bureau that partial compensation was sufficient since part of the meat was usually still saleable. All claims were required to be supported by statements by both a regional game warden and a recognized veterinary doctor. Since it was impossible to enforce effective surveillance over such a large region, the regional administration, like the state officers of the late Fascist era, believed that some form of compensation, even if not required by law, was necessary in order to strengthen the protection granted to bears by the Consolidation Act of 1939. The need for a legislative intervention, able to clarify the nature of the compensation, was also increasingly felt by the officers of the provincial hunting and fishing bureau.[57]

Nature conservationists, on the other hand, were convinced that shepherds often exaggerated their claims of livestock losses in order to justify armed intervention against the bears and to increase the value of damages awarded.[58] Vigilio Marchetti, for instance, claimed that the damage in the previous years had been on average 4–5 head of livestock per year, and that these were usually unattended sheep.[59] As a way to reduce the number of attacks – and incidentally making true the fears of the local community that the protection of the bear could thwart their rights to access natural resources – he also demanded that fewer herding permits be granted. Marchetti saw the shepherds as the main threat to the bears, 'both for the damages they actually suffer [...] and because they easily shift the blame on bears for losses caused by their own carelessness'.

Nonetheless, nature conservationists like Marchetti believed that a quick response to any possible incident was the only way to ensure the shepherds started to support the state's efforts for the protection of the brown bear. The conservationists had some sympathy for the shepherds' plight and they petitioned for a system that would both prevent bears being shot and grant that actual damages to the herds be compensated. Proposals to compensate in full as a way to limit social hostility to the preservation of the bear were also made by members of the regional commission charged with studying the opportunity to set up a natural park on the Adamello Brenta massif in 1950.[60] Vigilio Marchetti proposed a far-fetched plan, involving the deployment of four wardens who would follow the bears in their seasonal movements so that they could prevent any incidents with the herders and assess any claims for damages firsthand. Even if the president of the regional administration supported the plan, the game wardens, which preferred the improvement of permanent surveillance at the municipal level, contested it. One game warden stressed in particular that it would have been very hard for a single man, however 'brave, zealous, passionate, tireless, knowledgeable of the places where [the bear] hangs around' to shadow the bears wherever they went.[61]

Even the game wardens, which in general were supportive of the herders, sometimes expressed doubts about the truthfulness of the claims submitted. This was the case in an incident in which shepherds claimed that their livestock had been killed by a bear just steps from their tents without them noticing anything at all. On other occasions the game wardens reprimanded the herders for having abandoned their livestock over night to go to the village to sleep. In 1950, forest wardens sternly admonished one shepherd who claimed the loss of two sheep and two lambs and threatened to kill the bear himself.[62] In other instances, facing the shepherds' negligence, representatives of the regional administration tried to educate them about how to reduce the rate of bear attacks. On 1 July 1954, the regional hunting and fishing bureau sent a letter to a number of municipalities, asking the mayors to publicize the protected status of the bear. This was the first official recognition that the regional administration would compensate damages caused by bears. The letter detailed as well the minimum requirements of animal custody needed to ask for compensation in case of damage caused by a bear attack. In particular, it stressed how the protection of livestock should be achieved by any means to prevent bears from getting too close to livestock, while reminding herders that killing or capturing them was strictly forbidden by law.[63]

Predictably, perhaps, most of the local press was supportive of the claims made by the herders and stressed the dangerousness of the bear, although from time to time the conservationists' stance found its way into the newspapers. In 1952, for example, *L'Adige* doubted that any of the alleged attacks ever occurred and argued that the bears were essentially vegetarians. The anonymous journalist stressed that no bear had ever been caught in the act and that all attacks had fortuitously occurred at night. He was not alone in suspecting that most of these alleged bear attacks had actually been rather venal accidents, where livestock got lost and the herders were trying to retrieve some money by blaming their losses on the bears.[64] This article caused some debate in the following weeks: one response actually advised shepherds they could kill bears and not get caught by poisoning the remains of livestock and waiting for the bears to come back to finish their meal.[65]

One particularly interesting incident from September 1954 demonstrates how herders and the press used the bear as a scapegoat. A farmer claimed that he had to sacrifice his heifer in order to save his own life from a bear that was stalking him.[66] After further inquiries the regional game warden, Benuzzi, discovered that the claim was false. The farmer had lost the heifer and decided to go first home but search for her later. During his further search a bear and her cub followed him and he assumed that the cow had been attacked. He must have been quite surprised when he found her with the rest of his herd when he got back home.[67]

Shepherds and hunters alike stressed that while protecting the bear was a worthy endeavour, the protection of humans should not be forgotten either. In 1958, for example, the hunting association and the municipality of Livo denounced the presence of a big bear close to the village, reporting that many people were worried about what could happen to children and women. According to the association, fewer and fewer people were going to work the fields or to collect wood in the forests due to fear. The authorities were invited to intervene to get rid of the bear, since the hunting ban did not allow the members of the association to take the matter into their own hands.[68] The mayor of Livo wrote to the regional administration:

> If the presence of the bear can be tolerated in certain high mountain areas, very far from the village, where people go only rarely and usually in groups, it can certainly not be tolerated close to the village where it can be met by women and kids.[69]

There is no evidence that the authorities did reply, nor act, in any way. Most probably the bear just left the area and the issue was soon forgotten.

On 13 August 1956, apparently in an attempt to make the ban on bear hunting more effective and in accordance with requests made by a Committee for the Protection of the Brown Bear and the support of the Provincial Hunting Commission, the regional administration decreed that all forms of hunting were prohibited in the Val di Genova and the surrounding valleys – the bear's stronghold in the region. The only exceptions were made for chamois and roe, but only with a permit and only when accompanied by a game warden. This decree effectively instituted a reserve in the surroundings of the Val di Genova, granting a more strict preservation of the local bear population. The measure, which prevented bear poachers from roaming the valley under the guise of legally hunting other animals, was modified by a further decree just three weeks later on 3 September 1956, which allowed grouse and partridge to be freely hunted. Guns for birds and bears are quite different, but nonetheless the records tell us of incidents in which bears were killed with guns prepared for grouse hunting, so it can be said that this modification weakened the preservation potential of the decree.[70] In 1957, Alpinist and conservationist Fausto Stefenelli even announced that the region had created an 'oasis' where the bear could live in peace. He likely only meant the issuing of this ban, since there are no other references anywhere to the institution of an actual nature reserve.[71]

Conclusions

Early calls for the protection of the last colony of brown bears in the Italian Alps through the institution of a dedicated national park had little to no effect. Besides the institution of a number of commissions and the drafting of various plans to create a park to protect the brown bear, no bear sanctuary materialized until 1967, and then only as a provincial nature reserve. The only form of protection granted to the bear was thus the total ban on hunting and capturing in effect since at least 1936. The ban, however, proved difficult to enforce, showing the limits of state capacity in this regard, especially because of the limited number of available game wardens. In the long term, this preservation policy was ineffective in ameliorating the conditions that exposed the bear to the risk of extinction in the first place, namely local hunting and self-defence. During and after the Fascist regime the Italian state proved incapable of exerting the necessary control over its territory to check poachers, avoid vengeance kills and ease the fears of the local communities. Bear killings in fact continued to occur quite regularly, if at a reduced rate, in the following decades. Both the conservation movements and government officers, notwithstanding multiple attempts, failed to dispel claims made by representatives and members of the local communities that bears were a threat to biosecurity – that is, a danger to people, livestock and livelihoods. Popular hostility towards bears was probably the main motive delaying the creation of a park.

Moreover, since the hunting ban was necessarily enforced in areas of mixed land use where bears and livestock could easily meet, the risk of incidents involving livestock increased. In the 1940s and 1950s local farmers repeatedly reported that bear attacks were endangering their livelihoods. In the medium term, this encouraged the state and local administrations to set up a system to pay the farmers damages for livestock losses caused by the bears. The idea was that such a system could help preserve the local bear colony by preventing farmers and shepherds from illegally defending their herds by force of arms or by seeking revenge. In this case, counter to the classical Foucauldian narrative, state-led interventions did not reduce the insecurity of naturality, but rather increased it. If the measure of success lies in the security of human communities, rather than in any environmental metric, nineteenth-century bounties were more efficient in granting the normalization of the natural world desired by many local communities by leading the local bear colony to the brink of extinction.[72]

The complex, yet essentially informal, system of compensations and subsidies first set up by the central state and then continued by the regional administration in response to the perceived risks produced by the hunting ban transformed the existing conflict between herders and bears into a conflict of the herdsmen with the nature state. In the eyes of the local farmers and transhumant herders, the nature state defended what was widely considered to be a 'noxious animal' that put at risk the physical and economic safety of its own subjects. The number of reported incidents with bears and, consequently, of requests for compensation is consistent with the higher bracket of the estimated bear populations on the Adamello Brenta massif. Nonetheless, on occasion herders exploited conservation regulations to their economic advantage, as it seems still happens today: many claims resulting from alleged bear attacks were fraudulent and used by claimants to get compensation for livestock that was lost due to other causes. Without the necessary funds and the will to implement legislation, the hunting ban was not effective: the lack of a specific territory to be monitored, the difficulty in enforcing control, the existence of human/animal conflicts over resource access and popular discontent turned this promising tool into a blunt weapon under both Fascist and democratic rule. Herders, farmers and the nature state became involved in a struggle between the preservation of animals and the protection of human interests. Preserving the bear seems only to have been possible through a system of monetary exchange, in which government agencies effectively insured livestock holders against losses they might incur as a consequence of this policy. While past examples of monetary compensation for damages – such as those discussed in this chapter and those implemented in the royal hunting reserve of Abruzzo throughout the nineteenth century – differ substantially from recent discourse on the commoditization of conservation and environmental services, they can help to historicize current debates about the role of financial benefits in spurring conservation.[73]

In the face of the actual day-to-day tensions between conservation and biosecurity, the nature state has shown greater continuities in Italy than might be expected between the Fascist regime and the post-war democratic system. Hunting legislation was essentially maintained and informal policies of monetary compensation were refined in the passage from one regime to the other. The monetary model of conflict management, tentatively set up by Fascist administrators, has since gained momentum, becoming a central feature of pan-European reintroduction and preservation initiatives.[74] This is not to imply that the nature state does not respond and react to ideological changes in the overall structure of the state, but as the warfare state and the welfare state, the nature state shows a great level of resilience and stability. Once the state adds the management and preservation of nature and the environment to its responsibilities – indeed, once species preservation comes under its purview – certain ways of thinking and certain policy objectives can become so engrained that it requires great, conscious effort to overcome inertia and modify such approaches. Without a major paradigm shift with respect to both philosophies of nature and attitudes towards governance, even informal policies, like those analysed in this chapter, tend to remain unchanged or even to evolve independently. Over the years, the nature state can thus become autonomous enough to set it apart from, and in competition with, other sectors of the state and civil society. As the case of the bears of Adamello Brenta massif shows, the failure to create an actual conservation institution like a national park should not obscure the significance of the continuity in hunting legislation and policies intended to appease those whose biosecurity was apparently threatened by the ministrations of the nature state.

Notes

1 Luigi Boitani *et al.*, 'Potential Range and Corridors of Brown Bears in the Eastern Alps, Italy', *Ursus*, 11 (1999), 123; Claudio Groff *et al.* (eds), 'Rapporto Orso 2013 del Servizio Foreste e Fauna' (Trento, 2014), 19; Ufficio Faunistico del Parco Naturale Adamello Brenta, *L'impegno del Parco per l'orso: il Progetto Life Ursus* (Rovereto, 2010), 13–15, 29–31, 62, 76.

2 Henry Buller, 'Safe from the Wolf: Biosecurity, Biodiversity, and Competing Philosophies of Nature', *Environment and Planning A*, 40/7 (2008), 1583.

3 Charis Thompson, 'When Elephants Stand for Competing Philosophies of Nature', in *Complexities: Social Studies of Knowledge Practice*, ed. by John Law and Annemarie Mol (Durham, NC, 2002), 166.

4   Martin Knoll, 'Hunting in the Eighteenth Century: An Environmental History Perspective', *Historical Social Research/Historische Sozialforschung*, 29/3 (2004), 10; Robert Delort and François Walter, *Histoire de l'environnement européen* (Paris, 2001), 84.

5   Edmund Russell, 'Evolution and the Environment', in *A Companion to Global Environmental History*, ed. by J.R. McNeill and Erin Stewart Mauldin (Malden, MA: 2012), 382; Andrew G. Walder, *The Waning of the Communist State: Economic Origins of Political Decline in China and Hungary* (Berkeley, CA, 1995), 89.

6   'Orso – Biologia ed ecologia', Parco Naturale Adamello Brenta, www.pnab.it/natura-e-territorio/orso/biologia.html; Damiano Preatoni *et al.*, 'Conservation of Brown Bear in the Alps: Space Use and Settlement Behavior of Reintroduced Bears', *Acta Oecologica*, 28/3 (2005), 189–90; Boitani *et al.*, 'Potential Range and Corridors of Brown Bears in the Eastern Alps, Italy', 123–7; Petra Kaczensky, 'Large Carnivore Depredation on Livestock in Europe', *Ursus*, 11 (1999), 67.

7   Kai Curry-Lindahl, 'The Brown Bear (*Ursus arctos*) in Europe: Decline, Present Distribution, Biology and Ecology', *Bears: Their Biology and Management*, 2 (1972), 75–8; Boitani *et al.*, 'Potential Range and Corridors of Brown Bears in the Eastern Alps, Italy', 128; Ufficio Faunistico del Parco Naturale Adamello Brenta, *L'impegno del Parco per l'orso*, 64; Buller, 'Safe from the Wolf', 1585.

8   Aldo Oriani, 'Indagine storica sulla distribuzione dell'orso bruno (*Ursus arctos* L., 1758) nelle Alpi lombarde e della Svizzera italiana', *Il Naturalista Valtellinese – Atti Mus. Civ. Stor. Nat. Morbegno*, 2 (1991), 99–136; Fabio Osti, 'Gli ultimi orsi bruni nel Trentino', *Il Cacciatore Trentino*, 30 (1996), 45–9; Curry-Lindahl, 'The Brown Bear (*Ursus arctos*) in Europe', 74; Urs Breitenmoser, 'Large Predators in the Alps: The Fall and Rise of Man's Competitors', *Biological Conservation, Conservation Biology and Biodiversity Strategies*, 83/3 (1998), 281; Andrej Kobler and Miha Adamic, 'Identifying Brown Bear Habitat by a Combined GIS and Machine Learning Method', *Ecological Modelling*, 135/2–3 (2000), 291.

9   Kaczensky, 'Large Carnivore Depredation on Livestock in Europe', 61–2; Guido Castelli, 'In merito alla protezione dell'orso bruno ed all'istituzione di un Parco Nazionale dell'Adamello e del Brenta (1938)', in *Notizie storiche sul Parco Naturale Adamello Brenta*, by Franco Pedrotti (Trento, 2008), 493; Vigilio Marchetti to Regione Trentino Alto-Adige, 'Esposto', 28 March 1950, IRPC, 2.3.24, Archivio Provinciale di Trento (from hereon APT).

10 Danilo Mussi, 'Caccia e cacciatori d'orsi sull'Adamello Brenta', in *Sulla pelle dell'orso. La caccia nei documenti del passato e nelle memorie ottocentesche di Luigi Fantoma*, by Anna Finocchi and Danilo Mussi (Arco, 2002), 17–162; Agostino Bonomi, 'Invasione di orsi', *Bollettino del Naturalista di Siena*, 10/9 (1890), 107; Andreas Zedrosser *et al.*, 'Status and Management of the Brown Bear in Europe', *Ursus*, 12 (2001), 9, 15.

11 E.g. Benedetto Collini, 'L'orso bruno è onnivoro', *L'Adige*, 8 October 1952.

12 Buller, 'Safe from the Wolf', 1586.

13 Katarzyna Bojarska and Nuria Selva, 'Spatial Patterns in Brown Bear *Ursus arctos* Diet: The Role of Geographical and Environmental Factors', *Mammal Review*, 42/2 (2012), 122, 129; Curry-Lindahl, 'The Brown Bear (*Ursus arctos*) in Europe', 78–9; Kaczensky, 'Large Carnivore Depredation on Livestock in Europe', 66–7.

14 The only outlier not included in these averages is Norway. There the annual per capita livestock loss reaches an appalling 82.2. The country's geo-climatic and bio-geographical conditions, the fact that untended sheep rearing is quite common, and the fact that livestock losses due to wolves and lynxes are similarly high lead us to assume that this is a very particular case that cannot be included in the calculation

of a Europe-wide average. See also Kaczensky, 'Large Carnivore Depredation on Livestock in Europe', 64–6.

15 Justin Toland *et al.*, *LIFE and Human Coexistence with Large Carnivores* (Luxembourg, 2013), 15; Philip Bethge, 'Brown Bears in the Alps: The Great Bear Comeback', *Spiegel Online*, 3 November 2005.

16 Regarding the early realization of the risk that rare animal species such as the Marsican bear and the Alpine ibex could disappear, see Luigi Piccioni, 'Il dono dell'orso. Abitanti e plantigradi nell'Alta Val di Sangro tra Ottocento e Novecento', *Abruzzo Contemporaneo*, 2/2 (1996), 61–113; Emidio Agostinone, 'In Abruzzo: il parco nazionale dell'orso', *Emporium*, 60 (1924), 442–9; Lino Vaccari, 'Necessità di un parco nazionale in Italia', *Le Vie d'Italia*, 5, 1921, 489–95; G.B., 'L'isola degli stambecchi', *Le Vie d'Italia*, 12, 1925, 1402–8.

17 Wilko Graf von Hardenberg, 'A Nation's Parks: Failure and Success in Fascist Nature Conservation', *Modern Italy*, 19/3 (2014), 276–8; Wilko Graf von Hardenberg, 'Act Local, Think National: A Brief History of Access Rights and Environmental Conflicts in Fascist Italy', in *Nature and History in Modern Italy*, ed. by Marco Armiero and Marcus Hall (Athens, OH, 2010), 142–7. For a more accurate overview of the complex relationship between the nature conservation movement and the Italian government, see Luigi Piccioni, *Il volto amato della Patria. Il primo movimento per la conservazione della natura in Italia, 1880–1934* (Camerino, Italy, 1999), 190–206.

18 Luigi Vittorio Bertarelli, 'Due parchi nazionali nel Trentino', *Le Vie d'Italia*, 1, 1919, 1–12; Giovanni Pedrotti, 'Per l'istituzione di parchi nazionali nel Trentino', *Giornale d'Italia forestale*, 14 September 1919; James Sievert, *The Origins of Nature Conservation in Italy* (Bern, 2000), 144; Franco Pedrotti, *Notizie storiche sul Parco Naturale Adamello Brenta* (Trento, 2008), 23–4; Luigi Piccioni, *Primo di cordata. Renzo Videsott dal sesto grado alla protezione della natura* (Trento, 2010), 160–2. For an analysis of how the violence of the conflict modified the perception of mountain environments in Italy and fostered conservation, see also Marco Armiero, *A Rugged Nation: Mountains and the Making of Modern Italy: Nineteenth and Twentieth Centuries* (Cambridge, 2011), 99–108 and Wilko Graf von Hardenberg, 'Beyond Human Limits: The Culture of Nature Conservation in Interwar Italy', *Aether – The Journal of Media Geography*, 11 (2013), 48–50.

19 Oscar de Beaux, *Conserviamo alle Alpi il loro orso* (Trento, 1933); Guido Castelli, *L'orso bruno nella Venezia Tridentina* (Trento, 1935). Regarding the excellent reception of Castelli's book by the European scientific community and the Italian political elite, see the collection of reviews and letters in Pedrotti, *Notizie storiche sul Parco Naturale Adamello Brenta*, 464–74.

20 Guido Castelli to Benito Mussolini, 21 September 1935, PCM, 1934–1936, f. 3.1.5, n. 4989, Archivio Centrale dello Stato, Rome.

21 Castelli, *L'orso bruno nella Venezia Tridentina*, 153; Edmondo Rossoni to Arturo Marescalchi, 12 July 1935 in Pedrotti, *Notizie storiche sul Parco Naturale Adamello Brenta*, 463–4.

22 Law 24 June 1923, n. 1420 'Provvedimenti per la protezione della selvaggina e l'esercizio della caccia', art. 22(b) and Royal Decree 15 January 1931, n. 117, 'Testo unico delle leggi e decreti per la protezione della selvaggina e per l'esercizio della caccia', art. 36(d); ministerial decree of 10 July 1931, 'Calendario venatorio nelle nuove Provincie sino al 31 dicembre 1931', art. 5; ministerial decree of 30 November 1936, 'Divieto di caccia e di cattura dell'orsa bruno delle Alpi'; Royal Decree 5 June 1939, n. 1016, 'Testo unico delle norme per la protezione della selvaggina e per l'esercizio della caccia'.

23 Rossoni to Marescalchi, 12 July 1935.

24 Hardenberg, 'A Nation's Parks', 275–85; Peter Alagona, *After the Grizzly: Endangered Species and the Politics of Place in California* (Berkeley, CA, 2013); Piccioni, *Il volto amato della patria*, 86.

25 Wilko Graf von Hardenberg, 'Processi di modernizzazione e conservazione della natura nelle Alpi italiane del ventesimo secolo', *Percorsi di ricerca*, Working papers. Laboratorio di Storia delle Alpi – LabiSAlp, 3 (2011), 36.

26 Michele Corti, 'La reintroduzione sulle Alpi dell'orso e del lupo: le ragioni degli ecologisti e quelle dei pastori e alpigiani, ma non solo', *Confronti. Autonomia lombarda: le idee, i fatti, le esperienze*, 9/1 (2010), 100–1.

27 Bruno Parisi to Gian Giacomo Gallarati Scotti, 20 August 1938, in Pedrotti, *Notizie storiche sul Parco Naturale Adamello Brenta*, 496.

28 Castelli, 'In merito alla protezione dell'orso bruno ed all'istituzione di un Parco Nazionale dell'Adamello e del Brenta (1938)', 493.

29 Bruno Parisi to Gian Giacomo Gallarati Scotti, 21 October 1938, in Pedrotti, *Notizie storiche sul Parco Naturale Adamello Brenta*, 497; Piccioni, 'Il dono dell'orso', 61–113.

30 Commissario Ministeriale per l'applicazione della legge sulla caccia nelle Nuove Provincie to Regia Prefettura di Trento, 31 July 1939, IRPC, 2.3.24, APT.

31 Guido Castelli and Oscar de Beaux. 'Relazione, disegno di legge e regolamento per il Parco Nazionale dell'Adamello e del Brenta (1940)', in Pedrotti, *Notizie storiche sul Parco Naturale Adamello Brenta*, 500–9; Piccioni, *Il volto amato della patria*, 272–3; Sievert, *The Origins of Nature Conservation in Italy*, 201–8.

32 Guido Castelli, 'Pro memoria per la formazione di un comitato promotore del Parco Nazionale Brenta-Adamello (1946)', in Pedrotti, *Notizie storiche sul Parco Naturale Adamello Brenta*, 512–14. More sources to this extent, including proposals by mountaineer Fausto Stefenelli and General Aldo Daz may be found in Pedrotti, *Notizie storiche sul Parco Naturale Adamello Brenta*, 514–30.

33 Vigilio Marchetti to Alcide De Gasperi and others, 1 December 1949 IRPC, 2.3.24, APT.

34 Presidente del Consiglio Regionale del Trentino-Alto Adige to Paolo Videsott and Fausto Stefenelli, 30 May 1949, in Pedrotti, *Notizie storiche sul Parco Naturale Adamello Brenta*, 531; 'Probleme des Trentino', *Dolomiten*, 8 March 1950.

35 MIPN – Sez. Milano to Tullio Odorizzi – Presidente Giunta Regionale – Trento, 25 May 1950, IRPC, 2.3.24, APT.

36 Andrea Mattei, 'L'orso bruno, animale vegetariano?' *L'Adige*, 3 October 1952. A similar proposal was made in 'Nelle valli di Genova, Nambrone e d'Algone l'orso ha causato un milione di danni', *Alto Adige*, 8 October 1952.

37 P.F., 'Per gli ultimi orsi i giorni sono contati', *Il Corriere d'Informazione*, 1 June 1950; Geom. Leone Collini, Pinzolo to Ingegnere [Giulio Angelini?], 12 October 1950 IRPC, 2.3.24, APT; Andrea Mattarel, 'Ancora sull'orso bruno; considerazioni e proposte', *L'Adige*, 20 November 1952; 'Sbranate due bovine dagli orsi in una malga nell'alta val di Sole', *Alto Adige*, 26 July 1952.

38 'Storia del Parco Naturale dell'Adamello Brenta', Parco Naturale Adamello Brenta, www.pnab.it/chi-siamo/storia.html.

39 Vigilio Marchetti to Regione Trentino Alto-Adige, 'Esposto'.

40 Castelli, *L'orso bruno nella Venezia Tridentina*, 130–5; Mussi, 'Caccia e cacciatori d'orsi sull'Adamello Brenta', 156; Franco Pedrotti, 'Elenco di orsi bruni (*Ursus arctos* L.) uccisi in Trentino dal 1935 al 1971', in *Una vita per la natura. Scritti sulla conservazione della natura, in onore di Renzo Videsott nel cinquantenario del Parco nazionale Gran Paradiso*, ed. by Franco Pedrotti (Camerino, 1972), 225–40.

41 Ministero Agricoltura e Foreste, 'L'orso bruno delle Alpi: la conservazione della specie (1938)', in Pedrotti, *Notizie storiche sul Parco Naturale Adamello Brenta*, 494; Castelli, 'In merito alla protezione dell'orso bruno ed all'istituzione di un Parco Nazionale dell'Adamello e del Brenta (1938)', 493.

42 II Legione to Coorte Trento, 'Protezione dell'Orso Bruno delle Alpi nel Gruppo di Brenta', 25 April 1938, IRF, 4.130, APT.

43 Castelli, 'In merito alla protezione dell'orso bruno ed all'istituzione di un Parco Nazionale dell'Adamello e del Brenta (1938);' Guido Castelli, 'Uccisione di un orso bruno maschio in Val Rendena (1941)', in Pedrotti, *Notizie storiche sul Parco Naturale Adamello Brenta*, 510–11.

44 Marchetti to Alcide De Gasperi and others, 1 December 1949. It is worth noting that reportedly only a couple of bears were killed in these years. It is true, however, that the chaos of the war might have hidden a much bigger number of cases. See Pedrotti, 'Elenco di orsi bruni (*Ursus arctos* L.) uccisi in Trentino dal 1935 al 1971', 225–40.

45 Commissario Ministeriale per l'applicazione della legge sulla caccia nelle Nuove Provincie to Regia Prefettura di Trento, 31 July 1939, IRPC, 2.3.24, APT; Comune di Ossana to Regia Prefettura di Trento, 8 November 1939, IRPC, 2.3.24, APT.

46 Ministero Agricoltura e Foreste, Ufficio Centrale Pesca e Caccia to Capo dell'Ispettorato Provinciale dell'Agricoltura – Commissario straordinario del Comitato Prov.le della Caccia di Trento, 'Sussidio per danni causati dall'orso bruno', 23 October 1947, IRPC, 2.3.24, APT.

47 Castelli, *L'orso bruno nella Venezia Tridentina*, 86–135. Nonetheless, as shown by Franco Pedrotti, there were still a significant number of killings, both by hunting and because of the poisoned baits used to get rid of foxes. See Pedrotti, 'Elenco di orsi bruni (*Ursus arctos* L.) uccisi in Trentino dal 1935 al 1971', 225–40.

48 P.F., 'Per gli ultimi orsi i giorni sono contati'.

49 Only in 1978 the Province of Trento, however, definitely legislated the means by which the damages caused by bears should be compensated: Provincial Law 10 August 1978, n. 31 'Protezione dell'orso bruno nel territorio provinciale e risarcimento dei danni provocati dallo stesso e dalla selvaggina stanziale protetta.'

50 See a collection of articles of the local press on this topic preserved at the Archivio Provinciale di Trento, IRPC, 2.3.24. The same fact that these articles were collected by the provincial administration shows the interest of the latter for this issue and its wider relevance in local politics. For one of the few positive reports, see Artophylax, 'Il plantigrado del Brenta è un elemento faunistico prezioso', *Alto Adige*, 2 October 1954.

51 Kaczensky, 'Large Carnivore Depredation on Livestock in Europe', 64–6.

52 Before 1952 conflicts about who was responsible had allegedly interrupted the payment of compensation over a number of years. See Collini, 'L'orso bruno è onnivoro'.

53 As an example, see Assessorato Regionale Agricoltura e Foreste to Presidente Comitato Provinciale della Caccia presso Ispettorato Provinciale Agrario, 'Danni dell'orso bruno – domanda di sussidio di Bonetti Remo fu Emilio da Molveno', 20 November 1952, IRPC, 2.3.24, APT.

54 See archival documentation in Archivio Provinciale di Trento under 'Protezione orso e danni da orso, 1939–1959', IRPC, 2.3.24, and in particular the yearly list of granted settlements produced by the *Assessorato Regionale Agricoltura e Foreste* (Regional Department for Agriculture and Forestry) throughout the 1950s.

55 Hans Dietl to Giovanni Neri, 'Danni dell'orso bruno al bestiame all'alpeggio', 2 June 1954, IRPC, 2.3.24, APT; Istat, *Il valore della moneta in Italia dal 1861 al 2008* (Roma, 2009).

56 Ambrogio de Vigili to Capo Ufficio Caccia e Pesca, 10 September 1955, IRPC, 2.3.24, APT.

57 Assessorato Regionale Agricoltura e Foreste – Ufficio Caccia e Pesca to Giunta Regionale, 'Proposta di deliberazione – Sussidi speciali per danni causati dall'orso bruno a bestiame all'alpeggio in località varie di montagna del Trentino occidentale', 9 November 1953, IRPC, 2.3.24, APT; Capo Ufficio Caccia e Pesca to Hans Dietl, 'Relazione sui danni dell'orso bruno al bestiame all'alpeggio e sull'intervento della regione a parziale indennizzo dei danni stessi', 31 May 1954, IRPC, 2.3.24, APT.

58 Marchetti to Alcide De Gasperi and others, 1 December 1949.

59 As shown earlier, these numbers are much lower than those claimed by shepherds between 1952 and 1958, when the killing of, on average, 30 sheep, goats, and cows per year was denounced. Vigilio Marchetti to Regione Trentino Alto-Adige, 'Esposto'.

60 Giulio Angelini to Presidente della Giunta Regionale, 12 June 1950, IRPC, 2.3.24, APT.

61 Vigilio Marchetti to Regione Trentino Alto-Adige, 'Esposto'; Presidenza Regione Trentino Alto-Adige to Commissario del Governo in Trentino Alto-Adige, 'Orso bruno delle Alpi', 6 July 1950, IRPC, 2.3.24, APT; signed letter to Giulio Angelini, 'Conservazione orso bruno', 9 July 1950, IRPC, 2.3.24, APT.

62 Mario Tisi to Assessorato Agricoltura e Foreste – Ufficio Caccia e Pesca, 'Relazione danni dell'orso', 21 June 1955, IRPC, 2.3.24, APT; Mario Tisi to Assessorato Agricoltura e Foreste – Ufficio Caccia e Pesca, 'Relazione danni dell'orso', 7 July 1955, IRPC, 2.3.24, APT; Guardiacaccia Regionale to Assessorato Agricoltura e Foreste – Ufficio Caccia e Pesca, 'Gregge aggredito dall'orso bruno', 3 July 1953, IRPC, 2.3.24, APT; Guardiacaccia Regionale to Assessorato Agricoltura e Foreste – Servizi Forestali, 6 July 1953, IRPC, 2.3.24, APT.

63 Ufficio Caccia e Pesca to Sindaci delle Valli Giudicarie, Rendena, di Non e Sole, 'Danni dell'orso bruno: Custodia del bestiame all'alpeggio', 1 July 1954, IRPC, 2.3.24, APT. Similar letters were sent as reminders in the following years. See Assessorato Agricoltura e Foreste – Ufficio Caccia e Pesca to Comune di Ultimo-Ulten, 'Danni dell'orso bruno al bestiame all'alpeggio', 23 June 1955, IRPC, 2.3.24, APT.

64 'Gli sbranamenti di pecore realtà o fantasia di pastori?' *L'Adige*, 11 September 1952; 'Una pecora sbranata nella Malga Brialone', *Il Gazzettino*, 17 September 1954; 'Un contadino sul Monte di Cles si imbatte in un orso alpino', *Il Gazzettino*, 13 June 1958.

65 Benedetto Collini, 'L'orso bruno è onnivoro.'

66 'Per salvare la pelle sacrifica la manza alla belva che lo insegue', *Alto Adige*, 15 September 1954; 'Un'ora e mezza di fuga in montagna braccato da un'orsa e dal suo piccolo', *L'Adige*, 15 September 1954.

67 Bruno Benuzzi to Assessorato Agricoltura e Foreste – Ufficio Caccia e Pesca, 'Odorizzi Giorgio di Angelo da Mechel – Danni dell'orso', 21 September 1954, IRPC, 2.3.24, APT; 'La favola dell'orso feroce e della manzetta sbranata', *Alto Adige*, 18 September 1954.

68 Sezione Cacciatori Livo to Comune di Livo, 29 October 1958, IRPC, 2.3.24, APT.

69 Comune di Livo to Assessorato Agricoltura e Foreste – Ufficio Caccia e Pesca. 'Danneggiamenti dell'orso', 15 November 1958, IRPC, 2.3.24, APT.
70 Castelli, 'Uccisione di un orso bruno maschio in Val Rendena (1941)'.
71 Dino Buzzati, 'I protettori degli orsi fondano l'Ordine di San Romedio', *Corriere della Sera*, 14 May 1957.
72 Buller, 'Safe from the Wolf', 1592.
73 Piccioni, 'Il dono dell'orso', 61–113; Kathleen McAfee, 'Selling Nature to Save It? Biodiversity and Green Developmentalism', *Environment and Planning D: Society and Space*, 17 (1999), 133–54.
74 Kaczensky, 'Large Carnivore Depredation on Livestock in Europe', 61.

4 Conservation politics in the Madras presidency

Maintaining the Lord Wenlock Downs of the Nilgiris, South India, as a national park, 1930–50

*Siddhartha Krishnan**

Introduction

Since the early 1980s, Indian historians, availing themselves of an abundant archive of colonial records, have identified the state as one of the most powerful agents of both the transformation of nature and its conservation. It is in this dual yet paradoxical sense that one needs to invoke the nature state in India or its provinces. In the course of three decades of busy archival scholarship, the state has emerged as a much-maligned, monolithic entity. This chapter, which examines the management of the grasslands of the Nilgiris in southern India in the first half of the twentieth century, aims to complicate this discourse by revealing the variety of competing interests and perspectives which shaped official policy with respect to this one area. The Nilgiris represent an exceptional territory in relation to much of the rest of India. Prevalent explanations do not adequately describe the region's history, for nature conservation here was based on neither purely utilitarian (commercial) nor idealistic (environmental or conservationist) motivations, but a set of aesthetic and amenity-based judgements largely made by the colonial elite. Moreover, conflicts about the use of this land did not occur, as might be expected, between the state and local communities, but rather among bureaucrats pursuing different goals.

That the colonial state's conservation policy in India was commercial in orientation is a common assertion in Indian environmental historiography. Historian Ramachandra Guha and his ecologist collaborator Madhav Gadgilhave convincingly demonstrated how and why the management of nature in India arose out of the state's economic interest in forestry.[1] The rapidly expanding railway (which grew from 7,678 kilometres of line in 1870 to 51,658 kilometres in

* Early thinking and writing around the chapter were done at the RCC, Munich. The Carson fellowship is precious. For a largely applied and rights-based interdisciplinary research institution, ATREE is generous and tolerant towards archival work. Thanks, ATREE and RCC. This chapter adds to the countless anthropological and historical studies on the pastoral Toda of the Nilgiris. With no benefit, they continue to graze and farm, coping with afforestation, wildlife crop and livestock raids and climate change. A magnanimous folk, these, eager and happy to service the constant academic tourist. I remain embarrassed and indebted.

1910) required large quantities of timber, which in turn motivated increasingly active forest management.[2] Nearly one million railroad sleepers were required annually by railway companies, and Governor-General Lord Dalhousie, observing that forest conservancy was 'an important administrative question', called in 1862 for the establishment of 'a department that could meet the enormous requirements' of railways. According to Guha and Gadgil, Britain 'had no tradition of managing forests for sustained timber production', and German foresters were called in to assist with the establishment of a Forest Department in 1864. By 1900, 20 per cent of India's land was reserved as forest, greatly affecting the lives of rural residents because the required redefinition of property rights conflicted with the customary land and resource use of hunter-gatherers, pastoralists and shifting cultivators. Forests in the two major mountain ranges, the Himalayas in the north and the Western Ghats that rose along the western coast in the south, were being replanted with commercially valuable species such as pine, teak and cedar – species with 'little' rural value.[3]

In the Nilgiris, however, the story took a different turn. This district in the Western Ghats is a highland region with peaks rising up to 2,637 metres above sea level. Grasslands dominated, interspersed with stunted evergreen cloud forests called 'sholas' occurring sparsely in the folds of grassy undulations. For centuries this area had been grazed by the buffaloes herded by the pastoral Toda, who seasonally burned the grass before the monsoons.[4] While afforestation of a different kind – primarily pine, along with blue gum and wattle (*Acacia decurrens*) – would be undertaken here in the mid-twentieth century, around the turn of the century the British chose to allow a large area of nearly 20,000 acres, known as the Lord Wenlock Downs, to remain as grassland, in apparent contradiction of their commercially motivated policies everywhere else.

In 1843 and 1864, the British bestowed the Toda with a common land tenure of 2,949 acres, called the 'Toda Patta Land' (*Patta* meaning 'title'), including 40 *munds* (hamlets); this land had long formed, in Anthony Walker's phrase, the 'Toda heartland'.[5] In addition, the Todas had grazing and ritual privilege over 1,900 acres of Reserve forests and revenue lands; in 1893, when their land came under the management provisions of the Madras Forest Act (1882), these rights were institutionalized. This was an unusual decision at a time when most hill lands were either being reserved as forests or given to British settlers, both civilian and military, for residence and business. For the British, the Toda were of ethnographic interest, worthy of preservation on account of their unusual cultural and racial characteristics. They possessed a robust physique, a language that seemingly differed in sound and syntax from Dravidian languages, and their barrelled and thatched houses appeared architecturally atypical; also seemingly atypical was their pastoral routine and ritual.[6]

For the English gentry living in the hill station Ootacamund (Ooty), the summer capital of the Madras Presidency or administrative division, the Downs formed a vast recreational backyard, offering amenities such as riding, jackal hunting and picnicking. This transformation of the Toda heartland into *English* heartland became most palpable when the tract was reserved in 1900 under the

Forest Act (1878) for recreation and pasturage as the Lord Wenlock Downs.[7] They were named to honour Beilby Lawley, 3rd Baron Wenlock and Governor of Madras, 1891–1896 – 'the Prince of Sportsmen' – who had overseen the construction of the Nilgiri Mountain Railway. The familiarity of the landscape and its resemblance to English grassland bred a desire to cherish and preserve. As one British enthusiast for hunting with dogs wrote in 1908, the Downs 'not only preserved for ever a much-needed tract of grazing-land, but has provided the Hunt with a "home country" the like of which no other pack in India can boast'.[8]

Thus, when disagreements over the use of this land arose, as the examples examined in this chapter will show, they reflected *English* rather than Indian rural interests. Records suggest that conflicts over afforesting grasslands in the Nilgiris, and the need to protect them against such commercial schemes by designating such grasslands as a national park, did not reflect animosity between local communities and the nature state, but among the bureaucrats who administered the state's turn to nature. These efforts were responses to the 'rational' pursuit of profitable plantation forestry in the district, which contained all the trappings of a commercial nature state as configured by Guha and Gadgil. But the particular quality of the hill's nature also triggered a novel tendency of the state to preserve the landscape rather than profit from it by afforesting it. Amenity, accessibility, familiarity and aesthetics converged in triggering preservationist impulses among some sections of the colonial administration, especially the bureaucrats charged with producing revenue such as the collectors or district administrative heads. Thanks to the way the Downs fulfilled the recreational needs of the Ooty gentry nostalgic for home, the Nilgiris became an exception to the Forest Department's management of land for commercial ends.

Indeed, it is important to note that some historians have questioned the extent to which the utilitarianism analysed by Guha and Gadgil held sway throughout the empire; others have traced the conservationist motivations that underpinned the creation of forest reserves. As K. Sivaramakrishnan has argued, scholarship must also take account of 'idealist' as well as 'materialist' interpretations of colonial political economy, particularly with respect to the natural environment.[9] As Richard Grove argued in an influential thesis, the colonial period saw the emergence of 'dessicationism' as a discourse linking drought and soil erosion to deforestation's 'climate or atmospheric effect', and 'was to become so important in cultural and scientific terms in the tropical colonies during the late eighteenth century'.[10] He draws attention to the 'nonconformist' responses of six Scottish surgeons of the East India Company to a 'series of ecological, climatic and subsistence crises' in India and their concern about the state of the forests and the need to preserve them. Among the men advocating 'environmental interventionism as part of the responsibility of the colonial state' was Hugh Cleghorn, who became Conservator of the Madras Presidency's forests in 1856.[11] Building on Grove's work, others have discerned a 'green imperialism' in the apocalyptic and urgent concerns of surgeons-turned-conservationists for whom the failure to 'conserve' forests was to invite disaster, where such concern 'went beyond the considerations of legality or legitimacy'.[12] As we shall see, in the postcolonial period the idealism borne of colonial conservation was critiqued as green imperialism, and nationalist disdain for elitist pursuits on the Downs provided sovereign leverage for afforesting the tract with wattle, pine and blue gum.

Notwithstanding the extant studies, there remains much to historicize, in more geographically refined scales, on what specifically constituted the nascent nature state in colonial India. It may well be the case that the empire went environmental, but Grove's desiccationism does not exhaust the idealist repertoire: desiccationism had a substantial material bearing on concern over drought, but this was not the case in the Nilgiris. Here the amenity value of the Downs to the British administrative and civil gentry, rather than anxieties generated by deforestation and drought, formed the basis for 'idealist' efforts to preserve the Downs. While it is true that conservationists specifically sought out the sholas to be protected for their water storing and letting functions, it was the familiar beauty of the open grassy vistas and their recreational potential that triggered resistance to spoliation. By looking at the specific forms and content of the idealism that marked environmental concern for this remote but economically and symbolically significant terrain, this chapter will draw out how the tension between utility and beauty played a role in the colonial history of the provincial Indian nature state.[13]

There remains yet another idiosyncrasy, a twist to the conservation turn if you will, that adds to the Nilgiris' status as an exceptional territory. The Downs were, to the best of my knowledge, the only tract in India to be, in terms of policy and practice, *maintained* as a national park, and yet not officially designated as one. This disjunction is of analytical value in studying national parks as culminations of the nature state's conservation turn, because the case serves as a historical instance of how contemporary states manage their conflicting roles as economic and environmental agents.[14]

As a means of understanding this developing nature state, this chapter shall therefore follow the conversations between colonial bureaucrats, discernible both in calls for legislating the Downs as a national park and in decisions to merely maintain the tract as a park. Tethered as it is to geography – the Nilgiris and the Madras Presidency – and period – 1930 to 1950 – these conversations reveal the extant discourse in India that attributes either strategic or environmental intent to the nature state. Put differently, these conversations allow us to unpack an ostensibly public and benign preservationist intent that conflicted with strategic timber requirements of the empire.

Chronology provides context to these conflicts. The motivations that secured the reservation of the grasslands by the Forest Department in 1900 were reconfirmed in efforts to protect the Downs from commercial demands between 1920 and 1930. In the 1920s and 1930s, protecting their recreational value was posited as coterminous with maintaining the 'public interest', a notion that now assumed rhetorical significance. This sets the stage for an examination of how in the early 1930s the national park question arose in the guise of possibly designating the Downs as a game preserve. The national park question resurfaced again in full heft with the onset of the Second World War in 1939, when the pressure to afforest with wattle to meet leather tanning agent supplies was great. With preservationist sentiment to the fore, revenue bureaucrats urged the passage of legislation to designate the Downs as a national park, to which senior officials in the Forest Department and the Board of Revenue lent emphatic support. As a concession, the state allowed the Downs to be *maintained* as a park.

As these episodes suggest, the nature state, even as a provincial entity, was not a monolith but an amalgam of interests, with the executive managing competing interests. The need to designate the Downs as a national park arose one final time in 1946–7 and, despite legal support from Indian forestry superiors and elected Indian representatives, and the recruitment to the campaign of the pastoral interests of the Toda, the newly independent Indian government remained as unconvinced as its colonial predecessor of the need to pass an Executive Order.

'Let sleeping dogs lie': conserving recreation in the public interest, 1920–30

In the first decade of the twentieth century, wattle plantations were established in forest reserves near Ooty to meet local energy needs. Conservator Lodge noted in 1910 that the 'cry for establishment', by which he meant the greater governmental control, 'is as loud in the Nilgiris as elsewhere'. Fuel revenues were in decline because of the high rates charged by the ring of cart men who monopolized the wattle supply, and to regulate grazing of wattle plantations by Toda buffaloes required more foresters and guards, for which no resources were available. Taxing the Todas who were grazing their animals on wattle plantations that fell outside the lands allotted to them seemed one solution, while regulating grazing by creating big grazing blocks in densely populated areas of the plateau, and smaller blocks in 'immense and comparatively unpopulated' areas like the Wenlock Downs was another, but neither was possible. Taxing the Toda required special government sanction, and permitting grazing on the Downs contravened existing rules for their management.[15] In sum, the policies which aimed to preserve the Toda *in situ*, pursuing their traditional way of life, and the amenity value of the Downs, thwarted the expansion of forestry operations.

Even as forestry expansion was prevented, another interest group was staking claims over Forest Department lands. A circle of enterprising recreationists drew up plans in 1921 to establish a golf course on Toda land. Until this point, the Gymkhana Club had leased a part of the Downs on an annual basis, but they now wanted to make this a permanent holding and to build a modern golfing infrastructure. This attempted 'green grab' saw the Gymkhana Club request the deforestation of 28 acres and 183 acres of the Downs, for a golf club and a golf course, respectively. To accede to the request of the 'memorialists', Chief

Conservator of Forest (CCF) S. Cox explained to the Board, would involve an alteration of their public use, which was at odds with 'the public interest' and the 1900 reservation.[16] Cox's position was that the Wenlock Downs forest reserves should be treated by the government as a public recreation ground and not sequestered for private use; this was judged by the Revenue (Special) department as a correct interpretation of the law.[17] Although members of the council, including the governor, acknowledged that the Gymkhana Club's annual lease had not affected the public interest negatively, they nonetheless agreed with the CCF on principle that a significant portion of the Downs should not be alienated.[18] Nor was the council impressed when the Gymkhana Club cited the precedent apparently set by the Ootacamund Hunt Kennels, which held land on the Downs, for the club had prescriptive right of having used the lands before the Downs were reserved for recreation in 1900. By refusing the land request, the state asserted control over what was perceived to be one of the most 'valuable sites' on the plateau, although the annual lease would continue to be renewed up until the present day.[19]

In practice, the authorities had not always taken such a firm view. For instance, in 1911 the state assumed more power to 'govern the pursuit of game' on the Downs, introducing regulations which restricted shooting ibex to those with a well-marked saddle, and hunting small game with no more than eight dogs. However, hard-and-fast bureaucratic rules were considered an unsuitable way to govern sporting activity, being at odds with the general ethos underpinning the functioning of the colonial regime. In practice, rule infractions tended to be excused on the grounds of either excess enthusiasm or a symptom of plentiful game availability. Enforcement was made doubly difficult by the fact that regulations differed between forests rented from chieftains in the foothills and reserved forests, and Toda lands on the plateau, which included the Downs. Simplifying the regulations seemed one way to strengthen the nature state, and a legal notification of 1911 empowered the collector to issue uniform game rules.[20]

What is not clear from the archives is whether the Toda pastoralists who grazed specific portions of the Downs were a component of the 'public' whose rights the colonial authorities sought to protect. The suggested choice of a representative of the 'general public' for the proposed committee to look into the Gymkhana Club's memorandum was someone who is 'interested in hunting'.[21] But perhaps the most significant official rendition of the public interest clause was made by C.G. Todhunter, a council member (Revenue). He alerted the bureaucracy to a contradiction in how the Downs were codified as public space. As a 'revenue member', Todhunter could not object to the Forest Department divesting 'control over areas which were not required for forest purpose', but as a member of the 'interested' public he warned that they should 'let sleeping dogs lie' and 'not invite attention to the irregularity of the arrangement' that protected the Downs by allowing the Forest Department to 'secure control over a great public recreation ground that could not otherwise be secured'.[22]

Of preserves, a park and perturbed foresters: conserving nature or stature? (1930–47)

In July 1931, A.Y.G. Campbell, a revenue member, mentioned to the Nilgiri conservator, A. Wimbush, that game was being 'shot-out' on the Downs, just as it was in the Chamala Valley in Chittoor, a district in the Presidency. Campbell recalled how during his tenure as collector of the district, he could order that only he and the district forest officer (DFO) could shoot game, but now Campbell thought it unlikely they could do anything to stop the extinction of game, which increased Indian self-government – 'Indianization' – would soon make inevitable. Campbell considered the Presidency CCF Richmond's contention that 'ordinary measures' taken by 'protective staff' were sufficient to preserve game as nonsense. Wimbush agreed, mordantly observing that the collector 'will issue licences wholesale to anybody who wants one'. In a separate memo, Wimbush echoed Todhunter, admitting that there was 'a great deal of eyewash about the whole thing', as he understood that one of the 'main objects' of game preserves 'was to strengthen the hands of officials in resisting applications for the alienation of reserved forest for tea etc.'.[23] That September, in order to 'force the attention of successive generations of officials' to guard against 'disafforestation' and the further loss of fauna, the colonial government had indeed concluded that though every reserve forest was 'strictly speaking' a game preserve, there was now the need for the actual 'selection and declaration' of areas as 'game preserves'.[24]

In line with this government order, recommendations for areas in the Presidency for declaration as game preserves were solicited. Portions of the Nilgiris that comprised Toda land and around which the Toda had grazing privileges were recommended. These included the 'good tea land' in Ebanad in the east of the Nilgiris, and the Wenlock Downs in the west and north-west, which were recommended for the richness of their fauna.[25] Wimbush thought it was a good idea to classify grasslands and sholas as potential game reserves because they were prospective tea cultivation lands, an inclusion CCF Richmond encouraged. 'You may suggest any areas of reserved forest under your charge which contain game and which are likely to require a second line of defence from alienation', wrote Richmond to Wimbush.[26] Wimbush's concern extended beyond the alienation of forest: he hoped he was 'right in thinking that there is no question of a sanctuary', of the land being 'closed to shooting', and he asked whether the government order would make no change to the 'present position and is mainly intended to serve as a moral support for our successors'.[27] Richmond was reassuring, replying that there was 'no question, in this connection of sanctuaries', of barring shooting completely.[28] The protection of nature, it seemed, would not impinge on the recreational interests of the bureaucratic class.

Forestry yielded not just profit and power in British colonies, but also recreational privilege that colonial foresters valued and sought to safeguard. Foresters were equally perturbed that efforts to manage game hunting might be at the expense of their authority. Forestry experts in colonial Malaysia, for instance, were worried by a potential introduction of the North American national park conservation model and sought reassurance from their colleagues in India. J.G. Watson of the Forest Research Institute, Kepong, Malaysia, wrote about sanctuary policy and the 'effect of forest operations on the general distribution of game', explaining that a commission had been appointed to appraise Malaysian game preservation with an object to create 'one or more enormous sanctuaries which will be completely locked up and looked after by a special staff, presumably on the lines of similar areas in North America'. The Malaysian Forest Department's belief was 'that forest reserves will provide adequate sanctuaries for game and that we are the obvious people to look after them'. The claim that 'systematic forest management is not incompatible with game preservation' was something that the Malaysian forester wanted to 'corroborate'.[29] Richmond was reassuring, replying that he had 'successfully resisted the constitution of sanctuaries in this province' on the grounds that the 'protection of game … is obviously a duty of a Forest Department' and forestry operations had not been detrimental to game in any place.[30]

Still, Richmond's complacency belies the evidence that conservationist attitudes were shifting elsewhere in India, seeking more formal designations and stronger controls. Was he oblivious to the fact that India's first national park was designated in the United Provinces of the North in 1930? This seems unlikely. Named Hailey Park after Malcolm Hailey, governor of the United Provinces, the park was designated in the Ramganga-Dhikala forests of what is presently the Uttarakhand state.[31] Popular histories suggest that Jim Corbett, hunting legend and conservationist, after whom the national park was renamed in 1956, and Evelyn Arthur Smythies, forester and philatelist, influenced the government to set up the park.[32] As such, the sporting rifle might have still symbolized elite interests in the Madras Presidency in the 1930s, but as Mahesh Rangarajan argues, in the United Provinces of the North, elite 'attitudes began to change when the camera began to accompany if not rival the gun' in forest forays. 'Guilt' and 'awareness of species extinction made it easier to enforce bag limits'.[33] The Madras Presidency government could not remain immune to the tendency to re-imagine 'game' as 'wildlife', and although choosing not to authorize any sanctuaries, it formed an association for the preservation of wildlife in south India. One of its purposes was to advise the government on game preserves.[34]

The status of the Downs were not settled, as the outbreak of the Second World War quickly made clear. Pressure had already grown on the Nilgiris in general thanks to the tanning industry's insatiable demand for wattle bark, a tanning agent imported from South Africa. Seeking new places where wattle plantations could be established, the government consulted with C.C. Wilson, the CCF, in 1938. It subsequently authorized the Forest Department to establish large-scale wattle plantations.[35] Six thousand acres of 'unproductive' rocky, marshy and grassy land were identified in the Nilgiris and, though not explicitly mentioned, parts of the Downs, mainly catchments of the Pykara River, were identified as plantation regions. The scheme envisaged bringing 'further areas' under plantation in the future, which presently did not figure in the scheme because of the 'fear of undue interference with the grazing interests' of the Toda.[36]

Alarmed by these developments, P. Macqueen, collector, sought to prevent further encroachments, submitting a proposal to the government 'to preserve in perpetuity the natural features' of the Wenlock Downs. Macqueen wrote that the 'scenery is unique in the whole of India, perhaps in the world'; it boasted 'accessible beauties and amenities' hard to find in the rest of India. They not only provided 'fishing, shooting, and splendid riding country', but offered 'great opportunities' for naturalists to study an 'exceptionally interesting flora and fauna', and for 'anthropologists to study unique primitive races'. Peppering and pampering the Downs with superlatives – 'unique', 'splendid', 'exceptional' – Macqueen wrote that they 'offered a place of rest to the mere lover of natural beauty who wishes for a time to escape from the rush of modern life'. Not only was this one of the clearest descriptions of the qualities of the Downs to be gleaned from the archive, but it also chimed with the contemporary case being made in favour of the designation of national parks in the UK. Macqueen then listed the opportunities that the Downs offered for modern pursuits themselves, noting that well-to-do Indian visitors were increasing and that the business interests of Indian landlords, shopkeepers and transport vehicle owners benefited from 'attracting residents, permanent and temporary'. Retired Europeans and Anglo-Indians were drawn to the Downs not just by the excellent climate, but by their beauty and the recreation they afforded. But this beauty could be marred beyond repair if spoliations in the form of large-scale tea, wattle and cinchona cultivation and small-scale potato cultivation and cattle grazing continued, notwithstanding the unfortunate fact that limiting cultivation would represent a loss to the potential prosperity of the region.[37]

In a manner that paralleled the 'Indianization' fears of his predecessors, Macqueen wrote that the residents of the Nilgiris were apprehensive of afforestation or cultivation in the future. Once the slopes and summits of the open Downs were planted with trees, they could never be 'restored' to their 'original condition'. Given that deforestation could be effected through the Indian Forest Act or on an order of the provincial government, and without the Nilgiri public's knowledge, Macqueen explained, the only way one could be confident that the Downs could be protected in the future was if they were designated as a national park. Public opinion – or what constituted public opinion in the colonial context – was going this way. The collector enclosed a list of supporting private and public institutions, including municipal councils, European and Anglo-Indian associations, planters associations, the Ootacamund Club, and the Gymkhana Club, among others. He was also careful to note that designating the Downs as a national park would not interfere with existing interests, which perhaps explains why foresters seemed not to be worried. 'The administration of the tract will continue to be in the hands of the forest department', wrote Macqueen, 'subject to the condition that nothing should be done in future which adversely affected the characteristic scenery, flora or fauna of the area.' The rights of the Toda were marshalled by Macqueen in defence of the Downs. They had enjoyed apparently immemorial rights to graze and live on the Downs, but recent experience suggested these rights had been 'curtailed by gradual encroachments in the Downs' and now needed protection. In particular, the Second World War had increased demand for potatoes and the Toda intermittently petitioned the government to complain that their lands, which incidentally they too wanted to cultivate, were being clandestinely rented by government officials to others.[38] And defending the rights of the Toda was not just sentimentality or opportunism on the part of Macqueen, for the traditional use of the Downs helped create and maintain the landscape so valued by the colonial elite, just as the grazing regimes of upland farmers in Britain helped maintain celebrated landscapes there. Moreover, national park status would not negatively affect the rights of established associations and members of the public to continue to enjoy sport and recreation on the Downs, and the government would incur no additional expense. As far as Macqueen was concerned, the proposed bill would do no more than convert certain areas of reserve forest into a national park for the 'benefit of Indian people', ensuring things would continue much as they had before.[39]

Forest superiors and the Board of Revenue responded in ways that made Macqueen's case appear overwrought. Wilson (the CCF) sympathized but did not find it necessary to designate the Downs a national park. They were already titled a reserve forest and were protected from violations under the Forest Act. Regretting past disreservations, Wilson hoped that the government would place on record that no such disreservations could ensue in future. If the government felt the necessity, instructions might be issued that no new plantations would be formed on the Downs.[40] The Board agreed with Wilson, concluding that the area proposed as a national park should be demarcated by an executive order, allowing Wilson to deal with the Downs in a manner consistent with its '*maintenance* as a National Park'.[41] An advisory committee, with the collector as one of the members, was to be appointed to advise the CCF on how the Downs were to be maintained as a national park. Subject to these conditions, the Board accepted the collector's proposal to preserve the Downs and did not have them designated a national park.

Wartime applications to establish plantations on land in the Downs, promoted as a 'new and prosperous industry' for India, were indeed turned down owing to the informal status of the Downs as a national park.[42] Nonetheless, the Forest Department itself went on to plant nearly 1,900 acres of grassland, including in the Toda patta lands in the southern Nilgiris, with wattle bark, pyrethrum flowers and potato crops, each assuming economic significance with the onset of war. Pyrethrum has anti-malarial properties and government demand opened up the market for the insecticides that were needed to protect military personnel from malaria; the same protection was required by Forest Department personnel clearing malarial tropical forests in the Presidency as part of standard forestry operations and the 'Grow More Food' scheme to counter wartime scarcity.[43] Forest lands were leased for five years and interest-free loans included funds to clear sholas; lease clauses included the planting of wattle, potatoes and eucalyptus, the latter to check soil erosion caused by potato planting.[44] Wartime was also wattle-time as pressure to become 'self-supporting' grew.[45]

India was one year from independence when Macqueen's 1939 national park proposals were again discussed by the Wenlock Downs Advisory Committee. Carleston, collector and a member of the committee, wrote to Dyson that 'with a popular government in power', 'a formal Act of legislature' to constitute the Downs as a national park, 'should have popular appeal'. The committee opined that 'Macqueen's proposals in their entirety make out a strong case' and, in contrast to the Macqueen episode, when the then CCF sympathized with the national park proposal but reiterated that the Downs' reserved forest status would suffice to protect against their conversion, A.J. Master, the present CCF, supported Carleston's call for passing legislation to declare the Downs a national park.[46] Despite this, the Board still could not see 'how the present arrangements under executive orders are ineffective and why a formal Act of the Legislature is necessary'.[47]

Master's worries about the vulnerability of the 'executive order' that maintained the Downs as a park was broadly shared by political elites, who sought to buttress their interests by seeking legitimacy in 'Indian' and 'indigenous' contexts. V.I. Munnuswamy Pillai, the local Member of the Legislative Assembly (MLA), wrote to the collector that, as one 'born and brought up in the Nilgiris', he could vouch 'without fear of contradiction' for how people both of this district and those coming from other parts and provinces, enjoy 'the great natural scenery' encountered in the Downs. If the Nilgiris, the 'Queen of Hill Stations and Sanatorium', is not to 'lose all its natural charm, the beautiful Downs must be maintained as a national asset'. Munnuswamy Pillai supported a legislation scheme, whether by means of a 'bill or resolution'.[48] Master found this view of the 'Nilgiris-born resident who appreciates and values the principle and uniquely attractive amenities' to be a 'fitting answer' to a petition that claimed that the Wenlock Downs were 'preserved for the benefit of a privileged few'.[49] In making a case for legislation, Munnuswamy Pillai conveniently recruited the interests of the Toda, an expedient the CCF, collector and DFO would also adopt. The government is 'wedded to a policy of preserving and uplifting' the Toda 'aborigines' who were 'pastoral in occupation and picturesque in physical appearance', Munnuswamy Pillai wrote. 'Their population has greatly dwindled and further reduction, in grazing and other facilities in the year to come will practically wipe off this primitive and picturesque community.'[50] Though Munnuswamy Pillai mentioned the need to protect catchments in the Downs that would fall under the scheme of a proposed Pykara hydroelectric project, and the local DFO was careful to mention the scheme's 'public interest', both the political representative and the forester warned of the consequences inundation would have for Toda grazing.[51]

However, the strongest sentiments in support of passing legislation cited by Master belonged to the DFO. It 'would be an unforgivable act to permit the development of the Downs for selfish and utilitarian ends instead of preserving them for the enjoyment and benefit of posterity the District Forest Officer says', wrote Master.[52] The Presidency government, satisfied with how the Wenlock Downs Committee had maintained the Downs as an informal park since the 1930s, reiterated its commitment to preserve the Downs and allow no further disreseverations, but it did not support Master's initiative. Master, too, had recognized that 'the advisory committee is working satisfactorily and that the Downs are also in good condition', but this was to miss the broader principle at work. He argued that his proposal to have the Lord Wenlock Downs designated a national park 'will be a representation and expression of the popular will, whereas the present authority behind the advisory office is only an executive order'.[53] His voice was not heeded.

Maintaining the Downs as a national park: the politics of conservation

Much of the upper Nilgiri plateau has now been afforested for industrial supply, but since 1900 the western and north-western portions have been preserved as the 'Lord Wenlock Downs' for recreation and pasturage. Half of the commons tenured to the Toda were found here and this largely explains their use as pasturage. The Downs were proximate to Ootacamund and were an easily accessible amenity, which explains both the site's recreational popularity and historic efforts to resist spoliation. While grasslands on the rest of the plateau were utilized for commercial afforestation, the Downs were maintained for their amenity value.

The representation of the Downs as recreational, and thus a landscape to be conserved, was clearly influenced by economic and historical contexts. During pre-war, wartime and post-war periods, the Downs were very productive symbolically. As an open grassy biome they played multiple roles for the state. They were reiterated as state-stewarded recreational or public interest space that needed protection from commercial demands; they served as another bureaucratic turf war in a Presidency permeated with official insecurities; and when vulnerable to both colonial and Indian utility, their aesthetic and heritage values were amplified in making strong cases for their legislation as a national park.

Although the potential of the Downs as a national park were not invoked explicitly when the Gymkhana Club sought permission to establish a golf course on the terrain, national park thinking was nonetheless implicit to the bureaucratic defence of them as recreational space and thus a site of public interest. This episode demonstrated how the conservation of the Downs was predicated on a colonial perception of their value as a site of leisure, largely on the grounds of their aesthetic similarity to highly valued British landscapes. In this sense, the colonial elite wished to mobilize the authority of the state to preserve that in India which was most British. If much the same was evident during the debate provoked by the proposal to declare the Downs a national park during the Second World War, the alarm was then raised by both the threat posed to the Downs by the war effort and the possibility that an independent India might not continue to maintain the Downs virtually as a national park. Designating the Downs as a National Park was no longer a means to protect the landscape from colonial forestry, but from potential spoliation by the independent India to come.

As such, the debate generated by the Downs among colonial officials deployed the 'public interest' as a shorthand for elite interests, lacking in particular the broadly popular basis of national park lobbying in Britain but deploying broadly the same discourse of natural beauty and public access. While the virtual national park question arose in the 1930s in the guise of game preserves, the only suggestion that a distinctly national park style of management, drawing upon the American model, might be introduced was found in the context of worried queries from Malaysian forestry experts. Would game preservation require a separate wildlife staff? And would this set a wider precedent, likely to be introduced elsewhere in the British Empire? Nothing so sweeping was at stake in the discussions, though this was indicative of how vested interests were becoming alert in the 1930s to the possible extension of the nature state.

Clearly, conservation was not just about the state of nature. Conservation debates both concealed and revealed the nature of the colonial state as an amalgam of insecure and interested groups, worried about the loss of power and keen to safeguard the leisured privilege that came with their status. Apparently, national parks and game preserves were not favoured by the very bureaucracy whose mandate was conservation, namely, the Forest Department. As a timber-harvesting and revenue-generating entity, its control over vast landscapes yielded, besides timber, other resources such as game. By contrast, it was officials belonging to the revenue bureaucracy who worried most about decrease of game and afforestation of recreational space. With the outbreak of war, interests looking to commercially exploit the Downs were strengthened and it became more difficult to sustain the argument that its amenity value made it a form of productive space. Utilitarian reasoning, heightened by the pressures of war and manipulated by entrepreneurs, suggested the Downs needed to be converted into economically and militarily useful monocultural plantations. In this context, lobbying for the designation of the Downs as a national park saw them *counter-produced* as an aesthetic, ethnographic and naturalist space needing protective legislation as a national park.

Six years later, when Macqueen's proposals were revisited by the Downs Committee, it became clear to colonial officials that the prospect of independence posed potent risks to the landscape and the Toda, its oldest residents. Inundation by a proposed hydroelectric project would affect the Toda's grazing prospects; the indigenes, now cast as the likely victims of the developmentalism of the independent state, could only be protected if the Downs were declared a park by popular will. Under the new dispensation, it was clear that a colonial Executive Order would prove no match for the demands of an independent state: the Downs could be maintained as a national park under British rule, but it had to be legislated as one under Indian rule if there was any hope of resisting the advancing interests of the state–commercial nexus. And yet, in the dying days of British India, the renewed calls for the designation of the Downs as a national park still originated with the elites, albeit an elite that was less exclusively British, and did not include significant efforts to mobilize the Toda in defence of their rights and interests. An elitist paternalism remained the dominant note.

A debate in the mid-1950s sealed the fate of the empire's former sweet spot. In 1955, an argument broke out over the Downs between McLaughlin, the last British collector, who worried about the aesthetic effects of development, and Subramaniam, a South Indian CCF, who sought to tap the Downs' economic potential. The 1939 afforestation scheme had not progressed well, but began to gain traction after independence, and Subramaniam sought to accelerate its development. While McLaughlin believed that the Downs could be considered the most beautiful landscape in the world, Subramaniam and his subordinates saw in the Downs revenue and employment potential for an 'impoverished nation'. In a letter to McLaughlin, D.K. Dey, the Nilgiri DFO, made the case for allowing the development by combining utility with a long-established aesthetic and amenity-based defence of the Downs. Blue gum plantations, he argued, 'will enhance the aesthetics of Downs and enhance fauna', while connecting blue gum woodlets with metalled roads would render 'these beautifully wooded downs accessible to the not so robust visitor'. Rotational felling of the forests every 15 years was only an incidental advantage, Dey argued, though by no means a small one in a hungry and poverty-stricken nation. Newspaper and eucalyptus oil industries would grow and fuel needs would be met. K.N. Raghavan Nair, the provincial silviculturist, felt similarly, writing to the CFF:

> The indigenous sholas, though very picturesque and beautiful are of no economic value. On the other hand blue gum and wattle, besides serving the purpose of the sholas, will also provide valuable raw materials for vitally important industries.[54]

'Jolly good bird, this DFO', noted Subramaniam of Dey, and the plantations went ahead, effectively bringing to an end an episode in the history of India's nature state.[55]

Even if British interests in preserving the Downs were elitist, a colonial or post-independence consensus in legislating them a national park would have spared the Downs their contemporary fate. Today, eucalyptus woodlots stand tall amid wattle and the thorny gorse thickets that have invaded the Downs. Pine trees have desiccated marsh and peat bogs. Conservation biologists and ecologists are studying invasive behaviour and are attempting ecological restoration of grasslands. The now-wooded Downs also serve as a predatory habitat. Tiger and leopard attacks on Toda buffaloes are common, and there is anxiety when schoolchildren, working husbands and grazing buffaloes fail to arrive before the light fades. Consequently, the Todas are nostalgic for the grassy open land of the past.[56] In retrospect, the decision not to declare the Downs a national park, whatever colonial interests lay behind such proposals, proved catastrophic to the grasslands and enormously stressful for the Todas. Since the 1990s, the Downs have once again become the focus of sustained ecological concern, a reflection of both the wider critique of the developmental priorities of independent India and a concomitant new mood that permits a less ideologically heated appraisal of the colonial state. Since then, the accent has necessarily been placed on restoration rather than preservation and the possibility that English heartland might be not only a Toda heartland but an Indian heartland too. The revival of the nature state, at least in this part of India, can thus be projected less as postcolonial nostalgia for 'the Raj' and more as an assertion of popular sovereignty and the defence of traditional rights in the face of powerful commercial interests.

Notes

1 Ramachandra Guha and Madhav Gadgil, 'State Forestry and Social Conflict in British India', *Past & Present*, 123 (1989), 141–77.
2 Ibid., 145.
3 Ibid., 147.
4 For a detailed natural history of the Nilgiris, see William A. Noble, 'The Nilgiris of Tamil Nadu, India, as a Distinctive Upland Island', in *Cultural Geography, Form and Process: Essays in Honour of Prof. A.B. Mukerji*, ed. by Neelam Grover and Kashi N. Singh (New Delhi, 2004), 401–20.
5 Anthony R. Walker, *The Toda of South India: A New Look* (Delhi, 1986), 252.
6 Siddhartha Krishnan, 'Landscape, Labor, and Label: The Second World War, Pastoralist Amelioration, and Pastoral Conservation in the Nilgiris, South India (1929–1945)', *International Labor and Working-Class History*, 87 (2015), 95.
7 Siddhartha Krishnan, 'Woody, Thorny, and Predatory Forests: Grassland Transformations in the Nilgiris, South India', in *Unruly Environments*, ed. by Christopher L. Pastore, Samuel Temple, and Siddhartha Krishnan (Munich, 2015), 40–1.
8 W. Francis, *The Nilgiris* (Madras, 1908), 36.
9 K. Sivaramakrishnan, 'Landlords, Regional Development and National Forestry Projects: Midnapore, 1930s–1960s', in *A New Moral Economy for India's Forests? Discourses of Community and Participation*, ed. by Roger Jeffery and Nandini Sundar (New Delhi, 1999), 71–91.
10 Richard Grove, *Green Imperialism: Colonial Expansion, Tropical Island Edens, and the Origins of Environmentalism, 1600–1860* (Cambridge, 1995), 153–6.
11 Ibid., 461–2.
12 Ajay Skaria, 'Timber Conservancy, Desiccationism and Scientific Forestry: The Dangs 1840s–1920s', in *Nature and the Orient: The Environmental History of South and Southeast Asia*, ed. by Richard Grove, Vinita Damodaran, and Satpal Sangwan (New Delhi, 1998), 596–635.
13 The mention of beauty or even utility signals a landscape's influence on ostensibly rational bureaucratic decisions. Thus, in configuring the role of conservation in legitimizing state rule, or the state's role in the 'construction' of nature as exercise of power, one risks analysis being environmentally deterministic. But much environmental history now avoids the scorn reserved for determinism by concentrating on the cultural interpretations of politics behind landscape regulation

and re-ordering. Two such environmental histories that provide insight into the nineteenth-century colonial state's predicaments in the pursuit of legitimacy on the Nilgiris plateau are: Gunnel Cederlöf, *Landscapes and the Law: Environmental Politics, Regional Histories, and Contests over Nature* (Ranikhet, 2008); and Deborah Sutton, *Other Landscapes: Colonialism and the Predicament of Authority in Nineteenth-Century South India* (Copenhagen, 2009).

14 See Michael Redclift, 'Redefining the Environmental "Crisis" in the South', in *Red and Green: A New Politics of the Environment*, ed. by Joe Weston (London, 1986); cited in John A. Hannigan, *Environmental Sociology*, 2nd edn (London, 2007), 21.

15 'Inspection Notes of the Nilgiris District', by Lodge, the conservator, southern circle, enclosed in letter from Davidson, the collector, Nilgiris, to the secretary, Land Revenue Department (hereafter LRD), 16 November 1910, Forest, Miscellaneous Series (hereafter Ms. No.), file no. 311, Tamil Nadu Archives (hereafter TNA).

16 S. Cox, CCF to the secretary, Revenue (hereafter RD) (Special), 12 July 1920, Development Department (hereafter DD), Ms. no. 333 (Golf Links file), TNA.

17 'Notes Connected with Government Order (hereafter GO) No. 333, RD (Special) 28 February 1921', B. Rama Rao, 28 July 1920.

18 'Notes Connected with GO No. 333, RD (Special) 28 February 1921', J.M. Turing, 31 August 1920.

19 Note by C.G. Todhunter, council member, to the governor, 2 December 1920 (Golf Links file).

20 W. Francis, collector, Nilgiris, to the secretary to the commissioner, LRD, 7 May 1910; GO no. 1759, RD, 9 June 1911, LRD, F., Press Series, file no. 167, TNA.

21 Note by Todhunter to the Governor, 2 December 1920 (Golf Links file: see note 19).

22 Ibid.

23 'Memo for future reference', handwritten note by A. Wimbush, 22 July 1930; as a consequence of the ban, Richmond mentions that the DFO and he had 'a very nice Xmas camp there', FD, Ms. No. 381, 29 August 1933, TNA.

24 GO no. 1737 (ibid.).

25 'Good tea land' referred to lands that could be cleared for tea plantations. Wimbush to Richmond, 14 November 1930 (ibid.).

26 Richmond to Wimbush, 18 November 1930 (ibid.).

27 Wimbush to Richmond, 14 November 1930 (ibid.).

28 Richmond to Wimbush, 18 November 1930 (ibid.).

29 Copy of letter from J.G. Watson, Forest Research Institute, Kepong, Selangor, F.M.S., to H.G. Champion, silviculturist, Forest Research Institute, Dehra Dun, 24 January 1931 (ibid.).

30 Reply to Watson, 27 February 1931 (ibid.).

31 Mahesh Rangarajan, 'Nature, Culture and Empires', in *People, Parks, and Wildlife: Towards Coexistence*, ed. by Vasant K. Saberwal, Mahesh Rangarajan and Ashish Kothari (New Delhi, 2000), 23.

32 https://en.wikipedia.org/wiki/Jim_Corbett_National_Park#cite_note-Tiwari1-9

33 Rangarajan, 'Nature, Culture and Empires', 23.

34 Decision made in meeting presided by the governor, 7 June 1933.

35 GO no. 157, 19 January 1940; GO no. Ms. 3097, DD, 14 December 1938, TNA.

36 'Scheme for the Cultivation of Green Wattle (Acacia decurrens) in the Madras Presidency for Production of Tanning Bark' (ibid.).

92   *Siddhartha Krishnan*

37 Proposal from P. Macqueen, collector, Nilgiris, to the secretary, DD, 17 April 1939, DD, File no. 783, 4 April 1940, TNA.
38 Krishnan, 'Landscape, Labor, and Label', 92–110.
39 By the 'Indian Forest Act', perhaps Macqueen was referring to the Madras Forest Act. The latter was passed in 1882 and the former in 1878. See Kavita Philip, *Civilising Natures: Race, Resources and Modernity in Colonial South India* (Hyderabad, 2003) for a discussion of the four-year difference between these two Acts and whether the Madras Act was more reasonable towards customary rights than the Indian Act.
40 C.C. Wilson, CCF, Madras, to the secretary, DD, 14 June 1939, TNA.
41 GO No. Ms. 783, April 4, 1940 (emphasis added).
42 E.G. Cameron, planter, Ben Gorm Estate, Hullical, Nilgiris, to V.I. Muniswamy Pillai, MLA, Ootacamund, 29 June 1940, DD, GO No. 1552, TNA.
43 Wilson to Dewan Bahadur V.N. Viswanatha Rao, secretary, DD, 25 July 1939 (ibid.). In 1943, 3,200 acres were used for potato cultivation as part of the 'Grow More Food' campaign.
44 DD, GO No. 315, 13 March 1943, TNA.
45 R.S. Browne, 'Brief Summary of the Scheme' to cultivate green wattle (*Acacia decurrens*), 19 January 1940, GO No. 157, DD, TNA.
46 Report, 15 July 1947; Carleston, collector, Nilgiris, to A.J. Master, CCF, Madras, 3 September 1946, BR, Ms. No. 925, TNA. The committee met on 15 June.
47 Note by assistant secretary (special), Revenue, 30 May 1947 (ibid.).
48 Munnuswamy Pillai to the collector, Nilgiris, 24 October 1946 (ibid.).
49 Master to the secretary, DD, Fort St. George, Madras, 22 March 1947 (ibid.).
50 Munnuswamy Pillai to the collector, Nilgiris, 24 October 1946 (ibid.).
51 Report of the DFO, Nilgiris, 12 June 1947 (ibid.).
52 Master to the secretary, DD, Fort St. George, Madras, 22 March 1947 (ibid.).
53 GO No. 2474, DD, 4 June 1947. Note file, 9 July 1947, TNA.
54 Note from K.N. Raghavan Nair, the provincial silviculturist, to the CCF, 30 July 1953, CCF GO no. 319, 1954, TNA.
55 D.K. Dey, DFO, Nilgiris, to H.C. McLaughlin, collector, Nilgiris, 28 July 1953 (ibid.).
56 For more on how such transformation ensued, see my 'Woody, Thorny, and Predatory Forests: Grassland Transformations in the Nilgiris, South India', 39–44; for an essentialist but engaging account of the current plight of the Toda, see Michael Tobias and Jane Gray Morrison, *Why Life Matters: Fifty Ecosystems of the Heart and Mind* (New York, 2014), 337–45.

5 Negotiating the nature state beyond the parks

Conservation in twentieth-century north-central Namibia

Emmanuel Kreike

By the late 1980s, apartheid South Africa was in many ways the embodiment of the nature state, deriving significant legitimacy from its extensive efforts to conserve nature in parks and reserves, combat deforestation and desertification, and containing such dangerous livestock diseases as rinderpest and anthrax. Indeed, conservation practices in apartheid South Africa were held up as global models even after the fall of apartheid. Apartheid's nature conservation complex not only was kept in place after the 1994 fall of the white colonial state by the new successive democratic governments, but also exported to South Africa's neighbours, most notably through the Peace Park initiative, which effectively expanded the Kruger Park into neighbouring Mozambique and Zimbabwe. The (South African) nature state only unfolded in remote north-central Namibia (Ovamboland) after the National Party won South Africa's 1948 elections and the new apartheid government's subsequent de-facto annexation of Namibia. South Africa's conservation policies were then introduced wholesale in Ovamboland. Yet conservation beyond the parks was contested not only by non-state actors, including various factions among Ovamboland's inhabitants, but also from within the nature state itself.

Apartheid South Africa's conservation model in many ways embodied the dark side of the nature state. The apartheid colonial system violently suppressed the rights of the majority of its population to maintain the privileges of a white minority. Conservation legitimized colonial interference in rural lives and livelihoods, serving to restrict the mobility of African populations and their livestock. White South Africans enjoyed the national parks for leisure and education. The few non-whites who frequented the parks served as rangers, maids, servants or cooks; non-white tourism was rare.[1] Moreover, as elsewhere in Africa and beyond, the creation of the nature state facilitated twentieth-century (white and colonial) nation- and empire-building.[2] Nature conservation in South Africa also directly helped to maintain the integrity of the apartheid state during the 1960s–1990s liberation wars. The Kruger Park, which stretches along much of the border with neighbouring Mozambique, played a key role as a security buffer against infiltration by African National Congress (ANC) guerrillas. The park also served as a base for military operations to destabilize the pro-ANC government of Mozambique.[3] Similarly, Etosha Park in Namibia served as a buffer to prevent incursions into the white farmlands to the south by the guerrillas of Namibia's liberation movement, the South West African Peoples' Organization (SWAPO), which was based in Angola. In fact, throughout colonial Africa, conservation was mainly about protecting scarce natural resources (including wildlife, forests, pastures and farmlands) from Africans and making them into a state-controlled commons. In the eyes of the colonial pioneers and protagonists of the nature state, Africa's indigenous human populations and their livestock not only spread diseases, but also wrought environmental destruction.[4] Conservation therefore primarily was concerned with domesticating African populations by creating state-managed nature. Not surprisingly, the nature state developed as a consequence of a series of contestations between various groups claiming to represent the (colonial or postcolonial) state and local communities.[5] The process of creating the nature state was neither linear nor simply a struggle between the state and its subjects. Officials and subjects at times forged alliances across the state–subject divide and certain categories of people and individuals inhabited a middle ground as intermediaries, or they crossed sides altogether.[6] In Southern Africa, the nature state was heavily contested even within the colonial state, leading to contradictions in conservation policies and practices. Yet, this does not mean that the colonial (nature) state was weak or ineffective. South Africa's attempts to construct the nature state in today's north-central Namibia involved the Etosha National Park and Ovamboland. Ovamboland initially was designated as a 'native reserve' administered by a native commissioner and later as a Bantustan or homeland with very limited self-rule by the 'traditional' leaders. Both conservation policies in the Etosha National Park and beyond the park in adjacent Ovamboland from 1915 to 1980 are addressed. The case study demonstrates the need to differentiate the nature state in time and place, even within one particular region. In north-central Namibia, the nature state proved weak in some realms, but strong and hegemonic in others, and its effectiveness on the ground expanded and contracted over time, reflecting changes in the status of Namibia from conquest, to mandate, to annexed province.

South African forces occupied modern Namibia (then German South-west Africa) in 1915 after defeating the German colonial army in the first months of the First World War. After the war, the League of Nations entrusted the former German colony as a mandate territory to the Union of South Africa. The South African administration introduced conservation by creating parks during the First World War. But, beyond establishing the Etosha National Park, the implementation of South Africa's conservation laws and regulations in north-central Namibia was limited. In 1946, South Africa failed to persuade the United Nations, the successor body of the League of Nations, to award the territory to South Africa in recognition of its strong contribution to the allied war effort. The United Nations did, however, allow South Africa to continue its stewardship over Namibia. After South Africa's National Party won the 1948 elections and formalized racial segregation, it also de-facto annexed Namibia as the fifth province of South Africa. South Africa took over the direct administration of the territory in the 1950s, subsequently introducing its conservation policies and regulations in Namibia.[7]

The partial implementation of the South African nature state in Ovamboland was due to a number of factors, including the formal status of Namibia as a League of Nations mandate, its critical importance as a labour reservoir for Namibia's economy, and its strategic location on the border with Angola. Violence and taxation in the adjacent Portuguese colony of Angola led to a steady flight and migration from southern Angola into Ovamboland during the first half of the twentieth century. Some South African officials feared that the implementation of harsh conservation measures in Ovamboland would reverse the flow. Moreover, the inhabitants of Ovamboland had a history of tenacious armed resistance against colonial conquest and they were not fully disarmed until well into the 1930s.[8] The Ovamboland administration therefore was hesitant in implementing conservation measures that might trigger resistance.

With the introduction of full-blown apartheid in the 1950s, South Africa unfolded its nature state wings over Ovamboland even as its imposition remained contested and incomplete. It was not only challenged by local African subjects, but also divided the colonial state itself. By 1980, the nature state in Ovamboland was part reality and part fiction. Officials of both the Departments of Bantu Affairs and Agriculture warned that conservation measures championed by their colleagues from the Departments of Nature Conservation and Veterinary Services threatened colonial order and stability. A high-ranking Bantu Affairs official went so far as to recommend that the Department of Nature Conservation be banned from Ovamboland altogether. The official was not alone in opposing the expansion of the nature state into Ovamboland. The director of the Department of Agriculture warned that the implementation of further conservation measures would cause a revolt. His warning was prophetic: during the 1980s, Ovamboland turned into an outright war zone and conservation officials and projects became prime targets for the armed wing of the SWAPO, causing the total collapse of all conservation efforts. By tracing nature conservation efforts in north-central Namibia before and after the Second World War, the internal struggles within the nature state's institutions emerge.

Before the Second World War, the main concern of the colonial state was to control people through control over territory. In Namibia, this was accomplished through indirect rule, with local chiefs and headmen playing a key role. Establishing and maintaining parks and protecting select large 'royal' game was seen as integral to empire building and the consolidation of the colonial state.[9] Beyond the parks, conservation in north-central Namibia was considered to be of secondary importance. South Africa's economy had a voracious appetite for cheap African labour for its mines and settler farms. Protecting wildlife also served to mobilize labour by ending commercial and subsistence hunting as alternatives to engaging in wage labour.[10]

During the late 1800s, European and African hunters commercially hunted wildlife in the Angola–Namibia border region between the Kunene River and the Kavango River. During the dry seasons, wildlife and waterfowl concentrated along the Kunene River and south of Ovamboland at Etosha Pan or sought refuge in the Oshimolo marshes across the border in Angola. Herds of wildebeest, zebra and springbuck gathered at Etosha Pan, and buffalo, rhino, kudu, impala and wild boar drank from the Kunene River, where crocodiles and hippos swam. Elephants roamed north of Ovamboland in Angola.[11] Hunting and the late 1890s rinderpest epidemic, however, decimated the wildlife population.[12] The introduction of modern firearms in the region enormously increased the efficiency of hunting. By 1910, the approximately 300,000 inhabitants of the Ovambo floodplain on either side of the modern Angola–Namibia border owned an estimated 10,000 firearms, mostly breech-loading rifles that could be reloaded more quickly than the old muzzle-loaders and could kill an animal at far greater distances.[13]

After defeating the German army in 1915, the South African army marched north into the territory that subsequently became known as Ovamboland. German control over Ovamboland had never been effectively established. The South African administration proclaimed the Namutoni and Okaukuejo Game Reserves, which later merged into the Etosha Game Reserve. The South Africans established the Namutoni Game Reserve in 1916. In 1921, beacons marked the reserve's boundary north-west of Namutoni, where an old German colonial fort served as the game warden's base. The game warden answered to the native affairs' commissioner of Ovamboland. The colonial administration prohibited hunting 'royal game', including elephants and lions even outside of the game reserves.[14] The boundaries of the game reserves were ill-defined, however, and Ovamboland's elite challenged the new restrictions. King Martin of Ondonga claimed areas near Etosha Pan as his 'traditional' hunting grounds and sent his men to hunt there during the early 1920s.[15] King Iipumbu of Uukwambi equally ignored the new restrictions, which contributed to the events that led to his violent removal from office by the South African administration in 1932.[16] Poaching both inside and outside the game reserves continued to be a problem until at least the mid-1950s.[17]

The disarmament of the population of Ovamboland had a more profound impact on the conservation of the region's wildlife than contemporary colonial conservation regulations even though the effect was largely unintended. During the 1920s and 1930s, all but a few select kings, chiefs and headmen were forced to surrender their firearms. Those who retained firearms either hunted for themselves or sponsored professional hunters who used horses and guns supplied by their patrons to hunt large game and produce dried meat. Colonial officials allowed the practice as long as they hunted outside of the Etosha Park and observed the restriction against hunting royal game. A small number of professional hunters who produced dried meat remained active until the 1960s.[18] With the less-efficient bows and arrows and dogs, and faced with increased restrictions on hunting large game, the bulk of the inhabitants of Ovamboland were restricted to hunting small game except for the occasional herd of larger game that strayed close to the villages. Large flocks of migratory birds passed through Ovamboland during the rainy season and temporarily inhabited the breeding grounds between Oponono Lake and Etosha Pan.[19] Small game hunting around the villages, however, was little affected. Young boys trapped and killed rodents and birds while herding livestock near their homes; this provided food and limited the damage rodents and birds caused to crops and grain stores.[20]

The recovery of wildlife populations from the 1890s rinderpest, the reduction of commercial and subsistence hunting and the disarmament campaigns explain why wildlife had not entirely disappeared from Ovamboland (outside of Etosha) by the 1920s and 1930s. Some species actually may have increased in numbers or expanded their range. During the 1870s and 1880s, elephants, for example, were virtually extinct in Ovamboland. During the 1920s, 1930s and 1940s they reappeared in the floodplain, especially along wildlife migration corridors between Etosha and the Kunene River on the territory's western edge, and between Etosha and the Oshimolo swamps and the Okavango River in the east. Yet, even as overall numbers of wildlife in Ovamboland dropped, incidences of human–wildlife contact increased because a settlement frontier which expanded west- and eastwards beyond the Ovambo floodplain increasingly intersected with north–south wildlife migratory movements.[21]

The only figures available for the wildlife population of Ovamboland (which administratively included Etosha Park until the 1970s) are for 1930 and for 1938–43. A comparison of the 1930 figures with those for 1938 suggests a decline in the overall number of large game, including giraffe, zebra, kudu, gemsbok, wildebeest, hartebeest, springbuck, duiker and hyena. For most of the species, the decline was dramatic: the number of giraffes fell from 160 to 30 animals; the zebra population from 12,500 to 1,500; kudu from 3,000 to 500; gemsbok from 3,000 to 650; wildebeest from 7,000 to 2,500; and hyena from 800 to 220. Eland and steenbok increased in numbers from 200 to 400 and 4,000 to 4,500, respectively. Lions experienced a minor decline, from 50 to 35–45 animals, while the cheetah population remained stable at 50 animals and the number of leopards doubled to 150 animals. Between 1938 and 1943, after the disarmament of the population of Ovamboland had been completed, most animal species remained roughly at the same population levels.[22] Giraffe, zebra, eland, roan antelope, wildebeest, duiker, lion and cheetah populations grew.[23] Elephants seemed to have returned to Ovamboland's margins in the 1920s and 1930s. Significantly, predator populations remained relatively stable (lions) or increased (leopards). The figures are estimates but served effectively to legitimize conservation policies.[24]

The success of colonial conservation, however, ironically eroded any grass-roots support for conservation among the population of the colonial territory. Disarming Ovamboland and game conservation measures caused, especially, elephants and such dangerous predators as lions and leopards to venture closer to villages and cattle posts to seek food and water, dramatically increasing the incidence of human–animal conflict. Human–wildlife contact also increased during the late 1920s to the 1950s as a result of the influx of large numbers of refugees from Angola into Ovamboland. Moreover, internal migrations facilitated by increasing political security from the 1920s onwards encouraged individuals and families to settle new areas on the margins of Ovamboland in the uninhabited buffer zones that had existed between the precolonial polities. The net effect of these transboundary and internal migrations was that humans increasingly encroached on wildlife migration habitat and migratory routes. Colonial reports demonstrate that during droughts, elephants invaded villages, raiding crop fields, food stores, and fruit trees, as well as chasing livestock from scarce sources of water. Elephants sometimes maimed and killed livestock and destroyed precious water holes, as well as fences, fields, crops and fruit trees. Lions preyed on livestock at cattle posts and near villages. During the 1940s and 1960s leopard and lion attacks occurred regularly. Losses likely were underreported because no compensation was offered, but in 1940 alone predators killed over 200 head of livestock; in 1941, they killed 140 head of livestock. Sometimes, humans fell victim to predators, too. In 1939, a leopard mauled ten people in a single village and a hyena bit two people in another village. Two of the victims died of their wounds. In 1946, lions killed a village headman and wounded several others in a series of attacks on different villages. In 1948, a leopard attacked a man close to colonial administration's head office at Ondangwa. In 1953, a wild dog attack left ten people wounded and two dead, while elephants killed another three people. Ovamboland's officials rarely intervened, a fact that greatly disturbed the local chiefs. Herdsmen had to be extremely vigilant about predators; at night they secured their herds behind tall thornbush barriers and protected themselves by keeping huge fires burning.[25]

Perhaps not only the attacks themselves and the economic loss they caused, but also larger existential concerns about increased disorder and insecurity expressed themselves in the rare cases of direct indigenous critiques of colonial conservation recorded in the colonial archive. In 1949, in a letter overflowing with indignation, King Kambonde of Ondonga reported that he saw an elephant tear down a large mud-plastered granary in his neighbour's homestead, leaving her destitute. In 1952, King Shetuatha Mbashu complained bitterly that elephants had imposed a virtual reign of terror at the edge of his district, killing cattle at will while the colonial administration ignored his pleas for help. In 1958, during a large community meeting at Ondangwa, one among the assembled asked if the colonial administration would now finally allow lions and elephants to be killed when they threatened people's lives and livelihoods.[26] While Ovamboland's colonial administration proved inflexible and hegemonic in terms of wildlife conservation, the opposite was true in the realm of forest conservation. In the mid-1920s, missionaries warned that progressive deforestation in Ovamboland would cause desertification. In 1931, in his first report, a newly arrived junior officer expressed alarm about the dramatic levels of deforestation in his district.[27] Officials and missionaries alike ascribed the deforestation to the Angolan refugees and internal migrants who were settling new areas, clearing land for their fields and farms and protecting their homesteads with elaborate palisades.[28] Ironically, the vegetation-devouring palisades and fences around the farms were the only way to keep marauding wildlife at bay.

The head of the colonial administration in Ovamboland, Native Commissioner C.H.L. Hahn, however, thought that the assessments by his subaltern and the missionaries were overblown and alarmist. He acknowledged that Ovambo wood use wasted good timber and that the establishment of new homesteads led to a certain amount of deforestation. Nevertheless, in his confidential correspondence to his superiors in Windhoek, he noted that the imposition of restrictions on indigenous wood use might threaten the colonial order in the politically sensitive border region. On those grounds, in 1941 he argued strongly against introducing forestry conservation under the 1936 Native Land and Trust Act in Ovamboland, explaining that conditions in the area differed greatly from those in South Africa.[29] He warned that imposing limits on cutting trees for 'domestic purposes' would trigger political unrest.[30] Hahn's political instability argument struck a chord with his superiors because Ovamboland had only been partially pacified in 1917, and disarming the Ovamboland's former polities was a slow process. The former kingdom of Uukwambi was disarmed as late as 1932, and only with the aid of South African bombers and armoured cars that destroyed the king's palace. Moreover, migration, flight and arms smuggling across the border with Angola was rampant.[31] Hahn was not only successful in silencing his own subalterns and the missionaries, but, with the complicity of his superiors, he managed to prevent the introduction of most conservation policies that had been implemented elsewhere in the native reserves of South Africa and Namibia.[32]

The only forest conservation measures Hahn allowed in Ovamboland were a prohibition against setting forest fires, the imposition of limits on cutting timber trees by the missions, the protection of selected trees, and the establishing of village forest reserves. The prohibition against the use of fire to manage vegetation, pastures and wildlife had a limited impact because until well after the Second World War the colonial administration in Ovamboland lacked the staff to enforce the measure and local chiefs and headmen were reluctant to police it. Only timber cutting by the missions was regulated by the colonial administration. Any regulation of timber use by the local population for 'subsistence' was left entirely to the discretion of the local chiefs and headmen. Native Commissioner Hahn argued that no real intervention in the protection of the region's towering fruit trees was necessary because chiefs and headmen already protected the fruit trees in the villages.[33]

Subsequent attempts regarding tree conservation in 1957 (by a newly appointed agricultural officer for Ovamboland) and in 1978 (by the forestry officer) acknowledged that indigenous fruit trees already were protected under 'traditional law'. Nevertheless, in both cases the officials felt compelled to draw up a list of trees that they thought ought to be permanently protected.[34] Most large timber trees in the Ovambo floodplain occurred on the sandy ridges between the seasonal flood channels that cut through the region. The top of the ridges was less suitable for crop cultivation, and until the 1950s often remained covered by trees. These 'forests', which consisted of large trees interspersed with lower bush vegetation, served as sources of wood and marked the territorial boundaries between neighbouring villages. In the 1940s and 1950s, the colonial administration declared that the ridges would constitute formal village forest reserves, but enforcement proved difficult as land became increasingly scarce and village headmen allocated the land to young landless households instead of enforcing the forest reserves.[35]

Although fires were a regular occurrence during the late 1920s and 1930s, officials considered them to be dangerous and utterly wasteful of timber resources. Officials urged headmen to impose heavy fines on those accused of setting fires outside of the villages. King Martin of Ondonga district, however, claimed that he was utterly powerless to check the occurrence of fires and, despite the threat of heavy fines, fires continued to be a problem until the early 1950s.[36]

A third concern that emerged in discussions about conservation policies before the Second World War was the perceived explosive increase of indigenous livestock herds. During the 1930s and 1940s, colonial officials and experts across Africa identified indigenous livestock as a major environmental threat. From their perspective, not only did African livestock harbour dangerous microbes, including rinderpest, lungsickness and foot and mouth, but the overabundance of animals also caused overgrazing, deforestation and desertification. Livestock damaged full-grown trees and prevented tree regeneration. Conservation policies involving livestock consequently led to tensions not only between Ovamboland's population and its administration, but also among colonial officials and various departments within the colonial bureaucracy. During the 1920s and 1930s, Native Commissioner Hahn expressed concern about the issue, but he intentionally limited interventions that targeted indigenous cattle management. Hahn in public denied that overstocking was a problem in Ovamboland and he postulated that any grazing problems could be solved by developing water sources east of the Ovambo floodplain.[37] By the 1940s, however, he seems to have come privately to the conclusion that overstocking was becoming a real issue.[38] He prohibited the movement of cattle from Ovamboland to the south to prevent any infection of the herds of the white ranchers in the Police Zone (colonial Namibia south of Etosha Park). However, he allowed the unlimited import of cattle from the south into Ovamboland.[39] Like officials elsewhere, he maligned goats as a source of deforestation but otherwise ignored them.[40] His most interventionist policy regarding livestock was largely unsuccessful. It involved limiting the import of donkeys, arguing that they caused overgrazing.[41]

During Hahn's tenure, he actively sabotaged measures to limit the movement of cattle across the Angola–Namibia boundary or to introduce a cattle vaccination programme to eradicate livestock diseases. The transborder cattle movements were a key component of cattle transhumance: during the dry season, herdsmen drove the cattle herds away from the floodplain villages to seasonal pastures along the Kunene River to the west or to the Oshimolo swamps to the north-east, across the border in southern Angola. Rehearsing his argument that he did not wish to undermine traditional society and the tribal order in Ovamboland, Hahn successfully thwarted the introduction of any of the measures used elsewhere that affected indigenous livestock management in the name of conservation. Hahn refused to stop the transborder cattle transhumance despite the attempts by his Portuguese counterparts on the Angolan side to close the border for cattle movements. That a 1930s Portuguese attempt to prevent cattle movements culminated in threats and violence against its border guards, forcing the Portuguese officials to back down, served as grist on Hahn's mill. He cancelled carefully planned cattle vaccination projects during the 1920s and again in the 1930s, claiming that interference with transcolonial cattle movement would lead to political unrest and a reversal of human migrations from the Angolan side of the border to South African-controlled Ovamboland. Ovamboland by the 1930s had become not only a key labour reservoir for colonial Namibia but also for South Africa as a result of a massive influx of refugees and migrants from Angola. A 1946 foot-and-mouth disease outbreak just north of the border in Angola led to the addition of a veterinary official to Hahn's staff. The veterinary official recommended the urgent creation of a five-mile cordon zone along the border to prevent the spread into Ovamboland. The veterinarian also urged that cattle trespassing in the cordon should be considered infected and shot. Hahn rejected the institution of the cordon along the border, reiterating his stock argument that it would lead to political unrest. As a result, the veterinary cordon was located east–west, south of Ovamboland instead.[42] Soon thereafter, however, Hahn retired.

Until the mid–1920s, colonial conservation largely was limited to large game and parks, but this changed after the Second World War. Concerns about desertification (fuelled by local droughts and famines as well as the American Dustbowl) fed ideas about expanding conservation beyond the parks and led to the introduction of soil and water conservation projects throughout Africa.[43] The full implementation of these projects was delayed by the impact of the 1930s economic recession and the Second World War. After 1945, colonial governments energetically sought to implement their pre-war conservation agendas. Whereas for most of the pre-war era, territorial and population control had been the main objectives of colonial administrations, after the Second World War, the colonial state prioritized 'development'. Development required the conquest and domestication of tropical nature, and conservation was one of the principal tools to accomplish the subjugation of nature in the colonies, thereby unlocking the full potential of its natural resources.[44]

The consolidation of conservation areas led to the forced removal of entire communities. Outside of the parks, soil, forest and wildlife conservation, and veterinary programmes that aimed to reduce overgrazing and eradicate livestock diseases, dramatically affected land and resource use. Conservation policies resulted in land alienation, displacement and impoverishment, and triggered resistance. Often, the nature state was either depicted as overpowering and destructive or as inefficient and helpless in the face of resistance and evasion.[45]

The weakness of the nature state was not only attributed to resistance, but also to officials' lack of understanding of local environmental and social conditions, leading to the implementation of projects that were not only detrimental to the environment but also added to the workload of already overburdened African peasants, women in particular.[46] Sometimes, the very scientists who mapped out the new conservation projects even subverted colonialism by criticizing past and present policies.[47]

Whereas before the mid-1940s the South African administration of Ovamboland and Namibia seemed to prioritize maintaining order, conditions began to change when the United Nations nixed South Africa's attempt to annex South-west Africa/Namibia. The UN's rejection was a slap in the face for South Africa's Smuts government and contributed to his United Party's defeat in the 1948 elections and the victory of the opposition National Party. Native Commissioner Hahn had accompanied Smuts on his mission to the UN to support South Africa's claims to Namibia as a reward for South Africa's contribution to the war effort. Hahn retired soon after Smuts' diplomatic debacle and his former subordinate and nemesis Eedes succeeded him in 1947. In terms of livestock conservation, Eedes was much more interventionist than Hahn. Yet, in other respects, he echoed his predecessor's claims that Ovamboland was unique and that most conservation measures were inappropriate in the territory.[48] Aided by the outbreak of cattle disease epidemics across the border in Angola, Eedes introduced new livestock-related conservation measures but strong opposition voiced by the missionaries frustrated his projects.

Eedes identified two conservation priorities: overpopulation and overstocking. Both conditions, he argued, led to deforestation and overgrazing. He employed colonial statistics to demonstrate that cattle numbers had increased four-fold between 1926 and 1946, from 60,000 head to 250,000.[49] As an immediate measure, Eedes maintained the veterinary cordon south of Ovamboland near Namutoni even after the immediate threat of livestock diseases had passed.[50] Originally a temporary measure, during Eedes' tenure it evolved into what became known as the Red Line, which remains in place to the present.

At the time, Eedes' plan was to make Ovamboland livestock disease-free and to move the veterinary cordon north to the Namibia–Angola boundary. He sought to create a 5–10-mile livestock and settlement-free zone along the border to prevent any future infection from across the border with Angola. Executing the plan would have required removing up to 20,000 people from the densely settled border zone in the Oukwanyama and Ombalantu districts. In an unguarded moment, Eedes confessed to an official of the Church of England Mission (CEM) that his plan probably would be deemed too radical by South-west Africa's highest colonial official. The CEM officer leaked the plan to his bishop, George Tobias. Bishop Tobias tipped off his missionaries in Ovamboland, who then vehemently and publicly criticized the plan, warning that its implementation would spark a revolt in Ovamboland.[51]

Taken aback by the furore that his plans had caused, Eedes back-pedalled and implored his superiors to keep the plans secret for the moment. The latter ordered him to investigate the allegations by the missionaries that revolt was brewing. Eedes entrusted the task to his subaltern, C.S. Holdt, who was stationed in Oshikango on the border with Angola and responsible for the districts that would have been most affected by the plan. Holdt concluded that if the plan were to be implemented and the population removed from the cordon strip, the administration probably would have to resort to the use of force.[52] Eedes forbade Holdt to discuss the plan with the senior headmen of the Oukwanyama district (the largest district affected by the removals) and decided instead to temporarily shelve the plan until the missionary outcry had died down. Eedes assured his superior that he would be prepared to lie to the Ovamboland chiefs and headmen and tell them that the plans had been abandoned. His superiors accepted the strategy and Eedes subsequently informed the Oukwanyama tribal council that the reports about the plans were untrue and that the administration had never even discussed the idea of evacuating a border strip.[53] Secretly, and undoubtedly with Eedes' blessing, however, veterinarian Dr Zschokke, who had assisted Eedes with developing the plans, kept the idea alive.[54] A renewed outbreak of foot-and-mouth disease in Okavango to the east of Ovamboland in 1950 gave Eedes the excuse to reintroduce his radical plans. Claiming that the infection had originated in Angola, Eedes announced that the border would be closed for all transborder cattle movements. To placate the local headmen, who feared that they would be unable to enforce the measure, the native commissioner promised that armed police officers with vehicles would guard the border. Eedes threatened that any cattle found crossing the border would be shot on sight. He also announced that the border would soon be fenced. When his orders were defied, Eedes made good on his threat and personally shot several offending head of cattle. Yet, almost immediately thereafter, he withdrew the veterinary cordon from the border to its previous location south of Ovamboland. It is unclear if Eedes himself took the initiative to move the cordon or if his superiors ordered him to do so. In any case, he maliciously neglected to withdraw his orders prohibiting the transborder movement of cattle, even after being informed by the veterinary officials that what initially had been diagnosed as foot and mouth was not in fact the dreaded disease.[55]

Eedes' retirement as native commissioner in 1954 symbolically marked the imposition of the South African nature state in Ovamboland, with the introduction of the entire body of its conservation policies in the territory. In 1955, Ovamboland and the other 'native territories' of Namibia came directly under the control of South Africa's Pretoria-based Department of Native Affairs (soon renamed Bantu Affairs). But the political, administrative and economic annexation of Ovamboland and the imposition of the South African nature state had already been in the works. A 1950 report on the conservation of Ovamboland's forest resources foreshadowed how conservation would be used to broadcast state power. The report arbitrarily defined three-quarters of the approximately four million hectares of Ovamboland as 'true indigenous forest', effectively identifying most of the territory as an undeveloped natural resource and therefore a potential object for state intervention through forest conservation.[56] The nature state's creep in Ovamboland is more obvious in terms of wildlife conservation policies: human access to the Etosha Park was even further proscribed. The San population that had been allowed to reside in the park throughout the 1930s and 1940s was expelled in 1954.[57] The park's boundary with Ovamboland was fenced between 1971 and 1974, which hindered game migrations but did not stop elephants from leaving the park and raiding villages.[58]

The state and its local officials continued to privilege the conservation of royal game outside of the parks, despite continuing human–wildlife conflict, and wildlife conservation policies remained contested. During a 1958 public meeting in the Ondonga district, Johannes Kuandambi appropriated colonial definitions of which wildlife was precious and which a pest, and re-cast lions and elephants ('royal' game in colonial eyes) as vermin that needed to be eradicated. No doubt his opinion was inspired by the bottled-up frustration about the colonial administration's reluctance to act against marauding wild animals. By the late 1960s, no large game remained in the former wilderness areas that in the late 1800s had separated the Ovambo floodplain polities in the heart of the floodplain. Eland, kudu, gemsbok, hartebeest, wildebeest and springbuck, however, continued to roam the western and southern margins of the floodplain, while predators remained a threat at isolated cattle posts. Elephants continued to create havoc throughout the 1970s and 1980s.[59]

Throughout this era, conservation officers ignored complaints about wildlife threats to lives and livelihoods in Ovamboland. In 1977, a particularly insensitive nature conservation official admonished his audience of cattle-owners who had lost livestock to elephants, asserting that they needed to be more accommodating to elephants' needs. In a highly confidential 1960s report, the commissioner-general of South-west Africa (Namibia) advised the minister of Bantu agriculture and development in Pretoria that the Department of Nature Conservation should be expelled from Ovamboland and the other homelands because it was 'greatly despised'. The commissioner-general recommended that all conservation regulations and practices outside the parks be abandoned and that any predators and elephants that entered the inhabited regions of Ovamboland be shot on sight.[60]

By far the most intrusive conservation measures imposed in the 1950s related to livestock management. As had occurred under Eedes in the late 1940s and early 1950s, 'overgrazing' remained the main gateway for the expansion of the nature state in the name of development until the end of South African rule. A 1980s report, for example, concluded that livestock raising was primitive and involved the 'misuse and deterioration of natural grazing'.[61] In 1954, the administrator of colonial Namibia held a series of large public meetings in Ovamboland. Conservation issues featured prominently in his speeches. The highest colonial official in Namibia warned against deforestation, overstocking and desertification and called for the voluntary culling of donkeys and cattle. Officials and experts alike attributed overstocking to a 'cattle complex' and the lack of a cattle market.[62]

The conservation measures aimed at livestock management, which often combined development and conservation aims, in no small part contributed to the outbreak of open resistance and armed revolt in the 1970s. The goals of the projects were to improve what was seen as poor-quality livestock, ban livestock diseases and limit overgrazing. The undertaking involved increasing Ovamboland's livestock watering infrastructure, annual livestock inspections, livestock dipping and inoculations, and the introduction of scientific range management with fenced grazing camps.

Overstocking became the dominant conservationist concern in the 1950s and continued to be the most controversial manifestation of the nature state until the end of South African colonial rule. Whereas during the 1950s fears about overstocking were often expressed in such vague qualifications as 'overgrazing' and the 'denuding' of pastures, in the 1970s they were reformatted in more scientific terms. Statistical compilations from colonial reports demonstrated that cattle numbers in Ovamboland increased by nearly a factor of ten from 1925 to 1975.[63] Assessments of grazing pressure by using the scientific concept of 'carrying capacity' dramatically confirmed the earlier diagnosis of severe overgrazing. Based on 1977 figures, Ovamboland counted one cattle unit per 8.14 hectares, whereas the vegetation was thought to be able to sustain only one cattle unit per 12–16 hectares.[64] The conclusion that Ovamboland contained up to twice the number of cattle that it could support made the urgency of conservationist intervention only more apparent. A 1976 report claimed that soil degradation in Ovamboland was so dramatic that desertification could only be avoided through drastic measures.[65] Browsing by livestock was also considered to cause deforestation.[66] Extension officers in the 1970s urged cattle-holders to use modern livestock management, in particular culling and rotational grazing.[67] The canned meat processing plant in Oshakati, which opened in 1976 and was intended to encourage the sale of cattle to reduce its numbers, proved to be an abject failure. The prices offered were too low to entice Ovamboland's cattle-owners to part with their animals. Between 1976 and 1981, the plant processed just 500 head of cattle from Ovambo sellers.[68]

Eedes' plans to make Ovamboland livestock disease-free and to prevent cross-border cattle movements – thus moving the veterinary cordon (the Red Line) to the Angola–Namibia boundary – re-emerged again in the late 1950s. Although the decision to fence the Angola–Namibia boundary was made in the early 1950s, it took renewed foot-and-mouth outbreaks along the border in 1958 and 1959 to reignite interest in the project in 1959.[69] To prevent infection of cattle south of the border, the Department of Bantu Affairs and the Veterinary Department joined forces to proclaim a two-mile strip along the border a stock-free zone. Locally recruited border guards patrolled the stock-free zone. Any cattle found in the stock-free zone were subject to decimation.[70] The cattle killings caused great unrest and the Department of Bantu Affairs had to arm the border guards after they received threats from distressed cattle-owners. In 1960, soon after the measures had been implemented, South Africa's prime minister personally intervened to stop the cattle killings; henceforth, cattle could only be impounded and quarantined.[71]

By the late 1960s, and despite occasional cases of non-cooperation and frequent complaints by cattle-holders, most of Ovamboland's cattle had been vaccinated against the major diseases, making a fenced border critical to prevent reinfection from the Angolan side.[72] Ovamboland's administration permitted transborder movement of cattle when there were no active disease outbreaks, facilitated by the Department of Bantu Affairs, which maintained four border gates with quarantine camps for that purpose. Veterinary Department officials, however, disagreed with the practice and argued for a total ban on the cross-border movement of livestock.[73] Veterinary officials complained that any cattle that were impounded for illegal trespassing along the border were simply returned to their owners by the Bantu Affairs officials, frustrating the efforts by the Veterinary Department officials and their border guards. In 1969, Bantu Affairs officials openly protested against the Veterinary Department's continued attempts to close the border, arguing that doing so was practically impossible and would have serious political repercussions.[74] The Department of Agriculture sided with Bantu Affairs. In 1961, the Agriculture Department insisted that the prohibition of transborder cattle movements be removed.[75] In 1971, the director of agriculture for Ovamboland rejected the Veterinary Department's proposals to expand the use of fences to seal off Ovamboland's cattle not only from the surrounding regions, but also within Ovamboland to impose more scientific pastureland management. These plans would have effectively ended cattle transhumance. The director of agriculture emphasized that consensus in Ovamboland was strongly against the proposals and warned that the plans were resulting in rising resentment towards the Veterinary Department. Although his department agreed with the assessment that Ovamboland was overgrazed, he recommended abandoning plans for the creation of grazing camps within Ovamboland.[76] The resentment boiled over and culminated in the 1972 Ovamboland revolt. The veterinary services' infrastructure was a prominent target: in many places, the border fence was literally cut to pieces in a matter of days and most cattle inspection kraals were burned.[77]

Although the South Africans created the beginnings of what later became the Etosha National Park soon after taking control over German South-west Africa, they did not apply most of their conservation policies and regulations to Ovamboland until well after the Second World War. Concerns about the political fall-out in what was a sensitive border area in a League of Nations mandate territory prevailed to make the South African administration rule Ovamboland with a 'light touch'. In the second half of the 1940s, in the immediate aftermath of South Africa's failed attempt to have the UN formally transfer the Namibian mandate to its sovereignty, however, a new set of conservation measures regarding livestock management were introduced. The implementation of these measures faltered in the face of missionary protests.

A focus on conservation in and beyond the parks highlights both the hegemonic strength of the colonial state and the ambiguities and contradictions within it as the nature state reached down to the local level. By the mid-twentieth century, conservation policies within the parks had steamrolled all before it: the game in the park had become off-limits and any continued hunting was prosecuted as poaching. Beyond the Etosha Park, however, the contours of the nature state were frayed, and the battle lines of the contestation for the nature state were surprisingly fluid: until the mid-1940s, Native Commissioner Hahn prevented the implementation of most conservation policies in Ovamboland, even those that were common in other 'native territories' in Namibia and South Africa. His successor, Eedes, introduced radical conservation measures affecting livestock, but otherwise rejected most conservation practices, as had his predecessor. From the mid-1950s onward, the Veterinary and Nature Conservation Departments emerged as the most radical agents of the nature state, yet often found their plans thwarted by their colleagues from the Departments of Bantu Affairs and Agriculture, who warned that the full implementation of the nature state caused dangerous political unrest (in effect reiterating Hahn's arguments). The refrain that conservation could cause political destabilization in Ovamboland indirectly demonstrates how and to what extent colonial subjects shaped the face of the nature state. Colonial officials may frequently have used the spectre of conservation triggering rural revolt as ammunition in personal or interdepartmental rivalries, but instances of actual resistance suggest that it was merely rhetoric. Indeed, by the early 1970s, Ovamboland witnessed a rural revolt that directly targeted the key tools employed by the nature state in the territory: the border fence and the Veterinary Department's cattle inspection kraals.

Thus the implementation of the nature state on the ground fostered the seeds that undermined its very foundations, even as the conservation infrastructure constituted important physical tools for maintaining the colonial state (i.e. the parks as security buffer zones during the liberation wars) and legitimized it internationally (with South Africa's conservation as a model for national conservation). It is clear that the struggles about the nature state cannot simply be portrayed as occurring between 'the state' on the one hand and its 'subjects' on the other. Nor can internal struggles and contradictions (or the absence of evidence thereof) within the colonial state be taken as a manifestation of an overall weakness of the colonial state. The state in its local manifestation in 1920s and 1930s Ovamboland in many ways was rather weak; witness its failure to disarm the Ovamboland population. But that did not stop Native Commissioners Hahn and Eedes from imposing draconian game conservation measures. The 1950s and 1960s apartheid state in Namibia was in many ways a strong state with and through its wholesale introduction of South Africa's conservation policies and practices in Ovamboland after having annexed Namibia in the face of international condemnation. Yet, by the late 1960s, some of South Africa's own key officials argued for removing the vanguard of the nature state – the Department of Nature Conservation – from Ovamboland entirely. Effectively, they suggested that the modern apartheid state was incompatible with key aspects of the nature state, emphasizing that nature conservation in

Ovamboland needed to take a back-seat. Beyond the park, they concluded, nature conservation efforts merely interfered with development and apartheid order and security. At the same time, however, conservation writ large also trumpeted apartheid's legitimacy: the nature state was emblematic of the late twentieth-century modern state.

Notes

1 Some non-white tourism occurred in the case of the Kruger National Park, see Jacob S.T. Dlamini, '*Putting the Kruger Park in Its Place: A Social History of Africans, Mobility, and Conservation in a Modernizing South Africa, 1900–2010*' (unpublished PhD dissertation, Yale University, 2012).

2 See Jane Carruthers, *The Kruger National Park: A Social and Political History* (Pietermaritzburg, 1995).

3 See Stephen Ellis, 'Of Elephants and Men: Politics and Nature Conservation in South Africa', *Journal of Southern African Studies*, 20/1 (1994), 53–69.

4 See, for example, Paul R. Ehrlich, *The Population Bomb* (New York, 1968); Henry N. LeHouérou, *The Grazing Land Ecosystems of the African Sahel* (Berlin, 1989); Norman Myers, *Deforestation Rates in Tropical Forests and Their Climatic Implications: A Friends of the Earth Report* (London, 1989). For critiques, see, for example, Mary Tiffen, Michael Mortimore and Francis Gichuki, *More People, Less Erosion: Environmental Recovery in Kenya* (Chichester, 1994); James Fairhead and Melissa Leach, *Misreading the African Landscape: Society and Ecology in a Forest–Savanna Mosaic* (Cambridge, 1996).

5 For discussions of this view and criticisms, see, for example, David Anderson and Richard Grove, *Conservation in Africa: People, Policies, and Practice* (Cambridge, 1987); William Beinart and Colin Bundy, *Hidden Struggles in Rural South Africa: Politics & Popular Movements in the Transkei and Eastern Cape, 1890–1930* (London, 1987); John M. MacKenzie, *Imperialism and the Natural World* (Manchester, 1990); Richard Grove, *Green Imperialism: Colonial Expansion, Tropical Island Edens, and the Origins of Environmentalism, 1600–1860* (Cambridge, 1995); Nancy J. Jacobs, *Environment, Power, and Injustice: A South African History* (Cambridge, 2003); Roderick P. Neumann, *Imposing Wilderness: Struggles over Livelihood and Nature Preservation in Africa* (Berkeley, CA, 1998); James C. Scott, *The Art of Not Being Governed: An Anarchist History of Upland Southeast Asia* (New Haven, CT, 2009).

6 The creation of the Moremi Game Reserve in 1950s Botswana was championed by a coalition of international conservationists and local African leaders and opposed by colonial officials and African commercial ranchers, see Maitseo Bolaane, *Chiefs, Hunters and San in the Creation of the Moremi Game Reserve, Okavango Delta: Multiracial Interactions and Initiatives 1956–1979* (Osaka, 2013).

7 For an overview of Namibia's history, see Marion Wallace with John Kinahan, *A History of Namibia* (Auckland Park, 2011).

8 On Ovamboland's colonial history, see, for example, William G. Clarence-Smith, *Slaves, Peasants and Capitalists in Southern Angola: 1840–1926* (Cambridge, 1979); Patricia Hayes, Jeremy Silvester and Marion Wallace (eds), *Namibia Under South African Rule: Mobility & Containment, 1915–46* (Oxford, 1998); Meredith McKittrick, *To Dwell Secure: Generation, Christianity, and Colonialism in Ovamboland* (Portsmouth, NH, 2002); Emmanuel Kreike, *Re-Creating Eden: Land Use, Environment, and Society in Southern Angola and Northern Namibia* (Portsmouth, NH, 2004).

9 See, for example, William Beinart, *The Rise of Conservation in South Africa: Settlers, Livestock, and the Environment 1770–1950* (Oxford, 2003); James L. Giblin, *The Politics of Environmental Control in Northeastern Tanzania, 1840–1940* (Philadelphia, PA, 1992); James L. Giblin and Gregory H. Maddox, *Custodians of the Land: Ecology and Culture in the History of Tanzania* (London, 1996); James McCann, *Green Land, Brown Land, Black Land: An Environmental History of Africa, 1800–1990* (Portsmouth, NH, 1999); Kate B. Showers, *Imperial Gullies: Soil Erosion and Conservation in Lesotho* (Athens, OH, 2005).

10 See, for example, William Beinart, Peter Delius and Stanley Trapido (eds), *Putting a Plough to the Ground: Accumulation and Dispossession in Rural South Africa, 1850–1930* (Johannesburg, 1986); William Beinart and JoAnn McGregor (eds), *Social History and African Environments* (Oxford, 2003).

11 August Wülfhorst, *Schiwesa, ein Simeon aus den Ovambochristen* (Barmen, 1912), 8–9, 28; J. Chapman, 1903–16, 79, 83–4, A233, National Archives of Namibia, Windhoek, Namibia (henceforth NAN); B. Lau (ed.), *Carl Hugo Hahn Tagebücher 1837–1860* (Windhoek, 1985), Diaries, Part IV 1856–1860, entries 22 and 23 July 1857, 1040–5.

12 P. Duparquet, 'Notes sur les Bushmen', [Duparquet] to 'Monsieur le Directeur', s.l., s.d. and Funchal, 17 June 1881, 475, A IV, Archives Générales du Congrégation du Saint Esprit, Paris, France (General Archives of the Holy Ghost Congregation; henceforth AGCSE); Diary Jordan, Native Affairs Ovamboland (henceforth NAO) 104; J. Chapman, 1903–16, 45–7, 159–60, 167–9, A233 and Hahn, 'Notes on Ovamboland', Windhoek, 15 May 1924, NAO 18, NAN; Secretary for South-west Africa, 'Native Cattle', replies to Questionnaire by Dr G. Schmid, Government Veterinary Officer, n.p. (1932), to Secretary for External Affairs, Pretoria, vol. 456, South West Africa Administration (henceforth SWAA) Native Affairs, NAN; 'Ainda o Desastre do Humbe', and 'A Peste Bovina em Angola', *Portugal em África*, 5/5 (1898), 51, 128–36 respectively; Hugo Marquardsen, *Angola* (Berlin, 1920), 99–101; Alfred P.G. Schachtzabel, *Angola: Forschungen und Erlebnisse in Südwestafrika* (Berlin, 1926), 89–99; Antonio de Quadres Flores, *Recordações do Sul de Angola, 1914–1929* (Guimarães, 1952), 200.

13 Kreike, *Re-Creating Eden*, 26, 31–2.

14 Resident commissioner Ovamboland (henceforth RCO) to Officer Commanding 1st South African Mounted Rifles, 17 and 25 September 1916, RCO 3; Game Warden to Secretary SSWA, Namutoni, 9 September 1921 and RCO to SSWA, n.d, RCO 8; Monthly and Quarterly Reports Ovamboland, 1931, 1935, 1937, 1939–41, 1946, NAO 19–21; Quarterly Reports Ovamboland, 1947–9, 1952–4, NAO 60–1, NAN.

15 Timotheus Nakale, interview by author, Ekoka laKula, 21 February 1993; RCO to Officer Commanding 1st South African Mounted Rifles, 17 and 25 September 1916, RCO 3; Game Warden to SSWA, Namutoni, 9 September 1921 and RCO to SSWA, n.d, RCO 8; Monthly and Quarterly Reports Ovamboland, 1931, 1935, 1937, 1939–41, 1946, NAO 19–21; Quarterly Reports Ovamboland, 1947–9, 1952–4, NAO 60–1; Native Commissioner Ovamboland (henceforth NCO) to Chief Native Commissioner (henceforth CNC), Ondangwa, 26 August 1954, NAO 103; Hota 36/3/165: Statement 16 August 1954, NAO 92, NAN.

16 Administrator South-west Africa to Prime Minister Pretoria, Case of Ipumbu, Windhoek, 6 September 1932, A450 vol. 7 and NCO to SSWA, Ondangwa, 23 October 1930, NAO 9 f. 5/2, NAN.

17 Timotheus Nakale, interview by author, Ekoka laKula, 21 February 1993; Monthly and Quarterly Reports Ovamboland, 1931, 1935, 1937, 1939–41, 1946, NAO 19–21; Quarterly Reports Ovamboland, 1947–9, 1952–4, NAO 60–1; NCO to CNC, Ondangwa, 26 August 1954, NAO 103; Hota 36/3/165: Statement 16 August 1954, NAO 92, NAN.

18 Kreike, *Re-Creating Eden*, 360–408.

19 RCO to SSWA, 27 October 1918 and Extracts from RCO's Personal Diaries, entries for March 1917, for example, 10 March, RCO 8 f. 9, and RCO to SSWA, 24 September 1921, Tour to North-western Ovamboland and f. 3/1916/2, Ipumbu to Manning, Ukwambi, 2 January 1918, RCO 4; Monthly Reports Ovamboland, December 1932, February–March 1936 and January 1940, NAO 19–20; Acting Native Commissioner, 'Dietary: Oukwanyama, Ovamboland', appendix to NCO to CNC, Ondangwa, 4 October 1948, NAO 69 f. 25/6, and Quarterly Reports Ovamboland, January–March 1950, January–March and April–June 1954, NAO 60–1; Statements Johannes Shekudja, Ondangwa, 18–19 March 1952, NAO 90; Quarterly Report Ovamboland, January–March 1946, NAO 21 and Quarterly Reports Ovamboland, July–September 1953 and April–June 1954, NAO 61, NAN.

20 Interviews by author: Kanime Hamyela, Omutwewondjaba (Namibia), 15 June 1993 and Mateus Nangobe Omupanda (Namibia), 24 May 1993; Kreike, *Re-Creating Eden*, chaps 3–4.; H. Welsch, Quartalbericht, Omatemba, 30 March 1916, 2515 C/h 31, Archiv der Vereinigte Evangelische Mission, Wüppertal-Barmen, Germany (henceforth AVEM), Rheinische Missionsgesellschaft (henceforth RMG); Monthly Report Ovamboland, March 1925 and Hahn, Notes on Ovamboland, Windhoek, 15 May 1924, NAO 18; Monthly Reports Ovamboland, September–October 1931 and January 1932, NAO 19; Annual Health Reports 1933 and 1937, NAO 36–7; Rodent Inspector Ovamboland to District Surgeon Ovamboland, Ondangwa, 18 June 1948 and tribal secretary Ondonga to NCO, Okaloko, 20 July 1954, NAO 66; NCO to David Sakeus, Ondangwa, 28 January 1949, NAO 89, NAN.

21 Ibid., 26; Monthly and Quarterly Reports Ovamboland, July 1929, 1931, 1937, 1939–46, NAO 18, 20–1; Director Water Affairs to Director Water Affairs Windhoek, Ondangwa, 5 July 1965, WAT 145, NAN.

22 On the disarmament, see Emmanuel Kreike, *Deforestation and Reforestation in Namibia: The Global Consequences of Local Contradictions* (Princeton, NJ, 2010), 118–20.

23 Commander SWA Police Namutoni to Officer Commanding NAO, Namutoni, 11 August 1930, A450, 14, NAN. The 1938–43 figures are taken from the Annual Reports Ovamboland.

24 Kreike, *Deforestation and Reforestation in Namibia*, 101–11.

25 On human–wildlife conflict, see ibid., 101–9.

26 Kreike, *Deforestation and Reforestation in Namibia*, 101–9.

27 On the missionary reports, see a newspaper clipping of article by Tobias (1925), A450, 9; Report Ovamboland Cotton Prospects appendix to Alec Crosby to Bishop of Damaraland, St. Mary's Mission, 11 January 1924, NAO 26; South West Africa Commission 1935, NAO 104, NAN. On the assessment by the junior officer, see Officer Commanding Oshikango to NCO, Oshikango, 17 March 1931, SWAA 3, NAN.

28 On the palisaded homesteads, see newspaper clipping of an article by Tobias (1925), A450, 9, and Annual Health Report Ovamboland 1937, NAO 36, NAN. On the population movements and deforestation, see Kreike, *Deforestation and Reforestation in Namibia*, 23–43.

29 The 1936 Native Trust and Land Act of 1936 led to direct interventions in land use and triggered resistance, see Robert Ross, *A Concise History of South Africa* (Cambridge, 1999), 110.

30 NCO to CNC, Ondangwa, 2 June 1941, SWAA 3, NAN.

31 On the disarmament and actions against Uukwambi, see Kreike, *Deforestation and Reforestation in Namibia*, 114–20, 54, respectively.

32 Ibid., 66.

33 Emmanuel Kreike, *Environmental Infrastructure in African History: Examining the Myth of Natural Resource Management in Namibia* (Cambridge, 2013), 123–6.

34 Ibid., 47–9.

35 Ibid., 123–6.

36 On fires, see ibid., 156–73.

37 South West Africa Commission, Minutes of Evidence, vol. 12, Ukualuthi, 13 August 1935, Evidence Hahn and vol. 10 Agriculture, A450, 12, NAN. See also Kreike, *Re-Creating Eden*, 129–76.

38 A450, 10, NAN. The document is a draft of the 1942 Annual Report for Ovamboland.

39 Kreike, *Deforestation and Reforestation in Namibia*, 144–9.

40 Kreike, *Environmental Infrastructure in African History*, 152.

41 Kreike, *Deforestation and Reforestation in Namibia*, 92–101.

42 Government Veterinary Officer to Director Agriculture, 18 January 1946, and Quarterly Reports Ovamboland January–June 1946, NAO 15, NAN.

43 Beinart and Bundy, *Hidden Struggles in Rural South Africa*; David Anderson, 'Depression, Dust Bowl, Demography, and Drought: The Colonial State and Soil Conservation in East Africa during the 1930s', in *Colonialism and Nationalism in Africa*, ed. by Gregory H. Maddox (New York, 1993), II, 209–31; David Anderson, *Eroding the Commons: The Politics of Ecology in Baringo, Kenya, 1890s–1963* (Oxford, 2002).

44 Kreike, *Deforestation and Reforestation in Namibia*, 48–9, 66–8.

45 On the impact of conservation projects and resistance, see, for example, Greet Kershaw, *Mau Mau From Below* (Oxford, 1997); Ramachandra Guha, *The Unquiet Woods: Ecological Change and Peasant Resistance in the Himalaya* (Berkeley, 1989).

46 Showers, *Imperial Gullies*.

47 On scientists undermining the colonial project, see Helen Tilley, *Africa as a Living Laboratory: Empire, Development, and the Problem of Scientific Knowledge, 1870–1950* (Chicago, IL, 2011).

48 On Eedes' argument that Ovamboland was unique, see NCO to CNC, Ondangwa, 17 April 1948, NAO 101, NAN.

49 Kreike, *Deforestation and Reforestation in Namibia*, 150–2. Quarterly Reports Ovamboland, January–September 1947, NAO 60, NAN. For overstocking in Ovamboland, see also Quarterly Report Ovamboland, October–December 1952, NAO 60; Annual Health Report Ovamboland 1953, NAO 65; Agricultural Officer to NCO, Report Travel to the Northwestern Part of Ovamboland, 20–22 June 1956, Ondangwa, 4 July 1956 and Agricultural Report Ovamboland, 1956–1957, BAC 133, NAN.

50 Quarterly Reports Ovamboland, January–September 1947, NAO 60; Government Veterinary Officer Grootfontein, Annual Report 1947, NAO 59; Quarterly Report Ovamboland January–March 1946, NAO 21; Telegram NCO to Secretary Windhoek (October 1947) and Chief Ushona Shimi (to NCO), Ongandjera, 14 October 1947, NAO 58, NAN.

51 NCO to CNC, 2 July 1947; CNC to Bishop of Damaraland, 13 June 1947; Bishop of Damaraland to Additional Native Commissioner, Windhoek, 12 February 1948; Dymond to the Bishop of Damaraland, 27 January 1948; Bjorklund (FMS) to Dymond, undated, appendix, Bishop of Damaraland to Additional Native Commissioner, Windhoek, 12 February 1948, all NAO 59, NAN.

52 ANC to NCO, 21 February 1948, NAO 59, NAN.

53 NCO to CNC, 25 February and 8 March 1948, NAO 59, NAN.

54 Dr Zschokke to Director Agriculture, Windhoek, 26 October 1948, NAO 59, NAN.

55 NCO to the Headmen and People of Ukuanyama, 10 January 1950 and NCO to Dr Schatz (GVO Ovamboland), 11 February 1950; NCO to Commander South African Police Cordon Ovamboland; NCO to CNC, 12 January 1950; Telegram NCO to Secretary SWA, 14 February 1950; NCO to Dr. Schatz and to Noncommissioned Officer South African Police Cordon Ovamboland, 11 February 1950; NCO to CNC, 12 January 1950; NAO 59. ANC Tsumeb to NCO Ondangwa, 9 January 1950; NCO to CNC, 3 January 1950; Kaibi Mundjele to NCO, Ombalantu, 2 May 1950; ANC to Kwanyama Headmen, 29 November 1950; NCO to Chief Kambonde, 29 November 1950; NCO to Ombalantu Headmen, 9 May 1950; all NAO 58, NAN.

56 NCO, Ondangwa, 21 October 1950; Census of Agriculture, 1949–1950, NAO 103 f. 62/2, NAN.

57 Annual Report Ovamboland 1953, NAO 61, NAN.

58 Kreike, *Deforestation and Reforestation in Namibia*, 153, fn 48.

59 S. Davis, 'Tour of Northern Territories', WAT ww17 (ii); Commissioner-General SWA to Minister Bantu Administration, Windhoek, 21 January 1966, BON 1; Bantu Affairs Commissioner, 'Hoofman: Johannes Shekudja', 11 March 1968 and Form Vilho Weyulu, 11 March 1968, AHE (BAC) 1/2; Ovambo Government Items nrs. 38, 41, 42, OVA 54, NAN.

60 Kreike, *Deforestation and Reforestation in Namibia*, 101–11.

61 Keith Morrow, 'A Framework for the Long Term Development of Agriculture within Owambo', August 1980.

62 Minutes of Ukwanyama Tribal Meeting (12 July 1954) and Meeting Administrator with Ondonga Tribe, 12 July 1954, NAO 64, NAN.

63 Kreike, *Deforestation and Reforestation in Namibia*, 149–50.

64 Secretary Agriculture to Secretary Bantu Administration Pretoria, Ondangwa, 10 March 1977, OVA 26, NAN.

65 Agricultural Report Ovamboland, 1955–1956, BAC 133; Lueckhoff, report on a visit to SWA, 3–15 November 1969; Appendix to Regional Forester to Director-in-Chief Bantu Administration Pretoria, Grootfontein, 3 April 1970, OVA 57, NAN.

66 On livestock and deforestation, see Le Roux to Secretary Agriculture, Supply Inventory: Indigenous Forests Ovamboland, Ondangwa, 5 November 1976, OVA 57, NAN.

67 See, for example, Agricultural Officer Moses Nandjebo, Monthly Reports 1971, OVA 61, NAN.

68 Kreike, *Deforestation and Reforestation in Namibia*, 155, footnote 53.

69 Director Agriculture to Secretary SWA, Ondangwa, 13 January 1961, AGR 897 and Director Agriculture to Director Veterinary Services Pretoria, Ondangwa, 27 August 1959, AGR 125, NAN.

70 Director Agriculture to Secretary SWA, Ondangwa, 13 January 1961 and Director of Agriculture to Cattle Inspector Oshikango, Ondangwa, 8 November 1961, AGR

897; Director Agriculture to Director Veterinary Services Pretoria, Ondangwa, 27 August 1959, AGR 125, NAN. On the resulting livestock losses, see Magdalena Ndapohoni Emmanuel, interview with the author, Oihambo, Kunene, 4 April 2005.

71 Director Agriculture to Secretary SWA, Ondangwa, 13 January and 8 November 1961 and State Veterinarian to Bantu Commissioner Oshikango, Ondangwa, 12 June 1961, AGR 897, NAN.

72 On the protests against veterinary measures in particular, the recurrent inspections of cattle and their vaccination, see SWAPO to Chief Bantu Commissioner, Endola, Oukwanyama, 18 April 1961, and Acting Chief Bantu Affairs Commissioner to S.S. Kankungua and I.E. Tudaheni, Windhoek, 22 May 1961, AGR 897, NAN.

73 Chief Bantu Commissioner SWA to Chief Director Ovamboland, Windhoek, 18 December 1968, appendices I–II, OVA 56, NAN

74 Minutes of a Meeting in the Office of the Chief Bantu Commissioner, Windhoek, 9 April 1969, OVA 56, NAN.

75 Director of Agriculture to Cattle Inspector Oshikango, Ondangwa, 8 November 1961 and Memo Cattle Inspector to Dr Viljoen, Oshikango, 26 December 1961, AGR 897, NAN.

76 'Owambo Verslag' and Director Agriculture to Chief Director Ondangwa, Ondangwa (June or July 1971), OVA 49, NAN; Director Agriculture to Secretary Bantu Affairs Pretoria, Ondangwa, 17 November 1971, OVA 46, NAN.

77 On cutting the border fence, see Agricultural Officer to Director Agriculture Ondangwa, Ondangwa, Travel Report, 26–31 January 1972, OVA 40, NAN. On the burning of the cattle inspection kraals, see Department of Government Affairs and Finance, Ovambo Government to Director Agriculture, Ondangwa, 2 February 1972, OVA 50, NAN.

6   Conventional thinking and the fragile birth of the nature state in post-war Britain

*Matthew Kelly**

The origins of the desire to empower the British state to protect nature lay in the evolving sense of the public commons that can be traced to patterns in thought and sensitivity that reflected the effect of industrialization and urbanization. This included but was not limited to the development of natural science, radical responses to enclosure and agricultural improvement, sensibilities nurtured by the picturesque and romanticism, and middle- and working-class opposition to attempts by property holders to restrict customary rights of access.[1] By the twentieth century, the agenda was strengthened by concerns about the apparently negative effect urban living had on the health of the population, the emergence of a new leisure economy that reified the physical and psychological wellbeing nurtured by time spent in 'the country' and the freedoms brought by affordable railway travel and the private motor car, as exemplified by H.V. Morton's best-selling nationalist paean *In Search of England*.[2] Suburbanization and inadequately controlled development was also concerning. In 1926, the year the Campaign for the Preservation of Rural England (CPRE) was established, the Ministry of Health lamented 'the merging of town and country, and the consequent loss of identity of both'.[3]

Activists tended to emphasize the need to protect certain highly valued landscapes, all in private ownership of one sort or another, which were judged part of the national patrimony. This notion found early expression in Wordsworth's claim that the Lake District in the north of England was 'a sort of national property', and by the twentieth century an effective Lakes lobby existed.[4] As this suggests, relatively undeveloped and unenclosed upland landscapes, particularly those within easy reach of towns and cities that could be construed as wild, were the focus of preservationist and access lobbying, but the agenda was also applied to lowland landscapes of particular historical significance or natural beauty and a more general sense of the rural 'scene'. In the interwar years, this perspective was increasingly framed in terms of the social democratic right of the general public to enjoy beautiful places, which in turn saw the idea

* Research for this chapter was funded by a British Academy/Leverhulme Small Research Grant (SG142861). I much appreciated Emily Wakild's valuable feedback on early drafts.

that certain landscapes had high 'amenity' value as places of leisure become an established component of mainstream political discourse.

In 1931, the Addison Committee, established by Ramsey MacDonald's Labour government, recommended that the government establish national parks, distinguishing national reserves from nature sanctuaries. This met with a favourable response from government but soon fell victim to highly unfavourable economic circumstances and the successor National Government was more inclined to empower local authorities to protect amenity than to create a new national designation.[5] Despite this, the principle that the state should protect the natural environment and ensure rights of access had been established, and in the 1930s the national parks lobby enjoyed a period of consolidation. Much of this energy stemmed from civil society groups, notably the Friends of the Lake District, but the agenda also benefited from the sympathy of elite groups, including individuals close to government.[6] The failure of the Access to Mountains bill in 1939, the sixth attempt since the late nineteenth century to pass an access bill, proved but a hitch along the way. During the war, national park designation, thanks to the sympathies of Lord Reith, the minister of town and country planning, was a minor component of Whitehall deliberations over post-war reconstruction. As John Dower's *Report on National Parks in England and Wales* (1945) made clear, preserving natural beauty and wildlife against developmental pressures was judged inseparable from enhancing rights of access.[7]

National park advocacy often overlapped with the defence of the traditional farming practices that created and maintained valued landscapes, an assumption that informed the influential findings of the Committee on Land Utilisation in Rural Areas chaired by Lord Justice Scott. The Scott Report (1942) envisaged a post-war agriculture that combined traditionalism with a notional progressivism. Insisting the rural community was essentially agricultural and farmers the custodians of the land, Scott thought the mixed character of British farming should be revived by reversing the wartime shift to cereal production.[8] His thinking was shaped by his acute consciousness of the social desolation caused by interwar agricultural depression and his belief that the under-utilization of the land by farming in the 1930s had harmed the natural landscape: the 'busy prosperity' of wartime agriculture could only be maintained by sustaining the state intervention that had ensured 'fair' returns, price stability and a living wage and job security for farm workers during the war.[9] In other words, and here Scott sweetened the new dirigisme with a Wordworthian note, if the countryside was 'the heritage of the whole nation', then 'the cheapest way, indeed the only way, of preserving the countryside in anything like its traditional aspect would still be to farm it.'[10] As a later commentator observed, Scott 'accepted the corollary that there should be facility of access for all'.[11]

Scott's proposition that a desirable nature was created by agriculture, and state support for agriculture could help produce that nature, proved paradigmatic, making agricultural policy a component of the post-war nature state. Whether Scott's prognosis was a plausible basis for managing the agricultural component of the post-war economy was immediately in dispute. In his famous dissenting report, Professor S.R. Dennison argued that if the amenity value of the countryside could only be maintained through inefficient agricultural practices that could not guarantee sufficient income, then the agricultural worker 'should be paid in respect of his function as a landscape gardener and not as an agriculturalist'.[12] This seemed impractical, not least thanks to the acute financial pressures Britain would face after the war, and Dennison rightly anticipated post-war rural prosperity relying on a mix of agricultural subsidy, specialist intensive farming requiring fewer workers, and the introduction of light industry. Consequently, Dennison concluded that if rural Britain's amenity value, including its natural qualities, was to be protected, farming and forestry would need to be brought within the planning system. Austin Robinson, a Keynesian economist and economic adviser to the Ministry of Production, sympathized. He agreed that the state had a role to play, but what this would be with respect to the delicate question of private property rights remained unclear:

> Shall we attempt to make individual ownership compatible with public service by a system of rules and regulations and planning bodies? Shall we piously hope that where necessary communal ownership will be developed by the State, embodied, for example, in the National Trust? Or shall we encourage the State to act as organiser of this communal service?[13]

In the event, a satisfactory answer to Robinson's question was not found. The turn towards planning made by Clement Attlee's post-war Labour governments, as evident in the Distribution of Industry Act (1945), the New Towns Act (1946), the Town and Country Planning Act (1947) and the National Parks and Access to Countryside Act (1949), left farming and forestry outside of the new system.[14] The National Parks Commission, tasked with designating National Parks and Areas of Outstanding Natural Beauty in England and Wales, was duly established, and by the fall of the second Attlee government in 1951, national parks were designated in the Lake District, the Peak District, Snowdonia and Dartmoor. Six more would follow by 1956, totalling 10 per cent of the land surface of England and Wales, but as Brian Harrison notes, not one of the parks 'were in the farmed countryside of lowland England most vulnerable to agricultural change'.[15] Budgetary constraints combined with the government's reluctance to be seen to undermine the authority of elected local governments also ensured the early park authorities were not independent planning authorities possessed of statutory powers but committees of the county council, or joint committees where the park straddled county boundaries. As William Adams observes, the new parks were 'essentially planning designations', intended to help 'protect natural beauty and promote countryside recreation'.[16] Britain was doing national parks on the cheap and in a way that would minimize the nature state's capacity to intervene in agriculture.

Nonetheless, the birth pangs of the British nature state did not see nature conservationists of a more scientific bent wholly marginalized. During the war the emphasis placed on amenity was challenged by the Conference on Nature Preservation in Post-war Reconstruction, which urged the government to establish nature reserves under proper scientific guidance as a part of the new turn towards national planning.[17] Successful lobbying saw the 1949 national parks legislation make provision for the establishment by Royal Charter of the Nature Conservancy, a government research agency tasked with classifying and acquiring National Nature Reserves, designating Sites of Special Scientific Interest (SSSIs), and advising local and national government on the consequences for nature of any planning proposal. In the decades that followed, much Conservancy energy was spent surveying Britain's flora and fauna, creating an unprecedentedly full account of Britain's wildlife, and compiling reports on pressing environmental issues; what remained of its small budget was used to buy or lease land for designation as National Nature Reserves.[18] Lacking real power to protect the SSSIs, Nature Conservancy could only notify the local authorities of the importance of the land as nature in the hope this would be taken into consideration when planning decisions were made. Like the park authorities, Nature Conservancy could expect to be heard but not obeyed.

The creation of parallel agencies, one intended to protect amenity, the other to protect nature, institutionalized a 'somewhat perverse' division, establishing two quite distinct ways in which the state made the British landscape legible and its statutory obligations visible.[19] In theory, the gaze onto the environment resembled 20/20 vision, but in practice threats to amenity were easily appreciated by public opinion, whereas threats to nature were often only legible to expert eyes. Consequently, the decision to compartmentalize expertise has since been criticized for creating a false dichotomy between nature conservation and amenity that retarded the development of effective environmental protection in the UK.[20]

This institutional weakness, compounded by the amateurism of the National Park Commission,[21] was thrown into sharp relief by the powerful challenge the fledging nature state faced from within the social democratic state. The expansion and intensification of farming and forestry were actively incentivized by the subsidy regimes of the Ministry of Agriculture, Fisheries and Food (MAFF) and the Forestry Commission. The rapid intensification that would characterize the 'second agricultural revolution' proved less a spontaneous response to market forces by entrepreneurial farmers enthused by new technologies, and more a state-funded, social democratic enterprise catalysed by war, predicated on the politics of 'cheap food', and institutionalized by Labour's 1947 Agriculture Act. As Sue Elworthy and Jane Holder argue, 'the Town and Country Planning Act 1947 ensured security of land use for agriculture and unhampered agricultural development; the Agriculture Act 1947 achieved security of investment in farming'.[22] Price guarantees, government grants and fiscal incentives encouraged investment that significantly increased productivity, which was only intensified when the UK joined the European Common Market in 1973 and the largesse of the Common Agricultural Policy flowed into the pockets of UK farmers.[23]

By the early 1960s, Scott's claim that there was 'no antagonism' between agricultural use of land and its natural beauty was increasingly hard to sustain and the countryside lobby and the nascent environmental movement had grown very concerned by the material changes that state-driven agricultural intensification had wrought on the British landscape. Between 1946 and 1974, a quarter of the hedgerows in England and Wales had been grubbed up (some 120,000 miles), including innumerable trees, in order to create large, efficient fields, while much heathland had been ploughed and fertilized to 'improve' rough grazing or create new arable.[24] Ornithologists were particularly concerned by loss of avian habitat, but it was the sudden awareness in the late 1950s of the mortality among birds caused by artificial pesticides based on chlorinated hydrocarbons that really focused minds.[25] Rachel Carson's *Silent Spring* (1962), though written primarily from an American perspective, drew attention to the British case, and in his introduction to the British edition the Labour peer Lord Shackleton stoked the controversy, observing:

> The agricultural Establishment is so convinced of the great benefit in increased production through the use of these chemicals that when they come to balance the problem in utilitarian terms, they find it difficult to see the wider and longer-term consequences.[26]

As will be shown, despite the growing evidence to the contrary, the notion that agri-industry was the rightful custodian of British nature and thus integral to the functioning of the nature state proved peculiarly resilient.

The ministrations of the Forestry Commission equally exposed the limited capacity of the nature state to limit environmental change in the interests of maintaining flora and fauna. Tasked from 1919 with making Britain less dependent on timber imports, the Commission cultivated a softwood crop in place of the tendency to 'devastate' a natural resource. Government subventions made upland forestry more profitable than grazing sheep or cattle on acidic soils, and millions of hectares of agriculturally marginal land were thus afforested, transforming the look and ecology of great swathes of Britain's most cherished landscapes.[27] Lobbyists offended by regimented stands of conifers highlighted the seeming paradox that the Forestry Commission brought an unprecedented quantity of land under state control and yet was not subject to planning law. Rather than having recourse to law, local activists seeking to halt or limit new forestry developments relied on making life difficult for landowners or commercial forestry companies, not least by generating bad press and harassing government ministers.[28] By the 1960s, fiscal incentives and grants for planting had created a market for previously near-valueless land, prompting amenity societies or park authorities to sometimes purchase land to prevent either ecologically damaging afforestation or the felling of broadleaved woodland for re-planting with a softwood crop.[29] Relatively small conifer stands in highly valued landscapes like Dartmoor, Exmoor and the Lakes caused the most fuss, though the great state forestry enterprises at Kielder in Northumbria and Galloway in Scotland attracted significant adverse comment.

Add to the mix new reservoirs, quarrying operations, television masts, overhead electricity cables and housing, plus high-profile developments like the industrial complex established in Pembrokeshire National Park, the Ballistic Missile Early Warning Station on the North York Moors and the nuclear power stations in Snowdonia and a Kentish Area of Natural Beauty (AONB), and the source of the deep dissatisfaction that landscape preservationists and nature conservationists had with the performance of the nature state is easy to see. No designation had proved an adequate prophylactic against damaging developments. And this despite the centralizing tendencies of the period ensuring many contentious decisions ended up on the desk of the minister for housing and local government, or subject to parliamentary scrutiny. Due deference was paid to the claims of nature as a component of the national interest, but they rarely trumped the needs of statutory bodies like the water undertakers or local socioeconomic interests. The sense of crisis was compounded by anxieties about population growth, global food supply, car ownership, traffic congestion, not a little hatred of caravans and a patrician sense that the general public did not know how to behave in the countryside.

Robinson had wryly observed that Scott provided a seemingly unanswerable case: 'We see the English countryside fashioned out of the English landscape by the English farming tradition.'[30] When serious efforts were made to consider environmental concerns in the 1960s and 1970s, Scott's assumptions proved peculiarly resilient, despite the ecological effect of agricultural intensification. Nature Conservancy's determination to challenge conventional wisdom largely fell on deaf ears, exposing the degree to which the National Parks Commission was complicit in the custodial rhetoric of the farmers, if not always the foresters. The nature state in Britain was not stillborn, but as the following examination of these discussions show, it was a weak suckling.

The first concerted effort to respond collectively to the sense of crisis was made in November 1963 when Nature Conservancy hosted a high-profile Study Conference at Fishmongers' Hall in central London. Under the benevolent gaze of Philip, Duke of Edinburgh, the UK president of the World Wildlife Fund, this remarkable event saw representatives of some 90 organizations come together to discuss how they wished to see 'The Countryside in 1970'. Almost all aspects of British economic life and many wildlife and conservation bodies were represented. The published proceedings and discussion papers made it clear that the conference had no working definition of conservation and a particularly weak sense of what might constitute nature conservation. In the foreword to the published proceedings, Philip explained that they still needed 'an agreed body of criteria against which the pros and cons of any project affecting conservation can be measured'.[31] Philip left undisturbed the traditional notion that the natural environment was a resource to be exploited by humans and he did not challenge the working assumption that controversial developments could be resolved by 'balancing' interests, which in practice tended to favour developers and local commercial interests. Sir William Holford, a Whitehall adviser during the war and now the influential professor of town planning at University College London, argued that 'no yardstick to measure national interest' and 'none to measure amenity value' existed, adding that there could never be 'a permanent value for either'.[32] By this reading, an inherent value could not be imputed to nature, despite it being a component of the national interest, nor, a generation before biodiversity became a firmly established concept, was there a way of quantifying natural value.

Times, however, had changed, and Philip candidly admitted the likely 'head-on collision' between conservationists interested in landscape, wild places, birds, animals, insects or plants and 'those whose activities have a direct impact on nature, particularly modern agriculture, urban and industrial development'.[33] But even if it was accepted that modern farming was harmful to nature, the Study Conference generally did not challenge the idea that the farmers were the primary custodians of the land. Moreover, private MAFF correspondence suggested it had no intention of introducing 'conservation planning', which it judged 'a form of control which found no place in the philosophy of the present [Conservative] government'.[34] As the National Farmers Union explained to the conference, conservation, understood by them as maintaining an established rural aesthetic, required maintaining farm incomes, if 'more bracken, derelict buildings, de-population' and loss of national heritage were to be avoided.[35] Scott's lament for the decay caused by the agricultural depression of the 1930s was here restated, the amenity agenda deployed to justify the continued subsidy of farms that would be put out of business by more competitive neighbours or foreign imports.

Other sectional interests were less diplomatic. Sir Ronald German of the General Post Office, mindful of the controversies that had accompanied the erection of the television mast on Dartmoor, was adamant that expansion must continue, though he did acknowledge that more consultation was needed; J. Taylor of the Federation of British Industries baldly stated that minerals had 'to be dug from the ground from the place where nature had put them', dismissing opposition to new mines and quarries as 'emotional'; and L. Millis of the British Waterworks Association, rightly anticipating future conflicts over the location of new reservoirs, stated that 'hilly areas would have to make their contribution', a line of argument that rejected the segregationist outlook of the national parks lobby and implicitly rejected the notion that certain 'areas' should be afforded special protection.[36]

Then there were the self-conscious realists. L. Dudley Stamp, who played an instrumental role in drafting the Scott report and had insisted on the protection of commons on amenity grounds when chair of the Common Land Commission in the 1950s, coolly asserted that the needs of industry came before conservation, describing 'waste land' as 'a disgrace to the nation'. This echoed the lexicon and moral outlook of nineteenth-century improvement, ballasting a position that was stridently modernizing. To increase yields meant hedgerows would have to go and effective use made of fertilizers, insecticides and toxic chemicals for the removal of vegetable and animal pests. 'The agricultural worker of the past was fast disappearing', Stamp opined, 'the agricultural worker of the future would be the man in a white coat'.[37] The Country Landowners Association's paper on 'Man-Made Countryside' spun a suggestive line about how 'ideas of space, time, location and mobility must be changed', adding a cunning historicist twist in the observation that the hedges that were being 'grubbed up today' were only a few generations old and had been bitterly resented by those opposing enclosure.[38] Lowland preservationism did indeed seek to maintain the landscapes of enclosure, but here the Country Landowners Association (CLA) overlooked the importance of hedge cover as ecosystem. If not a full substitute for the open fields and scrub woodland of the old commons, hedgerows were a relatively biodiverse ecosystem, a claim that emphatically could not be made of the fenced monocultures of intensified agriculture. Above all, the CLA insisted on the rights of private property and, breaking with Scott, saw little reason why owners should not extract wealth from their soil however they saw fit, there being 'nothing particularly socially virtuous in farming land as compared to using it in some other way'.[39] It is striking how little consideration there was of whether subsidy and fiscal incentive had problematized the very notion of private property in land. G.B. Ryle of the Forestry Commission was similarly revealing. He struck the relativist note, arguing that the public's attitude to afforestation had divided along generational lines, with younger people appreciative of the recreation opportunities – walking trails and picnic spots – brought by conifer plantations.[40]

This was a classic expression of the shifting baselines phenomenon whereby successor generations have little sense of what is lost or the dramatic interventions that created familiar landscapes. But more than this, the failure of the Forestry Commission's amenity-based argument to take into account the ecological effects of large conifer plantations saw it contest preservationist rather than nature conservationist objections. Like all the contributions to the study conference summarized so far, the Forestry Commission implicitly testified to the weakness or absence of a sophisticated nature-based perspective, the challenge being to justify their actions in terms of competing human pressures. A richer perspective might have been expected from the National Parks Commission, but Lord Strang's submission on 'The Future of the National Parks' proved how the institutionalization of the amenity/nature conservation duality was determining perspectives. Echoing the fears of numerous amenity organizations, Strang is worth quoting at length:

> More nuclear and conventional power stations in hitherto unspoilt country; more overhead transmission and distribution lines stretched across the landscape; more masts on high ground for communication requirements of all kinds; continuing use of National Parks by the armed services for defence installations and military training; growing demand for water from upland areas; a change in the pattern of agriculture in the hill areas; the surge of caravans and the flooding in of cars to spread like a rash across the

open countryside and to jam the roads; the increasing influx of holiday-makers, with more time and more money to spend and therefore with increasing requirements for recreation, and an increasing need of guidance in the proper use of the countryside.[41]

Here the discontents of post-war preservationism were boiled down into a grumpy list that neatly encapsulated some of the principle developments of post-war industrial society: the Cold War context, increasing demand for electricity and water and the public's enjoyment of the motor car, television, increased leisure time and rising expendable incomes. All were having a profound effect on the British landscape, but if Prince Philip was right to argue that the 'Countryside in 1970' conferences were characterized by a cordial atmosphere, this was partly because most rural interests, the tourist industry excepted, found a common enemy in the leisure motorist, whose freedoms not only placed extraordinary developmental pressure on Britain's infrastructure, but also disrupted the social and cultural equilibrium long thought to characterize country life. In Strang's lament, the discursive shift from the list of state-inflicted interventions to the description of the behaviour and shortcomings of the general public is hard to miss, the language becoming metaphorical and emotive. This mix of snobbery and paternalism was typical of the preservationist milieu – the national parks were for people with walking boots and knapsacks, not motor cars and transistor radios – but the sense of affront was more widely shared, chiming with a broader strain of post-war cultural pessimism.

Strang's defeatist solution was that each Park needed to be surveyed in order to identify an 'inner zone of quiet, unspoilt country to be kept free from development and intrusive disturbance of any kind'. More controls needed to be imposed on agriculture, forestry, camping and caravanning, but as important was the need 'to inculcate, and wardens to enforce, good public behaviour'. Strang, too, was a modern, wanting to see the parks transformed from unruly space to disciplined place. Just as striking was the sentence that followed: 'Positively, there might be plans, in cooperation with the Nature Conservancy, to watch over the ecological balance of flora and fauna.'[42] And that was as much as he had to say on the matter.

Contrast Strang's treatment of the challenges faced by the parks with the paper submitted by Max Nicholson, director of the Nature Conservancy, and the gulf in understanding and perspective between the conservation scientists and the rest becomes very clear. Nicholson's eloquent screed avoided the quotidian self-interest of most other delegates, offering a paradigmatic overview of the challenges faced by humanity that started from the premise that, of all animals, humans were most able to modify their environment. Mankind, he argued, had created 'an increasingly vast, complex and artificial environment of his own', which was 'partly independent of, but also interdependent with, the natural environment'. This is not so different from historians Sverker Sörlin's and Paul Warde's recent description of the environment as 'a human product, an alloy of nature' or the tendency of environmental historians to characterize the natural environment as a hybrid production of human and non-human nature.[43] Nicholson urged that they extend their understanding of the immediate damage caused by particular developments to a broader understanding of how human actions unconsciously or indirectly undermined the capacity of the natural environment to sustain life. They must learn to minimize the negative effect human activities had on the natural environment, but this could only be the first step towards aiming to 'enrich its variety and maintain or enhance its long-term biological yield, in terms of wild as well as of domesticated or cultivated organisms'.[44] With greater understanding of natural processes and their interdependency, they could exercise 'effective national trusteeship for our whole natural environment and all that it contains'.[45] Here was an attempt to move the discussion on from the preservationist commitment to traditional agricultural practices as a way of maintaining desirable landscapes, often through statist solutions, towards the idea that the natural environment required active management that drew on the expertise of non-agriculturalists.

Nicholson's thinking largely fell on deaf ears. The Countryside Act of 1968 replaced the National Parks Commission with the Countryside Commission and empowered local authorities to develop parkland close to urban areas for amenity purposes, partly in the hope that this would ease congestion of the national parks. By widening rather than deepening the government's interest in the non-urban, the new Act strengthened the social democratic rather than the ecological pretensions of the 1949 legislation, gesturing towards a less segregationist but still largely amenity-based view of non-urban landscapes. It failed to satisfy those wanting to see enhancement of the capacity of the national park authorities (NPAs) to protect nature.[46]

That said, the Commission's decision in 1971 to order a study of Britain's 'New Agricultural Landscapes' did reflect growing public concern at the effect of agricultural intensification on lowland Britain. In the preface to the published report, John Cripps, chair of the Commission, wrote that the report provided 'fresh and deeply disturbing facts about the nature and scale of changes taking place in the appearance of much of the English countryside' and its 'greatly diminished scenic and wildlife interest'.[47] By foregrounding appearance and 'interest', Cripps reflected the anthropic orientation of the report, whose principle survey technique assessed landscape change in terms of visual effects on the 'horizon'.[48] Although the report conceded that agriculture, recreation and wildlife were no longer compatible, by failing to offer an ecological basis for why this was a bad thing, evasive conclusions could only result. It could hardly be denied, as the report admitted, that 'a serious depletion of wildlife habitat' had stemmed from loss of hedgerows, hedgerow trees, dykes and woodland, plus the infilling of ponds, the underdrainage of streamside meadows, the 'improvement' of stream courses, the reduction of permanent grassland, stubble burning and the extensive use of herbicides ('spray drift'). But could it really be claimed that there was 'no conclusive evidence' to back the view of ecologists 'that the stability of an ecosystem depends in some measure on its diversity' or that the 'long-term effects of specialised cereal production on wildlife' were 'not known'? A little educated guesswork could predict the long-term consequences of confining wildlife to farm and roadside boundaries, small woodlands, streams and ditches, the marginal terrain of the new agriculture landscape.[49] As such, the Countryside Commission's sympathy for farmers who found beauty in 'tidy' landscapes denuded of agriculturally non-functional features, and the recommendation that the state might offer grants to encourage the restoration of lost tree cover in marginal land, served only to highlight the straitened ecological perspective underpinning official thinking. The report suggested no real desire to significantly disrupt the intensification process or challenge the agricultural *habitus*, nor did it acknowledge that pockets of restored cover, as distinct from connected habitats, were of minimal wildlife utility.[50]

Broadly the same could be said of the submissions made to the National Parks Policy Review Commission chaired by Lord Sandford, undersecretary of state at the Department of Environment. Based on hearings held in each park between January 1972 and October 1973, it came at a moment when the performance of the nature state was coming under international scrutiny. The first European Year of Conservation in 1970 is widely acknowledged to reflect the broader environmental turn in popular political thinking, generating much newspaper comment and making it easier for parliament to reject controversial planning applications, notably bills to establish or enhance reservoirs at Calderdale and Derwent in the Peak District National Park, the Dowlais Valley in South Wales and Swincombe in Dartmoor National Park.[51] Other developments of the moment included the foundation of radical activist organizations like Friends of the Earth and Greenpeace in 1969 and 1971, respectively, the first publication of the long-running *Ecologist* magazine in July 1970, and the coming to prominence of ecologically minded lifestyles.[52]

The Sandford Report of 1974 was the most significant statement on the condition of the national parks since their formation. It is principally remembered for establishing the so-called Sandford Principle, which stated that when there is an irreconcilable conflict in the parks between the conservation of the landscape and its enjoyment by the public, conservation must take precedence. Wilson's third Labour government adopted this as a governing principle, though it did not find legislative form until the passage of the Environment Act in 1995, by which time the NPAs had already been strengthened. And although the Sandford Principle reflected the immediate concerns of the commissioners, as the emphasis placed on the rise of the private motorist in the initial briefing by the secretary suggested, it failed to do justice to the richness of the evidence received or the wide-ranging content and conclusions of the report itself.

Much brought to Sandford's attention was predictable. Few can have been surprised to learn that the NPAs were frustrated by the little control they could exercise over land use in the parks. Their complaints were familiar. Quarrying and forestry had wrought significant environmental change and brought heavy vehicles to primitive roads; new reservoirs (55 in the Peak District alone), as well as the development of tourist facilities, particularly new caravan sites, often went ahead regardless of their view; and they had almost no say over changes in agricultural practices, including those stimulated by state subsidy.

The gap between the amenity and the agricultural interest was also evident in the zeal with which landowners and farmers attacked the very notion of a *national* park, insisting the designation had created a false impression that the land was in public ownership and this gave the general public untrammelled rights of access. Anger that livestock had been worried or crops damaged by acts of trespass might have been justified in some instances, but there remained a fundamental refusal of the idea that the national parks were a part of the public commons: the land was private property, access agreements were voluntary and changes in land use should not be subject to planning law. Where the park authorities did exert some influence, such as over planning applications for new buildings, farmers resented meeting costs that did not always apply to neighbours outside the park boundaries. In essence, the rural propertied felt entitled to compensation for all costs or losses incurred by any conditions or restrictions imposed by the state on their activities.

In the main, the farmers had reason to feel entitled. For all the talk of conservation as a dynamic process predicated on managing change in the interest of the natural environment, almost every submission presented to the Sandford Committee, with the exception of those pushing a transparently commercial interest, promoted a broadly preservationist agenda. Industrial development should be halted, forestry brought under planning control and rough grazing preserved as a means of maintaining the look and, secondarily, the flora and fauna of existing landscapes. Farmers were criticized for converting rough grazing or heathland into grassland by, for example, the Exmoor National Park Joint Advisory Committee, but, echoing Scott, the old shibboleth that grazing remained necessary if the land was not to 'deteriorate to thicket, gorse and reed' went largely unchallenged.[53]

Amenity remained the abiding principle, the desire for tidy and aesthetically pleasing national parks the aim. Certain plants, like ferns or gorse, were judged unattractive and therefore bad, and others, most obviously heather, were thought attractive and therefore good. There was almost no consideration of the ecological significance of these choices, and it was assumed that the quality of the human experience, visual and physical, was the yardstick by which any development could be measured. By this thinking, a part of the national park that became difficult to hike through thanks to scrubbing up had by definition deteriorated, regardless of whether this improved wildlife habitats. And although the submission by the Forestry Commission obviously broke with the near-negative consensus with respect to forestry, its argument that 'there need be no intrinsic incompatibility between forestry and amenity and that the solution lies in determining the scale, location and nature of plantations in relation to their setting' lay within the dominant amenity discourse.[54]

As with the 'Countryside in the 1970' conferences, only the submission by the Nature Conservancy broke with the consensus. This 21-page typed document, with an additional ten pages or so of appendices, examined existing approaches or policies with respect not to amenity but to wildlife, thereby offering a fundamentally different way of making the performance of the national parks legible. If this approach reflected statutory responsibilities and the accumulated wisdom of 20 years spent identifying the most valuable natural or semi-natural landscapes in the country, there were passages in the submission that pointed to more unorthodox thinking, moments perhaps when suppressed desires surfaced.

Nature Conservancy made clear that it was disappointed with the performance of the national parks and frustrated that it had not been allowed to properly fulfil the advisory role promised by the 1949 legislation; it challenged land use orthodoxies, asserting in a key claim that 'nature conservation' itself should be considered a 'form or aspect of land use ... primarily for people and for their good'; and it argued that establishing national parks had been part of the general attempt to build 'a new and better Britain after World War II', which meant 'using the countryside beyond its immediate economic value, to the greater benefit of the nation'.[55] And although the 'natural scenic and amenity' value of the parks was indeed an 'expression of patterns of land use evolved by man through the centuries', Nature Conservancy insisted that the natural beauty of the parks stemmed from their 'basic ecological features to an especially marked degree'.[56] Developments that further distanced the terrain from its natural ecology undermined a park's status and were therefore at odds with the 1949 legislation.

Although these observations narrowed the gap in perspective between Nature Conservancy and the amenity societies, Nature Conservancy nonetheless gave the parks a relatively clean bill of health, suggesting that many of the developments the preservationists found objectionable did not particularly disturb the conservationists. Agriculture remained relatively marginal, coniferization was not extensive and building, including roads, was subject to stricter controls than elsewhere. Moreover, quarrying was in decline and military training, by reducing other kinds of disturbance, had probably benefited wildlife, whereas too many visitors congregating in the same places had damaged wildlife by disturbing nesting birds, damaging flora (picking wild flowers), trampling vegetation and causing erosion.[57] Moreover, the Conservancy accepted that the parks could not be 'managed as havens of wildlife and wilderness' as they were in the United States. Inhabitants had every right to modern amenities like electricity, sewage disposal and so on, and farming, forestry, water supply and mineral exploitation were likely to continue. But having made all of these concessions to modernity, the Conservancy expressed a different kind of modern desire, arguing that the most valuable ecological sites needed to be managed according to 'definable goals', which meant 'sustaining diversity in physical features, vegetation, flora and fauna, maintaining species population ... and preventing damage to fragile habitats'. What was more, if the primary aim was to 'maintain a balanced representation of desirable features in perpetuity', a secondary aim could be 'diversifying habitat so as to allow the increase of valued species or the entry of new species'.[58]

At the same time, by arguing that nature conservation 'may require the maintenance of largely man-made ecosystems resulting from particular forms of land use', the Conservancy merely articulated in more sophisticated language what many submissions had said about how it was necessary to maintain traditional grazing regimes;[59] similarly so, its concern about the use of insecticides and herbicides and the application of fertilizers to unenclosed land or the surface draining of bog and wet pasture. The parks might not have been subject to significant lowland-style intensification, but heathland was threatened almost everywhere, particularly because headage payments encouraged overgrazing and burning. Characteristically, Nature Conservancy added that heavy sheep mortality, a consequence of overstocking and over-wintering on exposed terrain, benefited carrion-feeding predators, such as ravens, buzzards and foxes.[60]

Much here would become orthodox conservationism, making the Conservancy argument stand out all the more amid the conventional thinking of most other Sandford submissions. Here was an approach to the Parks that measured their success not in terms of amenity or landscape beauty, but sustainability and biodiversity. But the Conservancy took the analysis a step further, considering the 'ecological change in the uplands' that would be caused if a stop were put to the Hill Sheep Subsidy when Britain joined the European Common Market. Reducing or removing flocks or other grazing animals from the hills would lead to a 'considerable increase in the luxuriance of vegetation, especially grasses and bilberry, and the recovery of heather moor where it is degenerating'. This would begin a more significant transformation.

> Trees such as rowan and birch would probably invade slowly and patchily, and it would likely be many years before anything approaching a woodland cover became established by natural means on the lower slopes. The increased luxuriance of grasses, bilberry and heather would make walking more difficult and give increased fire hazards, but would mostly be beneficial to wildlife. Field Voles and probably Rabbits would increase and provide alternative food (to carrion) for Buzzards, Ravens and Foxes, as well as attracting larger numbers of other predators such as Kestrels, Hen Harriers and Short-eared owls. On heather ground birds such as the Merlin and Stonechat would probably increase or reappear. Colourful flowers normally kept close grazed by sheep would at first flourish, but might eventually be overwhelmed by other vegetation, including scrub.[61]

Here, a patchy invasion would inhibit walkers, increase the risk of fire and might simply result in scrubbing up; there, increased tree cover and a greater flourishing and diversity of wildlife. Here, the responsibility to uphold national park ideals; there, barely suppressed excitement at the prospect of a revitalized nature, a rewilding *avant la lettre*.[62]

Without a break in the flow, without a new paragraph, the author continued, observing that if farmers were to sustain the agricultural practices that keep national park landscapes as the public like them, if they were to reject advances in agricultural methods used elsewhere, then they must be paid to do so. With this parental wag of the finger, the preservationist agenda is reasserted, an alternative conservation vision for the national parks of nature-at-will suppressed, and a degree of cognitive dissonance neutralized.

Less visionary but of more immediate practical significance, the Conservancy's discussion of woodland also raised questions about the negative effect of grazing. Few doubted that clear-felling broadleaf stands and replacing them with conifers impoverished flora and fauna, but as significant was the Conservancy's claim that grazing hill woods, again advocated by traditionalists, kept down or eliminated herbaceous plants and prevented the regeneration of trees and plants from seedlings.[63] As such, many grazed hill woods were 'virtually moribund', as the Countryside Commission's *New Agricultural Landscapes* report had said of lowland tree cover.[64] Again, interventionist management was needed if the effects of grazing were to be offset. Rotational fencing of blocks of woodland would allow saplings to become established, while at the other end of the life-cycle some trees should be allowed to become 'overmature' or even to die and rot, so that over the course of their lifetime they delivered their full ecological services.[65] Again, using the possible consequences of entry into the Common Market as an alibi, the Conservancy imagined tree cover increasing by natural means to such an extent that small flocks of herbivores might need to be re-introduced as a management tool. On uplands denuded of sheep, planting conifers could even be a first step in a programme of managed tree cover restoration. Broadleaved trees would be introduced during the second rotation, replicating in the short-term the longer-term effects of natural process.[66]

In the event, the Sandford Report neither conveyed these possibilities nor fully embraced the perspective of the professional conservationists. Its observations and recommendations were framed in terms of the possible conflict between 'the preservation of natural beauty' and 'the promotion of public enjoyment', concluding that 'where irreconcilable conflicts exist between conservation and public enjoyment, then conservation interest should take priority'. That at least was the official rendering of the Sandford Principle. In fact, the phrasing in the report was more far-reaching, more explicitly closing the gap between preservationist and conservationist.

> We have no doubt that where the conflict between the two purposes, which has always been inherent, becomes acute, the first one must prevail in order that the beauty and ecological qualities of the national parks may be maintained.[67]

Framing the recommendations in ecological terms gave greater force to the report's broad conclusion:

> The presumption against development which would be out of accord with park purposes must be strong throughout the whole of the parks; in the most beautiful parts which remain unspoiled it should amount to a prohibition to be breached only in the case of a most compelling national necessity.[68]

The report went on to recommend that a new designation, 'national heritage areas', should be applied to the 'very highest quality of landscape' in the parks. Here, amenity – or public enjoyment – would not be the priority, though farming and forestry 'would of course continue, but only by methods compatible with the main purpose of the area'.[69] Nature Conservancy might well have felt moved to respond that establishing National Nature Reserves or designating SSSIs already served this purpose, but by adopting the emerging discourse of 'heritage', the onus was placed on stewarding 'outstandingly beautiful landscapes' in a way that suggested natural beauty had a firmly ecological basis.[70] That might not seem a radical suggestion, but in terms of the potential working of the nature state, it again suggested a narrowing of the amenity–nature conservation divide, at least with respect to some particularly prized – and agriculturally marginal – terrains.

Despite this, the limitations of Sandford's 'national heritage areas' recommendation should not be obscured. Upholding the clear consensus that maintaining grazing was necessary if the purposes of the parks were to be fulfilled, Sandford expressed his sympathy for farmers who had taken advantage of MAFF grants, opting to 'intensify' the 'productive capacity' of rough grazing by ploughing, fencing and re-seeding. Although converting heathland to grassland might have changed the 'texture and character of the landscape', an aesthetic rather than an ecological claim, Sandford still insisted that 'for *most of the land* the best managers from every point of view will continue to be farmers earning their livings from farming'. Changing economic circumstances and new technologies would 'inevitably ... affect the pattern of agricultural use' but 'sound farming and national park purposes are normally in accord'.[71]

What was meant by 'sound farming' was not clear. Sandford argued that the public interest should be taken into account before any further 'improvement' of rough grazing took place, but the reluctance to be prescriptive remained. Better management of the commons was 'urgently needed' if the interests of 'agriculture, ecology and the public' were to be met, but it would be another 11 years before the most important common, that of Dartmoor, was made subject to a new management regime.[72] Sandford also thought there should be a strong presumption against the destruction of broadleaved woodland, but here again local voluntary agreements were preferred to government intervention and the onus was on the government and park authorities to find ways to counteract the profit motive of the landowner. The implication seemed clear. Having established planting grants and fiscal incentives to afforest, the government should compensate those asked by the NPAs not to exploit these opportunities.[73] The moral hazard does not need to be spelled out.

Sandford shared the fate of many government committees of inquiry. Its primary political purpose was served at the moment of its commissioning and its conclusions or recommendations proved to be of secondary importance. The Wilson government's decision to adopt the Sandford Principle was as much an exercise in political good manners as anything else, and although there is little reason to doubt Sandford's sincerity, the whole enterprise, from the submissions received through to the report itself, was significantly constrained by conventional thinking. Amenity remained the dominant discourse, the farmers reified as the true keepers of the parks, and tourists as the principal problem. Developments in agriculture and the encroachment of industry on the parks did not see the founding principles of the 1949 legislation or the possible role for government significantly rethought. As responses to the controversy over the 'improvement' of Exmoor or the controversy provoked by the 'improvement' clauses of the first Dartmoor Commons Bill (1977) demonstrated, the government, whether Labour or Conservative, preferred local voluntarist responses to immediate problems rather than the kind of sweeping solutions characteristic of the US nature state. It was thus with some justification that Ann and Malcolm MacEwen argued in their coruscating polemic of 1982 that the uplands 'are threatened, less perhaps by the local cataclysmic changes made by vast new engineering works (such as reservoirs and roads) than by the insidious widespread incremental changes wrought by modern farming and forestry'.[74]

Nonetheless, there were shifts in thinking. In 1977, M.J. Feist of the Countryside Commission could observe at an academic gathering that 'increased environmental consciousness among the public means that more people now associate an attractive landscape with one that has a high wildlife value and vice versa'.[75] That would gradually take legislative form and this discussion might be concluded by scrolling ahead, sketching a picture that takes in the Wildlife and Countryside Act 1981, which introduced new species-based wildlife protection and required MAFF to notify the NPAs when making grants for agricultural improvement,[76] the reaction against the extraordinarily wasteful and ecologically destructive consequences of the Common Agricultural Policy and its significant reform in the 1990s, the significance of the Rio Earth Summit in 1992, the Environment Act of 1995 and the role environmental stewardship grants came to play in maintaining hill farming on a reduced scale. Particular attention could be paid to how, after Rio, maintaining or enhancing biodiversity came to provide a means by which the nature state quantified environmental effect and was gradually established as a principle of governance, rendering a rare butterfly in a marginal habitat a more effective barrier against the bulldozer or the plough than any number of protestors or lobbyists. Nonetheless, no simple narrative of progress would suffice, for as the nature state was strengthened, often through the replacement of productivist subsidies with environmental management grants, the environmental harm caused by developmental pressure still did not abate.

A more immediately suggestive ending that captures something of the conflicted mood of the 1970s can be found by comparing two idiosyncratic but influential books. Nan Fairbrother's *New Lives New Landscapes*, published in 1970, is a sophisticated and iconoclastic example of post-war technocratic and social democratic optimism. To Fairbrother, British agriculture was a quaint survival that only began to modernize during the Second World War and had a long way to go. Fairbrother saw the 'old countryside' as a place of poverty, found forestry a 'promising alternative' to unprofitable hill farming, and insisted no more should be asked of farmers than that they 'create' from the land 'a good functional farmscape'.[77] Like the Nature Conservancy, she too pondered the ecological effect of a collapse of hill farming in the uplands, picturing 'the liberated hills and glens of the natural landscape', but this was of secondary importance to her story. New technologies must be embraced. They would secure farming's future and help to meet the nation's food needs. Fairbrother could be decidedly provoking, describing crops 'as prosperous as never before, thriving and exuberantly healthy: thousands of golden acres of cereals, lavish prairies of untrodden grass grown lush and green with nitrogen.'[78]

Her argument had an aesthetic dimension too: the land's new 'openness' had created a new rural beauty that allowed 'the shape of the land' to be seen, making for 'a bold and uncluttered composition of wide-views and clearly-defined effects', the 'best landscape' for those looking out of a car window.[79] Here was a modernist picturesque, satisfying 'a new-world aesthetic which admires aeroplanes and Swedish glass and modern architecture – simple, functional, sparse, elegant, bare of incidental decoration, and essentially large-scale even in small units'.[80]

Marion Shoard's *The Theft of the Countryside*, published in 1980, could not have been more different. The author had a background in zoology and planning, and had worked for the CPRE. The title of her book, of course, said much, as did chapter headings like 'Subsidies for Destruction' and 'Farming and Forestry – Above the Law'. Where Fairbrother exercised ironic detachment, Shoard was all passionate reaction; where Fairbrother's gaze onto the land embodied an aestheticized utilitarianism, Shoard's revived the radical traditional of the public commons. By what right, she asked, did farmers damage hedgerows, hedgerow trees, woods, roughlands, downs, moors and wetlands? Despite her palpable anger, she found the fuss amenity associations made about encroachments onto the national parks misplaced. Damage in the uplands was superficial, insignificant when compared to the real harm inflicted on the lowlands by agricultural intensification. Sanctifying landscapes least subject to developmental pressures had allowed a state-subsidized free-for-all elsewhere.[81]

Much of this rings true, but rather than choosing between Fairbrother or Shoard, the anthropic assumptions underpinning both might simply be registered. Even Shoard's lament for Britain's 'disappearing wildlife' is framed in terms of the pleasure the countryside provides human beings, particularly the right of children to experience this delight, rather than a broader sense of the need to sustain the world's life systems.[82] 'Rational' or 'radical', Fairbrother and Shoard were typically post-war, manifesting a particularly British distinction between ecology and amenity that long stymied the development of its nature state.

Notes

1 Paul Readman, 'Preserving the English Landscape, c.1870–1914', *Cultural and Social History*, 5/2 (2008), 197–218.
2 H.V. Morton, *In Search of England* (London, 1927). In general, see David Matless, *Landscape and Englishness* (London, 2001); on the optimism of those years, see David

Jeremiah, 'Motoring and the British Countryside', *Rural History*, 21/2 (2010), 233–50; and on H.V. Morton, see Michael Bartholomew, *In Search of H. V. Morton* (London, 2004).

3 Quoted in Gordon E. Cherry, *Environmental Planning, 1939–1969: Vol. II National Parks and Recreation in the Countryside* (London, 1975), 9.

4 William Wordsworth, *Guide to the Lakes* (London, 2004), 93; Wendy Joy Darby, *Landscape and Identity: Geographies of Nation and Class in England* (Oxford, 2000).

5 John Sheail, *Nature in Trust: The History of Nature Conservation in Britain* (Glasgow, 1976), 77–8.

6 F.R. Sandbach, 'The Early Campaign for a National Park in the Lake District', *Transactions of the Institute of British Geographers*, 3/4 (1978), 498–514.

7 Cherry, *Environmental Planning, 1939–1969*, 43–4; Sheail, *Nature in Trust*, 100.

8 During the war, the extent of land under cultivation increased from eight million to 13 million acres, often at the expense of meat production.

9 On mixed farming, see James Winter, *Secure from Rash Assault: Sustaining the Victorian Environment* (Berkeley, CA, 1999); on Scott, see Alun Howkins, *The Death of Rural England: A Social History of the Countryside since 1900* (London, 2003), 136–7.

10 Quoted in Cherry, *Environmental Planning, 1939–1969*, 34–5.

11 Ibid., 35.

12 Ann MacEwen and Malcolm MacEwen, *National Parks, Conservation or Cosmetics?* (London, 1982), 9–10; Dennison quoted in Sue Elworthy and Jane Holder, *Environmental Protection: Text and Materials* (London, 1997), 105.

13 Austin Robinson, 'The Scott and Uthwatt Reports on Land Utilisation', *The Economic Journal*, 53/209 (1943), 32.

14 Cherry, *Environmental Planning, 1939–1969*, 3.

15 Brian Harrison, *Finding a Role? The United Kingdom, 1970–1990* (Oxford, 2010), 66.

16 William Adams, *Future Nature: A Vision for Conservation* (London, 1996), 60.

17 Sheail, *Nature in Trust*, 95.

18 Ibid., 122ff.

19 William Adams, 'Rationalization and Conservation: Ecology and the Management of Nature in the United Kingdom', *Transactions of the Institute of British Geographers*, 22/3 (1997), 279.

20 MacEwen and MacEwen, *National Parks*, 18.

21 Ibid., 21.

22 Elworthy and Holder, *Environmental Protection*, 107.

23 There is an extensive policy-oriented literature on European agricultural subsidies, including Brian E Hill, *The Common Agricultural Policy: Past, Present, and Future* (London, 1984); Brian Gardner, *European Agriculture: Policies, Production, and Trade* (London, 1996).

24 David Evans, *A History of Nature Conservation in Britain* (London, 1992), 196.

25 In general, see Harrison, *Finding a Role?*, 56–68.

26 Rachel Carson, *Silent Spring* (Boston, 1962), xvii.

27 As late as 1977, a Nature Conservancy Council specialist observed that 'The ultimate profitability of upland forestry is still unknown and therefore essentially a gamble.' See A.N. Lance, 'Upland Wildlife: Some Future Conservation Problems', in *The Future of Upland Britain: Proceedings of a Symposium Held at the University of Reading in September, 1977*, ed. by R.B. Tranter (Reading, 1978), II, 451.

28 Matthew Kelly, *Quartz and Feldspar. Dartmoor: A British Landscape in Modern Times* (London, 2015), 244–67.

29 Lance, 'Upland wildlife', 451: 'The reafforestation of open moorland, especially by the State since World War I, has brought more change to the British uplands than any other recent factor. In most cases the impacts on wildlife have been absolute and not just a matter of degree; when a site is planted, its wildlife community become replaced with a different and more artificial one.'

30 Robinson, 'Scott and Uthwatt Reports', 28.

31 Nature Conservancy for the Study Conference on the Countryside, *The Countryside in 1970: Proceedings of the Study Conference Held at Fishmongers' Hall, London, E.C.4, 4–5 Nov. 1963* (London, 1964), xxi.

32 Ibid., 6–7.

33 Ibid., 1, 3.

34 Draft Report by the Joint Standing Liaison Committee of the Agricultural and Forestry Departments and the Nature Conservancy. Working Party on Land Improvement Grants and Sites of Special Scientific Interest, 3 October 1963, FT 41/61, National Archive London (henceforth NAL).

35 Nature Conservancy, *The Countryside in 1970*, 34.

36 Ibid., 24, 28.

37 Ibid., 27. Stamp had a habit of riling the preservationists, see Kelly, *Quartz and Feldspar*, 397.

38 Nature Conservancy, *The Countryside in 1970*, 223.

39 Ibid., 225.

40 Ibid., 27.

41 Ibid., 210.

42 Ibid., 211.

43 Sverker Sörlin and Paul Warde (eds), *Nature's End: History and Environment* (Basingstoke, 2009), 3.

44 Nature Conservancy, *The Countryside in 1970*, 201.

45 Ibid., 204.

46 MacEwen and MacEwen, *National Parks*, 23–4; Cherry, *Environmental Planning, 1939–1969*, 136–7.

47 Countryside Commission, *New Agricultural Landscapes: Report of a Study* (Cheltenham, 1974), i.

48 Ibid., 5.

49 Ibid., 2, 12, 17, 21.

50 Ibid., 44–5.

51 On Swincombe, see Kelly, *Quartz and Feldspar*, 293–303. More generally, see Harrison, *Finding a Role?*; or, for a characteristically amused account of emergent middle-class mores, see Dominic Sandbrook, *State of Emergency. The Way We Were: Britain, 1970–1974* (London, 2010).

52 On Greenpeace, see Frank Zelko, *Make It a Green Peace! The Rise of Countercultural Environmentalism* (New York, 2013).

53 Exmoor National Park Joint Advisory Committee submission to the National Park Policies Review Committee, 3–4, AT 38/1, NAL. So potent was the opposition to state-subsidized improvement on Exmoor that it was made subject to a separate inquiry chaired by Lord Porchester in 1977, which saw MAFF come in for some stinging criticism. See MacEwen and MacEwen, *National Parks*, 173–93.

54 Forestry Commission submission to the National Park Policies Review Committee, 2, AT 38/1, NAL.
55 Nature Conservancy submission to the National Park Policies Review Committee, 2–3, AT 38/2, NAL.
56 Ibid., 3.
57 Ibid., 3–4.
58 Ibid., 7–8.
59 Ibid., 9.
60 Ibid., 10.
61 Ibid., 10.
62 On rewilding, see Peter Taylor (ed.), *Rewilding: ECOS Writing on Wildland and Conservation Values* (Walton Hill, 2011); George Monbiot, *Feral: Searching for Enchantment on the Frontiers of Rewilding* (London, 2013).
63 A claim confirmed by a recent authority; see Derek Yalden, 'The Post-Glacial History of Grazing', in *Trees, Forested Landscapes, and Grazing Animals: A European Perspective on Woodlands and Grazed Treescapes*, ed. by Ian D. Rotherham (London, 2013), 66–7.
64 This was particularly mentioned with respect to the case studies on Preston on Wye in Herefordshire and Myton on Swale in Yorkshire, Countryside Commission, *New Agricultural Landscapes*, 29, 32.
65 Nature Conservancy submission, 12.
66 Ibid., 13.
67 Report of the National Park Policies Review Committee (1974) *or* Sandford Report, 10, AT 38/9, NAL.
68 Ibid., 11; italics in original.
69 Ibid., 12.
70 Ibid., 12.
71 Ibid., 61; italics added.
72 Ibid., 61, 65.
73 Ibid., 67.
74 MacEwen and MacEwen, *National Parks*, 63–4.
75 M.J. Feist, 'Landscape Conservation in Upland Britain', in *The Future of Upland Britain*, ed. by R.B. Tranter (Reading, 1978), I, 210.
76 A farmer who refused an agricultural grant because a development would harm wildlife was eligible for compensation payment. Many NPAs found it cheaper to buy land than to compensate. See John Blunden and Nigel Curry (eds), *A People's Charter? Forty Years of the National Parks and Access to the Countryside Act 1949* (London, 1990), 120–1.
77 Nan Fairbrother, *New Lives, New Landscapes: Planning for the 21st Century* (New York, 1970), 71, 122, 239.
78 Ibid., 244.
79 Ibid., 241–2, 245–6.
80 Ibid., 248.
81 Marion Shoard, *The Theft of the Countryside* (London, 1980), 140–1.
82 Ibid., 192–4.

7   Behind the scenes and out in the open

Making Colombian national parks in the 1960s and 1970s

*Claudia Leal**

In 1977, Julio Carrizosa, head of Colombia's National Institute for Natural Renewable Resources and the Environment, known by its Spanish acronym Inderena, presented the National Council for Economic and Social Policy with a proposal to create 20 protected areas. Accompanying Carrizosa was Jorge Hernández, a self-taught man who worked as the institute's chief scientist and who is a legend among Colombian biologists. In the council, the president and his ministers discussed critical policy issues and made some of the most important decisions of government, but that day most participants remained silent; only the minister of mines spoke up. He opined that protecting the environment was a luxury that only developed countries could afford, and went on to make several inquiries of Hernández, who obligingly provided detailed answers. After an hour of discussion, President Alfonso López Michelsen (1974–8) tacitly approved the proposal by reminding those present that there were other topics on the agenda and they needed to move on. In this expeditious manner, close to two million hectares were put under state protection, greatly increasing the few existing conservation units in the country and effectively establishing a national system of protected areas.[1]

This episode illustrates key aspects of the building of national parks in Colombia and Latin America. In the 1960s and 1970s, state structures that allowed important decisions to be made without much consultation or public negotiation facilitated the construction of networks of protected areas. Existing laws that defined procedures and institutions for the promotion and management of protected areas provided the basis for these sorts of agreements. In Colombia, the Code of Natural Resources (1974) and Inderena (created in 1968) backed the process of nationalizing nature in the form of national parks. Once a few well-positioned scientists and politicians agreed that national parks were an integral part of modern states, they could with relative ease work *behind the scenes* to grant certain tracts of land such status.

However, designating an area as protected was just a first step: parks on paper needed to be built on the ground. This meant demarcating their limits, making

* I thank Juan Sebastián Moreno for his assistance in retrieving information, Emily Wakild for her comments and the School of Social Sciences at Universidad de los Andes for providing funding.

them visible through wardens and landmarks, and effectively managing them so that flora, fauna, water, and spectacular scenery could persist. Furthermore, for a *national* park to truly come to life, it had to be publicly recognized and appropriated as such. Those living nearby, as well as citizens (and foreigners) at large, should come to acknowledge its existence and see parks in general as integral parts of the national territory.

Making national parks in Colombia has been tortuous and protracted, yet fundamental to building the nature state – the set of institutions, regulations and relations by which the state acknowledged its responsibility to care for, and not just use or overcome, nature.[2] These institutions and regulations emerged as part of the expansion of the national state. A robust enough state, as existed in most of Latin America by the 1960s, thus preceded the development within it of specialized divisions and rules devoted to the environment. The institutionalization of these new areas of state activity came about with the support of some state agencies and bureaucracies, and in opposition to others. Reconstructing the convoluted development of national parks contributes to our understanding of historical processes of state formation that undermine conceptions of the state as an abstract, homogeneous and coherent entity.[3] Furthermore, parks produced contrasting effects on state legitimacy (an inherent part of state building) as they favoured some constituencies while negatively impacting upon others.

This chapter starts by examining the creation of the national park system in Colombia, part of a Latin American trend. Working within a political system that concentrated key decision-making powers in the person of the president, ambitious new environmental institutions, armed with new environmental guidelines, advocated the designation of protected areas. The second part of the chapter moves the focus to Tayrona National Park to explain park formation beyond mere designation. It examines how, in the late 1960s and early 1970s, bitter struggles waged against settlers and tourist interests brought Colombia's most popular national park into existence. This story reveals how the national park system emerged with the support of certain national state institutions and in opposition to others. At the same time, it strengthened the central state by snatching authority over particular areas from the local and regional state.

The creation of national park systems

The first wave of South American park creation – in the 1930s – occurred in a few countries, mostly Chile, Argentina, Brazil and Mexico. By 1939, South American governments had established 20 parks, to which we should add the 40 parks created in Mexico during Lázaro Cárdenas' presidency (1934–40). Their designation was motivated by the need to provide recreation outlets for urban populations and establish control over border areas (as in Argentina and Chile's Andean highlands, and Brazil's south-eastern corner); in the Mexican case, park creation also served to advance a rural model of social justice.[4] The establishment of protected areas lost steam in the 1940s and 1950s, but had a steady growth afterwards. The first parks of many Latin American countries date from the 1960s, and resulted from varied disjointed initiatives. A Peruvian biologist and politician led a campaign to protect oilbirds (*guácharos*) from hunting, which resulted in the creation of his country's first national park in 1961.[5] In Costa Rica, the first initiative to establish a protected area had a different kind of lobbyist behind it: a Scandinavian couple, who had moved to a beautiful part of the country, was dismayed by the deforestation caused by settlers. Their proposal to create a reserve went through in 1965.[6]

Brazilian parks dating from those years share the same haphazard history and illustrate how, in a world of small elites and strong regional concentration of power, relationships between early conservationists and politicians could have long-lasting consequences. The eccentric president Jânio Quadros (1961), who seemed to have a soft spot for the environment, appointed as head of the Forestry Council a friend of his who had co-founded a pioneering environmental NGO three years earlier. Before Quadros' early resignation, less than one year into his term in office, his friend managed to convince him to establish nine parks. Most were relatively small, just 41,600 hectares on average, but one of them, Xingu, which is today an indigenous park, reached gigantic proportions at over 2.6 million hectares.[7] As most parks at the time, it had a singular story behind it: it was a belated result of a well-known expedition of the 1940s, and aimed at incorporating a distant Amazonian territory and its indigenous inhabitants into the Brazilian nation.[8]

This trend of parks sprouting piecemeal changed around the 1970s thanks to the slow building of the nature state in various countries, and with it the creation of national parks systems. The erection of an environmental establishment was part of the general expansion of the state and should be associated with the vast transformation Latin American societies experienced after the Second World War. Between 1945 and 1981, regional economies grew faster and at a steadier pace than before, then the debt crisis hit and growth stalled. Regional population increased rapidly – at a steady 2.7 per cent between 1950 and 1970 – and became increasingly urban: while 41 per cent of Latin Americans lived in cities at mid-century, three decades later more than 60 per cent did so.[9] But the formation of an environmental apparatus was not straightforward: no agreement existed about the need to alter developmental trends nor was there a generalized desire to set apart areas for nature conservation.

Inderena, the cradle of Colombia's national park system, exemplifies the emergence of nature states in most of post-war Latin America. The Colombian state underwent its most rapid growth in the 1960s and 1970s. The bureaucracy expanded at an unprecedented rate as the state became more centralized: in 1962, public employees in national institutions surpassed those working for local and regional ones.[10] Inderena emerged as part of the constitutional reform of 1968 that aimed to improve the state's administrative efficiency.[11] The reform strengthened the Ministry of Agriculture partly by creating three new development institutes within it: Inderena, in charge of natural resources, and two others devoted to agriculture and cattle ranching.[12]

This policy contained an unexpected contradiction: the institution created to develop Colombia's capacity to exploit its natural resources more effectively carried within it the seeds of nature protection. Inderena, which was initially called the Institute for the Development of Natural Renewable Resources, resulted from a contentious merger between the Ministry's Division of Natural Resources and the Corporation of the Magdalena and Sinú Valleys (CVM). The CVM had a small parks office responsible for three national parks created in 1964 (among them, Tayrona). This office became the new Division of National Parks within Inderena and clashed bitterly with those employees who had worked for the Ministry encouraging the exports of feline and caiman skins, as well as live animals. The conflict between these factions was only solved after 1974, when president López Michelsen assumed office and appointed Julio Carrizosa, a conservationist in the making, as head of Inderena. Carrizosa refashioned the institute towards a more determined conservationist stance to the point that, in 1976, *development* was dropped from its name and *environment* was added.[13]

In those same years, a similar hybrid institution emerged in Brazil, albeit one that did not break away from its developmental mandate. In 1967, the military dictatorship (1964–85) created the Brazilian Institute for Forestry Development (IBDF) by merging the Ministry of Agriculture's Department of Natural Renewable Resources with the two institutes in charge of the production of *yerba mate* and pinewood. Most of the bureaucrats of the IBDF were transferred from these institutes and the few conservationists in the staff were confined to the small and isolated Department for Forest Research and the Conservation of Nature (DN). Although this small group considered the creation of protected areas its principal mandate, until 1979 it advanced slowly, largely due to lack of support from the head of the institute and the minister himself.[14]

Both the Brazilian and Colombian cases demonstrate how multilateral institutions played crucial roles in the development of nature states. The 1972 the United Nations Conference on the Human Environment that took place in Stockholm was particularly influential, as Manuel Rodríguez, former minister of the environment of Colombia, explains:

> The [Code of Renewable Natural Resources and Environmental Protection] was the main response of Colombia to the agreements that stemmed from the [Stockholm Conference] two years before. It became the first General Law promulgated in Latin America, and marked the beginning of a movement to incorporate this kind of legislation into the juridical order of the countries in the region.[15]

In Brazil, the Stockholm meeting led to the creation, in 1973, of the small Secretariat of the Environment (SEMA) within the Ministry of the Interior. SEMA devoted much energy to designating protected areas and coordinated the enactment, in 1981, of a National Environmental Policy Law.[16]

As environmental institutions and regulations came to be part of Latin American states, international organizations and networks provided support and gave legitimacy to conservation efforts. Twenty-five representatives from 15 Latin American countries attended the First World Congress on National Parks (Seattle, 1962), organized by the world's leading environmental NGO – the International Union for the Conservation of Nature and Natural Resources (IUCN) – and co-sponsored by UNESCO and FAO.[17] The Latin American Committee on National Parks (CLAPN), established that year by the Latin American Forestry Commission of FAO, resulted from that meeting. In 1964, another committee with the same name was created in Quito; its meetings evolved into the Latin American Conferences on National Parks, which took place in Venezuela (1967), Ecuador (1970) and Colombia (1971). Members of CLAPN received constantly updated information about what was going on in other parts of the world in relation to nature conservation.[18] IUCN also organized a conference in 1968 on conservation in Bariloche, Argentina, which again had the support of UNESCO and FAO. With this experience in hand, the 39 Latin American delegates to the Second World Congress on National Parks (Yellowstone and Grand Teton National Parks, 1972) were much better prepared than their peers ten years before.[19]

Around the same time, courses contributed to professionalizing park management, particularly by disseminating lessons from the United States. In 1966, Argentina's park service led the way with a course offered in Bariloche. A year later, the future founder of the National Parks Department in Costa Rica, Mario Boza, got introduced to this topic in a course given by Kenton Miller – a consultant for FAO who later became president of IUCN – at the Inter-American Institute in Turrialba. Miller also taught a course in Valdivia, Chile, in 1969, attended by Chileans, Brazilians, Argentinians and a Paraguayan. Staff members from the park offices of various Latin American countries attended courses offered in the United States. Boza enrolled in a one-month course in Aspen, Colorado, while Heliodoro Sánchez, from Colombia, remembers his '40-day PhD', an official tour of various US parks in 1970. Two years later, Sánchez took a six-month course co-organized by the US Park Service.[20]

Additionally, the FAO provided conservation advice to various governments. Kenton Miller visited Chile and Colombia several times between 1966 and 1970 to assist with park management.[21] Along with two colleagues, in 1974 he published an FAO document in Spanish, with guidelines for drafting management plans for national parks.[22] That same year, Gary Wetterberg, who had just finished a dissertation on South American national parks, wrote a document for the Brazilian government on behalf of FAO on conservation priorities for Amazonia, which initiated conservation efforts in this region.[23] Members of the Peace Corps pitched in by working – at least in Costa Rica, Colombia and Chile – in chronically understaffed parks.[24]

These international efforts to foster conservation contributed decisively to a sharp increase in the number of conservation units and the area under protection in Latin America – as well as in other parts of the world.[25] Chile, a pioneer in national parks in the subcontinent, put more than twice as much land under protected status between 1965 and 1970 than in the 1930s–1950s combined.[26] Meanwhile, Colombia made up for its late start: it created six protected areas in the 1960s (while only one had been established before), amounting to 1,290,280 hectares, and 23 in the 1970s, totalling 2,680,458 hectares.

In Brazil, the institutional force behind the designation of protected areas consolidated in the 1970s, but the results could not be seen until the following decade. When the DN was created in 1967, Brazil had 14 national parks covering a little over 1.1 million hectares. The small DN staff was able to designate, between 1971 and 1974, three parks that doubled that area. But as support from above for the creation of additional parks subsequently weakened, for the next five years this group devoted itself to carefully designing a national plan for protected areas. When backing resumed in 1979, the DN created 11 parks in seven years – mostly in the Amazon – that added over six million hectares to the national park system, plus other conservation units that enlarged protected territory even more. Additionally, in 1973, the government had created SEMA to address pollution. However, its director, Paulo Nogueira Neto, one of the few experienced environmentalists in the country, considered nature conservation a top priority, so he invented a new category of protected area – the ecological station – with which he further expanded Brazilian protected territory.

In sum, the examples of Brazil, Colombia and Chile show how national park systems were put in place in the 1960s, 1970s and 1980s, when enough units covering sizeable areas in various geographies were designated as protected areas. The general growth of the state apparatus, which facilitated the creation of environmental institutions and legislation, was fundamental to this shift. Similarly, the international conservation network aided the process by providing instruments, some resources and legitimacy. However, someone had to decide or approve the creation of protected areas, which meant setting aside spaces where productive activities and human habitation were for the most part barred. In the absence of environmental movements that advocated the establishment of protected areas, and without any consensus over the desirability of such a policy, how was it possible to put thousands of hectares of land under state protection? The answer lies in the great powers wielded by presidents.

Gentleman's politics

The designation of national parks did not go through tough public debates; these decisions were taken within the executive branch by a small group of politicians and public servants, closely tied to the president. The heavy weight of the executive branch is best exemplified by the extraordinary presidential powers that have been a hallmark of Latin American states. Since independence, republics in this region have had presidential regimes, that is, they have directly elected presidents for fixed terms. As specialists in Latin American politics explain,

What appears to distinguish the Latin American variety [of this kind of regime] is a high degree of what we might summarize as executive law-making powers. Specifically Latin American constitutions are uniquely inclined to empower presidents to decree laws, initiate legislative proposals, and exert powers in emergency conditions.[27]

Moreover, in the 1970s, authoritarian governments that further concentrated power were the norm – only three Latin American countries were spared this misfortune; Colombia was one of them. This country illustrates how designating protected areas could be relatively straightforward if promoters managed to convince a small number of decision-makers to act.

Colombian political history of the 1950s and 1960s helps explain the country's heightened presidential powers. To end a bloody and protracted war between Liberals and Conservatives, the bosses of the two historical parties favoured military rule and backed general Gustavo Rojas Pinilla (1953–7), Colombia's sole twentieth-century dictator. A military junta followed until 1958, when the bosses devised another strategy to promote peace: alternate power between the two parties for four presidential terms, an arrangement known as the National Front (1958–74). The end of the war and the bipartisan arrangement, along with the growth of the state, contributed to a shift in the logic of people's political allegiances: from the quasi-religious party adscription of over a century to patronage networks.[28] In this context, members of Congress sought to secure resources to reward the narrow set of voters who supported them, rather than being accountable to the larger electorate. Presidential powers, then, served to further these clientelist interests by freeing congressmen from the burden of making policy. The 1968 reform expanded these powers (until the 1991 constitution constrained them). In the 1970s and 1980s, the president proposed nearly all substantive legislation, much of it under emergency powers, thus completely avoiding debates in Congress.[29]

In this context, the National Council on Economic and Social Policy (Conpes), which had the last word within the National Planning Department (DNP), operated as the president's advisory board. Central planning offices were created throughout Latin America in the late 1950s and early 1960s by recommendation of the UN Economic Commission for Latin America, as a tool for long-term development policy, and by the US Alliance for Progress, as a condition for aid reception. The 1968 constitutional reform that created Inderena also strengthened the Planning Department by giving it the responsibility of managing the central state's budget and overseeing the execution of the government's development plan.[30] Under President Carlos Lleras Restrepo (1968–72), the mastermind behind the reform, the Conpes started to meet weekly to 'consider and act upon policy papers prepared by the Planning Department', a tradition that 'lasted for almost 20 years and five administrations'.[31]

Aware of this institutional arrangement, Carrizosa, appointed head of Inderena in 1974, approached Miguel Urrutia, head of the Planning Department, to request funds. The two had already met, for Urrutia had been Carrisoza's professor in the master's programme in economics at the elite Universidad de los Andes. Urrutia made it a condition of granting funds that it be part of an investment proposal and even suggested that it could be centred on parks. Officials at Inderena's park office had already drafted a map with about 60 proposed protected areas. The Planning Department recommended prioritizing a smaller number using water as the main criteria for selection. In this manner, a team of three park officials, with the support of Carrizosa, Urrutia and the vice-minister of agriculture, agreed on the proposal to create 20 protected areas. After securing President López Michelsen's support, the proposal was presented to the Conpes in 1977. The decision did not come into effect through presidential decree, but through executive orders by the Ministry of Agriculture.

For this initiative to be successful, a few key gentlemen, especially the president, needed to believe in the desirability of national parks. In the initial months of his administration, President López Michelsen had been personally involved in drafting the Code of National Resources, and he considered the development of a national parks system as part of the Code's implementation.[32] He even went beyond endorsing the 1977 proposal by suggesting the inclusion of a place inhabited by flamingos in the Caribbean coast within the designated areas. Urrutia, the head of the Planning Department, also felt great affinity with the idea and proposed making parks the centre of Inderena's activities. When I asked Carrizosa why Urrutia cared about parks, he responded that '[Urrutia] was a very *cultured* fellow.'[33] Many of these elite men, who considered themselves well educated and cosmopolitan, shared the idea that parks were a characteristic of the modern world, which needed to be adequately implemented in the country. President Alberto Lleras Camargo (1958–62) is another example of such a gentleman; in a letter from 1960 he recalled visiting national parks in the United States and expressed his hope that Colombia might one day create them too:

> You are not mistaken that national parks stand out among my memories of traveling in the United States, and I feel that, despite the lack of precedent in Colombia, it is worth trying to awaken public consciousness in order to create some.[34]

In authoritarian regimes a few key players also proved crucial for the advancement of conservation policy. Within Brazil's 21-year dictatorship, park creation accelerated in 1979, when a new military president came to power and proved interested in the DN's proposals. Military brokers, who could navigate the regime, lobbied successfully, helping those civilians in charge of environmental policy. Admiral Belart, for example, had access to presidents and ministers and arranged decisive meetings; another admiral, Ibsen de Gusmão Câmara, befriended many conservationists and used his influence to promote a cause he made his own.[35]

Scientific backing and firsthand experience of the rapid changes occurring in the region help explain why influential men supported conservation initiatives.

Ecology legitimized conservation efforts: the identification of strategic ecosystems guided the DN's master plan in Brazil and was behind Inderena's map of protected areas.[36] The presence of Jorge Hernández, Inderena's leading biologist, at the 1977 Conpes meeting reinforces this point. Besides their faith in scientific knowledge, many of these men had seen cities grow and forests disappear, which made it easier for them to become convinced that nature protection was needed.

Gentleman's politics were at the core of park designation in Latin America and served to sidestep opposition. However, park designation was only a first step in the long process of building conservation units: executive orders had to be turned into realities. Tayrona National Park was formally created in 1964 and then built through fierce battles around occupation and tourism, which in part expressed the opposition that had been silenced before. These confrontations had many participants: the Park Service and other state agencies (which collaborated and also clashed with each other), plus settlers, landowners, journalists and politicians. Through their actions, all of them contributed to give concrete form to the abstract idea of a national park, and thus to build the nature state.

The struggle for territorial control in Tayrona National Park

'Paradise' is the most common word tourists writing on Tripadvisor.com use to refer to Tayrona National Park. Although some complain that it is no longer 'off the beaten track', that it can be uncomfortable, or that naked hippies dancing on the beach can spoil the experience, the words of a French visitor capture the general opinion: 'Spending a couple days in the middle of a humid tropical forest backed by the Sierra Nevada with white sand beaches and clear, warm waters is and will always be a unique and wonderful experience.' Tayrona comprises 12,000 hectares of land along the Caribbean, just east of the small city of Santa Marta, as well as 3,000 hectares of sea containing coral reefs. The park is known for its gorgeous bays surrounded by dry and humid tropical forests that creep up the foothills of the Sierra Nevada de Santa Marta, a massif towering to almost 6,000 metres. Pueblito, the archaeological ruins that stand two hours from the coast by a steep trail, add to its charm. The ancient Tayrona people who once inhabited the area give the park its name. Tourists may stay in the pricy five-star huts offered by the company that since 2005 holds a concession to provide services in the park. However, most visitors rent hammocks or use the camping grounds offered illegally by several small businesses. Fifty years have gone by since the creation of Colombia's most cherished national park and the Park Service has proved unable to control it: Besides prohibited facilities, the area has settlers and properties belonging to influential families from Santa Marta, plus a history tainted by drugs and paramilitaries.[37]

'Paper park', an expression often used to refer to conservation units that exist only in decrees, maps and government files, is too strong to describe Tayrona even if the Park Service has fallen well behind its own expectations of creating a place free of human dwellers under its tight control. In this respect, Tayrona hardly stands alone. In the early 1990s, 85.9 per cent of parks in South America had people living inside them – a situation that has probably not changed much. Park staff in many different countries have for long identified this issue as one of the main problems they face.[38] But Tayrona is atypical in that early on the state evicted most of the people living within it.[39] Paradoxically, dispossession made the park locally visible by significantly reducing the terrain's population and productive activities. Such a harsh policy stemmed from an idea – that parks are incompatible with human habitation – which gained much force in the late 1960s and clashed with the reality of a recently settled place.

Although the history of the designation of Tayrona National Park is rather murky, one thing is clear: no one consulted the peasants living there, nor the landowners, not even the municipality of Santa Marta, half of whose territory ended up as a *national* park. Tayrona is one of three parks created on the Caribbean coast near the city of Santa Marta in August 1964. At the time, rules for park establishment were vague. Law 2 of 1959 determined that the Ministry of Agriculture would designate national parks. However, it was the Institute for Agrarian Reform (Incora), an independent entity formed in 1961, that created these three Caribbean parks, based on its authority to establish 'reserves' in public lands for the conservation of natural resources. Incora worked in tandem with the CVM, which later became part of Inderena. Shortly after its establishment in 1960, the CVM emerged practically as the sole institution protecting natural resources in the country, particularly forests and fisheries, albeit only in its designated area. According to a key player in the formulation of agricultural policy in those days, the CVM found a 'powerful ally' in the first head of Incora, Enrique Peñalosa, 'a great conservationist'.[40] The CVM apparently found another powerful ally in Virgilio Barco, a prominent politician who between April 1963 and October 1964 acted as minister of agriculture, and two decades later became president of the republic (1986–90). Barco once said that the idea to create Tayrona National Park had been his, something that seems plausible given that he owned land north of the park and knew the area. Furthermore, as minister of agriculture he sat on the boards of both CVM and Incora, and was a personal friend of Peñalosa. So, in another example of gentleman's politics, Incora and CVM, with the support of the minister of agriculture, collaborated in the creation of the three parks.[41]

Tayrona was most likely included in the triad for being a stunning backwater. Fishermen from the small village of Taganga had been its most frequent users. Although in 1836 the most prosperous entrepreneur from Santa Marta bought over 1,000 hectares of land in what much later became the park – including Gairaca, Neguanje and Cinto bays – there is no evidence that he or his heirs ever made any use of this property before selling it in 1922.[42] Santa Marta historically lived off of commerce and to some extent agriculture. In the 1890s, coffee emerged as an important crop in the Sierra Nevada, inland from Santa Marta, and soon after bananas, grown in plains located to the south of the city, developed as the most significant regional crop. The area that became the park was too rugged for bananas and too low for coffee; but it was beautiful, so it could eventually attract visitors. But tourism in Santa Marta's surroundings was just taking off: as late as the mid-1950s, a neighbouring beach began to develop into the first local vacation spot.[43]

As Santa Marta discovered its tourism potential, the area to the east, which later became the park, was changing. One of the owners of the coffee haciendas in the Sierra opened a rough dirt road to connect another property of his that was located along the coast. That road served as an entry point for poor settlers and others with better means who cut down the forests to plant crops (see Figure 7.1). Meanwhile, a few influential families from Santa Marta started developing areas along the coast. Rafael Isidro Zúñiga, a member of one of these families, remembers that he began going to Cinto Bay in 1954 when he was seven, as his dad and uncle 'civilized' the land by planting grass and bringing in cattle. In a similar manner, the Sánchez Trujillo started works in Bahía Concha and the Valencia Piedrahita in Gayraca.[44] People from nearby villages such as Bonda, Mamatoco, and Taganga came to work in these properties, and to fish. Further east, in Cañaveral and Arrecifes, settlers from the interior of the country joined locals to open up lands. They subsisted by planting food crops such as manioc, yams and corn, and hunting agoutis and other animals, and they obtained cash by selling timber. A few of them worked tending coconut groves and cattle in the larger properties developed there.[45]

As was often the case in Colombia, the vast majority of these people did not have titles to the land. This situation might explain why the ordinance that created Tayrona explicitly presumed that the area was public land. Yet, more than describing a state of affairs, this assumption might be read as a prescription, for the ordinance also authorized Incora to buy or expropriate private properties within the park. Similarly, Law 2 of 1959 authorized the Ministry of Agriculture to expropriate land within areas designated as parks. The notion that parks should ideally be created in unsettled places dominated by nature, and still in the public realm, underlies these regulations, which also accommodated the possibility of forcing reality to fit the norm through purchase or expropriation. Even if these 'ideal' measures proved unfeasible, areas with crops and other uses were deliberately turned into parks as a way of arresting further development. As Carrizosa recently explained: 'Experience shows that declaring parks is urgent even if it is not possible to protect them immediately. Establishing legal protection prevents people and businesses who do not want to risk breaking the law from intruding.'[46]

In the first years of Tayrona's existence, the Park Service (initially housed within CVM and since 1968 within Inderena) devoted great efforts to creating a model protected area without residents or proprietors. In 1966, the CVM invited Kenton Miller, from FAO, to visit the three parks and propose management guidelines. Miller had two main suggestions for Tayrona. First, he recommended redrawing the park boundaries to exclude the fishing village of Taganga, as it was unfeasible to relocate it; Inderena followed this advice in 1969.[47] Second, he called for increased monitoring. The Park Service made 'control and vigilance' its motto and concentrated on trying to prevent activities that had become illegal. But, as Heliodoro Sánchez remembers, with just four of them supervising both Tayrona and Salamanca National Parks in 1968,

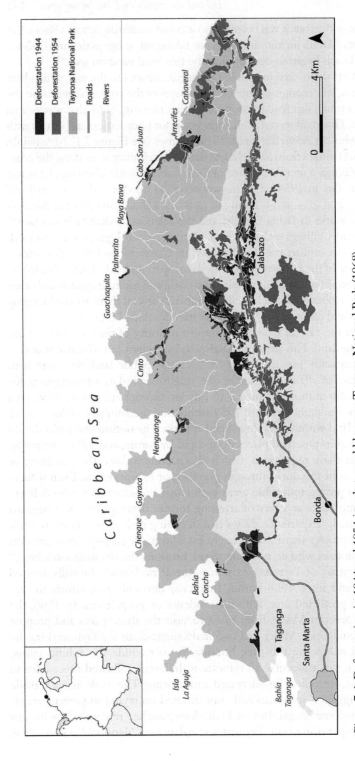

Figure 7.1 Deforestation in 1944 and 1954 in what would become Tayrona National Park (1968).

Note: not all the area depicted in the map was covered by the photographs, so deforestation outside of what became park is underestimated. I thank the IGAC for providing the photographs used to make this map.

Map by Christian Medina and Carlos Leopoldo Gómez, Cartography Lab, Universidad de los Andes, based on aerial photographs #2446–2451, flight M-27, 1954, Instituto Geográfico Agustín Codazzi, IGAC, and SNR–UAESPNN (2012), map p. 6.

results did not measure up to their expectations. By then, CVM had already decided to purchase all lands within the Park and had carried out a preliminary inventory of land use and land tenure.[48]

Between 1968 and 1970, two state agencies with headquarters in Bogota helped Inderena achieve the park ideal. The Geographical Institute carried out a detailed land registry; by July 1968, shortly before finishing, it had identified 70 units, seven of which had land titles. The institute appraised these few properties (since the last official appraisal was ten years old), as well as the many untitled farms it found.[49] That job served as a basis for Incora (the Agrarian Reform Institute) to buy settlers' crops and other improvements, for the land itself was not officially theirs. By early 1970, most people had sold and left, many against their will. A peasant from the area recalls that some people 'were given plots on the [southern] side of the road....While some were satisfied with the offer, others left empty handed.'[50] Most were probably not given the option of resettlement, since a year after their eviction some of the displaced told a reporter a different story:

> We lived off what we grew … and we also hunted. We did well, but then we were told that we had to leave Tayrona because it had been converted into a park.
>
> We told Inderena that we wouldn't leave. So they started harassing us: they burned our huts, destroyed our crops, confiscated our animals, and fined us … for planting new fields.
>
> Faced with that situation … we had no option but to sell our farms at ridiculous prices....They cheated us. ... We were promised land and credit … bullshit. ... Look at us: penniless and not knowing what to do.[51]

They also complained that unlike poor families who had been evicted, 'big landowners' were allowed to keep their properties. Aided by the confusion regarding land titles (manifest in the increasing number of properties), Inderena proved unable to return the parkland to the public domain. The owners' political clout, exemplified in the governor's plea to the president to find 'a fair solution' for them, must have contributed to this result.[52] In early 1970, Inderena's head informed that the possessions of about 200 small owners had been purchased, but not yet the lands of 23 larger owners, most of whom did not have proper titles. He announced that no private properties would remain within the park, and threatened to expropriate those who refused to sell.[53] However, more than two years later, 'the bigger properties … remained untouched'.[54] According to Inderena, by then 19 properties (a few of which apparently did not have appropriate legal backing) remained to be purchased.[55] But a map dating from that same year located 27 properties in the most valuable places of the park (see Figure 7.2).

Although settlers were expelled, the Park Service has been tormented by the multiplication of properties and residents ever since. The persistence of landowning allowed a few landless settlers to resist Inderena's policy. Medardo Ríos, for instance, who lives in Arrecifes, recently explained: 'I fell in love with

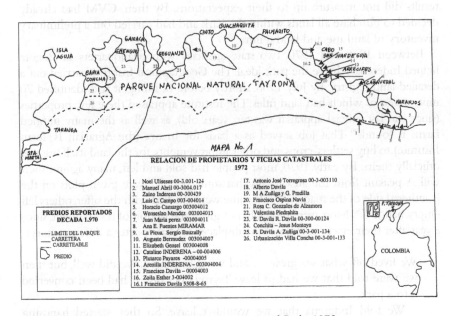

Figure 7.2 Private properties within Tayrona National Park, 1972.
Source: UAESPNN (1999), 'Parque Nacional Natural Tayrona. Situación de predios y tenencia', 7.

this place, so much that I am still here.' He worked in the coconut farms that were never bought out, and later in tourism. Little by little new settlers joined him and several people started selling food or offering lodgings for tourists. In 1986, given the persistence of properties and possessions in the park, Inderena requested another study that revealed the existence of 60 legal properties, which by 1999 had increased to 97 (see Figure 7.3).[56] The latest and most thorough study, from 2012, found that 18 properties covering an area of 3,395 hectares pre-dated the creation of the park. It also uncovered a series of legal anomalies that occurred after 1964: the state granted 11 properties totalling 329 hectares, while 172 land transactions occurred. One such case regards Antonio Torregrosa, who in 1970 refused to sell his farm, arguing that Incora's offer was too low.[57] For some years he used his land to raise pigs and, in 1991, sold it to a French man who built rustic cabins for foreign visitors. The 2012 report also described building permits, foreclosures and mortgages, all of which went against the law.[58]

The attempt to build a model park failed – but a park, however imperfect, was indeed created. Despite its shortfalls, Inderena eradicated cattle ranching and for the most part eliminated new plantings. The tractors that the Zúñiga family took with great pains to their farm in Cinto rotted for lack of use. In this manner, through the concerted efforts of no fewer than three agencies with headquarters in Bogotá, the nature state took concrete shape in Caribbean

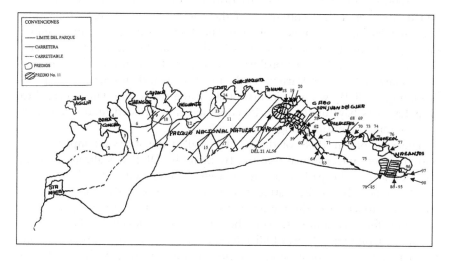

Figure 7.3 Private properties within Tayrona National Park, 1999.

Source: UAESPNN (1999), 'Parque Nacional Natural Tayrona. Situación de predios y tenencia', 11.

Colombia. But that limited success had a political cost. Although at the time agrarian reform was at its height, peasants did not secure access to land; instead, many were violently expelled and given token sums for the product of their labour. Owners fared better, but to this day they complain that the park's limits were drawn in such a way as to exclude the lands of influential bogotanos, located further east.[59] The municipality lamented having lost control of half its territory precisely when, as we will see, tourism prospects started to look good. Thus, in the eyes of peasants, local elites and the municipal administration, the central state violated local rights, so its legitimacy was eroded rather than enhanced. This tension built on a historical chasm between the Caribbean coast and a central state nested 800 km inland and 2,600 metres above sea level, in the Andean highlands.[60]

Since they could not do much with their properties, owners of land within the park kept their hopes up as the National Tourism Corporation (CNT) devised a plan for Tayrona's bays. In 1971, it proposed building hotels and cabins with 5,600 rooms and 10,180 beds, besides commercial areas, parking lots and recreation and sports facilities totalling 780 hectares.[61] But those plans generated a bitter public dispute through which Colombians elsewhere in the country began to regard the park as theirs.

A *national* park

The defeat of the project for upscale international tourism in Tayrona's beaches provides a more positive assessment of the accomplishments of park policy in the 1970s. President Misael Pastrana Borrero (1970–4) backed this initiative, which constituted the centrepiece of the state's attempt to make tourism a key force driving national development. The dispute that ensued pitted central state agencies and politicians against each other, while business interests backed the tourism plan and the national press opposed it. In the midst of the controversy, many Colombians learned for the first time that their country had parks belonging to all. By winning its first public battle the nature state managed to keep Tayrona's bays under its jurisdiction and thus avoided luxury buildings from tainting the breathtaking natural landscape.

The creation, in 1968, of the CNT signalled the state's attempt to seriously promote international tourism. By then, the DNP was already looking into developing the park as a way of strengthening Santa Marta's economy. A 1968 report began by stating that Tayrona National Park 'is the greatest tourist attraction in the region' and concluded that it was the area where '"stations" for international tourism should be first developed'.[62] CNT's predecessor, the Colombian Tourist Office (created in 1957), received proposals from national and international businesses interested in investing in the Caribbean coast: 61 per cent of the total value of such proposals corresponded to projects for Concha, Cinto and Arrecifes, some of the most beautiful spots within the park.[63] These early schemes became a full-blown plan when CNT hired Arthur D. Little, a famous consulting firm from Massachusetts, to work with a Colombian firm to draft a plan for tourist development in the Caribbean. In 1971, the firms produced a general proposal as well as a specific one for Tayrona National Park with the numerous rooms and beds mentioned above. The plan involved heavy state investment in roads, as well as water and sewage infrastructure, while private investors would develop the hotels and other tourist facilities under a concession. The CNT agreed with Inderena on the need to purchase private properties along the beachfront, but it wanted control of that narrow strip, which meant removing it from the Park. Inderena would be left in charge of the forests.[64] In March 1972, the DNP, the ministers of development and treasury and the CNT drafted a policy paper urging the government to proceed with the plan.[65]

In the meantime, Inderena – which had been left out of those discussions – produced a document, also published in March 1972, stating its opposition to the tourism plan.[66] Like all parties involved, Inderena was well aware of the bay's beauty and also wanted to attract visitors, a goal that appeared as 'recreation' in its plans. But this meant something completely different to what the CNT had in mind: rather than five-star hotels for foreigners, Inderena sought camping grounds largely for Colombian tourists. In his management guidelines for the park, Miller designated specific sites where picnic tables and camping spots should be built, and suggested that the existing cabins in Bahía Concha be allowed to function or be purchased to continue their use.[67] In 1971, an article in the leading national paper shared this general view, affirming that the park 'offers beautiful beaches that will be accessible to the public once the government builds roads and cabins, which will turn this place into the excursion center for all Colombians at moderate prices'.[68]

In May 1972, the dispute made the headlines. At a press conference the CNT stated that it had reached an agreement with Inderena to carry out the tourism plan, which Inderena denied emphatically.[69] Such an agreement seemed implausible after Inderena's heartfelt report from just two months prior. 'Tayrona National Park', read the report, 'constitutes one of the most sparkling gems in the crown of achievements ... of the arduous but exciting task that has been entrusted to Inderena.' The institute's highest officials argued that carrying out the plan would be tantamount to killing the goose that laid the golden eggs: paradise had to be protected to assure Santa Marta's future development, but most of all because it was a *national patrimony*. The report ended by calling for a coherent policy of natural resource protection.[70]

As the report shows, the self-styled defenders of the park used nationalist rhetoric to advance their arguments. Such was the case of Daniel Samper Pizano, a well-known journalist from the capital city, who expressed his position in the following manner:

> To whom does this unique natural treasure ... belong? To all Colombians, without exceptions of any kind. Who represents Colombians? The government. What does the government plan to do with this national property? Enclose it for the benefit of the grey-haired foreign tourists who will invade us as parrots from another world.[71]

By contrast, Santa Marta's newspaper – *El Informador* – acutely aware of the commercial possibilities at stake, criticized its peers from Bogotá: 'In a suspicious manner, the capital's press is echoing Inderena's vacuous and romantic, as well as unfounded concepts, which for us represents a serious abuse that we must vehemently reject.' It concluded: 'We will not allow [the tourist plan] to become, from one day to the next, a pipe dream simply due to the whim of an Inderena official.'[72]

Shortly after tourism in Tayrona was discussed in the national and regional press, Alegría Fonseca travelled to Stockholm to represent the Colombian Congress in the UN Conference on the Human Environment. This experience contributed to her determination to lead a debate in Congress, forcing politicians to publicly discuss for the first time an environmental issue even without having any decision power over the matter. Since she knew nothing about parks, she travelled several times to Tayrona and worked closely with Inderena's top officials. The debate developed in 1973 over several weeks.[73] Opponents to the plan secured backing from Prince Bernhard of the Netherlands, who, along with national environmentalists, activated his networks. As a result, renowned environmental NGOs, such as the WWF and the Sierra Club, as well as Colombian universities, sent letters disapproving of the project; Fonseca read them out loud to surprised members of Congress. 'Nobody knew anything', she told me, 'I was alone.'[74]

The debate produced a pronouncement from Congress (won by just one vote), which read: 'Tayrona National Park should be preserved and development of hotels prohibited.' However, the president did not receive the Congressional delegation that requested an appointment to deliver the recommendation. Furthermore, even though Inderena asked the government to reconsider the plan, it received instead a request to define the area to be given to the CNT. But within the government, support for the plan was not unanimous: the minister of agriculture threatened to resign and more than one head of DNP sided with Inderena. This opposition might have helped to deter supporters of the plan, but in any case it needed funding and they next targeted the banks. They sent copies of the debate in Congress to the Interamerican Development Bank (IDB), which had shown interest in financing the project. The IDB sent an auditor, and the Plan's prospects worsened. A change in government ended the controversy: President Alfonso López Michelsen decided to leave the Park undamaged.[75]

In 1974, Inderena built 70 camping spots in Cañaveral, along with bathroom and picnic facilities, fulfilling its vision of recreation in Tayrona National Park. It also continued erecting institutional facilities: the first two cabins had been built in 1969; six others followed, along with a lab, lodging for park rangers and administrative units, which made Inderena's physical presence more visible.[76] Tourism increased: in 1977 the park received 76,325 visitors, and 120,000 the following year.[77] The controversy made the park known and enticed people from several parts of Colombia to visit Tayrona.

Forests and at least one lone jaguar

Colombian academics have emphasized the absence of the state in many corners of the national territory (as a way of explaining how guerrillas and other illegal groups have secured spaces under their control).[78] Visiting Tayrona could lead to the same line of thought, for park rangers are rarely seen and no headquarters exist where visitors can find information and feel the presence of the state. Furthermore, as the Park Service failed to effectively manage the area, illegal services have sprouted along the beaches. Yet the impression of a place where the state has only had a marginal influence is deceiving. The nature state is powerfully and pervasively manifest here in the forests that dominate the park, and this imposing vegetation, with all the creatures that inhabit it, constitute the clearest result of the environmental policy that has shaped this corner of the country. That the forest has become such an obvious part of the park, one taken for granted, attests to the success of the Park Service.

In 2012, the image of a jaguar was captured by a camera trap. This imposing top predator of the Tropics can roam the forests of Tayrona thanks to a long process that involved a regime that gave much power to the president and encouraged a few *gentlemen* to decide behind the scenes the fate of certain tracts of land deemed naturally gifted.[79] That lone jaguar also symbolizes the conflicts that took place out in the open: forcible eviction and crop burning, congressional debate and the confrontations between state agencies that made the headlines. Tayrona, a territorial expression of the nature state in Caribbean Colombia, contributed to the breach between centre and region by alienating elites and peasants from Santa Marta and its surroundings. But as Tayrona gained status as a national symbol, the nature state acquired legitimacy for 'saving it' on behalf of the peoples of the Colombian nation and the international community.

Notes

1 Departamento Nacional de Planeación, DNP, 'Programa de Parques Nacionales Naturales', Documento CONPES 1408 (14 January 1977); interview with Julio Carrizosa, Bogotá, 13 April 2013.
2 See Matthew Kelly, Claudia Leal, Emily Wakild, and Wilko Graf von Hardenberg's Introduction to this volume.
3 Philip Abrams, 'Notes on the Difficulty of Studying the State (1977)' and Aradhana Sharma and Akhil Gupta, 'Introduction: Rethinking Theories of the State in an Age of Globalization', both in *The Anthropology of the State: A Reader*, ed. by Aradhana Sharma and Akhil Gupta (Oxford, 2006).
4 Gary B. Wetterberg, 'La historia y estado actual de los parques nacionales suramericanos y una evaluación de seleccionadas opciones de manejo' (unpublished PhD dissertation, University of Washington, 1974); Eugenia Scarzanella, 'Las bellezas naturales y la Nación: los Parques Nacionales en la Argentina en la primera mitad del siglo XX', *European Review of Latin American and Carribean Studies*, 73 (2002), 5–21; Emily Wakild, *Revolutionary Parks: Conservation, Social Justice, and Mexico's National Parks, 1910–1940* (Tucson, AZ, 2011); Frederico Freitas, 'A Park for the Borderlands: The Creation of the Iguaçu National Park in Southern Brazil, 1880–1940', *HIb: Revista de Historia Iberoamericana*, 7/2 (2014), 65–88.
5 Mary L. Barker, 'National Parks, Conservation, and Agrarian Reform in Peru', *Geographical Review*, 70/1 (1980), 1–18.
6 Sterling Evans, *The Green Republic: A Conservation History of Costa Rica* (Austin, TX, 1999).
7 Teresa Urban, *Saudade do Matão: Relembrando a Historia da Conservação da natureza no Brasil* (Curitiba, 2011 [1998]).
8 Seth Garfield, 'A Nationalist Environment: Indians, Nature, and the Construction of the Xingu National Park in Brazil', *Luso-Brazilian Review*, 41/1 (2004), 139–67.
9 Rosemary Thorp, *Progress, Poverty and Exclusion: An Economic History of Latin America in the 20th Century* (Baltimore, MD, 1998).
10 Fernando Uricoechea, *Estado y burocracia en Colombia, historia y organización* (Bogotá, 1986).
11 Jonathan Hartlyn, *The Politics of Coalition Rule in Colombia* (Cambridge, 1988).
12 Manuel Rodríguez Becerra, 'Ecología y medio ambiente', in *Nueva Historia de Colombia, Vol. IX: Ecología y Cultura*, ed. by Alvaro Tirado Mejía (Bogotá, 1998); Armando Samper Gnecco, 'Organización del sector agropecuario: El caso de Colombia', in *Panel sobre la organización y administración para el desarrollo agropecuario en América Latina, September 2–7, 1968* (Turrialba, 1968).

13 Decree 133 of 1976; interview with Julio Carrizosa; Julio Carrizosa Umaña, 'El Inderena, 1974–1978', *Revista Javeriana*, 89/444 (1978), 317–32.

14 Urban, *Saudade do Matão*; José Augusto Drummond, 'From Randomness to Planning: The 1979 Plan for Brazilian National Parks', in *National Parks Beyond the Nation: Global Perspectives on 'America's Best Idea'*, ed. by Adrian Howkins, Jared Orsi and Mark Fiege (Norman, OK, 2016).

15 Manuel Rodríguez Becerra, 'El Código de los Recursos Naturales Renovables y del Medio Ambiente: el conservacionismo utilitarista y el ambientalismo', in *Evaluación y perspectivas del Código Nacional de Recursos Naturales de Colombia en sus 30 años de vigencia* (Bogotá, 2004).

16 José Augusto Pádua, 'Environmentalism in Brazil: An Historical Perspective', in *A Companion to Global Environmental History*, ed. by John R. McNeill and Erin Stewart Mauldin (Oxford, 2012).

17 Alexander B. Adams (ed.), *First World Conference on National Parks: Seattle, Washington, June 30–July 7, 1962* (Washington, DC, 1962).

18 CLAPN Bulletins, Federico Carlos Lehmann's Archive, Instituto para la Investigación y la Preservación del Patrimonio Cultural y Natural del Valle del Cauca, Inciva, Cali.

19 Hugh Elliot (ed.), *Second World Conference on National Parks: Yellowstone and Grand Teton National Parks, U.S.A. September 18–27 1972* (Morges, 1974).

20 Evans, *The Green Republic*; Instituto Interamericano de Cooperación para la Agricultura (IICA) Zona Sur, 'Informe Final. Segunda reunión de la Comisión Asesora de Educación, Montevideo, 24–25 de julio 1969'; interview with Heliodoro Sánchez, Bogotá, 1 May 2013. See Terence Young and Lary M. Dilsaver, 'Collecting and Diffusing "the World's Best Thought": International Cooperation by the National Park Service', *The George Wright Forum*, 28/3 (2011), 269–78 for an initial exploration of the US National Park Service's Division of International Affairs, created in 1961.

21 Rodríguez Becerra, 'Ecología y medio ambiente'.

22 John J. Moseley, Kyran D. Thelen and Kenton R. Miller, 'Planificación de Parques Nacionales, guía para la preparación de planes de manejo para parques nacionales', *Documento Técnico de Trabajo* 15, FAO (1974).

23 Urban, *Saudade do Matão*.

24 Wetterberg, 'La historia y estado actual de los parques'; Evans, *The Green Republic*; interview with Heliodoro Sánchez.

25 Dan Brockington, Rosaleen Duffy and Jim Igoe, *Nature Unbound: Conservation, Capitalism and the Future of Protected Areas* (London, 2008).

26 Rafael Elizalde Mac-Clure, *La sobrevivencia de Chile: La conservación de sus recursos naturales renovables* (Santiago de Chile, 1970), 484–9.

27 José Antonio Cheibub, Zachary Elkins and Tom Ginsburg, 'Latin American Presidentialism in Comparative and Historical Perspective', *University of Chicago Public Law and Legal Theory Working Paper* 36 (2011), 3.

28 Francisco Leal Buitrago, *Estado y política en Colombia* (Bogotá, 1984).

29 Ronald P. Archer and Matthew Soberg Shugart, 'The Unrealized Potential of Presidential Dominance in Colombia', in *Presidentialism and Democracy in Latin America*, ed. by Scott Mainwaring and Matthew Soberg Shugart (Cambridge, 1997).

30 Luis Bernardo Mejía, 'The Changing Role of the Central Planning Offices in Latin America: A Comparative Historical Analysis Perspective, 1950–2013' (unpublished PhD dissertation, Maastricht University, 2014).

31 Miguel Urrutia, 'The Changing Nature of Economic Planning in Colombia', in *Development Planning in Mixed Economies*, ed. by Miguel Urrutia and Setsuko Yukawa (Tokyo, 1988), 170.

32 Manuel Rodríguez, personal communication, 30 April 2014.

33 Interview with Julio Carrizosa.

34 Letter from Alberto Lleras, president of Colombia, to Karl C. Parrish, Jr, 20 January 1960. Box 40, Lauchlin Currie Papers, 1931–94, and undated (bulk 1950–90), David M. Rubinstein Rare Book and Manuscript Library, Duke University. I thank Alejandro Camargo for bringing this document to my attention.

35 Urban, *Saudade do Matão*, 279.

36 Ronald A. Foresta, *Amazon Conservation in the Age of Development: The Limits of Providence* (Gainsville, FL, 1991); Timothy J. Farnhamn, *Saving Nature's Legacy: Origins of the Idea of Biological Diversity* (New Haven, CT, 2007).

37 I will not address in this paper how Tayrona's history is enmeshed with Colombia's armed conflict because it belongs to a later period that started timidly in the late 1970s.

38 Stephen Amend and Thora Amend (eds), *¿Espacios sin habitantes? Parques Nacionales de América del Sur* (Caracas, 1992); Wetterberg, 'La historia y estado actual de los parques'.

39 Although dispossession has not been the rule in the building of Latin American parks, Tayrona is by no means the only case. In his chapter in this book, Freitas informs of the removal of 2,500 settlers from Iguazu National Park in Brazil. Similarly, in the 1940s, people living within the recently created national reserve Payaca-Samiria in the Peruvian Amazon were relocated. Richard Bodmer and Pablo Huertas, 'Impacts of Displacement in the Pacaya-Samiria National Reserve, Peru', in *Protected Areas and Human Displacement: A Conservation Perspective*, ed. by Kent Redford and Eva Fern, Wildlife Conservation Society Working Paper (New York, 2007).

40 Samper Gnecco, 'Organización del sector agropecuario'.

41 Resolución 191, 1964, Incora. Tayrona was initially called Santa Marta and Sierra Nevada was called Los Tayronas. Interviews with Julio Carrizosa and with Carlos Lleras de la Fuente, Bogotá, 20 May 2014.

42 Joaquín Viloria de la Hoz, 'Empresarios de Santa Marta: el caso de Joaquín y Manuel Julian de Mier, 1800–1896', *Cuadernos de Historia Económica y Empresarial* 7 (2000); Superintendencia de Notariado y Registro (SNR) and Unidad Administrativa Especial del Sistema de Parques Nacionales Naturales (UAESPNN), 'Situación jurídica actual del Parque Nacional Natural Tayrona (Propiedad, tenencia y ocupación)' (Bogotá, January 2012).

43 Joaquín Viloria de la Hoz, 'Café Caribe: La economía cafetera en la Sierra Nevada de Santa Marta', *Documentos de Trabajo sobre Economía Regional* 1 (1997); Catherine C. LeGrand, 'Living in Macondo: Economy and Culture in a United Fruit Company Banana Enclave in Colombia', in *Close Encounters of Empire: Writing the Cultural History of U.S.–Latin American Relations*, ed. by Gilbert M. Joseph, Catherine C. LeGrand and Ricardo D. Salvatore (Durham, NC, 1998); Corporación Nacional de Turismo, 'Proyecto de utilización turística de las costas del Parque Tayrona: Zonificación, modelos y componentes físicos. Estudio turístico de la Costa Atlántica y de las islas de San Andrés y Providencia' (Bogotá, November 1971).

44 Interview with Rafael Isidro Zúñiga, Santa Marta, 15 July 2013.

45 Fabio Silva Vallejo and Deybis Carrasquilla, 'Rescate de la memoria histórica del PNN Tayrona: Santa Marta-Colombia', in *Gestión del Conocimiento Tradicional:*

Experiencias desde la Red GESTC (Bogotá, 2008); interview with Medardo Ríos (name changed to protect the interviewee's identity), Arrecifes, Tayrona National Park, 17 June 2013.

46 Angélica María Cuevas Guarnizo, 'Es hora de que en Colombia se funden nuevas ciudades', interview with Julio Carrizosa, *El Espectador*, 2 January 2014, 20.

47 Acuerdo 04, 1969, Inderena, and Resolución 292, 1969, Ministry of Agriculture.

48 Kenton R. Miller, 'Estrategia general para un programa de manejo de parques nacionales en el norte de Colombia', Instituto Interamericano de Ciencias Agrícolas de la OEA, Informe de Consulta 55 (Turrialba, May 1968); Habitar Ltda. et al., 'Proyecto de utilización turística'; Silva and Carrasquilla, 'Rescate de la memoria histórica'; interview with Heliodoro Sánchez.

49 Departamento Nacional de Planeación (DNP), 'Desarrollo turístico en el Parque Natural Nacional de Santa Marta', Documento CONPES 122 (8 August 1968).

50 Interview with Luis Eduardo Ibarra, Calabazo, 22 February 2013; 'Expropiarán tierras del Parque de los Tayronas', *El Tiempo*, 12 February 1970; One Redni, 'Tayrona: valiosa reserva natural', *El Tiempo*, 18 October 1968.

51 Guillermo Martínez, 'Pliego de cargos', *El Espectador*, 27 December 1970.

52 *El Informador*, 30 January 1971.

53 Ibid.

54 Eduardo Vargas Jiménez, '¿Bombardearon el Tayrona?', *El Tiempo*, 21 May 1972.

55 Fernando Ruan Ruan and Simón Max Franky, 'El Parque Tayrona para Colombia' (Bogotá, March 1972).

56 UAESPNN, 'Parque Nacional Natural Tayrona. Situación de predios y tenencia' (Bogotá, January 1999).

57 Martínez, 'Pliego de cargos'. See Palmarito in Figure 7.2.

58 SNR and UAESPNN, 'Situación jurídica actual'.

59 Interview with Rafael Isidro Zúñiga.

60 Eduardo Posada Carbó, 'La Liga costeña de 1919, una expresión de poder regional', *Boletín Cultural y Bibliográfico*, 22/3 (1985), 34–46.

61 Corporación Nacional de Turismo, 'Proyecto de utilización turística'.

62 DNP, 'Desarrollo turístico en el Parque Natural Nacional de Santa Marta', 6, 15.

63 Ibid.

64 Corporación Nacional de Turismo, 'Proyecto de utilización turística'; DNP and CNT, 'Recomendaciones al Consejo Nacional de Política Económica y Social sobre la formulación del Plan de Acción para el Desarrollo Turístico de la Costa Atlántica y el Archipiélago de San Andrés y Providencia', Documento CONPES 856 (17 March 1972); Vargas Jiménez, '¿Bombardearon el Tayrona?'

65 DNP and CNT, 'Recomendaciones al Consejo'.

66 Carrizosa Umaña, 'El Inderena, 1974–1978'.

67 Miller, 'Estrategia general para un programa de manejo'.

68 'El maravilloso Parque Tayrona', *El Tiempo*, 19 June 1971.

69 '"Se construirán hoteles en el Tayrona": Corturismo', *El Tiempo*, 26 May 1972; letters by Nicolás de Castillo, head of the CNT, and Daniel Samper Pizano, journalist, in 'Correo de El Tiempo', *El Tiempo*, 27 May 1972.

70 Ruan and Franky, 'El Parque Tayrona para Colombia', 31.

71 Daniel Samper Pizano, 'Un parque a dos aguas', *El Tiempo*, 27 May 1972.

72 *El Informador*, 30 May 1972.

73 *Anales del Congreso* 6 March 1973, 6 September 1973 and 12 September 1973.

74 Interview with Alegría Fonseca, Bogotá, 10 April 2014; Rodríguez Becerra, 'Ecología y medio ambiente'.

75 Carrizosa Umaña, 'El Inderena, 1974–1978'; interview with Alegría Fonseca; Rodríguez Becerra, 'Ecología y medio ambiente.'

76 Jesús Eugenio Henao Sarmiento, 'Parque Nacional Natural Tayrona: Infraestructura' (1981).

77 Fernando Irusta, 'Plan maestro del Parque Nacional Tayrona: propuesta técnica' (1979).

78 Comisión de Estudios sobre la Violencia, *Colombia, Violencia y Democracia: informe presentado al Ministerio de Gobierno* (Bogotá, 1987); Daniel Pécaut, 'Una lucha armada al servicio del statu quo social y político', in Comisión Histórica del Conflicto y sus Víctimas, *Contribución al entendimiento del conflicto armado en Colombia* (La Habana, 2015).

79 Parque Nacional Natural Tayrona and ProCAT Colombia, 'Monitoreo y creación de capacidades para la protección y manejo del Parque Nacional Natural Tayrona: Enfoque en mamíferos como herramienta de planificación' (Santa Marta, October 2012).

8 Ordering the borderland

Settlement and removal in the Iguaçu National Park, Brazil, 1940s–1970s

*Frederico Freitas**

Introduction

As the most-visited non-urban national park in Brazil, the Iguaçu National Park stands as a prime example of the role of the nature state in controlling, managing and producing nature. In 1939, the Brazilian government gazetted the park, the second in the country, as a response to the creation in 1934 of the similarly named, but completely independent, Iguazú National Park across the border in Argentina.[1] Initially, the goal of the Iguaçu National Park was to secure access to the Brazilian side of the monumental Iguazu Falls shared with Argentina, but in 1944 the area of the park was extended from 5,000 to over 160,000 hectares to protect an extensive area of subtropical Atlantic Forest. The subsequent processes of settlement, claims-making and conflict reveal how a sporadic approach to national park policy gave way to a vision that paired state conservation with federal initiatives designed to resolve broader agrarian conflicts.

In its beginnings in the 1930s, the park was part of a heavily forested border area whose low population density stemmed from a history of military conflicts and bonded labour that had pushed away many of its indigenous inhabitants. The opening of a highway in 1953 connected this borderland to Brazil's populated eastern and southern cores, attracting white Brazilian settlers in search of cheap land. Third- and fourth-generation German- and Italian-Brazilians, the sons and daughters of small proprietors trying their luck in a logging and agricultural frontier, comprised the bulk of the arriving population. Most farmers settled in the surrounding area of the park, felling trees and opening crop fields. However, uncertainty in public land tenure and disputes between federal and state governments allowed many of these migrants to settle inside the Iguaçu National Park, just 20 years after its establishment.

The first families of settlers arrived in the São José and Santo Alberto sections of the Iguaçu National Park in Brazil in the late 1950s, but the bulk of families moved into the area in the 1960s (see Figure 8.1, showing the settled area in

* Research for this chapter was funded through the Graduate Research Opportunity Funds from the School of Humanities and Sciences at Stanford University and the Albert J. Beveridge Grant from the American Historical Association.

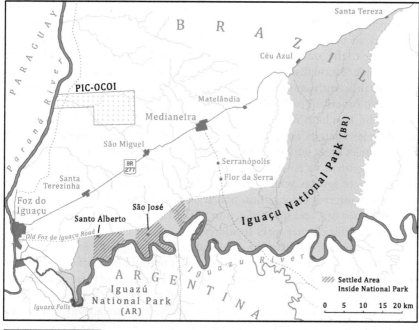

Figure 8.1 Iguacu National Park, Paraná, Brazil *c.*1970.

Sources: INCRA, 'Parque Nacional do Iguaçu', GIS Shapefiles (Curitiba, Paraná: INCRA-PR, 2010), INCRA-Curitiba; INCRA, 'Planta da Gleba de Mil Alqueires Colonia Silva Jardim', map, *c.*1970, PIC-OCOI files, INCRA-Cascavel; INCRA, 'Planta Silva Jardim', map, *c.*1970, PIC-OCOI files, INCRA-Cascavel; INCRA, 'Planta Santa Maria', map, *c.*1970, PIC-OCOI files, INCRA-Cascavel; INCRA, 'Planta Vila São José', map, *c.*1970, PIC-OCOI files, INCRA-Cascavel; IBRA, 'Parque Nacional do Iguaçu: Mapa de Situação', map, 1968, PIC-OCOI files, INCRA-Cascavel; SIB, Administración de Parques Nacionales, 'Limite del Parque Nacional Iguazú', GIS shape-file (Buenos Aires, 2013); Brazil, Serviço Geográfico do Exército, 'Foz do Iguaçu, SG-21-X-D', map (Brasília, 1980); Guaraniaçu, SG-22-VC, map (Brasília, 1980).

1970). By 1978, however, all but one family had been removed from the park by the Brazilian military government – the country was under military rule from 1964 to 1985. The mass relocation of settlers from a national park was a novelty in Brazil's environmental policy. Prior to the 1970s, the federal government had only removed a handful of proprietors and squatters in other national parks, and overlapping claims of land ownership and lack of enforcement were the norm in protected areas. This was all true for the Iguaçu National Park, and yet no other park in the 1970s presented such a challenge for land regularization as Iguaçu, due to the great number of settlers involved – the removal affected over 2,500 people. Notwithstanding the complications, the Brazilian state decided to engage in a costly and protracted process of eviction that had no parallel in other Latin American parks of the time.

How did hundreds of Brazilian farmers manage to settle inside a national park decades after its creation? Why did the Brazilian state undertake such efforts to evict these settlers? What caused the departure from previous neglect to an engagement in environmental policy implementation in Iguaçu? How can the case of Iguaçu, with its initial lack of federal control over public land and existing internal colonization policies, bring light to the conditions, institutional framework, and space of action of the Brazilian nature state? These are the questions this chapter seeks to address.

The exclusion of dwellers from national parks, although not initially codified in Brazilian law, was a staple of the discourse of national park officials since the establishment of the first parks in the 1930s. The legal basis of these designations was the forest code of 1934, which did not offer a clear definition of Brazil's putative national parks, but prohibited 'the exercise of any activity against the flora and fauna of the parks'. A revision of the code in 1965 rephrased the prohibition in terms of a ban on 'natural resource exploitation' inside national parks, but both pieces of legislation were silent regarding the presence of dwellers and the tenure of land by individuals inside national parks. The codes' brief definitions of the prohibited activities inside national parks were too vague. They allowed room, for example, for understanding subsistence agriculture in zones already modified by human activity as not being against the law. In sum, prior to the 1970s the Brazilian environmental legislation defined the state as the warden of the country's natural endowment, especially inside national parks, but had little to offer in terms of provisions on key issues like dwelling, land ownership and subsistence activities inside parks.[2] Yet, to many inside the state, it was clear that inhabitants should be excluded from existing or future parks and for years park directors in Iguaçu pressured the Forest Service to solve the problem of migrants settling inside the park. It was decades before the federal government addressed the issue, and then action stemmed from the alignment of national park policy with a new federal initiative devised to solve the agrarian problem in Brazil at large.

Like many other national parks in Latin America, Iguaçu presented a problem of uncertainty of land rights, and the occupation of the park demonstrates how the lack of control over public land can undermine the conservation mandate of a central state. *Grilagem*, the appropriation of public land through forged property titles, is a recurrent feature in Brazilian history and the source of many of the country's agrarian problems. In the case of Iguaçu, shady land agents took advantage of a dispute between federal and state governments over the ownership of the park's public land to forge land titles and sell parcels to incoming settlers. Ultimately, lack of federal oversight of public land made possible the settlement of sections of the park, and the removal and relocation of settlers in Iguaçu only occurred after federal officials reframed nature protection as part of the land conflict that plagued the Brazilian countryside. Since the Contestado War (1912–16), Western Paraná, where the park is located, had been a hotspot of violent land disputes that conflated legal insecurity with the excessive power of local potentates and the weak presence of the national state. In addition to that, the park, located along Brazil's international border with its main regional rival, Argentina, was considered part of a national security area. Thus, it was through the logic of territorial control that the proponents of settler removal engaged the resources and the sheer force of the state in solving the problem of settlers living inside Iguaçu.

After the creation of Brazil's first national park in 1937, conservation policy in the country was characterized by bursts of intense activity punctuating long interregnums of withdrawal. The eviction of settlers in the early 1970s, however, inaugurated a more concerted and sustained federal conservation strategy. A few years later a group of conservationists with good traction among the military would create several new national parks in the Brazilian Amazon and establish an integrated Brazilian national park system.[3] In Iguaçu, government officials managed to combine new policies of social and landscape reconfiguration (i.e. agrarian reform through colonization) with a federal mandate of nature conservation. The eviction of settlers from the Iguaçu National Park, therefore, evinces the way in which the Brazilian nature state's task of saving nature from its citizens was aligned with authoritarian policies of land reform pursued by the military dictatorship. Moreover, the institutionalization of the park system in the years that followed suggests the evictions helped catalyse a nature state mandate as a component of the expanded government powers introduced during the Brazilian military regime.

Whose public land?

The Brazilian government established the Iguaçu National Park in 1939 on lands donated by the government of the State of Paraná and located on the Brazilian banks of the Iguazu Falls.[4] From 1939 to 1944 the park was restricted to the 5,000-hectare area donated by the state government, but in 1944 the federal government decided to incorporate new land into the park, resulting in a 30-fold increase. The land used in the park expansion was granted by the Brazilian empire in 1889 to a railroad company as part of a concession for the building of new rail lines in southern Brazil. The railroads were never built, but the inheritor company, *Companhia Estrada de Ferro São Paulo-Rio Grande* (CEFSPRG), kept the lands until the company was nationalized by the regime of Getúlio Vargas in 1940. With the expropriation of the railroad company, officials at the National Park Section of the Brazilian Forest Service seized the opportunity to use a few of the renationalized land tracts to expand the park area and protect the groves of Brazilian pine (*Araucaria angustifolia*) located in the hills adjacent to the park. Both Octavio Silveira Mello, head of the National Park Section, and Mario Câmara Canto, the first director of the Iguaçu National Park, saw the incorporation into the park of the new public lands as a way of expanding its territory without incurring the expenses of compensating previous owners for the value of the land.[5]

Contrary to the plans of Canto and Mello, adding these new lands to the park proved to be a convoluted and protracted process. The land tracts incorporated by federal decree into the park in 1944 were already claimed by the State of Paraná, which had demarcated and transferred the lands to CEFSPRG in the 1920s. As the railroad was never built and the inheritor company nationalized, the land grants were set to return to the public domain. However, nationalization generated disputes over which governmental sphere was the legitimate owner of the land. State officials believed the railroad land grants had originated in lands owned by the State of Paraná, as after the Republican Constitution of 1891 all public land passed from the hands of the central government to the states' control. The federal government, on the other hand, claimed the original contract granting the lands to the railroad companies was signed before the transfer of the country's public lands to the states in 1891, which meant they were part of the nationalized assets to be assimilated by the federal government in 1940.[6]

After the fall of Getúlio Vargas in 1945, a legal dispute over the ownership of the railroad land put the government of the State of Paraná, where the park was located, in conflict with the Brazilian federal government. The land tracts in question included not only the area used for the expansion of the Iguaçu National Park, but also much of the land in the western half of the state. These were areas of recent colonization, ripe with grilagem and agrarian conflict where the federal government had consistently failed to impose a territorial order owing to the behind-the-scenes manoeuvring of local politicians, colonization companies and local land notaries.[7] The matter of the ownership of the railroad land was legally settled by a Brazilian Supreme Court ruling in 1963 in favour of the federal government. Debates within the state saw park officials at Iguaçu wait until 1970 for the federal government to initiate the process of eviction of the settlers living inside park boundaries.[8]

State-sponsored grilagem

Uncertainty in public land tenure persisted to the mid-1960s and created the conditions for the systematic grilagem that characterized the region where the Iguaçu National Park was located. In the 1950s, the political class in the State of Paraná was steeped in land speculation and grilagem, influencing the state government to illegally title public land to partners in the local business class. Others, encouraged by the state government's reckless behaviour, would sell land parcels as if they were twice or three times their actual size to absentee speculators from São Paulo or Curitiba. Many parcels already had one or two previous titles conveniently ignored by the state government or local land notaries. Deeds were stacked upon each other like a house of cards. The confusion in land titling also attracted shady developers seeking to take advantage of the situation to profit from their own forged deeds. Land surveys made by the local Department of Land and Colonization were purposely dubious, and many tracts were renamed in attempts to confound buyers and prevent future legal action.[9]

All this grilagem provided land for the many migrants arriving in the region. Most arrived with a small amount of capital and acquired parcels from land speculators or colonization companies deeply involved in the practice. Beginning in the late 1940s, Western Paraná became the prime destination for German- and Italian-Brazilian settlers coming from the southern states of Santa Catarina and Rio Grande do Sul. In the 1950s, the opening of a new road by the federal government, Highway 277, facilitated the arrival of thousands of settlers to an area of cheap and accessible land, but with precarious enforcement of property rights. Possession of a deed was not a guarantee of land ownership for settlers, as each piece of land was also claimed by other deeds, which were used by colonization companies to evict settlers, using an army of henchmen, before reselling the land to the next settler. Violence became widespread in this situation of generalized land tenure uncertainty, as land agents and colonization companies made use of arson, beatings, rape and assassination against those settlers who refused to recognize bogus claims to the land they had acquired in the region. Settlers also fought back, and in the 1950s two major land conflicts erupted in Western Paraná, pitting colonization companies against settlers.[10] Protesting against the harassment by local politicians and colonization companies, settlers took up arms in 1951 and 1957, occupying several towns and demanding federal intervention to resolve the land conflict.[11] Inside Iguaçu, land agents also thrived on this legal uncertainty, selling public park land to migrants from Santa Catarina and Rio Grande do Sul in the 1960s. Much like elsewhere in Western Paraná, inside the park land was sold by individuals who knew how to navigate the complexities of local land bureaucracy and take advantage of the inability of the federal government to enforce its claims over park land.[12]

The federal decision to remove settlers

At the beginning of 1966, two years into the 21-year military regime, the Ministry of Agriculture designated a committee to assess the status of the Brazilian national parks. The committee, led by the agricultural engineer Harold Strang, travelled throughout the country assessing *in loco* the status of 15 of the 16 parks existing in Brazil at the time. It was the first time technicians from the Ministry of Agriculture visited most national parks and it was part of a larger initiative by the military government to organize and restructure its environmental policy under a single national agency. In his report, Strang denounced the lack of a national park policy, which was reflected in the 'ineffective administrative organization [of national parks], the absence of specialized personnel, the chaos in the land tenure situation, the lack of vehicles and other resources, and the absence of research'.[13] A year later, in February 1967, the government created a new environmental and forestry agency, the *Instituto Brasileiro de Desenvolvimento Florestal* (Brazilian Institute for Forest Development (IBDF)), the result of the merging of several smaller agencies under the aegis of the Ministry of Agriculture.[14]

The creation of the committee in 1966 was in line with the move to organize the land situation in Brazil, a core issue for the military regime. The committee travelled more than 30,000 kilometres by aeroplane, automobile, boat and horse, through isolated areas with poor transportation infrastructure. In the Iguaçu National Park the members of the committee were informed of settlements by the park director, René Denizart Pockrandt. Before the committee's arrival, an attempt by Pockrandt to take a census of the families living in the park area was faced with fierce opposition as he and other park employees were furiously chased away by armed settlers. Nevertheless, Pockrandt reported to IBDF on the existence of hundreds of families living in the area. They had farms, crop and grazing fields and a village with a church and a school. Unsurprisingly, the park director was very pessimistic about the prospect of successfully removing the families, who he presented as 'quite stubborn and dangerous'. Pockrandt believed removal would demand the use of force, probably by the army itself, and the federal government would incur the cost of offering new lands in other areas. Influenced by Pockrandt, the national park committee suggested in its 1969 report that the park should be sectioned into two parts, with the exclusion of the settled area in the middle from the protected territory. The government then should build fences isolating the two distinct sections of the park from the settled area, providing settlers whose lands would then be located outside the new boundaries of the park with legal titles. Pockrandt believed the IBDF should prioritize the conservation of the old growth seasonal semi-deciduous forest and mixed ombrophilous forest (araucaria forest) in the eastern section of the national park instead of spending resources removing settlers from an area that had already suffered considerable human impact.[15]

The removal of settlers was not a consensus among federal officials, but the idea of a park without people was. Pockrandt believed the retracing of park boundaries could prevent the fierce conflict that would inevitably accompany a possible settler eviction. The park director, however, was unable to convince his superiors of the validity of his proposal. He met resistance from the newly appointed minister of agriculture, Luís Fernando Cirne Lima, who was adamant in his belief that the complete removal of settlers was the only way of dealing with the issue. The military government appointed Lima minister in October 1969, with the avowed mission of dealing with the land problem in Brazil. His grand plan was to parcel and colonize frontier areas – especially, but not only, in the Amazon. For this purpose, one of his first measures was the creation of a new federal land agency, the *Instituto Nacional de Colonização e Reforma Agrária* (National Institute for Colonization and Agrarian Reform (INCRA)). The creation of INCRA marked the commitment of the military dictatorship to solving the land question in Brazil through colonization projects that sent surplus rural populations to frontier areas. In the case of Iguaçu, the Ministry of Agriculture decided to use these new tools, an expropriation law tailored to promote agrarian reform and federal resettlement projects set in frontier areas, to solve the problem of settlers inside the national park. An agreement between INCRA and IBDF was signed on August 26, 1970, less than two months after the creation of the new land agency in July of that same year. The agreement offered an opportunity for the newly created INCRA to test its colonization programme on settlers at the Iguaçu National Park.[16]

To direct the eviction process, the military appointed the retired army Colonel Jayme de Paiva Bello, the former commander of the Army Border Division in Foz do Iguaçu, as the new park director in May 1971. Among Bello's new duties as the head of the park was the eviction of settlers from the protected area. He approached his new task from a military disposition, which gained him the hatred of many settlers. Bello was known among settlers as an authoritarian and irascible character who is said to have once stated that 'German-Brazilians were unfit to settle on the borderlands of Brazil for their lack of commitment to the nation, as demonstrated by the invasion of a national park.' Bello also accused the State of Paraná of promoting illegal colonization in federal lands since the 1960s. To him, the federal government had shown good faith through its decision to expropriate the land and compensate farmers instead of simply nullifying land titles. Settlers, in turn, were to be blamed for their own situation, as he insisted that 'Those who bought lands inside a national park should have known they were illegally acquiring federal land.' 'In the end', Bello continued, 'they bet on it and lost, it took a couple of years, but they lost.'[17]

Initial relocation

In 1971 the federal government enacted decree 69412, allowing the occupied section of the Iguaçú National Park to be expropriated for social interest (*desapropriação por interesse social*). This was a legal dispositive introduced by the military months after the 1964 coup to promote agrarian reform. Agitation in the countryside had provided one of the justifications for the overthrow of former president João Goulart in April 1964, and after the coup the military recognized that some form of agrarian reform was still badly needed to curb land conflicts and prevent the emergence of rural political movements.[18]

At that time, the area harboured hundreds of farms and two villages, Santo Alberto and São José.[19] In the meetings with INCRA and IBDF officials, settlers were informed that 'due to a decree of the president Emílio Garrastazu Médici' they would have to leave the area because 'the land where they lived was part of the park since the 1940s'. Foreseeing possible acts of resistance, the IBDF signed an agreement with the State of Paraná to deploy 50 state police officers – equipped with new weapons, vehicles and boats – to the Iguaçu National Park. Prior to that, it would have been impossible for the 16 ill-equipped and poorly trained park wardens to carry out the eviction of thousands of settlers. The 1970 agreement with the State of Paraná not only provided IBDF and INCRA with the manpower to enforce the new restrictive environmental regulations designed by Bello, but also signalled the new era of greater subordination of states to the federal government inaugurated by the military regime.[20]

The relocation plan laid out by INCRA and IBDF officials confused settlers, some of whom had probably first been introduced to the two agencies at the 1971 meetings.[21] INCRA established a colony for settlers from São José and Santo Alberto at the banks of the Ocoí River, just 30 kilometres north of the park (see Figure 8.1). The colony was referred to by INCRA officials with a perfunctory acronym, PIC-OCOI, which stood for *Projeto Integrado de Colonização do Ocoí* (Ocoí Integrated Colonization Project). The area chosen for the colony was a private 12,500-hectare land tract owned by an absentee speculator that was, along with part of the national park itself, one of the few extensive and continuous stretches of Atlantic Forest still left in Western Paraná. INCRA's plan was to expropriate the area for social interest, parcel the tract into lots, implement the basic infrastructure of roads and electricity, establish agricultural villages, provide settlers with technical advice and facilitate loans with banks. The guiding vision of INCRA technicians was switching prospective small farmers from crops such as corn and beans to more marketable ones like soybeans. This entire infrastructure was also meant to lure settlers to the new location and prevent their return to the park, giving an end to what park officials considered the 'vicious cycle of forest destruction' carried out by settlers in Iguaçu. Yet, the location chosen for the colonization project was itself a forested 'idle' area 'empty' of people.[22] The settlement of Iguaçu farmers at PIC-OCOI, with its effort to create a modern agriculture community in a forested area, reproduced INCRA's approach to other colonization projects implemented elsewhere in Brazil. The main difference was the origin of settlers: whereas other projects dealt mainly with landless peasants, at PIC-OCOI settlers had themselves been the object of a previous INCRA-led judicial expropriation that removed them from the Iguaçu Park.[23]

For the national park occupants, INCRA designed a plan of action in which all small and medium landholders in possession of some type of deed would receive compensation for their land and improvements. They would then be offered the option of buying a new lot in PIC-OCOI for subsidized prices.[24] Those who possessed deeds, about half of the families in Iguaçu, would be compensated for their land in the form of agrarian reform bonds, paid annually and fully redeemed in 20 years. INCRA also paid in cash for improvements, depending on the assessments made by the agency's officials. To remove settlers the federal officials chose the easier path of accepting the legality of settlers' claims to land ownership, despite the convoluted and dubious origin of most deeds in the area. In total, INCRA recognized 232 land parcels with deeds, out of a total of 447, which were owned by 227 different individuals and one company. Besides these, there were hundreds of individuals and families who lived in the park area but failed to present any type of deed and were thus barred from receiving indemnity for the land they occupied. The process of expropriation and compensation, therefore, was far from equitable, as it rewarded knowledge of land titling. It legitimized the land ownership of those in possession of land titles, however questionable these deeds might have been, at the same time that it transformed settlers without acceptable land papers into squatters.[25]

Unsurprisingly, many settlers were dissatisfied with the expropriation process owing to the differences in treatment and indemnity. Those with deeds were eligible for compensation for both estate improvements and land value, whereas those who failed to present land titles only received indemnity for improvements. Settlers with deeds were discontented with the 20-year payment timeline of the government bonds they received. Others who possessed purchase contracts without deeds felt wronged due to not receiving land compensation. A number of settlers had indeed received twice the amount of land at the PIC-OCOI, which helped assuage resistance to the expropriations. Some settlers meanwhile opted out of the PIC-OCOI: about 60 families moved to Mato Grosso; others crossed the border and immigrated to Paraguay; and yet others moved to the cities, mainly to Foz do Iguaçu, abandoning farming altogether. All in all, by 1976, there were still 90 landholders resisting eviction from the park. They were dissatisfied with the new location at PIC-OCOI, contested INCRA's assessment of the value of their properties and improvements, and required the payment of their land in cash instead of bonds. They also demanded the right to eventually sell their PIC-OCOI land to be free to move somewhere else if they so desired. Their lawyer summarized their situation in a 2010 interview: these 'were small farmers, with little capital, who should have received compensation in cash, especially because land was expropriated to be incorporated into the national park, not to promote agrarian reform.'[26]

The writ of *habeas corpus*

In the winter of 1976, settlers in the villages of São José and Santo Alberto started being arrested for routine activities such as preparing the land for summer crops. Around 4 p.m. on 30 June, Bruno Wagner, Urbano Diel and Armindo Criveler Diel were arrested for ploughing their lands. They spent the night in the Federal Police jail in Foz do Iguaçu. In their testimony they complained of being continuously harassed and beaten by the state police, which culminated with their imprisonment. A week later the police arrested two other settlers, Lucila Postai and Romeu Canicio Postai. According to the police report, the couple had been ploughing their fields for summer crops and at the moment of their arrest Lucila Postai verbally and physically assaulted the police officers. Ploughing the fields was not the only action leading to the arrest of settlers in 1976. Maurício Schossler, for example, was arrested at home by plain-clothes officers and charged with the possession of subversive materials. Officers accused him of keeping an audio tape with a manifesto inciting the upheaval of settlers. Schossler spent a night in the Federal Police headquarters in Foz do Iguaçu, where, according to him, he was forced to witness a torture session of an unknown prisoner before his own interrogation – a common procedure in many police stations during Brazil's military dictatorship. Until that point, arrests for planting crops and for subversive activities were unheard of for the settlers in the Iguaçu National Park. Prior to 1976, only clearing new areas had been prohibited on settler properties.[27]

On 9 July 1976, a local attorney, Antônio Vanderli Moreira, attempted a bold move by filing a petition for a preventive writ of *habeas corpus* at the Second Federal Court in Curitiba. The petition was made on behalf of 80 of the remaining farmers from São José and Santo Alberto against the director of the Iguaçu National Park. In the petition, Moreira argued settlers had suffered unlawful coercion and restrictions by the IBDF on their constitutional right to come and go, and thus needed *habeas corpus* to move freely. The substitute judge, Silvio Dobrowolski, expeditiously denied the petition, arguing that the 'expropriated parcels were part of the Iguaçu National Park', and that 'there was nothing strange in setting aside deforested areas for nature conservation' as such decisions were based on 'ecological studies' the IBDF had made of the affected areas. The judge, however, failed to present such studies; none were ever produced in the entire process of eviction of settlers. The removal originated in a political decision, not a scientific one.[28]

The resistance of the remaining settlers fed into public officials' fear of the repetition of the settler uprisings of the 1950s and early 1960s. The head of the IBDF in the state, Humberto José Jusi, for example, requested the federal intelligence agency (Serviço Nacional de Informações (SNI)) in 1976 to investigate a possible rebellion of settlers in the park and at PIC-OCOI. According to Jusi, several 'subversive activities' were being planned to take place between April and May, including

> the occupation of PIC-OCOI, the kidnapping of the PIC-OCOI director's son, the murder of the PIC-OCOI and Iguaçu National Park directors, and the murder of the two commanders of the state forest police platoon quartered inside the park.

The SNI office in Curitiba sent at least one agent to the area to investigate the situation. The investigator's report describes a meeting attended by 'people with low education uttering slogans against the government and the 1964 revolution [military coup]'. Local federal police agents also contributed to the general paranoia by reporting radicals preaching among the settlers for a peasant revolution on 1 May. Fearing for their safety, the head of the PIC-OCOI had already taken his family out of the region. The day of 1 May came, but nothing happened.[29]

On the settlers' side, discontent was much more grounded on what they saw as an unjust process of resettlement than on projected ideals of a general settler uprising. They considered the 1971 expropriation act null and void because it determined the land would be nominally expropriated for agrarian reform ends, when, according to the petition, the government's true intention had always been expropriation for 'ecological preservation'. To settlers it was clear that 'agrarian reform' implied the expropriation and parcelling of idle latifundia to be distributed to landless peasants and small farmers, or, as defined by the 1964 Land Act, to promote 'the better distribution of land through modifications in its ownership and occupancy regime to attend the principles of social justice and increase of productivity'. Expropriating small proprietors to cobble together an idle latifundium was exactly the opposite of what the law defined as agrarian reform, and ultimately that was how settlers and their lawyer understood the national park – an enormous latifundium of idle lands that would be in better use if put into production.[30]

A second item in the list of complaints, however, reveals the ability of settlers to contest the displacement not only under the letter of the law, but also through its political and technical justifications. Settlers saw a basic contradiction in their forced removal from a cleared area to one, PIC-OCOI, constituted of 'virgin forest'. The resettlement, they argued, meant a second and unnecessary cycle of deforestation in a new site. They claimed that the agency, according to what was acceptable in the environmental ideas of the time, could very well compensate for the loss in the occupied area inside the national park by transforming the PIC-OCOI estate into a protected area of its own. After all, the chosen area was also forested, largely 'empty' and even slightly bigger – 12,500 hectares against the 12,000 hectares occupied by settlers in the park.

Other complaints all related to alleged failures in the removal and resettlement process. The action of park rangers and police officials became more punitive as they started arresting settlers for the removal of tree stumps from the fields, a necessary step before ploughing. Settlers also accused local municipal governments of halting the maintenance of the dirt roads leading to communities inside the park, thus impeding their access to local markets. Through the hurdles imposed on cultivation and circulation inside the park area, the goal of authorities was to strangle the remaining settlers economically. 'We either have to wait for the court decision, or for the deterioration of living conditions inside the park – settlers will have to move out', confessed the head of INCRA-PR, Aroldo José Moletta, in an interview.[31]

A closer look at the legislation wielded to remove settlers from Iguaçu casts light on the meaning of the relocation programme. Instead of employing expropriation for public utility (*desapropriação por utilidade pública*), INCRA officials chose to use a new legal instrument introduced with the 1964 Land Act: expropriation for social interest (*desapropriação por interesse social*).[32] The difference between the two was found not only in the different compensations they provided to settlers but, more importantly, the logic behind them. Expropriation for public utility in Brazil was similar to the US institution of eminent domain – expropriation for the building of roads, dams and the establishment of parks for the common good. Expropriation for social interest, on the other hand, was designed to achieve agrarian reform goals, promoting access to land by putting idle properties to use. The choice of agrarian reform legislation was a clear indication that, in the eyes of top-level government officials, the removal of settlers constituted a social and political problem rather than an environmental one.

The resolution of land conflicts and the top-down pacification of the countryside were two of the self-assumed tasks of the military. The use of newly minted agrarian reform tools emerged as an obvious choice to impose territorial order on an unstable borderland. Ultimately the approach of the federal government paid off. Despite being contested by several different class-action lawsuits, both regarding the expropriation itself and the compensation, the removal was never judicially cancelled. By 1982 all settlers had reached amicable agreements with INCRA on the value and payment of compensation, and by then the expropriation was a given fact as the occupied area inside the park territory returned to the control of the federal government.[33]

Conclusion

Today, the 12,000-hectare area previously occupied by settlers in Iguaçu (7.5 per cent of a total of over 160,000 hectares of park lands) is almost entirely covered by a robust secondary forest. In the late 1970s the national park administration removed all facilities put in place by settlers and allowed the forest to regrow – a demonstration of the engagement of the Brazilian state in constructing the park as a space of nature. Indeed, from 1970 onward, the Brazilian federal government's actively pursued policy of settler removal was ultimately legitimized by a mandate to recreate the natural landscape that existed inside the park at the moment it was gazetted in 1939.

Iguaçu's history is hardly unique; the removal of dwellers and the physical and discursive erasure of their presence in protected areas is a staple of the establishment of national parks elsewhere. Moreover, the creation of the Brazilian national park repeated a pattern commonly found elsewhere in Latin America – the creation of parks on lands of disputed ownership where tenure uncertainty continues decades after the protected area's initial gazetting. Therefore, it comes as no surprise that agrarian reform informed national park establishment in Iguaçu, as redistribution of land was a recurrent issue in the history of Latin American governments from left to right in the twentieth century.

Yet, Iguaçu also differs from other instances of national park displacement in some key aspects, such as the presence of non-indigenous settlers who arrived years after the park's creation, or the scale and resources invested in their removal. Furthermore, in contrast to many other national parks, in Iguaçu displacement did not result in customary or land rights being stripped away in order to enable tourism, for in the case of the Brazilian park 95 per cent of its territory came to be classified under land use regimes that prohibit visitation. The park does not offer backcountry permits, forbids camping and bans the entrance of cars inside its territory. Despite being one of the most visited non-urban national parks in Latin America, Iguaçu only allows access to the Iguazu Falls, where visitors are hauled around in park buses directly from the park entrance. Tourists are banned in other areas and many ignore the fact that the falls are part of Brazil's second oldest national park. In this sense, the relocation of settlers from the park in the 1970s created a territory of nature mostly devoid of touristic use, a preserved area for nature's sake.[34]

A mass relocation of settlers like the one carried out in Iguaçu was not repeated in other Brazilian national parks. The specific conditions at Iguaçu – a decades-long history of violent agrarian conflict in a sensitive border zone, the great number of settlers involved and the novelty of a newly minted agrarian reform tool – were absent in other Brazilian national parks. But Iguaçu helped to galvanize the idea of national parks as spaces devoid of people in Brazil. In 1979 a new law introduced a national park definition – the first in Brazilian legislation – that, for the first time, defined the national state as the sole owner of national park land. It defined parks as inalienable and, as a public good, unavailable to individuals. The new law forbade most types of dwellings inside parks (except those related to the functioning of parks as such), and prohibited 'human access' to most national park areas. In sum, the new law gave the federal government absolute control over the land inside national parks. By defining park lands as antithetical to individual use, it gave the state the legal means to clearly prohibit logging, poaching, raising livestock, agriculture and dwelling inside national parks.[35]

The case of Iguaçu provides an example of how conservationist efforts can be aligned to agrarian policy in an authoritarian context. The removal was an opportunity for land officials at INCRA to put into practice a new strategy of agrarian reform through colonization. It served to test the new expropriation legislation on the people who claimed land inside the park. Some of them were real large landowners, but the great majority were small proprietors who, according to the letter of the new law, should not be the target of such provisions. Furthermore, the second portion of the eviction process, resettlement at PIC-OCOI, also served as a test for the type of colonization project Brazilian policymakers planned to implement in frontier areas in the country.

More important, however, was the use of these extraordinary powers of territorial and social control to promote the conservation of nature mandated by a nature state. The new Brazilian agrarian reform institutions provided environmental agents at the IBDF with the instrument and momentum to carry out their historical agenda of national parks without dwellers. Without a new land code that amplified the powers of the central state to intervene in the national territory, a new land reform agency with a top-down agrarian reform programme, and the engagement of important sectors of the military caste that governed Brazil in the 1970s, national park officials would be incapable of advancing the goal of reconstituting the settled area of the national park as forested landscape. Iguaçu demonstrates how territorial organization and nature protection overlap. Even before the consolidation of a conservationist paradigm in national legislation, park proponents in Brazil tapped into unrelated territorial tools developed by an authoritarian state to consolidate a territorial intervention typical of the nature state.

Notes

1 *Iguazu* is a term of Tupi-Guarani origin meaning 'big water'. In Spanish it is spelled *Iguazú*, and in Portuguese it was *Iguassú* up to the 1940s and *Iguaçu* from the 1950s onward. Iguazu is originally the name of the 1,300-kilometre river that serves as the boundary between Argentina and Brazil in its last 130 kilometres, before flowing into the mighty Paraná River. It is also the name of the large binational waterfall that justified the creation of the two national parks. In this chapter I chose to keep the Portuguese spelling 'Iguaçu' for the Brazilian national park, *Parque Nacional do Iguaçu* (Iguaçu National Park), the Spanish spelling 'Iguazú' for the Argentine national park, *Parque Nacional Iguazú* (Iguazú National Park), and the English spelling 'Iguazu' for geographical features (Iguazu River and Iguazu Falls).

2 Brazil, Law 23793, Forest Act, 23 January 1934; Brazil, Law 4771, New Forest Act, 15 September 1965; Albert Breton, *Environmental Governance and Decentralisation* (Northampton, MA, 2008), 52.

3 Brazil, Decree 84017, National Park Act, 21 September 1979; IBDF, *Plano do Sistema de Unidades de Conservação* (Brasília, 1979). See also Teresa Urban, *Saudade do Matão: Relembrando a História da Conservação da Natureza no Brasil* (Curitiba, 1998); José Luiz de Andrade Franco and José Augusto Drummond, 'Nature Protection: The FBCN and Conservation Initiatives in Brazil, 1958–1992', *Historia Ambiental Latinoamericana y Caribeña*, 2/2 (2013), 338–67.

4 Frederico Freitas, 'A Park for the Borderlands: The Creation of the Iguaçu National Park in Southern Brazil, 1880–1940', *HIb: Revista de Historia Iberoamericana*, 7/2 (2014), 65–88.

5 Francisco Iglesias, 'Parques Nacionais Existentes, Descrição e Relevância', in Bernardino José de Souza, Cristovão Leite de Castro and Alexandre Emílio Sommler, *Anais do IX Congresso Brasileiro de Geografia, Florianópolis, 7 a 16 de Setembro de 1940* (Rio de Janeiro, 1944), III; Octavio Silveira Mello, 'Parque Nacional do Iguaçu: Área a Ser Pleiteada', 3 June 1942, Fundo Parque Nacional do Iguaçu, Instituto Chico Mendes de Conservação da Biodiversidade (hencefort ICMBio); Mario Câmara Canto, 'Relatório que Apresenta o Administrador do Parque Nacional do Iguassú, Referente ao Corrente Ano, Bem Como Sugestões para 1944', 22 December 1943, Pasta 'Relatórios de Atividades', Parque Nacional do Iguaçu, Brazil; João Augusto Falcão, 'O Engrandecimento do Parque Nacional do Iguaçu', in *O Serviço Florestal no Biênio 1943–1944* (Rio de Janeiro, 1945), 119–20; Ministério da Agricultura, Brazil, 'Ministério da Agricultura: Revigoramento da Política Florestal', *Correio da Manhã*, 7 March 1945; Brazil, Decree-Law 2073, 8 March 1940; Brazil, Decree-Law 2436, 22 July 1940; Brazil, Decree-Law 6506, 17 May 1944; Brazil, Decree-Law 6587, 14 June 1944; Brazil, Decree-Law 6664, 7 July 1944.

6 Brazil, Decree 10432, 9 November 1889; Brazil, Decree 305, 7 November 1890; Brazil, Decree 305, 7 April 1890; Brazil, Decree 920, 24 October 1890; Brazil, Decree 397, 20 June 1891; Brazil, Decree 968, 1 August 1892; Brazil, Decree 1386, 6 May 1893; Cecília Maria Westphalen, Brasil Pinheiro Machado and Altiva Pilatti Balhana, 'Nota Prévia ao Estudo da Ocupação de Terra no Paraná Moderno', *Boletim da Universidade Federal do Paraná – Departamento de História*, 7 (1968); Antonio Marcos Myskiw, '*Colonos, Posseiros e Grileiros: Conflitos de Terra no Oeste Paranaense (1961/66)*' (unpublished MA thesis, Fluminense Federal University, 2002), 148–55; Rubem Murilo Leão Rêgo, '*Terra de Violência: Estudo Sobre a Luta Pela Terra no Sudoeste do Paraná*' (unpublished MA thesis, University of Sao Paulo, 1979), 90–5; Ruy

Christovam Wachowicz, *Paraná, Sudoeste: Ocupação e Colonização* (Curitiba, 1985), 140–8, 177–81; Joe Foweraker, '*Political Conflict on the Frontier: A Case Study of the Land Problem in the West of Paraná, Brazil*' (unpublished PhD dissertation, University of Oxford, 1974), 103–5.

7 In Brazil, land registry is performed by private agents, the *tabeliões*, who are empowered by public authorities to perform notarial activities.

8 Antonio Cordeiro de Jesus Espólio e outro v. INCRA, TRF-4 – APELAÇÃO CIVEL: AC 17258 PR 2004.04.01.017258-5, http://trf-4.jusbrasil.com.br/jurisprudencia/8879247/apelacao-civel-ac-17258-pr-20040401017258-5-trf4; Leandro de Araújo Crestani and Erneldo Schallenberger, 'Nas Fronteiras do Oeste do Paraná: Conflitos Agrários e Mercado de Terras (1843/1960)', *Revista Trilhas da História*, 2/4 (2012), 100–5; Foweraker, 'Political Conflict on the Frontier', 8–14, 114–18, 120–33; INCRA, *Livro Branco da Grilagem de Terras* (Brasília, 2012), 17–19; Emílio Stachowski (INCRA official) in discussion with the author, 10 October 2013.

9 Foweraker, 'Political Conflict on the Frontier', 116–18, 132–3; Myskiw, 'Colonos, Posseiros e Grileiros;' Processo no. 87.10.11573-0 – Ação de Desapropriação/INCRA vs. Colonos do PNI, Justiça Federal do Paraná, Foz do Iguaçu.

10 On violence at the Brazilian frontier, see Otávio Guilherme Velho, *Capitalismo Autoritário e Campesinato: Um Estudo Comparativo a Partir da Fronteira Em Movimento* (São Paulo, 1979); José de Souza Martins, *Fronteira: A Degradação do Outro nos Confins do Humano*, 2nd edn (São Paulo, 2009).

11 'Reforma Agrária no Paraná', *Nosso Tempo* 231, Foz do Iguaçu, Paraná, Brasil, 12 September 1986; Lindomar W. Boneti, '*O Significado Histórico do Levante Armado dos Colonos do Sudoeste do Paraná Ocorrido em 1957*' (Porto Alegre, 1988), 1–16; Westphalen et al., 'Nota Prévia', 38–48.

12 Processo no. 87.10.11573-0 – Ação de Desapropriação/INCRA vs. Colonos do PNI – Folders 12 and 13 (1987), Justiça Federal do Paraná, Foz do Iguaçu; Emílio Stachowski, INCRA, Memos OFÍCIO/AGU/PGF/PF-PR/NAGRA/59/2008, OFÍCIO/AGU/PGF/PF-PR/NAGRA/100/2008, 20 November 2008, and deeds for the Iguaçu National Park estates 1930, 1958, 1973, 1974, 1979, 1996, Fundo PIC-OCOI Files, INCRA-Cascavel; Gaspar Peixoto Costa, *Relatório Apresentado à Comissão Especial do Estudo da Faixa de Fronteiras do Paraná e Santa Catarina, pelo General Gaspar Peixoto Costa, diretor do DGTC, na qualidade de Representante do Estado do Paraná, junto ao IBRA* (Curitiba, 1966); Arnaldo Carlos Muller, *História Cronológica do Parque Nacional do Iguaçu* (Western and Southwestern Paraná, 1998); 'Anexo 6 – Histórico da Região do Parque', Fundo Parque Nacional do Iguaçu, ICMBio; Alvaro Loureiro Martins, 'Levantamento do Parque Nacional do Iguaçu', IBRA, Cascavel (Paraná), 9 August 1968, Fundo Parque Nacional do Iguaçu, ICMBio; Adilson Simão (Iguaçu National Park Director, 1974–86) in discussion with the author, 16 October 2013; Lara Luciana Leal Seixas, '*Memória dos Desapropriados do Parque Nacional do Iguaçu: As Fronteiras do Cotidiano em Terras (i)Legais?*' (unpublished MA thesis, State University of Western Paraná, 2012), 81.

13 IBDF and IBRA, *Parques Nacionais e Reservas Equivalentes no Brasil: Relatório com vistas a uma revisão da política nacional nesse campo* (Brasília, 1969), 95–6.

14 The Forest Service, which had been reintroduced as an agency within the Ministry of Agriculture in 1938, lasted until 1962, when it was substituted by the *Departamento de Recursos Naturais Renováveis* (Department of Renewable Natural Resources, DRNR). The creation of the IBDF in 1967 merged in the same agency

the DRNR and three other agencies created under Vargas: the *Instituto Nacional do Pinho* (National Pine Tree Institute (INP)); the *Instituto Nacional do Mate* (National Yerba Mate Institute (INM)); and the *Conselho Federal Florestal* (Federal Forest Council (CFF)). Brazil, Delegated-Law 9, 11 October 1962; Brazil, Decree 52442, 8 October 1963; Brazil Decree-Law 289, 28 February 1967.

15 IBDF and IBRA, *Parques Nacionais*, 61–2; René Denizart Pockrandt, 'Relatório das atividades e problemas do parque', Iguaçu National Park, 12 October 1967, PNIB-A; Parque Nacional do Iguaçu, 'Relatório', 1976, PNIB-A.

16 Parque Nacional do Iguaçu, 'Relatório', 1976, PNIB-A; Ministério da Agricultura, Divisão de Segurança e Informações, 'Pedido de Busca n° 05/PSI/DSI/MA/75 Desenvolvimento do Setor Primário – Colonização OCOI – 5.1', 28 February 1975, Pasta 2.6, Fundo Parque Nacional do Iguaçu, ICMBio; Alvaro Loureiro Martins, 'Levantamento do Parque Nacional do Iguaçu', IBRA, Cascavel (Paraná), 9 August 1968, Fundo Parque Nacional do Iguaçu, ICMBio.

17 'Os Inquilinos do Parque Estão Saindo', *Referência em Planejamento* 1, First Semester of 1976; Jayme de Paiva Bello, 'Parque Nacional do Iguaçu: Informação sobre o Parna', 2 July 1975, Parque Nacional do Iguaçu archive; Adilson Simão (Iguaçu National Park Director, 1974–86) in discussion with the author, 16 October 2013; Seixas, 'Memória dos Desapropriados', 150; 'Paraná: Proibido Plantar', *Veja*, 21 July 1976.

18 Brazil, Decree 69412, 22 October 1971.

19 These were mostly small family farms. Properties smaller than 20 hectares comprised 69 per cent of all farms.

20 Ministério da Agricultura, Divisão de Segurança e Informações, 'Pedido de Busca n° 05/PSI/DSI/MA/75 Desenvolvimento do Setor Primário – Colonização OCOI – 5.1', 28 February 1975, Pasta 2.6, Fundo Parque Nacional do Iguaçu, ICMBio; Eugenio Cichovski to Secretário Geral do IBDF, 299/68, 15 October 1968, Pasta 'Parque Nacional do Iguaçu – Informações Complementares', Parque Nacional do Iguaçu archive; Instituto Brasileiro de Desenvolvimento Florestal, 'Termo de Acordo', 7 May 1970, Pasta 'Termo de Acordo de Contrato IBDF com a Secretaria de Agricultura do Estado do Paraná', Parque Nacional do Iguaçu archive; 'Colonos no Parque', *Diário do Paraná*, 3 July 1971.

21 Brazil, Decree 69412, 22 October 1971; Brazil, Decree 69411, 22 October 1971; Seixas, 'Memória dos Desapropriados', 26–7; 127–8; Brazil, Decree 69411, 22 October 1971; Brazil, Decree 69412, 22 October 1971.

22 The area chosen for the resettlement of the settlers from Iguaçu was not actually 'empty', as it harbored a small Guarani population living on fishing and other subsistence activities. This generated a series of conflicts of its own. See Frederico Freitas, 'The Guarani and the Iguaçu National Park: An Environmental History', *ReVista: Harvard Review of Latin America*, 14/3 (2015), 18–22.

23 'Ministério da Agricultura, Divisão de Segurança e Informações, 'Pedido de Busca n° 05/PSI/DSI/MA/75 Desenvolvimento do Setor Primário – Colonização OCOI – 5.1', 28 February 1975, Pasta 2.6, Fundo Parque Nacional do Iguaçu, ICMBio.

24 Ibid.

25 Processo no. 87.10.11573-0 – Ação de Desapropriação/INCRA vs. Colonos do PNI – Folder 1 (1973), Justiça Federal do Paraná, Foz do Iguaçu.

26 Seixas, 'Memória dos Desapropriados', 26–7, 138–43.

27 Bruno Wagner, Urbano Diel, and Armindo Criveler Diel, 'Notarized statement', 1 July 1976, Habeas Corpus no. 00.00.27777-2 (PR), 1976, Justiça Federal do

Paraná, Curitiba; 'Paraná: Proibido Plantar', *Veja*, 21 July 1976; Forest Police of Paraná, 'Report no. 31/76', Foz do Iguaçu, 1976, Habeas Corpus no. 00.00.27777-2 (PR), 1976, Justiça Federal do Paraná, Curitiba; Seixas, 'Memória dos Desapropriados', 132–6.

28 Silvio Dobrowolski, 'Habeas Corpus Preventivo', autos no. 859/76, 2ª Vara, 17 July 1976, Habeas Corpus no. 00.00.27777-2 (PR), 1976, Justiça Federal do Paraná, Curitiba.

29 Humberto José Jusi to Aldyr Eduardo Martins, 26 April 1976, Serviço Nacional de Informações (ACT ACE 2234/82), 1982, Arquivo Nacional-DF; 'Atividades Subversivas no Parque Nacional do Iguaçu', memo, 28 April 1976, Serviço Nacional de Informações (ACT ACE 2234/82), 1982, Arquivo Nacional-DF; Serviço Nacional de Informações, 'Pedido de Busca no. 079/16/AC/76', 9 June 1976, Serviço Nacional de Informações (ACT ACE 2234/82), 1982, Arquivo Nacional-DF.

30 Antônio Vanderli Moreira, 'Pedido de Habeas Corpus Preventivo', 6 July 1976, Habeas Corpus no. 00.00.27777-2 (PR), 1976, Justiça Federal do Paraná, Curitiba; Brazil, Law 4504, Land Act, Art. 1, 30 November 1964.

31 'É Proibido Cortar Árvores no Parque', *Diário do Paraná*, 15 May 1974; Antônio Vanderli Moreira, 'Pedido de Habeas Corpus Preventivo', 6 July 1976, Habeas Corpus no. 00.00.27777-2 (PR), 1976, Justiça Federal do Paraná, Curitiba; INCRA, Proof of Payment of Rural Property Land Tax in Name of José Telmo Schneider, 10 October 1973, Habeas Corpus no. 00.00.27777-2 (PR), 1976, Justiça Federal do Paraná, Curitiba; IBDF-PR, Logging Authorization, Foz do Iguaçu, 24 May 1976, Habeas Corpus nº 00.00.27777-2 (PR), 1976, Justiça Federal do Paraná, Curitiba. Alvino Baltazar, Emilio Leichtweis, Eugenio Hilario Leichtweis, José Antônio Postai, 'Notarized Statement', 1 June 1976, Habeas Corpus no. 00.00.27777-2 (PR), 1976, Justiça Federal do Paraná, Curitiba; 'INCRA Desmente Coação', *Estado do Paraná*, 14 July 1976, Dossiê PIC-OCOÍ, 1974–8, INCRA-Curitiba.

32 Brazil, Decree-Law 3365, Expropriation for Public Utility Act, 21 June 1941; Brazil, Law 4504, Land Act, 30 November 1964.

33 Processo no. 87.10.11573-0 – Ação de Desapropriação/INCRA vs. Colonos do PNI – Folder 5 (1987), Justiça Federal do Paraná, Foz do Iguaçu; Humberto José Jusi to Aldyr Eduardo Martins, 26 April 1976, Serviço Nacional de Informações (ACT ACE 2234/82), 1982, Arquivo Nacional, Brasília.

34 As a park closed to backcountry visitation, Iguaçu bears some resemblance to the model of science park established by the Swiss National Park. See Patrick Kupper, *Creating Wilderness: A Transnational History of the Swiss National Park* (New York, 2014); IBDF, *Plano de Manejo Parque Nacional do Iguaçu* (Brasília, 1981); IBAMA, *Plano de Manejo do Parque Nacional do Iguaçu* (Brasília, 1999).

35 Brazil, Decree 84017, 21 September 1979.

9 Discovering China's tropical rainforests

Shifting approaches to people and nature in the late twentieth century

*Michael Hathaway**

In 1986, a British visitor strolled through the steamy forests of Southwest China's Yunnan Province, walking on a trail later named in his honour. The day before, as he crossed an old Soviet-designed bridge across the Mekong River, his Chinese hosts told him politely but firmly to take no photos of it, as the Cold War legacy meant the Chinese were still nervous about foreign knowledge of their infrastructure that might be of military value. As he stopped and gazed into the trees, avidly searching for birds with his binoculars, he asked his hosts a wide array of questions. Many of these men, Chinese scientists and translators, wore a full suit as they trudged along the trail on what was, for most of them, their first day in this rainforest environment and their first day spent in the company of a foreigner. He was no ordinary tourist, though, for this was HRH Prince Philip. When I interviewed some of these scientists in 2000, they admitted they were quite nervous during his short trip to Yunnan, worried he might stumble or get sick from bad food. The stakes were much higher than entertaining royalty, however, as the Prince's trip to Yunnan was not merely for pleasure or rugged adventure in what was still called a 'leach-infested' place.[1] He was sent to adjudicate a contentious claim made by some Yunnanese officials that their province contained ecologically valuable tropical rainforest. Government officials in Beijing, eager to prove their county's ecological wealth and promote international connections, scrambled to assemble a team that could safely take a high-level visitor through an area with barely any tourist infrastructure. Although Beijing was able to provide excellent translators, few of them possessed much knowledge of the kind desired by the Prince. One researcher, however, Yang Yuanchang, stood out as possessing the richest scientific knowledge of the area. Professor Yang participated in some of the earliest scientific expeditions in the 1940s that began to create species inventories for

* I would like to thank the Rachel Carson Center for sponsoring the initial workshop, as well as the excellent work of Claudia Leal, Emily Wakild, Matt Kelly and Wilko Graf von Hardenberg in shepherding these papers with dedication and panache. To carry out this work, I received funding from the Social Sciences and Humanities Research Council, support from Simon Fraser University and my department chair Dany Lacombe, research assistance from Grace Zhang, and editorial assistance from Shiho Satsuka and Leslie Walker Williams.

this terra incognita. Thus, he helped make this tropical area legible to the fledgling state of the People's Republic of China, which had just begun on October 1, 1949. Four decades later, he worked to make this place legible to a rising and increasingly influential transnational group of nature conservation organizations, depicting it in a new frame: as a site with high levels of biological diversity.

Philip was not only royalty, but since 1981 was the head of the World Wildlife Fund (WWF), the largest conservation organization on the planet. The WWF had just signed an agreement with China for one of its largest projects, to protect the giant panda bear in neighbouring Sichuan Province.[2] The Chinese hosts deliberated: they knew that WWF officials felt the need to conserve their panda mascot, which had been the WWF's symbol since soon after it began in 1961. China was the only country in the world where wild pandas still lived.[3] Pandas had become a global symbol of wildlife conservation, the first species described as 'charismatic megafauna'.[4] Yet, there was no indication that the WWF would expand its operations beyond Sichuan.

The hope was that these Chinese hosts could convince the Prince that Yunnan possessed ecologically valuable rainforest and he would encourage the WWF to start a second conservation project. At the time, Yunnan's scientists and conservationists were poorly paid. Many had newly found jobs, after their universities were closed, especially during the turbulent Cultural Revolution, from 1966 to 1976. A WWF project could provide invaluable opportunities, especially so for Yunnan, often described as a backwards, economically poor region, where 'the mountain is high, and the emperor is far'. Yet Chinese scientists' efforts to substantiate their claim was challenging: they heard that Western scientists doubted them. Sceptics said that Yunnan was too far north of the equator to be tropical, not wet enough, or too stripped of its biodiversity by conversion into farmland.[5] Yunnan's scientists were eager to have the Prince verify their claims, and worked hard to show him their most impressive sites. They were delighted when he later supported them, describing the towering dipterocarp trees (long regarded as emblematic of tropical rainforests), and the existence of wild elephants, which surprised many Westerners who imagined these massive beasts had been eliminated from the Chinese landscape.[6]

Ultimately, the Prince's trip precipitated the travels of the many Westerners who flocked to Yunnan during the 1980s and 1990s, setting up a series of nature conservation projects first by the WWF (based in Geneva), then the World Bank's Global Environment Fund, the Dutch government, the Nature Conservancy (based in Arlington, Virginia) and others. Whereas some scholars of China have focused almost entirely on how the Chinese government created a 'nature state' as an internal phenomenon, many have seen the development of conservation as driven by external concerns, in particular as following a Western template of modernity.[7] In this chapter I argue that neither vision of the nature state is accurate.

In exploring the rise of nature conservation in China in the late twentieth century, this chapter argues that conservation was always built through transnational exchange. This should not be regarded, however, as an inevitable sequence of stages, as an inevitable result of 'modernity'. Such a position goes against much writing on global conservation, where the spread of conservation ideas and practices is often presented as a kind of one-way flow, developed in the United States or 'the West' and gradually absorbed throughout the world.[8] Richard Grove, however, has explicitly argued against such America-centric narratives.[9] Grove argues that many US-based scholars assume that the US pioneered this movement, and that this now forms a global template. In support of Grove's claims, John M. MacKenzie suggests that such scholars' knowledge is 'blinkered' by a focus on key American players, such as George Perkins Marsh, Henry David Thoreau, Aldo Leopold and John Muir.[10] A number of accounts describe how these men's 'wilderness ideals' are exported around the world.[11] In contrast, Grove contends that internationally circulating conservationism neither emerges from the late nineteenth-century American experience or the European metropole, but from the imperial periphery.[12] Although some scholars challenge Grove's alternative thesis, he nonetheless offers a voice of caution and helpful scepticism towards dominant narratives.[13]

This chapter is divided into two sections. The first section describes some of China's early conservation efforts. This history has often been ignored by dominant historical narratives that characterize Mao-era China as antithetical to conservation. China is often imagined as one of the world's least environmentally friendly countries, yet there was a time when it was celebrated by some international organizations as a leader in tree planting and soil and water conservation.

The second section explores in more detail how in the 1980s China began a serious engagement with international environmental organizations. I argue that Chinese scientists did not merely reproduce an existing global template as part of modernity. Rather, such engagements took place on a complex terrain, as governmental ministries reached out to international players and attempted to push and pull them in various directions. In my other work, I argue that China, as well as other places, does not merely receive global mandates, but actively works to produce what becomes understood as 'the global'.[14] In this chapter I examine a case study of the WWF's project to protect China's tropical rainforest. I combine interviews and participant observation with villagers and WWF staff from 1995, and from 2000–2, as well as archival study in WWF headquarters, and at the Yunnan Provincial Library. During the 2000–2 trip, I conducted 18 months of ethnographic research while living in one of these project villages; I've made several follow-up visits over the last decade.

Understandings of nature conservation in China are deeply shaped by widely held Western assumptions that the country is a 'Bad Earth',[15] a zone of ecological devastation. China is often described as a place where the environment was devastated through deliberate attack or through neglect as human-centred utilitarianism reigned supreme. Influential scholarly accounts, such as Judith Shapiro's *Mao's War Against Nature*, support the former view and Elizabeth Economy's *The River Runs Black* supports the latter perspective.[16] Yet even in the first decade of the People's Republic of China (PRC), scientists expressed much interest in protecting some places and animal species, such as the giant panda, which in the 1950s was becoming a key international symbol of Chineseness and a potentially useful player in 'panda diplomacy'.[17] This happened, it should be noted, while the fledgling country faced tremendous struggles in nation-building and supported extensive military struggles in the north (the Korean War) and south (the Vietnam War).[18] As Elena Songster points out, such conservation efforts are rarely discussed in the scholarly literature.[19]

Even though the PRC claimed a vast territory, it knew little about it, especially western China, when it began in 1949.[20] Over the last millennia, imperial territory ebbed and waned, and at this moment, the land that became 'China' was relatively large. Although Mao's Long March had exposed many farmer-soldiers to the great size of the nation, there were precious few written materials or experts with firsthand knowledge about its minerals and ores, animals and plants, rivers and mountains. Mao's army had encountered many different ethnic groups in western China, but officials had only rough guesses about their total population, or even how many ethnic groups existed or what languages they spoke.

In the first decade of PRC rule, later described by some historians as the 'honeymoon period' of PRC science, scientists were buoyed by a new-found sense of their social importance after decades of war. By 1950, officials had already created the Chinese Academy of Sciences. Experts returned from overseas, lured by the promise of overturning China's long-standing reputation as the 'sick man of Asia' and building a strong country.[21] Within a decade, the Academy of Sciences created approximately 100 institutes and often looked to the USSR, their closest ally, for guidance and support in scientific endeavours.[22]

With great enthusiasm, Beijing sent experts to survey their territory and resources. Although finding strategic resources such as coal and mineral ores to build China's economy was critical, this was also a time of interest in nature conservation.[23] In the Soviet Union, the nature reserve movement was part of a governmental mandate since the 1930s,[24] and although little is known of how the Soviets influenced conservation efforts during the Mao era, Soviet botanists and ornithologists worked in southern Yunnan, among other places.

In 1956, the State Forestry Department declared the PRC's first officially protected space at Dinghu Shan Nature Reserve in Guangdong Province.[25] Just two years later, in the year following a major Sino-Soviet biological expedition, China created a nature reserve in southern Yunnan Province's tropical forest, in a region called Xishuangbanna. The expedition took place over a two-year period, with top Soviet and Chinese botanists (such as Andrey Federov and Wu Zhengyi) collecting over 10,000 botanical specimens. The team was motivated to find plants suitable for industry and sites for creating rubber plantations, but they were also keenly interested in plants for basic science, and fostered efforts to preserve some of China's remnant tropical rainforests.[26] Also, ornithologists created baselines of bird species that have proved increasingly useful to twenty-first-century studies of biodiversity loss.[27]

In the same year as the Dinghu Shan reserve was established, Mao gave his famous 'Let a hundred flowers bloom' speech, asking China's experts for constructive criticism. Afterwards, many critical of his rule were punished and a climate of fear followed. The next major campaign, the 'Great Leap Forward', China's rush towards development, was predicated on a radical increase in iron and grain production. To make iron, rural residents hastily constructed millions of backyard furnaces and felled many trees to fuel the furnaces. To grow more grain, people carried out vast agricultural experiments, such as digging deep and planting closely; many of them failed. As projects such as building canals and dams occupied the labour of vast numbers of people, the output of grain fell precipitously. The Great Leap soon led to the world's largest famine, killing as many as 40 million people by 1962. A temporary hiatus from dramatic government campaigns followed, but during the Great Cultural Revolution of 1966–76 officials paid little interest to creating or maintaining protected areas. Conservation-minded scientists, especially those who saw promise in the early 1950s, had to negotiate a social climate that was quite chilly to their concerns.

These events caused great pressures for the ecological reserve designated in southern Yunnan, especially on two fronts. First, this was some of China's only suitable land for strategic tropical crops, such as rubber. Second, for over a decade it was a vital military staging ground for supporting the North Vietnamese. China desperately needed rubber after a US-led embargo cut-off almost all of its supplies; it was a critical resource for domestic and military uses. A number of Western scientists declared that Yunnan, lying to the north of the Tropic of Cancer, was too cold to grow rubber; no country had successfully grown rubber that far north. Yet, armed with 'revolutionary Mao Zedong thought', Chinese scientists discovered warm microclimates and bred new cold-hardy rubber varieties.[28] The trees, however, suffered. The winters were dry and cold, and trees would shed their leaves (in places with steadier rainfall and higher temperatures, rubber trees maintain their leaves year round) and hibernate, reducing production. Worse yet, in the winters of 1972 and 1974, freezing temperatures killed off thousands of acres of rubber trees, many of them over a decade old and gaining in productivity. Scientists decided that rubber should only grow up to 1,000 metres in elevation: above this point it was too vulnerable to cold snaps. The state set up more large-scale plantations, employing tens of thousands of ethnically Han workers relocated from Central China, seen as more reliable workers than the local ethnic minorities. Before the beginning of the PRC, this area was ruled by the ethnic Dai, who are linguistically and culturally related to the neighbouring Thai and had their own kingdom. After the PRC usurped their power,[29] Chinese officials attempted to restructure the Dai's Buddhist society around state-based atheism.[30]

During the 1960s and 1970s, some of the designated nature reserves were used for other purposes; as lowland forests were cleared and replanted with rubber, soldiers used some of the upland zones for training grounds. During the 1960s, China sent over 25,000 troops to Vietnam, many trained in Xishuangbanna.[31] Although the United States had left Vietnam by 1975, just four years later the

Chinese military invaded Vietnam and Xishuangbanna was again used as a staging ground.

Mao died in 1976, and by 1979, as Deng Xiaoping gained power, China reached out to the world and the US ended its embargo. Soon after, Deng signed international treaties and agreements, including environmental ones, and his government became increasingly open to connections with the West.

The WWF was the first major conservation organization to work in China; after choosing the panda as its symbol in 1961, WWF had tried in vain to establish connections with China. After nearly two decades of fruitless efforts to make connections, Nancy Nash, a WWF public relations consultant, facilitated the first negotiations, asking Wu Tai Chow, a friend in Hong Kong and an editor of a progressive newspaper with important contacts in Beijing, to help. Wu had some of his contacts read Nash's proposal, and in 1979 the WWF was invited to Beijing. WWF staff looked for a Western scientist to join the efforts of Hu Jinchu, China's main panda researcher.[32] Fortunately, the WWF's top candidate, Dr George Schaller, was available. Schaller was famous for his long-term research projects in India and Central Africa, studying Indian tigers and their relationship to deer, snow leopards in the Himalayas and other charismatic megafauna. He had just applied for a research project in India, but his visa was rejected by a bureaucracy that increasingly favoured Indian rather than foreign scientists.[33] Heading to China rather than India, George Schaller's joint research with Hu Jinchu helped galvanize massive public support for the panda, both domestically and internationally. Their efforts helped turn the panda into China's unofficial mascot and made the WWF's panda among the world's most recognized symbols.

Yunnan officials hoped to attract the WWF through their claim of having tropical rainforest. During the 1980s, years before 'climate change' became important, fear of 'tropical deforestation' mobilized support to 'save the world's rainforests'. During the 1980s, tropical rainforests were newly seen as uniquely valuable and vulnerable. Some described the rainforests as the 'lungs of the earth', key to producing the world's oxygen and influencing rainfall patterns.

The WWF raised significant funds in North America and Europe to address tropical deforestation, and they wanted to expand their efforts in China, one of the countries least known to Western science.[34] For over a millennium, China's northern-based rulers saw the area around Xishuangbanna as dangerous and miasmic, more of a place to banish criminals than a desirable site for settlement.[35] Even into the 1950s, this region was so little known to Beijing that many were shocked to discover that China still harboured herds of wild elephants, which were thought to be extinct.[36] The continued presence of wild elephants inspired the WWF representative, the Prince, to report positively about this place. With much haste, they sent another prominent Briton, the famed biologist John MacKinnon, to survey these tropical landscapes. MacKinnon was helping the WWF with their panda research, and was well-known for his work in Southeast Asian tropical forests, including studies of wild orangutans. This, as well as his extensive knowledge of regional bird species, made him highly regarded.

In his original project plans, MacKinnon characterized Xishuangbanna as 'a rich biodiverse landscape under threat'.[37] Then current ecological theory supported the idea that of all ecosystems, the tropical rainforest was one of the most fragile and susceptible to harm from human actions such as farming. Many biologists conceived of rainforests as a 'counterfeit paradise' whereby an apparently robust fecundity masked a true vulnerability – a thin layer of topsoil.[38] If this layer of soil supporting the vegetation was removed, many worried that the rainforest might never recover and, instead, turn into a permanent wasteland. According to many scientists at the time, 'slash and burn agriculture' was the worst possible threat to the rainforest. In this technique, farmers cut down a section of forest, wait for the trees to dry out, burn the felled trees (called 'slash') and plant crops in the cleared fields, fertilized by the tree ash. These slash-and-burn farmers, estimated at over 600 million, were described as ecological criminals or 'arsonists of the world's rainforest'.[39] These negative evaluations started becoming common in China in the 1980s. For example, in 1988 a Beijing journalist described a village in Xishuangbanna using a language of crisis, suggesting that 'in a small village like this [of 66 people], tens or even hundreds of acres of woods are destroyed every year' through slash and burn farming.[40] The author predicted a catastrophe:

> In addition, local peasants and nearby farm units destroy 16,000 to 33,000 acres of forest in Xishuangbanna every year. If this situation continues, the area is doomed, and Xishuangbanna, now rich and beautiful, may become a desert.[41]

These fears resonated with Western scientists, who began to see a solution to the problem of slash and burn: agroforestry. Agroforestry was regarded as transforming the peasantry from being wasteful and destructive into an efficient and beneficial force for, rather than against, the environment. After discussing the widespread damage created by slash and burn, one prominent public figure in rainforest conservation argued that:

> Nonetheless solutions are emerging, in the form of agroecosystem strategies that allow the cultivator to convert his agricultural lifestyle from a migratory to a stabilized, that is stationary affair; from extensive to intensive agriculture; and from wastefully inefficient to permanently productive agriculture. These solutions are becoming available in the forms of agroforestry.[42]

This statement vilifies mobility and valorizes stabilization. Agroforestry was the next hope and it was not surprising, then, that the WWF's John MacKinnon saw agroforestry as the main goal of their project in Xishuangbanna.

To carry out the agroforestry project, MacKinnon hired Jack Bentley, an American rancher who had taught agroforestry in the Philippines. Western conservationists who work in developing countries are often described as arrogant, harsh and elitist,[43] but Bentley's work was driven by a sense of empathy and self-reflection. For instance, in a conversation in 1995, Bentley said that he was disturbed that villagers were relocated by the Xishuangbanna Nature Reserve Bureau. I later found that between 1987 and 1990, the Bureau re-settled over 800 people from ten villages.[44] Bothered though he was by this, Bentley believed there was no way to challenge the government's decisions, which were 'always final in China'. He did not mention, however, that the WWF had actually encouraged relocations from the nature reserve, a fact I assume he knew. The WWF had lauded these relocations as 'indicative of the seriousness of the attention paid to conservation by the local government'. By 1996, however, WWF staff were committed to opposing relocation: the moral grounds of conservation were starting to change.[45]

Bentley said that the lands 'given' to these relocated villages were relatively small, and that their old ways of slash-and-burn agriculture were no longer viable. He believed it best, in general, to help villagers use their lands intensively with agroforestry, and teach them to plant and graft tropical fruit trees with high-yielding varieties. Bentley expressed interest in the tropical forests, as well as concern for soil erosion, but these were clearly not his only or chief concerns, and he mainly identified as a people's advocate. Among expats Bentley was unusual in referring to those he worked with not as 'peasants' but as 'villagers', a term in China with much less patronizing associations.

Agroforestry became an appealing intervention to both WWF and Chinese officials, a kind of awkward collaboration.[46] Agroforestry appealed on several levels to the WWF and regional government officials, in part because it was not antagonistic towards local people *per se*, yet it presumed that local people harmed the environment and needed to be reformed. It seemed like a method to increase agricultural productivity and decrease environmental degradation. It was especially targeted for the high mountains, which were seen as particularly vulnerable to erosion, important for watershed health and inhabited by peoples who were especially ignorant of scientific thinking and were undisciplined, as imagined in relation to the more sophisticated villagers living in the plains. Agroforestry seemed to offer a solution, for like other scientific methods it was reputed to be universal, requiring only slight modification for local conditions.

Agroforestry's status as scientific was a crucial element of its acceptability to each side of the partnership. It was important to the WWF because, by identifying itself with science, the WWF could claim to be 'apolitical' within China, a highly charged context. The WWF had already struggled for years to carry out its panda project, sparring with national and local officials. Western organizations working in China were nervous they would insult their host and be expelled.[47] The WWF was still based in Hong Kong, yet hoped to move their office to Beijing, so it was trying to find politically expedient strategies. In most scholarly accounts, international NGOs are taken to be wealthier than the national governments of the developing countries where these organizations work. This was not the case for China, however, for NGOs, including the WWF, were relatively weak and precariously positioned. The WWF could bring in substantial funds and opportunities at a local scale, but at a national scale its efforts paled in comparison to state projects. It should be remembered that the WWF was not just an international NGO: even though it was based in Geneva, it was seen as an American organization.[48]

Agroforestry's claim to science also appealed to Chinese government agencies, for whom it was imperative during the post-Mao era to demonstrate that their work was based on scientific understanding rather than political calculation. Nonetheless, reactions varied between the Ministry of Agriculture and the Ministry of Forestry. Foresters approved of agroforestry's scientific status and the goal of stabilizing agricultural plots so that local farmers would not slash and burn the ministry's forest lands. Conversely, agricultural extension agents largely saw agroforestry as a distraction. They advocated that farmers focus, instead, on year-round cropping in the paddy fields. One agricultural agent said that his peers saw agroforestry as relatively unproductive; nitrogen-fixing trees could not compete with chemical nitrogen fertilizer. He rhetorically asked why the WWF should keep farmers at a subsistence level. Instead, he suggested that farmers should embrace cash cropping, which was a very different vision than Bentley's.

As mentioned earlier, Bentley saw agroforestry as mitigating the restrictions imposed on these villages, such as the new nature reserve boundaries where slash and burn was no longer allowed. This perception was based on Bentley's understanding that these new boundaries would be inviolate, and thus villagers would be forced to confine their activities within a tightly confined space. This perspective, however, was not shared by local residents. Without a strict demarcation and frequent patrols by reserve guards, villagers understood these boundaries as essentially flexible and thus they were not as desperate for agricultural land as Bentley assumed.

Even though they did not always agree with Bentley's perceptions or find his teachings directly applicable, villagers largely welcomed him and the WWF. They were more worried about being forgotten than they were about being controlled by the heavy hand of governance. Although many of the middle-aged or older generation were familiar with government campaigns that required long periods of daily sacrifice during the Mao era, they saw the WWF's mandates as relatively light in comparison. Much scholarship on the Global South assumes that villagers wished for autonomy and are engaged in a war of everyday resistance against state forces, but I did not see such dynamics during my fieldwork in 2000–2.

In 1994, Bentley's project came to an end, and in 1995 the WWF conducted an assessment; during the five-year period of the life of the project, a veritable paradigm shift had taken place. In the late 1980s, WWF staff largely saw the problem in terms of scientifically ignorant villagers. By the mid-1990s, however, the team wondered in fact if the village was inhabited by knowledgeable indigenous people. Peoples regarded as indigenous were increasingly seen by global conservationists as possessing knowledge that was vital to finding new ways to live sustainably. Before the 1990s, almost no one was making a case for the value of indigenous knowledge or, indeed, that indigenous peoples even existed in China. Beijing might have acknowledged that China has many different ethnic groups, but they were labelled 'ethnic minorities' and almost always regarded as less 'advanced' than the ethnic Han majority; it was rare to see ethnic minority practices romanticized or even valorized.

Outside of China, international conservation organizations like the WWF and Conservation International were increasingly under fire around the question of indigenous rights. These organizations were accused of conservation efforts that often harmed indigenous groups.[49] Indigenous advocacy groups persuaded conservation NGOs to move from creating wilderness zones evacuated of local people to respecting and even fostering indigenous land rights.

At the same time, the WWF's main target for their interventions in Yunnan, slash and burn agriculture, was being rethought. In English-language documents, WWF staff began to use a new term, 'swidden agriculture', which was growing in popularity around the world as a replacement for 'slash and burn'.[50] Whereas the term slash and burn carried negative connotations of waste and destruction, the term swidden was a neutral one, invented in the 1950s, that encouraged scientists to study it with less stigma and bias.[51]

Such reconsiderations of swidden also paralleled changes within China, as some Chinese scientists were challenging older claims about swidden. First, whereas earlier research compared the erosion levels from swidden against those of natural forest, new experiments compared erosion with other forms of agriculture, such as rubber or tea plantations. Thus, in the older research, swidden looked quite damaging in terms of soil erosion, yet in the newer experiments it was often viewed as favourable to planting rubber or tea, for it resulted in less erosion. Second, swidden's relationship to biodiversity was also being rethought. New research showed that when swidden plots regrew, they could have levels of biodiversity just as high as the 'natural forest'.[52] For instance, there was growing appreciation of swidden as a form of agriculture that maintained biodiversity, especially as compared to cash crops grown in monocultures. Such rethinking was not only happening in China. Chinese biologists interacted with others investigating these topics: much work was being translated into Chinese for domestic consumption and being written in English for foreign consumption.[53]

In other countries, scientists started to investigate places long seen as exemplary sites of wilderness, without human influence. In the Amazon, for example, researchers found that the particular suite of tree species and even the existence of certain rivers might have anthropogenic origins.[54] Thus, these scientists increasingly questioned the division between the 'human-made landscape' and the 'natural landscape' as part of a new move to foster 'environmentally friendly agriculture'. With these new kinds of perspectives, the hegemony of research against slash and burn began to break down. In 2002, during a lecture to a large audience at the University of Michigan, David Pimental, a well-respected scholar at Cornell, shocked the audience by declaring that swidden was not the 'bogeyman of the world's tropical forests', as they had been trained to view it, but perhaps the world's most energetically efficient and ecologically sustainable form of farming.[55] In Yunnan, the WWF's new plan in 1995 shows evidence of a similar shift in perspective.[56]

By 1995, the evaluators now accused the WWF of committing a colossal mistake. The final report stated that local farmers were not destructive but were actually practising 'indigenous shifting cultivation', which the evaluators considered the most sophisticated and suitable land use for the tropical forest. Rather than working with the state to restrict local people, the evaluators wrote, WWF staff should learn from local people and try to expand locals' rights to land and resources. The EU team offered the following counsel:

> As a general rule indigenous shifting cultivation is both more sophisticated and sustainable than many settled monocultural alternatives in the tropics....
> There is a considerable amount that WWF and others can learn from [local people about] indigenous agroforestry and biodiversity management.[57]

The team advocated that the WWF should essentially invert its role from teacher to student in a new relationship with the local people, who were no longer to be seen as peasants but as indigenous peoples. For many WWF staff, the report was surprising. The WWF's field staff, both expatriate and domestic, were hardly stereotypical development agents who disparaged local people; the staff had a sincere interest in local livelihoods and appreciated the quandaries faced by local farmers. In fact, many were worried about the eviction of local people as China developed its nature state. Although scholars have celebrated states that take pollution seriously, arguing that such moves have widespread positive social consequences, benefiting industrial workers, as well as breathers and drinkers of less polluted air or water,[58] the state's turn to nature conservation nonetheless often entails costs and benefits that are quite uneven in their distribution. In this case some rural peoples have faced eviction or severe restrictions on their livelihoods that rely on access to these lands for grazing, farming, hunting and gathering edible and medicinal plants.[59] Ironically, communities that have protected their surrounding environments over the millennia are particularly vulnerable to such actions, as ecologically intact places are much more likely to come under plans for strict nature protection than areas re-made into farmland; thus, those who have protected forests are more likely to be locked out of them.[60]

From my perspective, we should not see the consultants' recommendations as one more example of Western knowledge formations flowing in a single direction towards the non-West. Indeed, their report was far more surprising to WWF expatriates than to some Chinese experts. The latter had already been promoting a new approach to conservation.[61] In fact, the European evaluators had read English-language reports written by these same Chinese experts, who had described neighbouring villages using the vocabulary of 'indigenous knowledge'. Chinese experts' multipronged efforts to unseat the previous framework and its predicates – the ignorant and destructive peasants in need of scientific agricultural techniques – directly led the European evaluators to 'discover' indigenous people in China who used sophisticated methods of environmentally friendly agriculture.

In a remarkable turn of events, older plans that tried to replace slash and burn with agroforestry, declaring that it created permanent wastelands, were superseded by new plans calling for villagers to be paid to carry out swidden. According to the new logic, swidden enhanced landscape heterogeneity and improved habitat for wild animals, especially for elephants. Many villagers were offended by this plan, especially when it suggested they travel back to old village sites in the nature reserve that others had been forcibly relocated from and that had been burned to the ground by park guards. These places were now talked about as haunted, as places to be avoided. A number of villagers were surprised by these quick changes: from stopping swidden to paying for swidden, and deliberately growing food for elephants, after centuries of trying to keep elephants away from their crops.

Villagers were emboldened by this show of concern for their livelihoods, and realized their proximity to the reserve created greater scrutiny but might also offer other possibilities. Some villagers had taken advantage of what Bentley offered, such as courses on fruit tree grafting. They selectively engaged with his offerings, rejecting many of his suggestions but embracing others. Several years after Bentley left, they wrote a letter to the Forestry Bureau to ask for a loan to buy tea-processing equipment for a village-based enterprise. Their letter borrowed language from Bentley's discussions, as he had suggested that their proximity to the nature reserve caused undue hardship, especially from state-protected animals such as wild elephants, which ate their crops and destroyed their fences. They received their loan, and built a profitable tea factory, reinforcing the idea that although there were some difficulties associated with their close proximity to the reserve, it also expanded their network of connections, which they could use in different ways. They were able to take potential forms of repression, and re-route them, thus enriching their life possibilities.

Conclusion

The WWF's entry into China reveals a number of conservation dynamics in the era of the nature state. The WWF was not the first to bring conservation to China, but built on existing legacies. Within the first decade and a half of the PRC, scientists had successfully protected 19 areas throughout the country.[62] A number of these scientists, who suffered in the 1960s and 1970s, were politically rehabilitated in the 1980s and became critical to rebuilding China's conservation system in the 1980s and 1990s. These scientists did not wait passively to receive mandates from international organizations; instead, they actively reached out to and negotiated with international conservation organizations. Although there were many projects during the Mao era that can be seen as 'environmental disasters', it should also be remembered that globally the protection of endangered species had not yet achieved much political traction. Instead, the expansion of agriculture was a key priority and human hubris was at a global highpoint, before the worries of the 'silent spring' and the damage to the ozone layer initiated a time of much greater caution and scepticism about the capacity of science to solve its own problems. Thus China was not so much an exception, but followed the rule of the rapid expansion of farmland after the Second World War, albeit following a different developmental path than the capitalist Green Revolution in neighbouring countries.

The history of China's nature state is frequently overlooked, especially with many reports in 2011 claiming that China had just created its 'first national park',[63] which was not entirely true. Also, several lingering and misinformed understandings of China continue to haunt efforts to understand what is happening there. First, in particular, Western reporters and scholars have often understood China as a 'Bad Earth', a place of destruction. Second, more generally, many attribute the existence of environmental concerns in the Global South to the flow of international influence from the Global North, or merely see this as an inevitable stage in the modern evolution of society.[64] Flow-based models of global change still tend to reinforce such assumptions. Rarely, for example, do we explore how countries like China, India and Indonesia are actually contributing to the global itself and not just 'becoming globalized'.

In terms of its project in Yuannan Province, we can see how the WWF, as the world's largest conservation organization, which to date has allocated more than $1 billion dollars, was not able to impose itself on China in a top-down manner. Instead, the WWF was attracted there and had to constantly negotiate its projects. Its vision of the landscape and people there changed relatively quickly and dramatically. The government had long been involved in agricultural expansion, but historically was primarily interested in encouraging the conversion of wastelands into agricultural areas and promoting advanced inputs such as hybrid seeds, chemical fertilizer and pesticides. Agroforestry, especially when seized upon by conservationists, had a different priority, as it was aimed more at subsistence than commercial production and it tried to find substitutes for chemical inputs, working more towards stabilization than expansion.

The response of the Chinese state was not unified and coordinated; instead, WWF staff worked with a number of state agencies, which often had different goals. In partnership with these agencies (such as the Ministry of Forestry and the Ministry of Agriculture), the WWF tried to establish a politically viable 'middle ground'.[65] These dynamics were made more challenging by the larger shifts in understanding of people and nature that occurred during the early 1990s, shifts in part precipitated by the increasing force of indigenous rights. In the present era, efforts by the state to enforce or expand nature conservation are always scrutinized in relation to indigeneity and the question of indigenous rights. Even though the Chinese state refuses the category of indigenous peoples within its own territory, nonetheless for international conservation groups like the WWF such sensibilities continue to shape their concerns and practices in China and elsewhere. Overall, then, international groups such as the WWF are shaped by both their own legacies and through their ongoing encounters with the practices and politics of nature in China itself.

Notes

1 His Royal Highness, Prince Philip, 'The Sixth World Conservation Lecture Conservation in China', *Environmentalist*, 7 (1987), 250.
2 George B. Schaller, *The Last Panda* (Chicago, IL, 1993).
3 Lifeng Zhu et al., 'Conservation Implications of Drastic Reductions in the Smallest and Most Isolated Populations of Giant Pandas', *Conservation Biology*, 24 (2010).
4 Devra G. Kleiman and John Seidensticker, 'Pandas in the Wild: The Giant Pandas of Wolong', *Science*, 228/4701 (1985), 875–6.
5 Kou, Zhengling, 'Xishuangbanna: Tropical Rain Forest.' *Beijing Review*, 14 (1997).
6 Mark Elvin, *The Retreat of the Elephants: An Environmental History of China* (New Haven, CT, 2004).
7 F.H. Buttel, 'Ecological Modernization as Social Theory', *Geoforum*, 31 (2000); Maarten A. Hajer, *The Politics of Environmental Discourse: Ecological Modernization and the Policy Process* (Oxford, 1995); Graeme Lang, 'Forests, Floods, and the Environmental State in China', *Organization and Environment*, 15 (2002).
8 This includes notions of the 'wilderness concept' or the 'Yellowstone model'. Roderick Nash, *Wilderness and the American Mind* (New Haven, CT, 1967); Roderick P. Neumann, *Imposing Wilderness: Struggles over Livelihood and Nature Preservation in Africa* (Berkeley, CA, 1998); Ramachandra Guha, 'Radical American Environmentalism and Wilderness Perservation: A Third World Critique', *Environmental Ethics*, 11/1 (1989), 71–83; Peter Coates, 'Creatures Enshrined: Wild Animals as Bearers of Heritage', *Past & Present*, 226/suppl. 10 (2015), 272–98.
9 Richard Grove, 'The Origins of Environmentalism', *Nature*, 345/6270 (1990), 11–14.
10 John M. MacKenzie, 'Empire and the Ecological Apocalypse: The Historiography of the Imperial Environment', in *Ecology and Empire: Environmental History of Settler Societies*, ed. by Tom Griffiths and Libby Robin (Seattle, WA, 1997), 217.
11 Nash, *Wilderness and the American Mind*.
12 Richard Grove, *Green Imperialism: Colonial Expansion, Tropical Island Edens, and the Origins of Environmentalism, 1600–1860* (Cambridge, 1995).
13 James Beattie, *Empire and Environmental Anxiety: Health, Science, Art and Conservation in South Asia and Australasia, 1800–1920* (New York, 2011); Juan Martinez Alier, *The Environmentalism of the Poor: A Study of Ecological Conflicts and Valuation* (Northhampton, MA, 2002); Greg Barton, *Empire Forestry and the Origins of Environmentalism* (Cambridge, 2002).
14 Michael J. Hathaway, *Environmental Winds: Making the Global in Southwest China* (Berkeley, CA, 2013).
15 Vaclav Smil, *The Bad Earth: Environmental Degradation in China* (Armonk, NY, 1984).
16 Judith Shapiro, *Mao's War Against Nature: Politics and the Environment in Revolutionary China* (Cambridge, 2001); Elizabeth Economy, *The River Runs Black: The Environmental Challenge to China's Future* (Ithaca, NY, 2004).
17 See, for example, Elena Songster, *Panda Nation: Nature, Science, and Nationalism in the People's Republic of China* (Oxford, forthcoming); Michael J. Hathaway, *Environmental Winds: Making the Global in Southwest China*. According to Noelle O'Connor, there are no known realistic images of pandas produced in China until the twentieth century, even though there are ancient traditions in painting its favourite food, bamboo. It really only started to gain iconic status in China after its image was commissioned for a set of stamps in 1963. Noelle O' Connor, 'A Quest for Pandas in Chinese Art', *ZooGoer*, 21 (1992).

18 As is well known, China faced Korean and American troops at its northern border and French, Vietnamese and later American troops at its southern border, which drew off tens of thousands of newly conscripted troops and vast amounts of equipment. China depended on the Soviet Union for equipment, and paid with grain, causing huge strains on food supplies for years, making officials leery of setting aside lands and money for nature conservation.

19 Songster, *Panda Nation*.

20 One scholar to examine this gradual process of building knowledge is Judd Kinzley. See Judd C. Kinzley, 'Crisis and the Development of China's Southwestern Periphery: The Transformation of Panzhihua, 1936–1969', *Modern China*, 38 (2012); Judd C. Kinzley, '*Staking Claims to China's Borderland: Oil, Ores and Statebuilding in Xinjiang Province, 1893–1964*' (unpublished PhD dissertation, University of California at San Diego, 2012).

21 Peter Neushul and Zuoyue Wang, 'Between the Devil and the Deep Sea: C. K. Tseng, Mariculture, and the Politics of Science in Modern China', *Isis*, 91/1 (2000), 59–88. This was difficult work as most of China's main scientific institutes were along the east coast, where the Japanese took over, destroying and removing books and equipment. Before the Japanese entered, scientists relocated a number of labs, including precious books, specimens and microscopes, sometimes travelling for over 1,000 miles inland by oxcart, train and human-powered watercraft in heroic efforts to reestablish themselves in Yunnan and Sichuan Provinces. During the 1990s, I heard many oral accounts of these times, first- and secondhand, from elderly scientists in Kunming.

22 The Soviets likely influenced China's emerging nature conservation policy, just as they shaped almost all aspects of Chinese science and education. The Soviet effort to remove designated places from human activity to use them as an ecological baseline for scientific study is well documented. See Brian Bonhomme, 'A Revolution in the Forests? Forest Conservation in Soviet Russia, 1917–1925', *Environmental History*, 7/3 (2002), 411–34; see especially work by Douglas R. Weiner, such as his books *A Little Corner of Freedom: Russian Nature Protection from Stalin to Gorbachev* (Berkeley, CA, 1999) and *Models of Nature: Ecology, Conservation, and Cultural Revolution in Soviet Russia* (Pittsburgh, PA, 2000).

23 The most impressive study on this topic is Elena Songster's forthcoming book, *Panda Nation*.

24 Weiner, *A Little Corner of Freedom*.

25 In some ways, protected areas drew on older precedent of making reserves for the royal elite (especially hunting grounds), and preserving lands around temples and monasteries. In ancient China, some lands were also claimed by urban centres, especially as sources of lumber. See N.K. Menzies, *Forest and Land Management in Imperial China* (London, 1994) and Edward H. Schafer, 'Hunting Parks and Animal Enclosures in Ancient China', *Journal of the Economic and Social History of the Orient*, 11/3 (1968), 318–43.

26 A.A. Fedorov, 'The Tropical Rain Forest of China. (Russian with English Summary)', *Bot. Zh. SSSR*, 43 (1958); Mark C. Tebbitt and Guan Kaiyun, 'Emended Circumscription of *Begonia silletensis* (Begoniaceae) and Description of a New Subspecies from Yunnan, China', *Novon*, 12/1 (2002), 133–6.

27 T.C.P Cheng, 'On Birds from Hsi-shuan-pan-na Area and Vicinity in Yunnan Province', *Acta Zoologica Sinica*, 13 (1961), 53–69 [in Chinese]; Rachakonda Sreekar, Kai Zhang, Jianchu Xu and Rhett D. Harrison. 'Yet Another Empty

Forest: Considering the Conservation Value of a Recently Established Tropical Nature Reserve', *PLoS One*, 10/2 (2015).

28 Janet C. Sturgeon, Nicholas K. Menzies, and Noah Schillo, 'Ecological Governance of Rubber in Xishuangbanna, China', *Conservation and Society*, 12/4 (2014), 376–85.

29 The Dai had tributary relations with the Chinese empire, as well as others such as rulers in present-day Thailand and Burma.

30 Vinya Sysamouth, '*Dai People's Indigenous Knowledge System of Communal Irrigation: A Case Study of the Adjustment of the Tai Lue to Centralized Policies in Xishuangbanna, Yunnan, China*' (unpublished PhD dissertation, University of Wisconsin-Madison, 2005).

31 Chen Jian, 'China's Involvement in the Vietnam War, 1964–69', *The China Quarterly*, 142 (1995).

32 Schaller, *The Last Panda*.

33 Michael L. Lewis, *Inventing Global Ecology: Tracking the Biodiversity Ideal in India, 1947–1997* (Athens, OH, 2004).

34 Daniel Viederman, President of the World Wildlife Fund, China (pers. comm. 1994); Alexis Schwarzenbach, *Saving the World's Wildlife: WWF – the First 50 Years* (London, 2011).

35 C.P. Giersch, *Asian Borderlands: The Transformation of Qing China's Yunnan Frontier* (Cambridge, MA, 2006).

36 Michael J. Hathaway, 'Wild Elephants as Actors in the Anthropocene', in *Animals in the Anthropocene: Critical Perspectives on Non-Human Futures*, ed. by Human Animal Research Network Editorial Collective (Sydney, 2015).

37 John Ramsay Mackinnon and Geoff Carey, *A Biodiversity Review of China* (Hong Kong, 1996).

38 Betty J. Meggers, *Amazonia: Man and Nature in a Counterfeit Paradise* (Chicago, IL, 1971).

39 William O'Brien, 'The Nature of Shifting Cultivation: Stories of Harmony, Degradation, and Redemption', *Human Ecology*, 30 (2002), 483.

40 Tang Xiyang. *Living Treasures: An Odyssey Through China's Extraordinary Nature Reserves* (New York, 1987).

41 Lu Junpei, and Qingbo Zeng. 'Hainan dao jianfeng ling ban luoye ji yulin "daogenghuozhong" shengtai houguo de chubu guance' [A Preliminary Observation on the Ecological Consequence After 'Slash and Burn Cultivation' of the Tropical Semideciduous Monsoon Forest on the Jian Feng Mountain in Hainan Island.] [In Chinese], *Acta Phytoecologica Sinica*, 4 (1981).

42 Norman Myers, *The Primary Source: Tropical Forests and Our Future* (New York, 1992), 48.

43 Guha, 'Radical American Environmentalism and Wilderness Perservation', 71–83.

44 Xiaogang Yu, '*Protected Areas, Traditional Natural Resource Management Systems and Indigenous Women: Case Study in Xishuangbanna, PR China*' (unpublished MA thesis, Asian Institute of Technology, Bangkok, 1993).

45 'Integrated Nature Conservation and Community Development Project in Xishuangbanna, Yunnan Province, China' (unpublished report for the WWF, 1996).

46 Anna L. Tsing, *Friction: An Ethnography of Global Connection* (Princeton, NJ, 2005).

47 Some were worried about WWF-affiliated staff making remarks that could insult their hosts. At one point, the Chinese government proposed a $100 million dollar panda plan, with substantial outside funding. MacKinnon responded, saying: 'It's a hostage situation. The Chinese are pointing a gun to the head of the panda and saying, "If you want to keep it, fund it. Otherwise we're going to let it go"'. Lena H.

Sun, 'Can Giant Pandas Survive the Effort to Save Them?', *The Washington Post*, 27 December 1993.

48 The WWF-US office played a disproportionately important role in international funding. As well, George Schaller was a naturalized US citizen, the head of WWF-China was an American and Bentley was American. There was also a strong British role as well, but no one in Yunnan thought of the WWF as a British organization.

49 Alexis Schwarzenbach, *Saving the World's Wildlife*.

50 Chris Elliot, Sejal Worah, and Geoff Carey, '*WWF Tropical Forest Conservation Projects, Xishuangbanna, China*' (Hong Kong, 1994).

51 Christian Erni (ed.), *The Concept of Indigenous Peoples in Asia: A Resource Book* (Copenhagen, 2008).

52 Jianchu Xu, '*Study on Indigenous Agroecosystems in a Hani Community*' (Chinese Academy of Sciences, Kunming Institute of Botany, 1991). Jianchu Xu, 'Understanding the Dynamics of Forest and Swidden Cultivation in Xishuangbanna, Southwest China: A GIS Application', *Community Forestry Development Experiences in Asia* (Kunming, 1994). S.Y. Chen, S.J. Pei and J.C. Xu, 'Indigenous Management of the Rattan Resources in the Forest Lands of Mountain Environment: The Hani Practice in the Mengsong Area of Yunnan, China', *Ethnobotany*, 5/1–2 (1993), 93–9.

53 Luo Yiqun, 'Miaozu bentu shengtai zhish yu senlin shengtai de huifu yu gengxin' [Local Ecological Knowledge of the Miao Ethnic Minority and the Restoration and Renewal of Forest Ecosystem] [In Chinese], *Journal of Tongren University*, 6 (2008).

54 See William Balée, 'Indigenous Transformation of Amazonian Forests: An Example from Maranhão, Brazil', *L'Homme*, 33 (1993); D. Posey, 'A Preliminary Report on Diversified Management of Tropical Forest by the Kayapó Indians of the Brazilian Amazon', *Advances in Economic Botany*, 1 (1984), 112–26; William M. Denevan, 'The Pristine Myth: The Landscape of the Americas in 1492', *Annals of the Association of American Geographers*, 82/3 (1992); Kat Anderson, *Tending the Wild: Native American Knowledge and the Management of California's Natural Resources* (Berkeley, CA, 2005); Hugh Raffles and Antoinette M.G.A. Winkler Prins, 'Further Reflections on Amazonian Environmental History: Transformations of Rivers and Streams', *Latin American Research Review*, 38/3 (2003), 165–87.

55 Pimentel (pers. comm., 2002).

56 Sejal Worah, 'WWF Project Identification Report: Xishuangbanna, China' (1995).

57 Steven Mark Newman and Bert Seibert, '*Malaysia, Vietnam, China: Evaluation of Conservation Strategies in Asian Countries*' (unpublished report for the WWF, 1995)

58 David John Frank, Ann Hironaka and Evan Schofer, 'The Nation-State and the Natural Environment over the Twentieth Century', *American Sociological Review*, 65/1 (2000), 96–116.

59 Charles Geisler, 'A New Kind of Trouble: Evictions in Eden', *International Social Science Journal*, 55/175 (2003), 69–78; Mark Dowie, *Conservation Refugees: The Hundred-Year Conflict between Global Conservation and Native Peoples* (Cambridge, MA, 2009); Nancy Lee Peluso, 'Coercing Conservation? The Politics of State Resource Control', *Global Environmental Change*, 3/2 (1993), 199–217.

60 Hathaway, *Environmental Winds*.

61 Shaoting Yin, *Yige Chongman Zhengyi de Wenhua Shengtai Tixi: Yunnan Daogeng Huozhong Yanjiu* [A Highly Controversial Cultural-Ecological System: Studies in Swidden Agriculture in Yunnan] [in Chinese] (Kunming, 1991); Xiaogang Yu, 'Shui

Zhiling Lai Zi Lijiang Lashi Hai Liuyu De Baogao' [Lashi Hai: The Soul of Water] [in Chinese] *Huaxia Ren Wenhua Dili* [*China Cultural Geography*] (2001).

62 Division of Wildlife Protection, SFA, *Study on China's Nature Reserves Policies* (Beijing, 2003), 236.

63 Mike Ives, 'Nosing into the Emerging National Parks of China's Yunnan Province', *Los Angeles Times*, 9 January 2011.

64 See Steven R. Brechin and Willett Kempton, 'Global Environmentalism: A Challenge to the Postmaterialism Thesis?', *Social Science Quarterly*, 75/2 (1994), 245–69; Steven R. Brechin, 'Objective Problems, Subjective Values, and Global Environmentalism: Evaluating the Postmaterialist Argument and Challenging a New Explanation', *Social Science Quarterly*, 80/4 (1999), 793–809.

65 Richard White, *The Middle Ground: Indians, Empires, and Republics in the Great Lakes Region, 1650–1815* (Cambridge, MA, 1991).

10 Nature, state and conservation in the Danube Delta

Turning fishermen into outlaws

Stefan Dorondel and Veronica Mitroi[*]

In the summer of 2001 a fisherman approached Stefan Dorondel in a bar in Jurilovca, a village located in south-east Romania at the border of the Danube Delta Biosphere Reserve (hereafter the Biosphere Reserve). Co-villagers told the man a researcher from Bucharest was asking around about fishing practices. After some small talk the fisherman offered Dorondel his services. To the fisherman, 'a man from Bucharest' with supposedly national connections was a potential 'fishing partner' who could help him sell his catch. 'I know other people who can help us too. In a few months we will be rich; I know the best places for fishing and they [the authorities] would never catch us', he assured Dorondel. The fisherman's proposal should be understood in the context of wider complaints about restraints imposed by the state on the rights of people living in the Biosphere Reserve: 'We have always explored and maintained the delta for the advantage of the state', claimed the fisherman, 'now they [the state authorities] forbid us to enter certain channels and to fish even for our families. Tourists who visit the Delta will end up having more rights than we locals do.'[1] The fisherman's proposal reflected some of the persistent peculiarities that shape fishing activity in this huge wetland, not least the restrictions imposed on locals by the enlargement of protected areas in the Delta. In response, fishermen attempt to bypass state-imposed restrictions out of frustration with state conservation policies that clash with their knowledge of the Delta as a natural ecosystem shaped for centuries by human activity.[2]

In 1990, not long after the overthrow of Nicolae Ceauşescu, members of the Romanian Academy and employees of the Danube Delta administrative body suggested the Romanian government expand the nature reserve from the existing 41,500 hectares to the entire Delta territory.[3] The Romanian Parliament

[*] Partially, this work was supported by a grant from the Ministry of National Education, CNCS – UEFISCDI, no. PN II-ID-PCE-2012-4-0587 (2013–16). Stefan Dorondel thanks also the Institut für Ost-und Südosteuropaforschung Regensburg – he wrote parts of this chapter while he was a Fellow there. We also thank Mihai Popa and Oana Mateescu for their comments and suggestions. Wilko Graf von Harderberg, Matt Kelly and Emmanuel Kreike read earlier versions of the chapter and helped us sharpen the argument. We alone are responsible for any misinterpretation or flaw this chapter may have.

vote to designate the Biosphere Reserve was followed in 1991 by international recognition of the worldwide ecological importance of the Delta by UNESCO and the Ramsar Convention.[4] International recognition of the value of the area allowed the Romanian government to attract significant financial support from global environmental institutions like the World Bank and the Global Environment Institute, which would allow it to radically change the 'face' of the Danube Delta. As a consequence, the centralized control once exercised by the socialist state has been maintained in the postsocialist years, reconstituting the Romanian nature state. Since 1990, nature conservation and restoration have been the main goals of the newly created authority that administers the entire Delta territory. The Danube Delta Biodiversity Reserve Agency (hereafter the Agency), a state agency, is tasked with both managing fishing activity, restoring those areas considered ecologically degraded and preventing the further degradation of the natural resources within the reserve.

In the name of biodiversity conservation, the Agency progressively restricted several 'traditional' fishing practices. The Agency's restrictive policy was backed by the central government, which publicly declared in 2007 that the Delta could be saved only if commercial fishing was banned and the waters were repopulated with fish. These restrictions had a major impact on the local economy, not least because few other economic activities are possible. Tourism and subsistence agriculture have not assured a sufficient livelihood for the population living in or around the reserve. The situation had already worsened by 1997, when the state fishing enterprises were privatized. Until 1997, Piscicola Jurilovca, one of the largest state fishing enterprises in the country, employed 1,200 people. After privatization, the company employed only 176 people.[5]

Deploring the privatization of the state fishing enterprise and the extension of conservation laws, a villager firmly stated to Dorondel: 'The lakes and swamps belong to God, thus the state or any other authority should refrain from imposing restrictions on us.' In the imaginary of these local men, fishing, after more than two centuries as the main economic activity for communities living there, cannot be simply interdicted.

This chapter offers a historical and ethnographical account of the appropriation of the Danube Delta's space and resources by different state agencies and representatives from the presocialist regime until the present time. We make two important claims: first, that although the character of the nature conservation policies in the Danube Delta has changed with changing political regimes, since the interwar years Romania has gradually constructed a nature state. We show that the interwar Romanian state established the delta's first nature reserves and protected areas as part of an attempt to establish its authority over this recently acquired territory. However, the early and initial construction of the nature state focused on forested areas rather than the aquatic landscape; biodiversity priorities reflected this preference. The socialist regime enlarged the protected natural areas but this protection existed more 'on paper' than on the ground. In the Delta, the nature state only became the main sociopolitical territorial organization in the postsocialist period. The second claim we make is that to understand the nature state enterprise in the Danube Delta, we need to look not only at policies of nature protection, but the way these were implemented on the ground, including how local inhabitants reacted to the impositions of the nature state. Consequently, we analyse the tensions between environmental policies and people living in the Delta over the course of the twentieth century. In order to distinguish the postsocialist environmental protection of the Danube Delta from previous periods we need to consider three distinct historical periods: presocialist (1878–1947), socialist (1945–89) and postsocialist (after 1990). By doing so, this chapter also explores how the fishermen themselves interpreted the growing presence of the state in their midst and how they acknowledged its legitimacy, accommodated its ministrations or critiqued its authority and judgements by word and deed. This chapter contextualizes recent ethnographical research in the Delta, drawing on interview material as a way of historicizing the relationship between the Delta, the fishermen and the state, past and present.[6] By combining ethnographic observations with the historical approach, we seek not only to disentangle the presumptions and the mechanisms deployed by the Romanian state during the last century in its efforts to control this fluid territory, but also to show how these policies were imperfectly implemented in the field and were often challenged by local people. State-oriented historical accounts, we contend, can run the danger of merging intention and implementation, thus exaggerating the extent to which the state implemented its environmental policies. Finally, a historical analysis of the development of the nature state in the Delta offers insight into the development of the capacity of the modern Romanian state from its founding in the late nineteenth century until the present time.

The development of the nature state in a newly acquired territory (1878–1947)

The Romanian state's first attempts to control and manage the Danube Delta for nature conservation reasons unfolded in the context of wider attempts by the state to organize a newly acquired territory. The composition of the territory matters to this story.

At about 6,000 km^2, the Danube Delta is by far the largest wetland area in Europe. It is situated at the border between Romania (which claims 82 per cent of the Delta's territory) and Ukraine (which claims 18 per cent). For centuries, the rich biological productivity of its numerous freshwater lakes connected by narrow channels has been exploited.[7] Specialist commentators highlight the Delta's great variety of fish, birds and aquatic vegetation, observing how the diversity of this interconnected aquatic environment (sea, ponds with different depths and degrees of salinity, channels, etc.) has shaped the development of a complex system of small-scale multi-species fisheries.[8] Historically – and to this day – fishing was the emblematic activity of local communities, both economically (the main revenue source for locals over the past two centuries) and culturally (as a dominant dimension of local identity). The Romanian part of the

Danube Delta includes various socioethnic groups such as the Russian Lipovans called *Starovieri* ('Old Believers' in Russian) and the Ukrainian 'Cossacks'. Both groups settled in the area during the eighteenth and nineteenth centuries.[9] The number of inhabitants today is almost unchanged since the beginning of the twentieth century: 15,000 people living in 23 localities.[10] At two habitants per square kilometre, the Danube Delta has one of the lowest population densities in Europe.

Until 1878 the province that shelters the Danube Delta, called Dobroudja, was part of the Ottoman Empire. Following the latter's defeat by Tsarist Russia in 1877, the Treaty of San Stefano saw Dobroudja – including the Delta – ceded by the Ottomans to become part of the Romanian state, itself having only been established in 1859. After the incorporation of Dobroudja in 1878, successive Romanian governments sought the 'internal colonization' of the province.[11] In 1878, Dobroudja formed the proverbial melting pot, with ethnic Romanians comprising only 10 per cent of the population, whereas the majority was Turkish. Bulgarians, Russian Lipoveni, Greeks and Armenians also lived in the province. All these former citizens of the Ottoman Empire became Romanian citizens in March 1880. As a consequence of intensive internal colonization over the course of the twentieth century, the Romanians have become the majority of the population in this province.

From the point of view of the Romanian state during this acquisition, the Danube Delta represented an 'empty space', an underdeveloped and underexploited area, ethnically diverse and isolated from the rest of the country by the Danube River.[12] Some populations, like the Turkish and the Circassians, were considered too 'primitive' or 'savage' to be incorporated into the new state's civilizing mission. Some commentators even asked whether the poor quality of the land meant it made a useful territory at all.[13] One of the first concerns of the Romanian state after 1878 was to introduce a new administrative organization, establish Romanian land property rights and extend the taxation system into the region. Under Ottoman rule the agricultural land, ponds, lakes and water channels were the property of the sultan, who further leased the right to use these to different persons from the province.[14] The province was governed by *caimacam*, who exerted, on behalf of the sultan, a single tax called *dijma*. Once Dobroudja passed under Romanian rule, all natural resources passed from the sultan's property to the Romanian state. The regions of the province were governed by a *prefect*.

If a nature state redefines rights and re-values territories under the umbrella of national interest, the Romanian state did just this in Dobroudja: the state was convinced that the Delta, on account of its important natural resources, should be subject to the new state. In 1893, the Romanian king empowered Grigore Antipa, a Romanian naturalist, to design a system for the sustainable exploitation of the Delta's natural resources based on his scientific knowledge about the area.[15] Agreeing that 'for economic and political reasons it is in the interest of the national state to sustain the development of fishing in the Danube Delta', Antipa designed a modern fishery in the Delta.[16]

Describing the social and economic relations between fishermen and the private entrepreneurs who held fishing rights and monopolized the fish-related commerce, Antipa noticed that the intermediaries who controlled the local and regional markets were in the main responsible for overfishing.[17] For instance, fishermen who caught small sturgeons that had no value to the merchants simply threw them away. If the sturgeons had reached maturity, not only would they have been worth a small fortune, but they would also have contributed to the perpetuation of the species.[18] This practice was very common until after the Second World War. Old fishermen remember that in one day a fisherman could throw away up to 150 kg of small sturgeon.[19] Merchants were accused of maintaining low fish prices, which pushed the fishermen to fish as much as possible, even during the closed season, using very small-maze fishing nets.[20] Local memories of sharp social inequalities between fishermen and their 'masters' are still vivid in many villages. One elderly fisherman from Jurilovca village remembered that 'All fish was given to the *masters* at a very small price. We were paid twice a year for our catch. The master knew how to make the calculation so the payment was extremely low.'[21] Another said that 'there was so much fish but it was poorly paid. Some fish as roach (*babuşca*) had no commercial value at all. We were always in debt to our masters'.[22] One outcome of this unbalanced economic relationship was a sharp decline of fish stock.

In 1896, Antipa introduced a law that sought to organize fishing in the Romanian national interest by banning intermediaries' activities, establishing local fishing rights and introducing new controls over fishing tools and practices. The reform was dedicated to the rational exploitation of the fish in the Danube Delta and attempted to reverse the environmental damage. Fishing had to develop as a lucrative economic activity but within the framework of long-term sustainable exploitation. As Antipa stated, 'the state introduces order in a disorderly place'.[23] The state, he continued, could not allow 'everyone to fish anywhere' as in the Ottoman period.[24] Antipa insisted that the Danube Delta had a natural dynamic that had to remain undisturbed despite fishing activities. In fact, he pleaded for economic activities that did not disturb the biological rhythm of the fish or its ecology. At the same time, the fishery reform inspired by him became a multifaceted political tool of nationalization and capitalization of the fish as an economic and natural resource. The Romanian state tried to organize the new territory by attempting to rationalize and homogenize a multitude of messy local fishing practices. In James C. Scott's terms, state modernization centres on making a space, economy and society 'legible', a process that involves the simplification of the landscape in order to facilitate the state to control and tax the territory. Under the pretext of improving human life, the state imposes control over natural resources and rules out all the practices that are difficult to codify and thus to tax.[25] As Antipa put it, 'the rational exploitation of these waters will bring the state a considerable amount of money'.[26] The fishing law of 1896 formalized some existing local fishing practices, but it also proscribed those considered damaging to natural resources; by seeking 'to draw a line between protecting nature and defending livelihoods', Antipa's reforms were a manifestation of the nature state.[27]

Establishing protected areas was another way to build the authority of the young Romanian nature state. In the early 1920s, a conservation movement started in Romania and in 1928 the first congress of Romanian natural scientists demanded a new system of laws and regulations. In 1930, the first Romanian 'natural environments' protection law was passed by parliament and, soon after, the Committee for Protection of Natural Monuments was established.[28] In the next decade, 36 protected areas were established totalling 15,551 ha.[29] In 1938, the Romanian Academy declared Letea forest a protected area. Located in the northern part of the Danube Delta, this 5,200 ha forest was considered a 'monument of nature' that needed to be protected due to its mixture of river marine sand dunes and a forest mixture of oak, ash and alder (*Alnus glutinosa*) with climbing lianas (*Vitis vinifera, Priploca graeca*) on trees.[30] In those first years of nature conservation in Romania it was mostly forests that were targeted for protection. A characteristic of conservation in the Danube Delta was that the policies for conservation unfolded concomitantly with the organization of fishing production – an activity that had to be organized and controlled in order to respect the hydrological and ecological equilibrium of this immense wetland.

Nature conservation 'on paper' (1947–89)

This section shows that the socialist environmental policies regarding the Delta were very strong on paper, but hardly implemented on the ground or followed by authorities and locals.

Romania became a socialist state in 1947. In 1949 all 'means of production' were nationalized, including industrial enterprises in conjunction with the collectivization and the de-kulakization of rural society. The economic and political socialist project was also meant to industrialize the country and improve the agricultural sector.[31] The Delta was especially attractive to socialist ambition since it was a vast territory, scarcely inhabited, with an apparently underexploited richness of natural resources. At 22 inhabitants per square kilometre, this represented a much lower density than the Romanian average of 73.6 inhabitants per square kilometre.[32] After 1953, the socialist state granted fishing rights exclusively to state companies and reorganized the activity according to socialist objectives. The state banned any private productive activity and declared fishing with private tools illegal. The fishermen became employees of the enterprises and obliged to meet a 'fishing production quota'.

The socialist state invested significantly in the 'integral exploitation' of the Delta's resources and a large number of scientists and technicians were invited to contribute, under political control, to improving the productivity of the wetland. Based on the hydrography of the Delta's territory, a plan for its complex reorganization was elaborated in 1962 and six large economic enterprises were established with the aim of exploiting the natural resources of the area. Whereas the higher land was targeted for agriculture, the marshes, channels, ponds and lakes were dedicated to fishing and reed exploitation.[33] A pharaonic landscaping programme started in 1982 envisaged 244,000 ha, including 144,000 ha of wetlands, for planned agricultural development, fisheries and forestry. By the end of 1989, 100,000 ha were dammed and drained, 42,000 ha of which were transformed into agricultural fields.[34] The industrial exploitation of reeds, used for cellulose extraction, which started in the 1960s, and the organization of fishing teams unfolded within the new state enterprises. Since 1980, the 20 state companies that had each been assigned a part of the territory of the Delta were managed by the *Centrala Deltei*, a hyper-centralized administrative institution managing all economic activity and investments.[35]

Paradoxically, the fierce exploitation of the Delta's resources unfolded at the same time as the extension of protected areas throughout Romania. From a little over 1,550 ha of protected areas in the 1940s, the socialist state expanded this to 43,683 ha in 1970 and 222,545 ha in 1985.[36] In September 1973, the Romanian government adopted Law 9 (the law on environment), which regulated the organization of conservation ecosystems (reserves and 'monuments of nature'). The international context for building a socialist nature state was important. A first impulse came from the International Union for the Conservation of Nature (hereafter IUCN), which recommended a long-term plan for the conservation of the Delta's environmental richness after 1971.[37] Another impulse was represented by the Danubian Cooperation among the riparian states that aimed at a better scientific knowledge of the Danube River; it started work in 1971.[38] Despite the international agreements Romania signed, Law 9 remained ineffective until 1990 for at least two reasons. One is that no institution existed to manage and enforce the law in protected areas. Second, the law was never accompanied by a detailed legal framework of action. The protected areas in the Delta had the same fate. In December 1961, four natural reservations encompassing 33,500 ha were established in the Danube Delta[39] However, the protected areas were not protected at all on the ground since no administration was appointed to manage these areas.[40] As one fisherman put it in an interview with Mitroi in early 2000, conservation during socialism was 'just on paper' and had no impact on the way local people interacted with the Delta.

Some dissident scientists openly criticized the 'productivist' approach taken by the state to the Danube Delta, highlighting the unfortunate 'consequences for biological equilibrium in natural reservations and the damage brought to birds and to the landscape by neglecting nature protection'.[41] They also criticized the 'irrational exploitation of the delta's natural resources'.[42] Levees built in 1967 and 1968 and the exploitation of reeds using heavy machines degraded the natural habitats of fish and birds, undermining their reproductive cycle; the agriculture practised in the nature reserves, including the use of insecticides and pesticides and overgrazing by sheep, had a negative effect on rare birds' nesting habits; and legal and illegal fishing drastically reduced the fish populations.[43] The intensive industrial development along the Danube's banks in Hungary, Serbia, Bulgaria and Romania poisoned the Danube and the delta's waters with heavy metals, nitrates and phosphorus.[44]

The collective environmental record is appalling. The physical transformation of the environment through damming, channelling, the creation of polders, pollution and biological perturbations (provoked by the introduction of alien fish species) led to a degradation of fish populations and the decline or even the disappearance of certain species.[45] Consequently, by the 1980s, the 'productivist' approach of the socialist state was only tenable thanks to state subsidy of the fishing industry. Fish capture decreased by half between 1960 and 1980; the requirement to fulfil 'production plans' and meet fishing quotas saw environmental degradation on a large, if largely unnoticed, scale.[46]

The socialist nature state was profoundly contradictory. One the one hand, in some areas the state took legal measures to forbid productive activity and protect some fish species (such as sturgeon).[47] On the other hand, fishermen – who were all employees of the Romanian state – fished in those areas. The socialist state viewed fish as a commodity, not a part of a larger ecosystem. Nature protection remained largely 'on paper'.

Conservation policies and knowledge vs local interests (1990 to present)

In 1991, a state decree transformed the Centrala Deltei into the Biosphere Reserve.[48] The postsocialist governments considered the socialist state's policy of intensified exploitation of the Delta's natural resources an 'economic disaster'. Consequently, as early as February 1990 the government decided to halt all work in progress and state investments in that area. The initiative was prompted by biologists and ecologists, who during socialism were afraid to openly oppose the government's policies in the Delta. The employees of the Centrala joined this initiative first and foremost for the fear of losing their jobs now that the investments and the works were suspended. Among them were also several conservationists who understood the environmental disaster they had helped to produce and decided to speak up once there was no political threat.[49] The employees and the 'non-productive' infrastructure were transferred to the newly created Agency. The economic infrastructure, lands and polders were placed under the administrative responsibility of the Tulcea County Council.[50]

Since the end of the nineteenth century, the Romanian state had been the main planning actor in the Danube Delta; in the 1990s, international recognition of the ecological value of the area by global institutions such as UNESCO and the IUCN turned international institutions into important actors in the governance of the area. In contrast to previous periods, the internationalization of the nature state made it more effective with respect to implementing policies on the ground. International governance has been manifest especially through financial aid from the World Bank and IUCN and the imposition of UNESCO's organizational and zoning models into the Delta.[51] Conservation programmes oriented towards ecological restoration and international cooperation benefited the most from international funding.[52] The conventions and contracts established between the international institutions and the national authorities often neglected local participants and their existing rights. The lack of any consultation with local communities and the absence of elected local representatives in the new Administrative Council of the Reserve gave local people the feeling that they had been 'placed' into a reserve, and their interests ignored. Actually, many locals acknowledged the existence of 'the Delta' only after the imposition of conservation policies by the Agency in 1997.[53]

Lower official fish catches during the first postsocialist years – the catch decreased by half between 1989 and 1997 – meant fishing was identified as one of the main threats to the ecosystem.[54] Moreover, scientists estimated that between 30 and 50 per cent of the real fish catch was sold on the black market.[55] Consequently, state ministries and agencies imposed restrictions on fishing, which included introducing fishing quotas and fishing licences, prohibiting the fishing of species now categorized as endangered, standardizing fishing tools in order to increase their selectivity and establishing strictly protected areas. In the 1990s, the Agency employed up to 150 environmental guards to control fishing.

Communities received no compensation for loss of income from these prohibitive measures. The only ameliorating social measure allowed is known as the 'familial fishing right', an old customary right that recognizes the right of any family living in the Delta to fish up to 3 kg per day for home consumption and allowed only in particular areas close to the villages. These restrictions inevitably contributed to conflict between the Agency and local populations in relation to poaching.

State restrictions on local fishermen were not matched by comparable treatment of the new private fishing companies. Based on the neoliberal mantra that it was in the interests of private firms to exploit the natural resources of the Delta's large ponds and lakes sustainably, significant concessions were made for external entrepreneurs.[56] This measure was justified by the government and the Agency to obtain a better protection of, and control over, resources, in a context of rising poaching and black market activities.[57] In fact, between 1990 and 1997 newly created private fishing companies worked in a legal vacuum with no enforcement upon them and with very relaxed environmental laws. They had only to respect a few state-imposed regulations such as the registration of all the fish quantities sold by the fishermen to the companies and to respect the prohibition period. Only in 1997 did the state attempt to implement a new legal framework for fishing activities adapted to the emerging free market context. The lease of fishing territorial rights to external investors (between 2003 and 2005) imposed even more limits on local rights and access to natural resources. However, after Romania joined the EU in 2007, the concessions were declared illegal and the Romanian government had to hurry the creation of fishermen associations. According to EU rules, the only institutions allowed to access European funds for fishing are professional associations. Despite a slight increase in local fishermen's participation in the management of the Delta's natural resources – almost all fishermen associations have, at least technically, a representative on the board committee of the Agency – the associations have little capacity to influence resource use and very limited access to markets.

In this context, the prevention of the degradation of natural resources in the Danube Delta is still a key part of the official discourse of both state authorities and environmental NGOs. Frequently, those involved in protecting biodiversity and the natural environment have turned their arguments against the local population. Local and national journals regularly claim: 'There is no more fish in the pool', 'The Danube Delta is cleared of fish by poachers!' or 'The paradise of [the] Danube Delta [has been] abandoned in the hands of poachers'.[58] As poaching came to be an essential component of an official discourse of environmental degradation in the Danube Delta, so anti-poaching discourse easily became anti-local. For instance, in spring 2012 attendees at a seminar organized in Crişan, a village in the Delta, were greeted by a huge banner as they landed on the pier, declaring: 'Poachers from the Danube Delta, a species which is an endangered species!' The banner was put there by a very active NGO called Save the Danube and the Delta.[59] The logic of the argument was simple: restrictions on commercial fishing were already extended, yet poaching continued, meaning poaching must be causing the continuing fish stock degradation.

The Agency has nothing left but to attack family fishing rights, arguing that the fishermen must be taking more than was their due, stigmatizing this ancient right as little different from poaching. Consequently, new regulations introduced in 2010 directly affect family fishing: the use of the small traditional nets (*setca*) for capturing the daily 3 kg of fish per family is now forbidden.[60] This means that the national government equates fishing by tourists with fishing for subsistence by the population that makes a living from this very activity – both groups are allowed to fish only using a fishing rod. The difference between fishing with a rod and fishing with a net is radical in terms of time and labour involved. A setca is a traditional professional tool that is adaptable to different water depths or the types and size of fish one is intending to catch.[61] This regulation triggered a riot among villagers, who saw their traditional economic activity jeopardized by the new rule. In a meeting at the Tulcea County Council, between all stakeholders involved in fishing management, local mayors – representing villagers of the Delta – lamented that the new regulation hit hard the locals of the Delta and 'risks losing the only fishing tool which still distinguishes the inhabitants of the delta from tourists: the setca'.[62] The way this meeting unfolded demonstrated another important thing: inhabitants of the Delta were just informed about the new rules; they were not consulted before the government approved them. The new rules aimed at 'protection, conservation, management and the exploitation of living aquatic resources'.[63] As one attendee put it, 'Fishermen were informed by the state officials about the new fishing rules and interdictions. I think they [the government] think that people living in the delta would not actually understand the content of the law and the interdictions they imposed.'[64] Fishermen protested against the new rules but also ignored them, continuing their activities.

State authorities justified the exclusion of fishermen from the legal definition of fishing rules by privileging expert over local or traditional knowledge. Emphasizing scientific knowledge and ignoring fishermen's traditional understanding of the Delta's ecology represents one way in which the nature state came to exclude a certain population from using a natural resource, or at least to restrict their right to use it. Fishermen of the Delta learn to fish from their fathers and forefathers – 'they were born in the boat', many of them told us – and they have a knowledge passed from one generation to the other, central to which is a sophisticated understanding of the wetland ecosystem in which they work and the ecology of the fish. They have what anthropologists call traditional ecological knowledge.[65] By 'tradition' we understand the 'cultural continuity transmitted in the form of social attitudes, beliefs, principles, and conventions of behaviour and practice derived from historical experience'.[66] Often, traditional knowledge conflicts with the scientific knowledge mobilized by the state in the definition of fishing rights. Fishermen harshly contest this 'official' knowledge. For example, the Emergency Ordinance promulgated in March 2008 aimed to conserve, protect and manage the living aquatic resource. Experts from the National Agency for Fishing and Aquaculture (NAFA), which regulates fishing activities and the conservation and management of living aquatic resources and promotes policies concerning these domains, identified the Danube River as among the country's important spawning areas. Thus, the governmental interdictions against the setca included the Danube.

Fishermen accused experts of not understanding the reproductive ecology of the Danube fish: shallow, warm waters are the nursery for spawning, not the ten-metre deep waters where fishermen set up their fishing tools. Moreover, fishermen use setca in the river mostly in winter, when the lakes, channels and marshes of the Delta are frozen. The fish spawn in spring, when the ice is long gone and fishermen return to the Delta's lakes. Thus, fishermen accuse the state agency and its 'experts' of a double ignorance: they neither understand fish ecology nor the fishing practices along the Danube and in the Delta.[67] Another fisherman from Sfântu Gheorghe village fiercely criticized the Agency's actions, which aim to turn the Delta into a natural habitat with no human intervention at all. He said:

> How can they promote a 'no human intervention' policy while 14,000 people live inside the Biosphere Reserve? Before communism, our grandparents used to clean and dig the channels with their bare hands and there was plenty of fish for everybody.[68]

The fisherman accused officials of a flagrant misunderstanding of the Delta's hydrology and ecology. If the channels are not maintained, the fresh water supply halts and they quickly degrade to swamps. Fish suffocate due to lack of oxygen, obviously no longer spawning, and this is the main cause of population decline.[69] The protectionist policies of the reservation also strictly forbid the burning of reeds in winter. Fishermen consider this interdiction silly because burning the reed facilitates also burning the vegetation which otherwise would overgrow, and helps prevent silting, a permanent risk in the Delta.[70]

Fishermen say that the equilibrium of the Delta was always maintained by human intervention. Protecting fish-eating birds, such as cormorant, pelican, wild ducks or the wild goose, the fishermen claim, produces an ecological disequilibrium. Before the state's involvement in bird protection, fishermen destroyed their nests and stole their eggs, keeping their numbers under control. Once the state became involved in establishing protected areas, as in the case of forest Letea, where birds nest in great numbers, disequilibrium has been produced. The number of birds has continued to grow and they consume a huge quantity of fish. As one fisherman put it:

> One single pelican eats 1.5 kilos of fish. Before [during socialism] we used to crash their nests but now you cannot touch them or else you may get into trouble. As long as one can see only birds on the surface of the lake and they eat all the fish. Birds [in large numbers] ruin the equilibrium of the Delta.[71]

Increasingly, this local ecological knowledge is supported by scientific observations.[72] Conflict between 'scientific' or 'official' and 'local' knowledge need not be absolute and, as Michael Hathaway has shown in this volume, they can be reconciled, but only when state authorities overcome their institutional bias.

The Agency fiercely protects the birds, especially the pelican, the symbol of the reservation, and promotes an idea of the Delta as untouched by human activity. The area is portrayed by UNESCO, national institutions, the Agency, tourist agencies and ecological associations as a 'paradise of the birds', a sanctuary for biodiversity, an untouchable ecological system.[73] The two visions of the Delta, the fishermen's and the Agency's, are mutually exclusive and difficult to integrate into a single workable definition of this wetland. For villagers, policy based on scientific knowledge harms rather than protects the environment. By challenging the 'official' arguments, fishermen challenge the very rationale of the fishing quota and consequently the very underpinnings of the management of the protected areas. For many inhabitants of the Delta, the Agency and its protective environmental policies are just the latest in a long line of external authorities imposing restrictions of long-established and seemingly sustainable ways of extracting a livelihood from the Delta.

Conclusion

This historical and ethnographic chapter has mapped the nature conservation policies implemented by the Romanian state in the Danube Delta from the beginning of the twentieth century up to the postsocialist transformation. By sustaining a certain form of protection for the different zones of the Delta, the state produces over time certain types of nature. By creating 'sanctuarized' nature, the state also imposes its authority on those marginal places it struggled for a long time to appropriate. The first attempt to protect nature in Dobroudja province unfolded concomitantly with the organization of this newly acquired territory by the Romanian state. Through Antipa's fishing reform at the dawn of the twentieth century, the state aimed to preserve the natural dynamics of the Delta and its rich biodiversity, albeit within the context of organizing sustainable fishing industry. The socialist state, in its attempt to re-organize the entire Romanian society, economy and nature, enlarged the protected area, but this policy was in open conflict with the productivist and strongly interventionist approach of the same state. During socialism, the conservation of nature was discursive, inspired by the conservation movement – reflected in the quantity of scientific work on this subject – but never really implemented on the ground. From this point of view, the socialist nature state was largely illusory. Only the postsocialist state, with its support from the international institutions such as the World Bank, UNESCO and the Ramsar Convention, has succeeded in institutionalizing the nature state in Romania.

As we know from other protected areas around the globe, there are often tensions between the state's attempt to protect an area and the people who inhabit it.[74] However, as this close examination of the Danube Delta shows, the nature state may well be legislated without ever existing on the ground. By examining this tension we detected the paradoxical nature of the nature state: it establishes a protected area that needs to be guarded against the very citizens the state claims to represent. The Danube Delta's fishermen are citizens of the Romanian state but they feel totally unrepresented and excluded from the valorization of the nature in the area. In the words of a frustrated fisherman: 'The state protects pelicans but it is insensitive with the delta's inhabitants who are poor and hungry.'[75] This tension is also expressed through a conflicting vision over the natural equilibrium: the state agencies argue that the ecosystem does not need humans to maintain its diversity whereas fishermen claim the opposite: humans maintain it. In Romania, the nature state has sought to minimize human intervention in the natural world, whereas people living in that area for at least three centuries claim that non-intervention causes serious disequilibrium in nature.

The historical evidence shows that the Romanian state has shifted its discourse on natural resources and on nature itself since the early twentieth century. A way to observe this change is through looking at how the state defined the fish and the fisherman. The new nation-state, built at the end of the nineteenth century, defined fish as a commodity *and* a natural resource at the same time. The socialist state turned fish into a commodity, neglecting its nature and place within the ecosystem – it might have extended the protected area's acreage, but it also intensified the exploitation of the natural resources of the Delta. The postsocialist state defines fish solely as a natural resource, instituting a regime of high protection for the entire Delta, which ignores the local population's dependence on this resource. Concomitant with the changing definition of the fish were changes to the definitions of fishermen and fishing. Before socialism, a clear rift existed between fishermen and the state: the state perceived fishermen as those who disturbed the natural dynamics of the Delta through their unsustainable fishing practices. Fishermen perceived the Romanian state as an external oppressor that instituted interdictions. The socialist regime radically changed this. The state made the fisherman part of the state. Clearing vegetation, burning reeds and clearing silt were all part of the job of the fisherman, essential to maintaining the productive potential of the wetland – that is, essential to maintaining a certain kind of nature. In postsocialist times, conservation policies established non-human priorities, restoring the presocialist rift between fishermen and the state. However, where the presocialist nature state also had nationalist intentions with respect to territorial security, the postsocialist nature state is motivated only by concerns regarding the protection of nature. The development of the postsocialist nature state is no longer solely a national project but is also an international one.

Not only has the state sought to impose on fishermen its understanding of fish ecology, but also the idea of the fish as the commodity that mediates the relationship between the Delta's inhabitants and the state. This resonates with Chapter 3, where Wilko Graf von Hardenberg shows how attitudes towards the bear mediate the relationship between the Italian state and farmers in the Italian Alps. In the case of the Danube Delta, the fish and its ecology form the locus for the clash between the interests of the state and the villagers. Natural elements mediating the relationship between state and local people mean in fact that the distinction between nature and society, between 'natural' places and 'social' ones, are continuously blurred. The distinction between 'natural' and 'social' places is a mechanism of nature conservation that criminalized ancient local practices.[76] The postsocialist state marginalizes local people in order to stress the naturalness of the delta – and thus sets a distinction between human activities and undisturbed nature, a continuous source of conflict between locals and conservation authorities. Following a long tradition of scholarship on conservation, we have outlined the historical, social and political mechanisms of how state policies identified and redefined nature, criminalizing local fishing practices in the process. The policies of nature protection in the twentieth century and the responses of fishermen to these policies reflect how nature and the state constitute each other in modern times.

Notes

1 Citation obtained in a formal interview with a fisherman from Jurilovca, by Veronica Mitroi in 2008.
2 William Cronon, 'Introduction: In Search of Nature', in *Uncommon Ground: Rethinking the Human Place in Nature*, ed. by William Cronon (New York, 1996); Emmanuel Kreike, *Environmental Infrastructure in African History: Examining the Myth of Natural Resource Management in Namibia* (Cambridge, 2013).
3 The new Biosphere Reserve covers all the Danube Delta's territory, including the Razelm-Sinoe lakes. That is 591,200 ha according to the World Bank Danube Delta Biodiversity Project (2005).

4   Ramsar is the international convention on wetlands, signed in Ramsar, Iran in 1971, www.ramsar.org/about/history-of-the-ramsar-convention.

5   Stefan Dorondel, 'The "Voices" of the Romanian Integration into EU: Land and Environmental Practices in a Village from Dobroudja', *The Anthropology of East Europe Review*, 23/2 (2005), 35; today, most villagers from the Delta live on meagre pensions and social benefits offered by the state: Ştefan Dorondel and Mihai Popa, 'Workings of the State: Administrative Lists, European Union Food Aid, and the Local Practices of Distribution in Rural Romania', *Social Analysis*, 58/3 (2014), 124–40.

6   Stefan Dorondel has carried out ethnographic and archival research in Jurilova village intermittently between 1997 and 2002; Veronica Mitroi carried out ten months of fieldwork between 2005 and 2008.

7   Édouard-Philippe Engelhardt, *Études sur les embouchures du Danube* (Galatz, 1862); J.J. Nacian, *La Dobroudja économique et sociale son passé, son présent et son avenir* (Paris, 1886); Tudose Tatu, *Tradiţia, promotoare a pescuitului gălăţean* [Tradition as the Promoter of the Fishing Activity in Galaţi County] (Galaţi, 2015).

8   Petre Gâştescu, 'The Danube Delta Biosphere Reserve. Geography, Biodiversity, Protection, Management', *Romanian Journal of Geography*, 53/2 (2009), 139–52.

9   For a more detailed history of the Danube Delta and its populations, see Frédéric Beaumont, 'Les Lipovènes du delta du Danube. Chronique d'une société théocratique russe des Balkans', *Balkanologie: Revue d'études pluridisciplinaires*, 10/1–2 (2008).

10   Aurel Banu and L. Rudescu, *Delta Dunării* [The Danube Delta] (Bucureşti, 1965), 231.

11   Catherine Durandin, 'La Russie, la Roumanie et les nouvelles frontières dans les Balkans: Le cas de la Dobroudgea', *Cahiers du monde russe et soviétique*, 20/1 (1979), 61–77. See also Constantin Iordachi, 'The California of the Romanians: The integration of Northern Dobrogea into Romania, 1878–1913', in *Nation-Building and Contested Identities: Romanian and Hungarian Case Studies*, ed. by Balász Trencsény, Dragoş Petrescu and Cristina Petrescu (Iaşi, 2001).

12   Francis Lebrun, *La Dobroudja; esquisse historique, géographique, ethnographique et statistique* (Paris, 1918). See also Engelhardt, *Études sur les embouchures du Danube*.

13   Constantin P. Scheletti, *Dobrogea organisarea* (Tulcea, 1879), III.

14   Scheletti, *Dobrogea organisarea*, 5. For the radical changes in property rights over the land, see Ion N. Roman, *Studiu asupra proprietăţii rurale din Dobrogea urmat de codul proprietăţii fonciare otomane din 1858 şi de legile romîneşti referitoare la proprietatea imobiliară rurală din Dobrogea* [A Study on Landed Property in Rural Dobroudja followed by the Ottoman Laws from 1858 and the Romanian Laws Concerning Property over Buildings in Rural Dobroudja] (Constanţa, 1907).

15   Grigore Antipa (1867–1944), a specialist in zoology, ichthyology, ecology and oceanography dedicated a great part of his work to the study of the Danube Delta and the Black Sea.

16   Grigore Antipa, 'Câteva probleme ştiinţifice şi economice privitoare la Delta Dunărei' [Several Scientific and Economic Problems Concerning the Danube Delta], *Analele Academiei Române*, 36 (1914), 17.

17   Grigore Antipa, *Pescăriile statului din Tulcea* [The State Fisheries of Tulcea] (Bucureşti, 1911), 26.

18   Grigore Antipa, *Studiu asupra pescăriilor din România* [The Study of the Fisheries of Romania] (Bucureşti, 1895), 44.

19 Osip Petrov, born in 1894 in Jurilovca village. He started to fish for his master, Taras Vlas, in 1914. From 'Autobiographies', 1970, Dorondel's collection. When the state fishing enterprise was privatized, the new owners threw the archive away. While in the field, Dorondel collected several valuable documents, including the *Autobiographies*.
20 Fishing is forbidden during the period the fish spawns.
21 'Autobiographies', Osip Petrov.
22 Ibid. Ignat Procop, born in 1901 in Jurilovca village. He was 15 when he started to work with his father.
23 Grigore Antipa, *Pescăriile statului*, 17.
24 Ibid., 9.
25 James Scott, *Seeing like a State: How Certain Schemes to Improve the Human Condition Have Failed* (New Haven, CT, 1998).
26 Grigore Antipa, *Pescăriile statului*, 29.
27 See p. 2 of the Introduction to this volume.
28 Corneliu Maior, Petru Aurel Darau and Viorel Soran, 'The History of Biodiversity in Romania', *Studia Universitatis – Seria Ştiinţe Inginereşti şi Agro-Turism*, 3 (2008), 7–13.
29 Ibid., 10.
30 G.F. Borlea, S. Radu and Doina Stana, 'Forest Biodiversity Preservation in Romania', *Notulae Botanicae Horti Agrobotanici Cluj-Napoca*, 34 (2006), 26; Sanda Vişan, 'Environmental Management Issues Prevailing in the Danube Delta Biosphere Reserve', *Review of International Comparative Management*, 15/1 (2014), 118.
31 Katherine Verdery and Gail Kligman, *Peasants Under Siege: The Collectivization of Romanian Agriculture, 1949–1962* (Princeton, NJ, 2011); Dorin Dobrincu and Constantin Iordachi (eds), *Transforming Peasants, Property and Power: The Collectivization of Agriculture in Romania, 1949–1962* (New York, 2009).
32 Banu and Rudescu, *Delta Dunării*, 231.
33 Aurel Banu and L. Radulescu, *Amenajarea complexă a Deltei pentru punerea in valoare a resurselor naturale* [The Complex Re-zoning of the Delta for the Valorisation of Natural Resources] (Bucureşti, 1965).
34 The Development Programme for Integral Exploitation of the Territory of the Danube Delta. See Michel Cernea and Cosima Ruhinis (eds), *Danube Delta Biodiversity Project: Local Benefits Case Study* (Stockholm, 2005).
35 Petre Gâştescu and Romulus Ştiuca, *Delta Dunării – Rezervaţie a Biosferei* [Danube Delta – Biosphere Reserve] (Tulcea, 2006).
36 Florin Ioras, 'Trends in Romanian Biodiversity Conservation', *Biodiversity and Conservation*, 12/1 (2003), 9–23; Viorel Soran, Jozef Biro, Oana Moldovan and Aurel Ardelean, 'Conservation of Biodiversity in Romania', *Biodiversity and Conservation*, 9/8 (2000), 1187–98.
37 David Turnock, 'Cross-border Conservation in East Central Europe: The Danube–Carpathian Complex and the Contribution of the World Wide Fund for Nature', *GeoJournal*, 55/2 (2001), 655–81.
38 Domokos Miklós, 'History and Results of the Hydrological Co-Operation of the Countries Sharing the Danube Catchment (1971–2008)', in *Hydrological Processes of the Danube River Basin: Perspectives from 10 Danubian Countries*, ed. by Mitja Brilly (Dordrecht, 2010), 1–23.
39 Ion Gh. Petrescu, *Delta Dunării – Aspecte, resurse* [The Danube Delta – Aspects, Resources] (Craiova, 1973), 118.

40 Veronica Mitroi interview with the former head of the Centrala Deltei in August 2008.

41 Valeriu Puşcariu, 'Conservarea naturii în Delta Dunării şi complexul Razelm' [The Nature Conservation in the Danube Delta and Razelm Lake], *Peuce*, 1 (1971), 506 (all translations from Romanian are ours).

42 Ibid. See also Valeriu Puşcariu, 'Observaţii asupra unor păsări rare din delta şi lunca Dunării' [A Notice on Rare Birds in the Delta and the Floodplain of the Danube], *Ocrotirea naturii*, 8/2 (1965), 201–17; Valeriu Puşcariu, 'Der Schutz der Vogelfauna im Donaudelta und das Überschwemmungsgebiet der Donau', in *Limnologische Berichte der X Jubiläumstagung Donauforschung Bulgarien, 10–20 Oktober 1966* (Sofia, 1968), 455–9.

43 Puşcariu, 'Conservarea naturii în Delta Dunării', 503–22.

44 Mircea Staras and Ion Navodaru, 'Schimbări în structura ihtiofaunei ca efect al modificării caracteristicilor biotopului' [Changing Fish Communities as a Result of Biotope Features Changes], *Analele Ştiinţifice ale Institutului Delta Dunării*, 4/1 (1995), 233–9; V. Bostan et al., 'Forms of Particulate Phosphorus in Suspension and in Bottom Sediment in the Danube Delta', *Lakes and Reservoirs: Research and Management*, 5 (2005), 105–10.

45 Ellen E. Wohl, *A World of Rivers: Environmental Change on Ten of the World's Great Rivers* (Chicago, 2010), 103–37.

46 INCPPDD, Raport de activitate al INCPPDD, Sinteza lucrărilor de cercetare executate în trimestrul IV. 1989 [INCPPDD Activity Report. Summary of the research activities in the fourth quarter. 1989] (Tulcea, 1989); Ion Navodaru, Mircea Staras and Irina Cernisencu, 'The Challenge of Sustainable Use of the Danube Delta Fisheries', *Fisheries Management and Ecology*, 8 (2001), 324.

47 The Fishing Law of 1974.

48 The Government Decision 983 of 14 September 1990 for the organization and functioning of the Ministry of the Environment. A series of legislative acts will subsequently ensure strengthened state control over the Delta.

49 Veronica Mitroi interview with the former technical director of the INCPPDD and with a former employee of the Centrala.

50 In Romania, every county has an elected council which assures the administrative coordination of public affairs. The communal and city councils, also elected, are subordinated to the county council. For more about the institutional transformation in the Danube Delta after 1990, see Veronica Mitroi, 'Le Delta du Danube, entre enjeux socio-économiques et préservation des ressources naturelles : exemple d'une « double transition »', *Pour*, 217 (2013), 115–24.

51 World Heritage Nomination. IUCN Summary prepared by IUCN (April 1991), based on the original nomination and summary submitted by the Government of Romania (1991). A cached version is available at www.webcitation.org/6m5eqcm33.

52 Kristof Van Assche et al., 'Delineating Locals: Transformations of Knowledge/Power and the Governance of the Danube Delta', *Journal of Environmental Policy & Planning*, 13/1 (2011), 8–10.

53 Constantin Iordachi and Kristof Van Assche, *The Biopolitics of the Danube Delta: Nature, History, Policies* (Lanham, MD, 2015). The same restrictive laws have been imposed on the Ukrainian part of the Delta as well. See Tanya Richardson, 'On the Limits of Liberalism in Participatory Environmental Governance: Conflict and Conservation in Ukraine's Danube Delta', *Development and Change*, 46/3 (2015), 415–41.

54 IUCN, *Conservation Status of the Danube Delta* (Cambridge, 1992). See also a multitude of studies realized by the experts from Danube Delta Research Institute, the main consultation institution for the Agency: Mircea Staras, Ion Navodaru and Ion Cernisencu, 'Aprecieri privind starea şi exploatarea unor stocuri de peşti din Rezervaţia Biosferei Delta Dunării' [Considerations Regarding the Status and the Exploitation of Fish Stocks in the Danube Delta Biosphere Reserve], *Analele Ştiinţifice ale Institutului Delta Dunării*, 3/1 (1995), 227–32; Ion Navodaru and Mircea Staras, 'Conservation of Fish Stocks in the Danube Delta, Romania: Present Status, Constraints, and Recommendation', *Italian Journal of Zoology*, 65 (1998), 369–71.

55 Mircea Staras, Ion Navodaru and Ion Cernisencu, 'Calitatea datelor statistice, o problemă a pescăriilor din Rezervaţia Biosferei Delta Dunarii [The Quality of Statistical Data, a Problem for the Fisheries from the Danube Delta Biosphere Reserve], *Analele Ştiinţifice ale Institutului Delta Dunării*, 6/2 (1998), 319–23; Ion Cernisencu, Mircea Staras and Ion Navodaru, 'Surse de eroare în estimarea capturilor durabile în pescăria din complexul Roşu-Puiu Rezervaţia Biosferei Delta Dunarii' [Errors Concerning the Sustainable Catches in the Roşu-Puiu Fishery of the Danube Delta Biosphere Reserve], *Analele Ştiinţifice ale Institutului Delta Dunării*, 5/2 (1997), 177–83.

56 There is a large neoliberal ideological current that minimizes the role of the state in protection and exploitation of natural resources, considering privatization of resources and their marketization as the only way to sustainably exploit a certain natural resource. For more in this regard, see Noel Castree, 'Neoliberalism and the Biophysical Environment 3: Putting Theory into Practice', *Geography Compass*, 5/1 (2011), 35–49.

57 Institutul Naţional al Deltei Dunării, *Imbunătţirea managementului pescăriilor din Rezervaţia Biosferei Delta Dunarii, cuprinzând Planul de acţiuni pe privatizarea dreptului de pescuit şi constituirea asociaţiilor de pescari* [Improvement of Fishing Management within the DDBR Including the Plan of Action for Privatizing the Right to Fish and the Constitution of Fishermen Associations] (Tulcea, 1997), 283.

58 *Ziare.com*, 10 February 2009, www.ziare.com/social/capitala/jaf-pe-apele-deltei-dunarii-668520; *Ziare.com*, 2 December 2008, www.ziare.com/social/capitala/braconierii-au-pescuit-ilegal-sute-de-tone-de-peste-din-delta-514150; *Ziare.com*, 15 May 2010, www.ziare.com/social/capitala/braconierii-au-pescuit-ilegal-sute-de-tone-de-peste-din-delta-514150.

59 This NGO has significant social and even political power. For a period of time, one of the leaders of this association was appointed the governor of the Agency.

60 Decision 975/2010 for the approval of standards regulating the practice of familial fishing in the DDBR.

61 Grigore Antipa, *Pescăria şi pescuitul în România* (Bucureşti, 1916), 508–12.

62 The new regulation that triggered the riot of fishermen was Emergency Ordinance no. 23 from 23 March 2008, which stipulated: 'The fishing with setca on the territory of the Reserve [...] represents a felony which is punishable with prison from one to three years and the suspension of fishing rights for a period from one to three years.'

63 Emergency Ordinance no. 23, art. 1.

64 Vera Mitroi interview with the representative of the fishermen from Dunavăţul de Jos village, Tulcea County, August 2008.

65 There is a growth in anthropological works on local (or traditional) ecological knowledge. The literature will not be reviewed here. For more on this, see Christian Bromberger, 'Les savoirs des autres', *Terrain*, 6 (1986), 3–5; Arturo Escobar, 'Whose Knowledge, Whose Nature? Biodiversity, Conservation and the Political Ecology of Social Movements', *Journal of Political Ecology*, 5/1 (1998), 53–82; Arun Agrawal, 'Classification de savoir autochtones: la dimension politique', *Revue internationale des sciences sociales*, 173/3 (2000), 325–36.

66 Fikret Berkes, *Sacred Ecology: Traditional Ecological Knowledge and Resource Management* (Philadelphia, PA, 1999), 4.

67 Veronica Mitroi interview with a fisherman from Jurilovca village, Tulcea County, August 2008.

68 Oana Ivan, 'Cultural Change in a Fishing Village in the Danube Delta: The Consequences of Environmental Protection and Tourism' (unpublished PhD dissertation, University of Kent and Babeş-Bolyai University Cluj-Napoca, 2012).

69 Idem.

70 Veronica Mitroi, 'Une pratique sociale à l'épreuve de la conservation de la nature. Incertitudes et controverses environnementales autour de la dégradation de la pêche dans la Réserve de la Biosphère du Delta du Danube' (unpublished PhD dissertation, University of Paris-Ouest Nanterre la Défence, 2013).

71 Veronica Mitroi interview with a fisherman from Jurilovca village, Tulcea County, August 2008.

72 Ion Navodaru, J. Botond Kiss, Irina Cernisencu, 'Fishery and Piscivorous Birds Forced to Sustain Together in Danube Delta, Romania (Review)', *Studii şi Cercetări Biologie*, 8 (2004), 128–39.

73 Mitroi, 'Une pratique sociale à l'épreuve de la conservation de la nature'.

74 Louis S. Warren, *The Hunter's Game: Poachers and Conservationists in Twentieth-Century America* (New Haven, CT, 1997), 11; Stuart Franklin, 'Białowieża Forest, Poland: Representation, Myth, and the Politics of Dispossession', *Environment and Planning A*, 34/8 (2002), 1459–85; Paul Greenough, '*Naturae Ferae*: Wild Animals in South Asia and the Standard Environmental Narrative', in *Agrarian Studies: Synthetic Work at the Cutting Edge*, ed. by James Scott and Nina Bhatt (New Haven, CT, 2001), 141–85; Monica Vasile, 'Nature Conservation, Conflict and Discourses on Forest Management: Communities and Protected Areas in Meridional Carpathians', *Sociologie Românească*, 3–4 (2008), 87–100.

75 Veronica Mitroi interview with a fisherman from Jurilovca, Tulcea County, in summer 2008.

76 Kreike, *Environmental Infrastructure in African History*.

Selected bibliography

Abinales, Patricio, and Donna J. Amoroso, *State and Society in the Philippines* (Lanham, MD, 2005).

Adams, William M., *Future Nature: A Vision for Conservation* (London, 1996).

———, *Against Extinction: The Story of Conservation* (London, 2004).

Agrawal, Arun, *Environmentality: Technologies of Government and the Making of Subjects* (Durham, NC, 2005).

Alagona, Peter, *After the Grizzly: Endangered Species and the Politics of Place in California* (Berkeley, CA, 2013).

Amend, Stephan, and Thora Amend, *National Parks without People? The South American Experience* (Gland, 1995).

Andermann, Jens, *The Optic of the State: Visuality and Power in Argentina and Brazil* (Pittsburgh, PA, 2007).

Anderson, David, *Eroding the Commons: The Politics of Ecology in Baringo, Kenya, 1890s–1963* (Oxford, 2002).

Anderson, David, and Richard Grove, *Conservation in Africa: People, Policies, and Practice* (Cambridge, 1987).

Armiero, Marco, *A Rugged Nation: Mountains and the Making of Modern Italy: Nineteenth and Twentieth Centuries* (Cambridge, 2011).

Balogh, Brian, *A Government out of Sight: The Mystery of National Authority in Nineteenth-Century America* (Cambridge, 2009).

Barton, Greg, *Empire Forestry and the Origins of Environmentalism* (Cambridge, 2002).

Beattie, James, *Empire and Environmental Anxiety: Health, Science, Art and Conservation in South Asia and Australasia, 1800–1920* (New York, 2011).

Beinart, William, *The Rise of Conservation in South Africa: Settlers, Livestock, and the Environment 1770–1950* (Oxford, 2003).

Beinart, William, and Colin Bundy, *Hidden Struggles in Rural South Africa: Politics & Popular Movements in the Transkei and Eastern Cape, 1890–1930* (London, 1987).

Bennett, Tony, and Patrick Joyce, Material Powers: Cultural Studies, History and the Material Turn (Hoboken, NJ, 2013).

Berkes, Fikret, *Sacred Ecology: Traditional Ecological Knowledge and Resource Management* (Philadelphia, PA, 1999).

Betts, Paul, and Corey Ross, 'Modern Historical Preservation – Towards a Global Perspective', *Past & Present*, 226/suppl. 10 (2015), 7–26.

Blackbourn, David, *The Conquest of Nature: Water, Landscape, and the Making of Modern Germany* (New York, 2006).

Blunden, John, and Nigel Curry (eds), *A People's Charter? Forty Years of the National Parks and Access to the Countryside Act 1949* (London, 1990).

Bolaane, Maitseo, *Chiefs, Hunters and San in the Creation of the Moremi Game Reserve, Okavango Delta: Multiracial Interactions and Initiatives 1956–1979* (Osaka, 2013).

Brockington, Dan, Rosaleen Duffy, and Jim Igoe, *Nature Unbound: Conservation, Capitalism and the Future of Protected Areas* (London, 2008).

Buller, Henry, 'Safe from the Wolf: Biosecurity, Biodiversity, and Competing Philosophies of Nature', *Environment and Planning A*, 40/7 (2008), 1583–97.

Camus Gayán, Pablo, *Ambiente, bosques y gestión forestal en Chile, 1541–2005* (Santiago de Chile, 2006).

Carruthers, Jane, *The Kruger National Park: A Social and Political History* (Pietermaritzburg, 1995).

Cederlöf, Gunnel, *Landscapes and the Law: Environmental Politics, Regional Histories, and Contests over Nature* (Ranikhet, 2008).

Chakrabarty, Dipesh, 'The Climate of History: Four Theses', *Critical Inquiry*, 35/2 (2009), 197–222.

Clarence-Smith, William G., *Slaves, Peasants and Capitalists in Southern Angola: 1840–1926* (Cambridge, 1979).

Coates, Peter, 'Creatures Enshrined: Wild Animals as Bearers of Heritage', *Past & Present*, 226/suppl. 10 (2015), 272–98.

Cronon, William, *Uncommon Ground: Rethinking the Human Place in Nature* (New York, 1995).

Cruikshank, Julie, *Do Glaciers Listen? Local Knowledge, Colonial Encounters, and Social Imagination* (Vancouver, 2005).

Darby, Wendy Joy, *Landscape and Identity: Geographies of Nation and Class in England* (Oxford, 2000).

Dilsaver, Lary M., and William Wyckoff, 'The Political Geography of National Parks', *Pacific Historical Review*, 74/2 (2005), 237–66.

Dobrincu, Dorin, and Constantin Iordachi (eds), Transforming Peasants, Property and Power: The Collectivization of Agriculture in Romania, 1949–1962 (Budapest, 2009).

Dorondel, Ştefan, 'The "Voices" of the Romanian Integration into EU: Land and Environmental Practices in a Village from Dobroudja', *The Anthropology of East Europe Review*, 23/2 (2005).

Dorondel, Ştefan, and Mihai Popa, 'Workings of the State: Administrative Lists, European Union Food Aid, and the Local Practices of Distribution in Rural Romania', *Social Analysis*, 58/3 (2014), 124–40.

Dowie, Mark, *Conservation Refugees: The Hundred-Year Conflict between Global Conservation and Native Peoples* (Cambridge, MA, 2009).

Duffy Burnett, Christina, and Burke Marshall, *Foreign in a Domestic Sense: Puerto Rico, American Expansion, and the Constitution* (Durham, NC, 2001).

Duit, Andreas, Peter H. Feindt, and James Meadowcroft, 'Greening Leviathan: The Rise of the Environmental State?', *Environmental Politics*, 25/1 (2016), 1–23.

Economy, Elizabeth, *The River Runs Black: The Environmental Challenge to China's Future* (Ithaca, NY, 2004).

Edgerton, David, *Warfare State Britain, 1920–1970* (Cambridge, 2006).

Ellis, Stephen, 'Of Elephants and Men: Politics and Nature Conservation in South Africa', *Journal of Southern African Studies*, 20/1 (1994), 53–69.

Elvin, Mark, *The Retreat of the Elephants: An Environmental History of China* (New Haven, CT, 2004).

Escobar, Arturo, 'Whose Knowledge, Whose Nature? Biodiversity, Conservation, and the Political Ecology of Social Movements', *Journal of Political Ecology*, 5/1 (1998), 53–82.

Evans, David, *A History of Nature Conservation in Britain* (London, 1992).

Fairhead, James, and Melissa Leach, *Misreading the African Landscape: Society and Ecology in a Forest–Savanna Mosaic* (Cambridge, 1996).

Farnham, Timothy J., *Saving Nature's Legacy: Origins of the Idea of Biological Diversity* (New Haven, CT, 2007).

Ford, Caroline, 'Nature, Culture and Conservation in France and Her Colonies 1840–1940', *Past & Present*, 183 (2004), 173–98.

Foresta, Ronald A., *Amazon Conservation in the Age of Development: The Limits of Providence* (Gainesville, FL, 1991).

Freitas, Frederico, 'A Park for the Borderlands: The Creation of the Iguaçu National Park in Southern Brazil, 1880–1940', *HIb: Revista de Historia Iberoamericana*, 7/2 (2014), 65–88.

———, 'The Guarani and the Iguaçu National Park: An Environmental History', *ReVista: Harvard Review of Latin America*, 14/3 (2015), 18–22.

Giblin, James L., *The Politics of Environmental Control in Northeastern Tanzania, 1840–1940* (Philadelphia, PA, 1992).

Giblin, James L. and Gregory H. Maddox, *Custodians of the Land: Ecology and Culture in the History of Tanzania* (London, 1996).

Gilbert, Jess C., *Planning Democracy: Agrarian Intellectuals and the Intended New Deal* (New Haven, CT, 2015).

Gissibl, Bernhard, Sabine Höhler and Patrick Kupper (eds), *Civilizing Nature: National Parks in Global Historical Perspective* (Oxford, 2012).

Griffiths, Tom, and Libby Robin (eds), *Ecology and Empire: Environmental History of Settler Societies* (Seattle, WA, 1997).

Grove, Richard, 'The Origins of Environmentalism', *Nature*, 345/6270 (1990), 11–14.

———, *Green Imperialism: Colonial Expansion, Tropical Island Edens, and the Origins of Environmentalism, 1600–1860* (Cambridge, 1995).

Guha, Ramachandra, 'Radical American Environmentalism and Wilderness Preservation: A Third World Critique', *Environmental Ethics*, 11/1 (1989), 71–83.

———, *The Unquiet Woods: Ecological Change and Peasant Resistance in the Himalaya* (Berkeley, Ca, 1989).

Guha, Ramachandra, and Madhav Gadgil, 'State Forestry and Social Conflict in British India', *Past & Present*, 123 (1989), 141–77.

Guldi, Jo, and David Armitage, *The History Manifesto* (Cambridge, 2014).

Hardenberg, Wilko Graf von, 'Act Local, Think National: A Brief History of Access Rights and Environmental Conflicts in Fascist Italy', in *Nature and History in Modern Italy*, ed. by Marco Armiero and Marcus Hall (Athens, OH, 2010), 141–58.

———, 'Beyond Human Limits. The Culture of Nature Conservation in Interwar Italy', *Aether – The Journal of Media Geography*, 11 (2013), 42–69.

———, 'A Nation's Parks: Failure and Success in Fascist Nature Conservation', *Modern Italy*, 19/3 (2014), 275–85.

Harrison, Brian Howard, *Finding a Role? The United Kingdom, 1970–1990* (Oxford, 2010).

Hartlyn, Jonathan, *The Politics of Coalition Rule in Colombia* (Cambridge, 1988).

Hartwig, Fernando C., *Federico Albert: Pionero del desarrollo forestal en Chile* (Talca, 1999).

Hathaway, Michael J., *Environmental Winds: Making the Global in Southwest China* (Berkeley, CA, 2013).

————, 'Wild Elephants as Actors in the Anthropocene', in *Animals in the Anthropocene: Critical Perspectives on Non-Human Futures*, ed. by Human Animal Research Network Editorial Collective (Sydney, 2015).

Hayes, Patricia, Jeremy Silvester and Marion Wallace (eds), *Namibia Under South African Rule: Mobility & Containment, 1915–46* (Oxford, 1998).

Hays, Samuel P., *Conservation and the Gospel of Efficiency: The Progressive Conservation Movement, 1890–1920* (Cambridge, MA, 1959).

Howkins, Adrian, Jared Orsi and Mark Fiege, *National Parks Beyond the Nation: Global Perspectives on 'America's Best Idea'* (Norman, OK, 2016).

Howkins, Alun, *The Death of Rural England: A Social History of the Countryside since 1900* (London, 2003).

Hurst, James Willard, *Law and Economic Growth: The Legal History of the Lumber Industry in Wisconsin, 1836–1915* (Cambridge, MA, 1964).

Iordachi, Constantin, 'The California of the Romanians: The Integration of Northern Dobrogea into Romania, 1878–1913', in *Nation-Building and Contested Identities: Romanian and Hungarian Case Studies*, ed. by Balász Trencsény, Dragoş Petrescu and Cristina Petrescu (Iaşi, 2001).

Iordachi, Constantin, and Kristof Van Assche, *The Biopolitics of the Danube Delta: Nature, History, Policies* (Lanham, MD, 2015).

Jacobs, Nancy J., *Environment, Power, and Injustice: A South African History* (Cambridge; New York, 2003).

Jacoby, Karl, *Crimes against Nature: Squatters, Poachers, Thieves, and the Hidden History of American Conservation* (Berkeley, CA, 2001).

Jeffery, Roger, and Nandini Sundar (eds), *A New Moral Economy for India's Forests? Discourses of Community and Participation* (New Delhi, 1999).

Joseph, G.M., Catherine LeGrand, and Ricardo Donato Salvatore, *Close Encounters of Empire: Writing the Cultural History of U.S.–Latin American Relations* (Durham, NC, 1998).

Josephson, Paul R., *Industrialized Nature: Brute Force Technology and the Transformation of the Natural World* (Washington, DC, 2002).

Keller, Robert H. and Michael F. Turek, *American Indians and National Parks* (Tucson, AZ, 1998).

Kelly, Matthew, *Quartz and Feldspar: Dartmoor – A British Landscape in Modern Times* (London, 2015).

Klubock, Thomas Miller, *La Frontera: Forests and Ecological Conflict in Chile's Frontier Territory* (Durham, NC, 2014).

Kohler, Robert E., *All Creatures: Naturalists, Collectors, and Biodiversity, 1850–1950* (Princeton, NJ, 2006).

Kreike, Emmanuel, *Re-Creating Eden: Land Use, Environment, and Society in Southern Angola and Northern Namibia* (Portsmouth, NH, 2004).

————, *Deforestation and Reforestation in Namibia: The Global Consequences of Local Contradictions* (Princeton, NJ, 2010).

Krishnan, Siddhartha, 'Landscape, Labor, and Label: The Second World War, Pastoralist Amelioration, and Pastoral Conservation in the Nilgiris, South India (1929–1945)', *International Labor and Working-Class History*, 87 (2015), 92–110.

————, 'Woody, Thorny, and Predatory Forests: Grassland Transformations in the Nilgiris, South India', in *Unruly Environments*, ed. by Christopher L. Pastore, Samuel Temple and Siddhartha Krishnan (Munich, 2015), 39–44.

Kupper, Patrick, *Creating Wilderness: A Transnational History of the Swiss National Park* (New York, 2014).

LeHouérou, Henry N., *The Grazing Land Ecosystems of the African Sahel* (Berlin, 1989).

Lekan, Thomas, *Imagining the Nation in Nature: Landscape Preservation and German Identity, 1885–1945* (Cambridge, 2004).

Levene, Mark, 'Climate Blues: Or How Awareness of the Human End Might Re-Instil Ethical Purpose to the Writing of History', *Environmental Humanities*, 2 (2013), 153–73.

Lewis, Michael L., *Inventing Global Ecology: Tracking the Biodiversity Ideal in India, 1947–1997* (Athens, OH, 2004).

Loo, Tina, *States of Nature: Conserving Canada's Wildlife in the Twentieth Century* (Vancouver, 2006).

López, Susana Mabel, *Representaciones de la Patagonia: colonos, científicos y políticos, 1870–1914* (La Plata, 2003).

Lorimer, Jamie, *Wildlife in the Anthropocene: Conservation after Nature* (Minneapolis, MN, 2015).

MacEwen, Ann, and Malcolm MacEwen, *National Parks, Conservation or Cosmetics?* (London, 1982).

MacKenzie, John M., *Imperialism and the Natural World* (Manchester, 1990).

Martinez Alier, Juan, *The Environmentalism of the Poor: A Study of Ecological Conflicts and Valuation* (Northampton, MA, 2002).

Matless, David, *Landscape and Englishness* (London, 2001).

McAfee, Kathleen, 'Selling Nature to Save It? Biodiversity and Green Developmentalism', *Environment and Planning D: Society and Space*, 17 (1999), 133–54.

McCann, James, *Green Land, Brown Land, Black Land: An Environmental History of Africa, 1800–1990* (Portsmouth, NH, 1999).

McCoy, Alfred W., and Francisco A. Scarano (eds), *Colonial Crucible: Empire in the Making of the Modern American State* (Madison, WI, 2009).

Miller, Char, *Gifford Pinchot and the Making of Modern Environmentalism* (Washington, DC, 2001).

Mitroi, Veronica, 'Le Delta du Danube, entre enjeux socio-économiques et préservation des ressources naturelles: exemple d'une « double transition »', *Pour*, 217 (2013), 115–24.

Monbiot, George, *Feral: Searching for Enchantment on the Frontiers of Rewilding* (London, 2013).

Moss, Chris, *Patagonia: A Cultural History* (New York, 2008).

Nash, Roderick, *Wilderness and the American Mind* (New Haven, CT, 1967).

Nelson, Michael P., and J. Baird Callicott, *The Wilderness Debate Rages On: Continuing the Great New Wilderness Debate* (Athens, GA, 2008).

Neumann, Roderick P., *Imposing Wilderness: Struggles over Livelihood and Nature Preservation in Africa* (Berkeley, CA, 1998).

Opie, John, *Nature's Nation: An Environmental History of the United States* (Fort Worth, TX, 1998).

Pádua, José Augusto, 'Environmentalism in Brazil: An Historical Perspective', in *A Companion to Global Environmental History*, ed. by J.R. McNeill and Erin Stewart Mauldin (Oxford, 2012).

Palacio, Germán, 'An Eco-Political Vision for an Environmental History: Toward a Latin American and North American Research Partnership', *Environmental History*, 17/4 (2012), 725–43.

Pedrotti, Franco, *Notizie storiche sul Parco Naturale Adamello Brenta* (Trento, 2008).

Perry, Richard O., 'Argentina and Chile: The Struggle for Patagonia 1843–1881', *The Americas*, 36/3 (1980), 347–63.

Piccioni, Luigi, 'Il dono dell'orso. Abitanti e plantigradi nell'Alta Val di Sangro tra Ottocento e Novecento', *Abruzzo Contemporaneo*, 2/2 (1996), 61–113.

———, *Il volto amato della Patria. Il primo movimento per la conservazione della natura in Italia, 1880–1934* (Camerino, 1999).

Rangarajan, Mahesh, 'Nature, Culture and Empires', in *People, Parks, and Wildlife: Towards Coexistence*, ed. by Vasant K. Saberwal, Mahesh Rangarajan and Ashish Kothari (New Delhi, 2000).

Readman, Paul, 'Preserving the English Landscape, c.1870–1914', *Cultural and Social History*, 5/2 (2008), 197–218.

Ritvo, Harriet, *The Dawn of Green: Manchester, Thirlmere, and Modern Environmentalism* (Chicago, IL, 2009).

Rome, Adam, 'What Really Matters in History: Environmental Perspectives in Modern America', *Environmental History*, 7/2 (2002), 303–18.

Runte, Alfred, *National Parks: The American Experience* (Lincoln, NE, 1979).

Safier, Neil, *Measuring the New World: Enlightenment Science and South America* (Chicago, IL, 2008).

Sandbrook, Dominic, *State of Emergency: The Way We Were – Britain, 1970–1974* (London, 2010).

Schaller, George B., *The Last Panda* (Chicago, IL, 1993).

Schulman, Bruce J., 'Governing Nature, Nurturing Government: Resource Management and the Development of the American State, 1900–1912', *Journal of Policy History*, 17/4 (2005), 375–403.

Scott, James C., *Seeing like a State: How Certain Schemes to Improve the Human Condition Have Failed* (New Haven, CT, 1998).

———, *The Art of Not Being Governed: An Anarchist History of Upland Southeast Asia* (New Haven, CT, 2009).

Sellars, Richard West, *Preserving Nature in the National Parks: A History* (New Haven, 1997).

Shapiro, Judith, *Mao's War Against Nature: Politics and the Environment in Revolutionary China* (Cambridge, 2001).

Sharma, Aradhana and Akhil Gupta (eds), *The Anthropology of the State: A Reader* (Malden, MA, 2006).

Sheail, John, *Nature in Trust: The History of Nature Conservation in Britain* (Glasgow, 1976).

Showers, Kate B., *Imperial Gullies: Soil Erosion and Conservation in Lesotho* (Athens, OH, 2005).

Sievert, James, *The Origins of Nature Conservation in Italy* (Bern, 2000).

Skaria, Ajay, 'Timber Conservancy, Desiccationism and Scientific Forestry: The Dangs 1840s–1920s', in *Nature and the Orient: The Environmental History of South and Southeast Asia*, ed. by Richard Grove, Vinita Damodaran and Satpal Sangwan (New Delhi, 1998), 596–635.

Skocpol, Theda, 'Bringing the State Back In: Strategies of Analysis in Current Research', in *Bringing the State Back In*, ed. by Peter B. Evans, Dietrich Rüschemeyer and Theda Skocpol (Cambridge, 1985), 3–37.

Smil, Vaclav, *The Bad Earth: Environmental Degradation in China* (Armonk, NY, 1984).

Sörlin, Sverker and Paul Warde (eds), *Nature's End: History and Environment* (Basingstoke, 2009).

Sparrow, Bartholomew H., *The Insular Cases and the Emergence of American Empire* (Lawrence, KS, 2006).

Spence, Mark David, *Dispossessing the Wilderness: Indian Removal and the Making of the National Parks* (New York, 1999).

Sutter, Paul S., David Igler, Christof Mauch, Gregg Mitman, Linda L. Nash, Helen M. Rozwadowski, *et al.*, 'State of the Field: American Environmental History', *Journal of American History*, 100/1 (2013), 94–148.

Sutton, Deborah, *Other Landscapes: Colonialism and the Predicament of Authority in Nineteenth-Century South India* (Copenhagen, 2009).

Takacs, David, *The Idea of Biodiversity: Philosophies of Paradise* (Baltimore, MD, 1996).

Thompson, Charis, 'When Elephants Stand for Competing Philosophies of Nature', in *Complexities: Social Studies of Knowledge Practice*, ed. by John Law and Annemarie Mol (Durham, NC, 2002), 166–90.

Thorp, Rosemary, *Progress, Poverty and Exclusion: An Economic History of Latin America in the 20th Century* (Baltimore, MD, 1998).

Tilley, Helen, *Africa as a Living Laboratory: Empire, Development, and the Problem of Scientific Knowledge, 1870–1950* (Chicago, IL, 2011).

Tilly, Charles, 'Reflections on the History of European State Making', in *The Formation of National States in Western Europe*, ed. by Charles Tilly (Princeton, NJ, 1975).

Tsing, Anna L., *Friction: An Ethnography of Global Connection* (Princeton, NJ, 2005).

Tucker, Richard P., *Insatiable Appetite: The United States and the Ecological Degradation of the Tropical World* (Berkeley, CA, 2000).

Turner, Frederick Jackson, *The Frontier in American History* (New York, 1920).

Tyrrell, Ian, *True Gardens of the Gods: Californian–Australian Environmental Reform, 1860–1930* (Berkeley, CA, 1999).

———, *Crisis of the Wasteful Nation: Empire and Conservation in Theodore Roosevelt's America* (Chicago, IL, 2015).

———, *Transnational Nation: United States History in Global Perspective since 1789*, rev. edn (Basingstoke, 2015).

Van Assche, Kristof, Martijn Duineveld, Raoul Beunen, and Petruta Teampau, 'Delineating Locals: Transformations of Knowledge/Power and the Governance of the Danube Delta', *Journal of Environmental Policy & Planning*, 13/1 (2011), 1–21.

Verdery, Katherine, and Gail Kligman, Peasants Under Siege: The Collectivization of Romanian Agriculture, 1949–1962 (Princeton, NJ, 2011).

Wakild, Emily, *Revolutionary Parks: Conservation, Social Justice, and Mexico's National Parks, 1910–1940* (Tucson, AZ, 2011).

Warren, Louis S., *The Hunter's Game: Poachers and Conservationists in Twentieth-Century America* (New Haven, CT, 1997).

Weiner, Douglas R., *A Little Corner of Freedom: Russian Nature Protection from Stalin to Gorbachëv* (Berkeley, CA, 1999).

———, *Models of Nature: Ecology, Conservation, and Cultural Revolution in Soviet Russia* (Pittsburgh, PA, 2000).

White, Richard, 'Environmental History, Ecology, and Meaning', *The Journal of American History*, 76/4 (1990), 1111–16.

Williams, Raymond, 'Ideas of Nature', in *Problems in Materialism and Culture* (London, 1980), 67–85.

Winter, James, *Secure from Rash Assault: Sustaining the Victorian Environment* (Berkeley, CA, 1999).

Worster, Donald, 'The Ecology of Order and Chaos', *Environmental History Review*, 14/1–2 (1990), 1–18.

Worster, Donald, Richard White, Carolyn Merchant, William Cronon, Stephen Pyne and Alfred Crosby, 'A Round Table: Environmental History', *The Journal of American History*, 76/4 (1990), 1080–420.

Young, Terence and Lary M. Dilsaver, 'Collecting and Diffusing "the World's Best Thought": International Cooperation by the National Park Service', *The George Wright Forum*, 28/3 (2011), 269–78.

Zelko, Frank, 'The Politics of Nature', in *The Oxford Handbook of Environmental History*, ed. by Andrew C. Isenberg (Oxford, 2014).

Zimmerer, Karl S., 'Human Geography and the "New Ecology": The Prospect and Promise of Integration', *Annals of the Association of American Geographers*, 84/1 (1994), 108–25.

Index

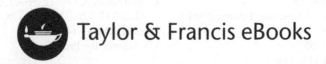

For Product Safety Concerns and Information please contact our
EU representative GPSR@taylorandfrancis.com
Taylor & Francis Verlag GmbH, Kaufingerstraße 24, 80331 München, Germany